ROUTLEDGE LIBRARY EDITIONS: COLD WAR SECURITY STUDIES

Volume 22

THE DEFENSE OF WESTERN EUROPE

THE DEFENSE OF WESTERN EUROPE

Edited by
L. H. GANN

LONDON AND NEW YORK

First published in 1987 by Croom Helm Ltd

This edition first published in 2021
by Routledge
2 Park Square, Milton Park, Abingdon, Oxon OX14 4RN

and by Routledge
52 Vanderbilt Avenue, New York, NY 10017

Routledge is an imprint of the Taylor & Francis Group, an informa business

© 1987 L.H. Gann

All rights reserved. No part of this book may be reprinted or reproduced or utilised in any form or by any electronic, mechanical, or other means, now known or hereafter invented, including photocopying and recording, or in any information storage or retrieval system, without permission in writing from the publishers.

Trademark notice: Product or corporate names may be trademarks or registered trademarks, and are used only for identification and explanation without intent to infringe.

British Library Cataloguing in Publication Data
A catalogue record for this book is available from the British Library

ISBN: 978-0-367-56630-2 (Set)
ISBN: 978-1-00-312438-2 (Set) (ebk)
ISBN: 978-0-367-63392-9 (Volume 22) (hbk)
ISBN: 978-1-00-311899-2 (Volume 22) (ebk)

Publisher's Note
The publisher has gone to great lengths to ensure the quality of this reprint but points out that some imperfections in the original copies may be apparent.

Disclaimer
The publisher has made every effort to trace copyright holders and would welcome correspondence from those they have been unable to trace.

THE DEFENSE OF WESTERN EUROPE

Edited by L.H. Gann
Hoover Institution, Stanford University

CROOM HELM
London & Sydney

AUBURN HOUSE PUBLISHING COMPANY
Dover, Massachusetts

© 1987 L.H. Gann
Croom Helm Ltd, Provident House, Burrell Row,
Beckenham, Kent BR3 1AT
Croom Helm Australia, 44-50 Waterloo Road,
North Ryde, 2113, New South Wales

British Library Cataloguing in Publication Data

The Defense of Western Europe.
   1. Europe — Armed Forces
 I. Gann, L.H.
   355'.0094   UA646

  ISBN 0-7099-1194-7

Auburn House Publishing Company,
14 Dedham Street, Dover, Massachusetts 02030

Library of Congress Cataloging-in-Publication Data

The Defense of Western Europe.

   Includes index.
   1. Europe — Armed Forces. I. Gann, Lewis H., 1924-
UA646.D429   1987   355'.0332'4   86-22321
ISBN 0-86569-159-2

Printed and bound in Great Britain by Mackays of Chatham Ltd, Kent

CONTENTS

List of Figures
List of Tables
Preface
L.H. Gann

1.	Western Europe and its Armies, 1945–85 *John Keegan*	1
2.	The British Armed Forces since 1945 *Roger Beaumont*	24
3.	The Danish and Norwegian Armed Forces *Nigel de Lee*	58
4.	Austria and Switzerland: the Defense Systems of Two Minor Powers *H.R. Fuhrer*	95
5.	The Spanish and Portuguese Defense Forces *Matthew Midlane*	126
6.	The Italian Armed Forces *Vittorfranco S. Pisano*	158
7.	French Defense and the Gaullist Legacy *Douglas Porch*	188
8.	The Bundeswehr of the Federal Republic of Germany *Dennis E. Showalter*	212
9.	The Defense Forces of the Low Countries *John H. Skinner*	255
10.	United States Armed Forces in Europe *Harry G. Summers, Jr.*	286

Notes on Contributors 310
Index 313

FIGURES

4.1	The Swiss Territorial Defense Concept	103
4.2	The Austrian Strategic Defense Concept	107
4.3	Potential Invasion Routes into Western Europe	107
4.4	Potential Invasion Routes into Austria and Switzerland	109
4.5	Principles of Territorial Defense	110
4.6	The Central Mountain Barriers	116
4.7	Openings into Switzerland and Main Roads in South Germany	117
4.8a	Switzerland's Topographic Structure	119
4.8b	Disposition of the Swiss Army	119
9.1	Outline Organization of Belgian Ministry of Defense and Principal Army Commands	260
9.2	Outline Organization of Dutch Ministry of Defense	271
9.3	Outline Organization of the Royal Netherlands Army	278
9.4	Dutch Manning System as Illustrated in a Battalion-Size Unit	280

TABLES

2.1	British Forces' Strength and Distribution, 1984	35
5.1	The 1977 Spanish Defense Budget	141
5.2	Spanish Defense Budget (Selected Years)	141
5.3	Portugese Defense Budget (Selected Years)	153
9.1	Organization and Tasks of General Staff Branches	261

PREFACE

At the end of World War II, much of Western Europe lay in ruins. The traditional European state system had broken down, so much so that, according to Ludwig Dehio, a German historian, all the European states, except Great Britain, had lost their traditional sovereignty. A speedy revival of the Western European economies seemed impossible, given both the destruction incurred in wartime and their many long standing weaknesses. The Western European states mostly suffered from severe internal dissensions and, in many cases, from a profound sense of pessimism. Western Europe henceforth was to face the overweening power of the Soviet Union; many Western Europeans, not necessarily Communists or Communist sympathizers, had become convinced that the future lay with the East.

Western Europe, however, confounded the pessimists' forecasts. To a greater or lesser extent, all Western European countries experienced an astonishing recovery, one that would have appeared incredible at the end of World War II. Democratic government, gravely challenged during the 1930s, was re-established. Western Europe passed through a new industrial revolution and through profound societal changes that left Europe much more prosperous than before. Western Europe and the US became closely linked, militarily through NATO, economically and culturally through a great variety of new associations within the Atlantic Community. Their safety and well-being turned out to be inextricably interlinked.

Nevertheless, a great deal of ignorance persists on both sides of the Atlantic concerning the respective partners overseas, and sometimes even next door. The striking growth of Western Europe's power in international affairs enhanced, if anything, this widespread mutual incomprehension, as evidenced by a great deal of mutual recrimination — sometimes justified, often without adequate grounds. All too many Americans, to give just one example, remain to this day woefully ignorant concerning the size of Western Europe's defense effort, or the importance of Western Europe to US prosperity.

In 1984, the Hoover Institution embarked on a new research project, under the general editorship of Peter Duignan and L. H. Gann, designed to contribute to Western European studies in the US, to stress the importance of Western Europe for the US, and to illustrate their mutual

Preface

interdependence in the Atlantic Community. The project is of an interdisciplinary character. At the time of writing, a collaborative volume on politics in Western Europe, edited by Gerald Dorfman and Peter Duignan, both Senior Fellows at the Hoover Institution, was in press and, a collaborative volume on the economies of Western Europe was being edited by Elliot Zupnick, Professor of Economics and Director of the Institute on Western Europe at Columbia University. Volumes are also planned on the societies and culture of Western Europe. L. H. Gann and Peter Duignan have begun to write an interpretive history on the Atlantic Community since 1945; the first volume will focus on the recovery of Western Europe after World War II.

The present volume will cover the military aspect. The volume covers the defense forces of Western Europe, including the US contribution to NATO. Austria and Switzerland have been included; neither of them form part of NATO; both, however, are of special interest. They provide alternative models of defense worthy of study for neutralists. Both moreover are of importance to NATO in an indirect fashion, by virtue of the manner in which they geographically separate NATO's northern and southern components in Central Europe. In general, the role of smaller countries, such as the Netherlands, Belgium, Norway, and Denmark, has been given due weight, given their strategic importance, and given the lack of easily available literature in English on their respective defense systems. The defense forces of Turkey and Greece, by contrast, have not been included, since both these states — though NATO members — do not form part of Western Europe.

All collaborators to this volume were asked to emphasize certain themes. These included a brief history from the end of World War II to the present, an appraisal of the relations between the armed forces and the societies that sustain them; an account of the military doctrine; the armaments used, and, their organization; the ability or otherwise of the various armed forces to carry out their assigned tasks; their structure and their manpower; and their relations with NATO.

In carrying out this task, collaborators received considerable latitude regarding the manner in which they would approach their respective themes. Some diversity in approach seemed desirable in view of the regional and national differences between the various Western European countries. NATO, after all, is quite unlike the Warsaw Pact. NATO's members all have their separate national styles and traditions. They are fully sovereign states. They are united in a common effort, not by the overweening power of a foreign occupant, but by voluntary agreement — so much so that a partner such as Norway excludes atomic weapons from its territory, an arrangement that would be unthinkable for Poland or the German Democratic Republic. There are many disparities in equipment, tactical doctrine, and organization. There are the traditional weaknesses that beset every great alliance, described with much force in a different context by Lord Macaulay nearly a century and a half ago. "Jealousies inevitably spring up. Disputes engender disputes. Every confederate is tempted to throw on others some part of the burden which he ought himself to bear. Scarcely one honestly furnishes the promised contingent. Scarcely one observes the appointed day."[1] But such weaknesses are partially balanced by the fact that the partners freely cooperate in a common endeavor to maintain peace, an endeavor that up to now has been unexpectedly successful.

But a great deal remains to be done — as the present contributions indicate. In many respects — the point bears repeating — the West has been incredibly successful, given Western Europe's military, political, and economic impotence at the end of World War II. Today, the European Economic Community alone is a global giant. In 1984, its gross domestic product amounted to two-thirds of the US's ($2,400.4 billion as against $3,627.9 billion). Its population was larger than the US's (272 million as against 232 million). Its exports were larger than those of the US ($227.2 billion as against $217.88 billion). Western Europe's economic progress over the last forty years has been astounding — despite many setbacks during the last decade. It is one of the world's great manufacturing centers; it commands a vast reservoir of scientific and technological skills. Indeed the Western powers between them remain the main source of technical and scientific creativity and innovation for the world at large. The European Economic Community alone is a major food producer and a major donor of food aid, as well as one of the most important sources of capital and technical assistance and a huge market for the developing world. Its combined military strength could be formidable. It produces some of the world's best military equipment. Its members between them maintain as many men under arms as the US (2,109,000 as against 2,350,000). If the Western alliance were willing to translate its economic strength into equivalent military power, the Soviet Union would form no threat to the rest of the world.

But the Western allies have as yet failed to match their economic superiority over the Soviet Union with corresponding military capability. NATO remains beset by serious problems that will emerge in the subsequent pages. Over the last decade, the balance of military power has shifted in the Soviets' favor. Soviet forces are greatly

Preface

superior to NATO's in terms of tanks, artillery, and combat divisions ready for deployment. The Soviets have improved their missile and their anti-ballistic missile strength. The US and Western Europe, despite their scientific and technological pre-eminence, have not as yet taken adequate steps to protect themselves even partially against missile attacks. Western Europe and the US moreover have for long been engaged in a massive long-term, one-way transfer of resources to the Soviet Union, a transfer that has involved them in furnishing expertise, technology, food, and credits to a potential enemy. The Western Europeans have been reluctant, in many cases, to back the US in strategic areas outside Europe, yet of essential concern to Western Europe's safety.

As the various contributors show, there is not the slightest reason for complacency — any more than for defeatism. Western Europe and NATO at large continue to face grave problems. Hopefully this volume will make a contribution toward a better understanding between the partners in a common defense. It is on their joint strength and their ability to cooperate that the future of world peace will depend in the foreseeable future.

The various authors' opinions expressed in this volume are purely their own and do not in any way commit their respective institutions.

L. H. Gann

Note

1. Thomas Babington Macaulay, *The History of England from the Accession of James II,* Belford, Clarke, Chicago, 1867, vol. 4, p. 123.

1 WESTERN EUROPE AND ITS ARMIES, 1945–85

John Keegan

Western Europe's principal achievements since 1945 have been, first, to right those self-inflicted economic wounds which were the most tangible result of its near-suicide in two world wars; second, to combine economic recovery with economic co-operation in the name of a hoped-for social and political unity which has so far escaped it.

But, though unity of the federal sort desired by the most "Europeanist" of the "Europeans" continues to elude it, the degree of social or political integration already achieved would, to a time traveller who had heard nothing of the continent since, say, 1938, seem little short of astonishing. Parliamentary institutions common to all members of the Economic Community now provide a forum for continental debate, if not yet for the enactment of political legislation. Free movement of labour between member states has been partially achieved. The abolition of internal passport restrictions and the introduction of common citizenship are within sight. Access to welfare facilities on a joint basis is already partially available. The homogenization of educational methods and qualifications is anticipated. Militarily and diplomatically, moreover, Europe has achieved a degree of voluntary integration unknown in any other region of the world. The traditionally or statutorily neutral states apart — Switzerland, Ireland, Sweden, Austria — the whole of Western Europe now belongs to a common military organization and organizes its continental defense through a single alliance system.

In a sense, however, among the least "European" of modern European institutions are Western Europe's armies. Like all armies, they bear close external and internal resemblances to each other. Hierarchical, disciplined, uniformed, they are all clearly the same sort of institution, formed in the same way and maintained for the same broad purpose. Nonetheless it can be argued that the relationship that subsists between each European army and its parent state is a unique one unlike that between any other pair, and unlike that between the parent state and any other institution within it. How, indeed, could it be otherwise? An army is the only state maintained institution which harbors the potentiality to overthrow the state by a singlehanded act of its own will. Both parties to the partnership — state and army — are aware, cannot ever forget, its ambiguous nature. Hence the issues of its singularity.

2 Western Europe and its Armies, 1945–85

Europe's armies have, since 1945, played an extensive range of variations on their relationship with the state, as also with the peoples from which they are recruited. Some — the British, the Belgians — have passed through the stresses of a decolonization process without deviating from a political docility which has been their admirable hallmark. Others — the French, the Portuguese — have been driven by the stress of decolonization into the rupture of their constitutional role and made direct attack on the government. Two armies, the Spanish and the Greek, have fallen out of sympathy with current political and social movements in domestic affairs and attempted — in the Greek case successfully — to exercise political power directly and on their own account. Another, Italy's, is held by the left-wing opposition in that country to be temperamentally opposed to any radical alteration of traditional political balances within the state and to stand ready to oppose it by force.

How are such variations of behavior to be explained? It is promising, on the face of it, to look for explanations in the institutional character of the countries themselves, since the differences between them, like their similarities, are very marked. Traditionally there have been six methods of recruiting armies. The first may be called the warrior method; it is characteristic of those societies dedicated to survival by struggle, in which all able-bodied males, not otherwise disbarred by social or religious taboo, habitually bear and use arms. Such societies — the Mongols or the Vikings are examples that spring to mind — stand usually at a low level of economic or social development. Few remain in the contemporary world and none in Europe. A second system is the slave army, usually chosen by societies which shun the shedding of blood between those who share the same code of values. Little known outside the Muslim world, it dominated the political arrangements of the early Caliphates and persisted into the Ottoman empire, where slave armies — at Damascus, Cairo, and Istanbul — exercised large and at times total power for long periods of history. Although the slave system undoubtedly had influence upon the Tsarist empire, whose common soldiers were exclusively recruited from the serf population during the eighteenth and part of the nineteenth centuries, it never took hold in Western Europe and, needless to say, is both unknown there today and wholly repugnant to its civic philosophy. A third method, characteristic of societies at a high level of political culture — though not necessarily at a consonant level of social equality — is the militia system. Under such arrangements, all fit males enjoying full political rights incur a liability to bear arms throughout active adulthood. It differs from the conscript system because of its close identification of political rights with military duty.

Because the army is the embodiment of the political notion, conflicts between army and nation are not theoretically feasible; theory is validated in practice, notably in the current cases of Switzerland or Sweden, by the absence of a professional military class institutionally able to mobilize *raison d'armée* against *raison d'état*. This lacuna principally differentiates the militia from the widespread conscript system, in which the army subsists in some degree of separation from the political nation, on which it levies a tax of the adult male's time, rather than money, to make good its manpower needs. Constitutionally, conscript armies ought to display a pattern of political propriety identical to that of militias. In practice, because they are directed by a professional military leadership distinct from a political one, they may at times invoke *raison d'armée* to oppose the sovereign will.

A fifth method of raising or maintaining an army is the mercenary principle. By that principle, a state provides for its external or domestic security by purchasing or subventing the services of military tradesmen. They may or may not be citizens or subjects of the paymaster state; whichever the case, the relationship is fraught with political risk, since the loyalty of the mercenary is instinctively assured only by regularity of payment and the degree of satisfaction it purchases. Even regular payment may fail to satisfy a mercenary where appetite for reward grows *en mangeant*, a phenomenon that states which have entrusted their defense to hired fighters have frequently encountered to their surprise and disadvantage. Only two European armies, the British and the French, continue to employ mercenaries and then in such small proportions that the political risk their engagement constitutes can be totally discounted.

The sixth or final method of raising soldiers is by regular enlistment. Regular or enlisted soldiers may be defined as full citizens of the employing state who agree to perform military service for salaried reward, with all the fringe benefits — security of tenure, pension rights, welfare and medical benefits — that salaried employment is conventionally understood to carry with it. Regular and mercenary enlistment clearly converge in character; they are differentiated chiefly by ethos, the regular or volunteer soldier being almost always a citizen of the employing state, and imbued during training and throughout his service by reiteration of his obligations of obedience and loyalty to sovereign authority.

Some of the foregoing systems are antipathetic and may not co-exist.

Others are not and may. In particular it is perfectly feasible for an army simultaneously to contain soldiers recruited on the conscript, regular, or mercenary principles or any two of those. Both the British and French armies have done so during the period under review. The British army, though largely regular at the present moment, contains a mercenary element — its Gurkha regiments. The French army, though conscript by majority, maintains a number of regular elite units, and one wholly mercenary contingent, the Foreign Legion. Even the West German army, organized on a strictly "citizen in uniform" basis, draws a few of its parachute units exclusively from regulars.

It might also be fruitful from a behavioural point of view to examine varying patterns of officer recruitment — since it is almost always the atitudes of officers which determine the political involvement or forebearance of an army. Much has been made, for example, of the fact that both Greek and Spanish officers tend to be drawn from an economically disfavoured social stratum — the lower middle class of the provinces. Neither group traditionally has been well rewarded and in Spain the custom of holding a second job used to be normal. The disparity between low financial reward and high social status — high at least by selfperception — is commonly held by military sociologists to explain the propensity of Greek or Spanish officers to play politics. Analysts of the French officer behavior have equally made much of the unequal geographical and social spread displayed in their recruitment pattern. A disproportionate number of French officers are drawn from the eastern provinces along the German frontier, where an untypical though understandable militarism flourishes, and also from the backward and strongly Catholic Breton West. Even more strikingly, the French officer corps is strongly self-recruiting. Currently almost half the entrants are the sons of officers or non-commissioned officers, either from the army itself or from the gendarmerie, constitutionally if not adminstratively part of the army also.

In Britain, officers are also drawn in unrepresentative proportions from limited social and economic sectors. Wales, the Midland cities, and the manufacturing North supply very few. The Home Counties, around London, the "feudal" West of England, the Scottish Highlands and such odd outposts as the Channel Islands and the still anglicized groups in the Republic of Ireland provide the majority. Almost half the British officer intake, moreover, continues to be recruited from young men educated at British "public" (i.e. private) schools, a group which accounts for less than 10 percent of the school population. In West Germany, it has been noted that "aristocratic" society — those families entitled to bear the particle "von" in their names — have strongly reasserted their former hold on officer entry. Something between 10 and 20 percent of regular officers are currently recruited from this "old" society, a resurgence quite out of character with trends in the development of German society elsewhere.

The operational experience of European armies since 1945 must also be taken into account in assessing the nature of their varying relationships with the states or societies to which they belong. The largest, strongest, and by many judgements the most effective, the West German, has had no operational experience at all. Re-activated only in 1956, it has dedicated itself in the intervening thirty years to demonstrating its willingness to undergo subordination to civilian, constitutional, and democratic control. West Germany's military establishment, to quote Dennis Showalter, has spent "most of its public energy demonstrating innocuousness . . . The Bundeswehr's operational efficiency is discussed far less than its commitment to democracy, its role in institutionalizing civic virtues, its contribution to the mastering of Germany's past". The French army, by contrast, has been intimately involved in the management of the Republic's present ever since 1946. A principal instrument, via its engagement in the defeat and occupation of Germany in 1944–45, of de Gaulle's claim to equality with the Big Three (Britain, the US and the USSR), at the settlement of the peace, it found itself immediately commited thereafter to the re-establishment of national control over the pre-war empire. The assertion of French imperial competence was judged by all post-war governments up to 1958 a prerequisite of French international credibility. As a result, the French army found itself committed first to a long and exhausting war against the nationalist movement in Vietnam, 1946–54, and then to an equally debilitating and ultimately morally corrupting war against the Algerian nationalists, 1954–62.

The British army, during the same period, underwent a similar imperial experience, on an even wider world front. Its colonial engagement entailed campaigns against Communist insurgents in Malaya, tribal nationalists in Kenya, Greek irredentists in Cyprus, Arab Marxists in Aden (South Yemen), Zionists and their Arab opponents in Palestine, and, most recently, Irish anti-Unionists in Ulster, to say nothing of minor campaigns and altercations elsewhere. Unlike the French army, however, the British was undisturbed in spirit by the process, in part because of post-war governments' stated commitment to decolonization, beginning with the grant of independence to India in 1947, and in part because of the army's unique ethos, to be discussed below.

Among other armies with operational experience, that of the Portugese is clearly of the greatest significance; the frustrations of its campaign against the freedom fighters of Angola was the precipitating element in its decision to overthrow the right-wing dictatorship at home in 1974. At a less extreme level, the peacekeeping experience, generally under United Nations' aegis, of the Irish, Norwegian, Swedish, Austrian, and other armies has also been an important influence on their outlook and performance in the post-war years.

Ultimately, however, neither institutional character nor recent experience truly helps us to understand how West European armies differ from each other, and remain so distinctively and irredeemably national in character. Each is a special case, to be understood in its domestic context chiefly through the historical experience that binds it to state and society. These contexts we must now review.

Historically, the senior West European army — it would make an ampler claim itself — is the French. Tracing its origins to the raising of certain regular infantry companies — *les bandes de Picardie* — by the crown in 1475, it regards itself as having had a permanent existence as an instrument of state since that date. The claim can certainly be disputed, largely because of the troubles besetting the authority of the French crown in later years. But the dispute is irrelevant to an analysis of civil–military relations in France, which for our purpose may be taken to begin with the Revolution in 1789. For it was then that the distinctive element in the relationship first made itself evident. That element is the propensity of the French army to take sides in disputes between governmental and popular power in France — particularly in Paris — and to play a decisive role in the outcome. Hence the suspicion which both governments and people harbor for the army, and the strong internal tensions to which it is subject.

Decisive in the overthrow of the absolute power of the monarchy in 1789 was the failure of its Household troops to oppose the Paris mobs in July. Similar desertions — admittedly accompanied in the first and last case by circumstances of military defeat — precipitated Napoleon's first abdication in 1814, Charles X's in 1830 and Napoleon III's in 1870. It is these memories that have imbued successive French governments with mistrust of military reliability. Popular memory still resents the repressive behavior of the army in 1851, when President Louis Napoleon made himself Emperor Napoleon III by military *coup de force*, and in 1871, when the Versailles army of the new Third Republic put down the Paris *communards* with brutality and bloodshed; it also cherishes the belief, widely held by Republicans at the turn of the last century, that the army's disposition towards the Third Republic's practice of democracy was a hostile one. Government and people both feel disquiet at the behavior of the army in 1958. Even though ushering in the revivifying Gaullist era, its action is widely judged to have been selfish and sectional in motivation.

For its part, the army would deny that it is or has been consciously a political force — as some Latin American armies may be characterized. Rather it would say that the successive resolution of the French political powers into intractable conflict between governmental and popular power impels it, as the custodian, like it or not, of armed force, to throw its weight in a crisis in one direction or another. It has done so in the past in what seemed, at the time, the best interest of the nation. Nevertheless it admits that its record, if not its inclinations, necessarily invests it with a degree of menace in the eyes of both government and people. By compensation, it would argue, it imposes on itself a strict code of apoliticality by which it successfully abides in all but the most troubled times. It would cite, by way of exemplification, its soubriquet of *la grande muette* in the period 1880–1900, its strict abstention from political involvement during the heated left–right exchanges of the 1930s and its acquiescence in de Gaulle's devaluation of land power — in order to create the *force de frappe* — during the mid-1960s.

Keen-eyed observers would nonetheless note that French governments of whatever complexion have taken their own precautions throughout the last hundred years to re-insure themselves against the army's misuse of its own power, that these precautions remain in force today and that they have been augmented since the troubled Algerian–OAS period of 1958–62. They include the maintenance of a large paramilitary police force, the Gendarmerie nationale, on which primary responsibility for the guarantee of this order has always fallen; a ban on the stationing of the Foreign Legion in metropolitan France (though since the loss of Algeria its depot has perforce had to be located on metropolitan territory); and, since 1958, strict limitation on the number of years which officers may serve in the parachute regiments, the spearhead of the anti-constitutional activity of the army in 1968–70. In some sense, it may be concluded, French governments seek to assure the political neutrality of the army by imposing its structural divisions within its organization that automatically constitute checks and balances.

The British army is a fascinating example of a military society of which structural subdivision, and thereby automatic check and balance, is the dominant feature. Historically, it makes no claim to equal the

French army in antiquity, since its foundation dates only from 1660, the year of the restoration of Charles II, who brought with him from exile the regiments which constitute its nucleus. Continuity of institutions being the keynote of British public life, however, it is not surprising to discover that the constituent units of the British army are, in unbroken descent, far older than those of the French, older indeed than those of any other European army, with the possible exception of the Swedish. "Regimentality" is, in consequence, the essence of British army life. It defines the context in which the officer or soldier performs his service. It also narrowly predetermines the courses the army will plot in its relationship with state and society.

Take, as an example of the continuity and contextuality of the regiment, the Royal Scots, the senior British infantry regiment. Raised originally on the mercenary principle by a Scottish aristocrat in 1633, it served first in the Swedish army, then in the French. It was not until 1683 that it entered the service of the British crown, and then on the same basis as it had served Gustavus Adolphus and Louis XIV. It might, presumably, have resumed its travels at a later date. But, as things turned out, it has remained in British service from that day to this, bearing the number 1st Foot and becoming attached, at the end of the nineteenth century when the British infantry regiments acquired a local affiliation, to the city and district of Edinburgh. During its three hundred years of crown service it has campaigned in almost every continent and major war, its colors are encrusted with battle honors and it has buried its dead in fifty countries. But, travelled though it is, the regiment remains not merely Scottish but deeply Edinburghian. Its officers are drawn from the professional middle class of the city and the squirearchy of its environs, its soldiers from the local working class. No city event is complete without the presence of a party of Royal Scots to represent the military element in the capital's life; the regiment, wherever it is stationed, equally expects constant attention and visits from the city's hierarchy. The First of Foot is as central an Edinburghian institution as the city's famous university or its international festival of the arts.

The position is repeated throughout the British Isles. Every region and major conurbation has its local infantry regiment, all of antiquity and military distinction. And so successful has the association between infantry regiment and locality proved that in more recent times the cavalry and artillery have adopted it. The result is that, in the combatant arms, the majority of officers and soldiers will now spend the whole of their years of enlistment in the same society of six hundred fellows.

The effect of this pattern of social stability on "combat performance" is now widely recognized. Enhancing as it does what military sociologists call "small unit cohesion", it is now being widely imitated, not least by the United States army. The influence of regimentality extends far beyond the purely military sphere, however. For the consequences of confining the personnel of combat units within a complex of watertight compartments, as the regimental system effectually does, are that the corporateness of the army as an institution is greatly diminished and its inclination and ability to act as a political force in historical life are thereby minimized. The British army is famously unpolitical. A single incident apart — the so-called but misnamed "Curragh Mutiny" of 1914, when a handful of officers voiced their objection to imposing the Irish Home Rule Act on reluctant Ulster — the army has played no overt political role in British life throughout its three hundred year history. Taking Professor S. E. Finer's two indications of politicality — "mood" and "motive" — as guides to an explanation of its tradition of detachment, one would concede that, for long and continuous periods, no motive was present. The bulk of the army, throughout the imperial period, was employed overseas, and too busy, operationally and emotionally, to play politics, even had it so chosen. But the structural guarantee against its so choosing — the specific against its falling into a dangerous "mood" — was provided by regimentality. That condition enlarged the soldier's sense of difference and separation from other soldiers — in the case of the Royal Scots, for example, a difference from non-Scots, differences between Highlanders and Lowlanders, differences between city and countryside, differences between the very ancient and comparatively newborn regiment — and thereby undermined, indeed positively eliminated, the possibility of officers developing that *esprit d'armée* leading to *raison d'armée* which has so frequently animated the French army, for example, in its dealings with state and society.

Regional and social particularity, of which regimentality is an expression, is a deeply British characteristic. Britishness, though one of the most powerful nationalisms of the modern world, is a sum of local patriotisms of high intensity. Britain's army may therefore be judged one of the country's most successful institutions, approximating as it does so closely to the country's preferred national model of what a national organization should be. Though in no sense planned, Britain's military arrangements are clearly among the most successful in Europe, if not the world.

It is illuminating to turn from the example of an army which has grown comfortably into a successful relationship with state and society to one whose relationship has been determined by thought and precept. That is the West German — the Bundeswehr. Its constitutional position could have been determined in no way other than legal enactment, for the old German army, which dissolved in defeat in 1945, was then formally abolished by the victor powers. Only the collapse of goodwill between West and East caused its recreation to be considered. And when the decision to bring it into being again was eventually taken in 1955, it led to the birth of a creature quite different from the one that had dominated so much of German life during the previous hundred years. It was to be an army whose soldiers were to preserve their civic rights while in uniform, in which there was to be no place for a system of military justice separate from the law of the land, and in which soldiers were taught to put the voice of informed conscience above the orders of authority — the last concept called, untranslatably, *Innere Führung*.

All this is made understandable through the briefest review of Germany's — and its *Urstaat* Prussia's — relationship with the Bundeswehr's ancestor. "The national industry of Prussia", wrote Mirabeau in the eighteenth century, "is war" — a permissible exaggeration of Prussia's successful military aggrandizement under Frederick the Great. He admittedly had inherited an efficient army already overlarge for the size of state that supported it, with a record of victory behind it. But under his rule it was to come to dwarf the state, both materially and, more important, morally. The landed class, formerly reluctant to leave their (often tiny) estates to do duty as officers, found no escape from Frederick's insistence. When led, as they were, consistently to victory, they not merely forgot their reluctance but learnt patriotic and authoritarian values that shortly made them the most militaristic group in Europe. Having previously not wished to be officers, Frederick's Prussian aristocracy soon refused to be anything but officers, while insisting that the ranks be held closed against any candidate from beyond their own narrow circle.

The onset of war usually caused the social barriers to be breached, as they were inevitably after Frederick's death, in the wars of the French Revolution and empire. But the return of peace always led to the old institutions being renewed, with strangely distorting and damaging effects on the development of Prussian and then German society during the nineteenth century. For while Prussia/Germany began to emerge as the dynamic economy on the European continent, spawning entrepreneurial, creative, and artisan classes of the greatest energy,

Prussian/German society failed to find from within its resources the means to reward and promote the leaders of the new society as they deserved. Social position was reserved for the military aristocracy which had laid the foundation for the state's rise during the Seven Years War. It was determined to cling to this status, however altered the circumstances it found around itself in the new Germany.

To reinforce and justify its monopoly of social position the officer class exercised two principal instruments. The first was universal military service, which extended the officer's authority over the whole of German manhood in the most formative years of life. Exposure to military service taught the young German unquestioning acceptance of authority, routinized discipline, and fervent patriotism. The lessons were validated by the absolute right of the officer to impose his will on that of the conscript, limited only by a prohibition on inflicting wounds or death. The causal infliction of blows and kicks on soldiers whose "attitude" offended the officer was commonplace and against it there was no redress in civil or military law.

The second instrument was the practice of victory in the field. An officer class living only on its past reputation would have lacked the standing to insist on the social privilege the Prussians had between 1815 and 1870. Indeed, it may be thought that the impatience shown by the new middle class with Prussian social immobility in the 1840s was in part encouraged by the length of the peace since 1815. But, after those dissatisfactions had come to a head and been extirpated by brute force in 1848, the army was thrice enabled to demonstrate — in 1864, 1866, and 1870 — that its claim to pre-eminence rested on supreme professional competence. The victories of the Franco-Prussian war of 1870–71 validated that claim beyond the power of contemporaries to question it — and led directly to the unification of Germany under a Prussian monarch who was also by convention the chief of the Prussian officer corps.

The identification of the head of state with a socially exclusive officer corps, in a relationship ungoverned by strict legal definition, was to prove one of the factors that would drive Germany to disaster in the twentieth century. Its undesirability in class terms has already been indicated. In political terms, it conferred on both parties, monarch and officer class, the unfettered right to determine military and ultimately foreign policy in the light of their wishes. Because the German officer corps regarded political control of the army as belonging jointly to the Kaiser and the *Generalität* — from which it insisted that the Minister of War be chosen — the empire's feeble parliamentary system was never allowed to bring military policy within its purview. It could, through budgetary restriction, impose some limit on the size of the army, though it acquiesced nonetheless in successive increases in army size from 1890–1914. But it was allowed no right of consultation in the making of war plans, the writing of military doctrine or even of the army's deployment in peace. Two states, as it were, co-existed within the German regime of 1871–1914, one military, one civilian. The latter offered its deference and the astonishing product of its wealth-creating capacity to the former, which accepted the tribute as its natural right and planned to dispose of it as thought fit.

The outcome is too well known to be reviewed in detail. Persuaded in 1914 that threats to the stability of the 'other' Germany — Austria-Hungary — threatened the interests of the empire itself, Kaiser and army prevailed on the civilian politicians to risk a war against Russia, even though that enterprise was known to carry with it the chance of war also with France. When the two-front war supervened, casting unbearable burdens on Germany's industrial and financial capacity to sustain the effort, the general staff responded by bringing first Germany's economic and then its political structures under its direct control. Ultimately, when the general staff's dictatorship proved unavailing as a means of delivering victory, Germany's military leaders resolved on the most radical decision ever contemplated within the German state: to rid themselves of the emperor as a means of winning from their enemies concessions that would leave state, but also army, to survive intact beyond defeat.

Their betrayal of the military oath, by which the Prussian/German officer corps had charted its course for nearly two hundred years, failed to evoke the outcome for which the generals had hoped. That failure cast the army into a new relationship with the German state, teaching it to shun direct political intervention but to conserve nonetheless its role as ultimate source of authority. *Überparteilichkeit* (above party) became its watchword; with the reservation that the army itself constituted a sort of non-ideological party ready if need be to throw its weight in the direction best calculated to protect the conjoined destiny of the nation and its soldiers.

During the Weimar period and the first years of the Hitler regime that followed, it succeeded admirably in preserving its commitment to *Überparteilichkeit*, even though in its officer recruitment policy it returned to principles of social exclusivity scarcely known since the reign of Frederick the Great. Limited as it was by the terms imposed at Versailles to a strength of four thousand career officers (overseeing an enlisted complement of 96,000 men), it could afford to be choosy in picking its officer candidates. Social exclusivity went by the board as soon as Hitler revoked the Versailles Treaty and committed his armed forces to large-scale expansion after 1935. But as the war to which Hitler's policies led took a turning towards disaster after 1942, the implications of *Überparteilichkeit* and social exclusivity reasserted themselves. Just as Hindenburg or Ludendorff had decided in the autumn of 1918 that their oath to the Kaiser counted for less than the survival of nation-army, and was an impediment to it, so in mid-World War II the pre-Hitler officer corps decided in significant numbers that their oath to him must be abrogated in the interests of nation-army also. The outcome was the July Plot of 1944, the failure of which did not disguise from Hitler its significance as a fundamental confrontation between the principles of military and political sovereignty within the German state. Heroes though the instigators of the plot are held to be by post-war democratic Germany, their readiness to challenge the power of constituted authority, even in the name of justice, bears out, in the eyes of cautious observers, the incurable propensity of the old army to see itself as a force existing beyond the ambit of law and custom. It is surprising, therefore, that when the West German state was obliged after 1949 to consider how and what sort of army it might raise in the future, it set subordination to the Constitution and to the government as the supreme value to be transmitted to its next generation of soldiers. The question of the exercise of command has been solved for it by the dictate of the former occupying forces: it would be vested in the (American) Supreme Commander Europe. Even administrative command was not to rest with the Federal President, but with the Minister of Defense. This solution of the troubled old question of supremacy allowed the emphasis on where the army's duty lay to be put where the constituting authorities wished it to be: in obedience to the Federal Constitution and laws, and to the army's own code of practice drawn up in conformity with the Constitution's spirit.

The attempt to make the Bundeswehr a constitutional force must be judged an unqualified success. In its thirty years of existence, it has given neither the German state nor German society the least cause for complaint, or even disquiet, by its public behavior. Meanwhile it has successfully achieved the highest standard of military efficiency within the NATO alliance.

The Spanish, Greek, and perhaps even the Italian governments might privately envy the opportunity that West Germany has had to start afresh in determining army–state relationships in the modern world. The Spanish army has been a particular thorn in the side of

Spanish democracy, which has come erratically back to life since the death of Franco in 1976. One overt and apparently large-scale attempt at a military *coup* and rumors of at least two others have marred Spain's progress from dictatorship to liberal democracy during the intervening period. Yet the wonder is that the army has not caused more trouble than it has, for it maintains an ethos as interventionist as the former German army's, with a record of political activity which has no parallel outside Latin America.

The Spanish kingdom's troubles with its army date from the beginning of the nineteenth century, when the old royal army was first forced to absorb a troublesome complement of former guerrilla fighters against Napoleon, and was then embroiled in a series of civil wars over succession to the crown. The accession of Alfonso XII appeared to settle divisions within the officer corps. But the disastrous war with America over Cuba and the Philippines in 1898, entailing acute material humiliation and frightful suffering among the conscript masses, made the army very unpopular; and its prestige was further damaged by its inept conduct of the Rif war in Morocco during 1918-22. Its leadership reacted by losing patience with civilian government and establishing a military dictatorship. It proved incapable of dealing with Spain's internal problems, largely those of economic decline and extreme social inequality, which it abdicated in 1934 to a republican regime. The Republic's programme — anti-clerical and mildly Socialist — made little impact on the country's difficulties, while inflaming the army's traditionalist prejudices. In 1936 the African garrisons, under the leadership of the most successful of the colonial generals, Francisco Franco, initiated a revolt, which led instantly to civil war.

The Civil War of 1936-39, besides causing a million deaths, opened wounds so deep in the Spanish social body that the forty-year Franco dictatorship to which it led takes on in retrospect the quality of a peace of exhaustion. During its course Franco was careful to preserve the army's social position and privileges. But, for all his military power, he also took trouble to isolate it absolutely from political involvement. The army, deprived of function and starved of funds, drifted into a state of hopeless inefficiency, the implications of which were disguised by the high esteem which the regime continued to accord it. Franco's death, the restoration of the monarchy, the re-establishment of democracy, and the admission of Spain to a full place in European life, marked by its entry first to NATO and then to the EEC, progressively awoke the buried fears and rancors of the traditionalist element in the officer corps. Democracy brought in its train concessions to minorities and regions that the army, as the most powerful centralizing force in the country, had always seen as its duty to repress. Europeanism cast into sharp relief the army's unfitness to take its place alongside those of its NATO partners, who had kept abreast of contemporary military trends. The result was the outbreak of military dissent that culminated in the assault on Parliament in 1982.

Fortunately for the future of Spain, the mutineers were quickly exposed as representing only a minority within the army, lacking the support to outface the loyal majority, the outrage of the population, and the King's adamant devotion to democracy. Their collapse was as total as it was sudden, and led rapidly to the institution of measures designed to draw the army's fangs that might formerly have been impossible. These measures included the retirement of many of the old guard of generals, and absolute reduction in the swollen size of the officer corps, and the institution of a new system of military education calculated to induce constitutionalism in the army's future leaders.

It may be judged that Spain has now made a successful transition from an era in which the army, though outwardly docile, nevertheless retained a latent capacity to negate all political and social change of which it disapproved, to one in which it is bound by the same duty of subordination to political authority which prevails in northern Europe.

The army of Spain's neighbor, Portugal, has traversed a similar course during the same period, though from a different starting point. Its vain attempt to oppose the struggles for national independence in its African colonies of Mozambique and Angola — particularly the latter, where resistance was strongest — led to the emigration in the early 1970s of 25 percent of Portuguese males of military age, determined to avoid the long periods of conscription the effort entailed, and the increasingly grave economic strains. In 1974 the army initiated a revolution that toppled the country's long established right-wing dictatorship and ushered in a period of domestic upheaval. The complexion of the new democratic government and of the army's new leadership was originally Socialist, but to an idealistic or unrealistic degree. Subsequently a more centrist government restored internal political stability and displaced the army from the political role it had chosen for itself. The contemporary Portuguese army, much reduced in size, now occupies a place in national affairs more consonant with that thought appropriate elsewhere in Europe.

Overlarge size was also one of the most salient defects of the postwar Italian army. Its role, ever since the establishment of a unified Italian kingdom in 1870, had been to act as a means of diminishing the regionalism endemic in Italian national life. As a result, the post-war Italian army continued to conscript the great majority of Italian youth, even though it was unable to provide a role for the mass of manpower thus mobilized, or to extract funds to finance it from the budget. A largely unemployable, purposeless, and discontented army thus emerged, to constitute a material incubus on the state; and the situation was exacerbated by the suspicion in which the non-Christian Democrat opposition held the military leadership, believing it to be intransigently opposed to any transference of power to anti-conservative forces within society. The military intelligence service in particular was believed by the left to maintain plans and "hit lists" that were to be implemented in an emergency should the transfer of power from right to left — even by democratic process — impend. It may well be that there was substance to the left's belief. Italy is a country in which scandal is endemic, and the scandals that erupt partake amply enough of the macabre to validate those that remain merely rumors. Nevertheless, it must be said that, whatever the attitude of the army, its behavior has given no cause for complaint since the inauguration of the Republic in 1945; that a peaceful shift of power from the right to the center and in the direction of the left has recently taken place; and that the state has imposed on the army a radical revision of its structure and diminution of its size during the 1980s without provoking from it the least hint of unconstitutional behavior. The Italian people, comparing their experience with that of their Greek neighbors during the last two decades, may well feel that their army's fundamental character has suffered an unjust misrepresentation.

It is with relief that the political scientist or military sociologist will turn from the case of Greek colonels or Spanish generals to the unsensational affairs of Europe's militias, notably the Swiss or Swedish. Of these the Swiss army must stand as the exemplar — as it does to the armies of all democracies that organize themselves on militia lines. The roots of the Swiss system are very deep, descending to the origins of the state as an association of free men, bearing arms as a symbol of their liberty and equality, in their struggle for freedom from foreign monarchical rule. Until the end of the eighteenth century Swiss military activity was frequently and massively directed into mercenary channels, simply as a means of winning revenue for an impoverished mountain people. With the rise of domestic prosperity in the nineteenth century, however, mercenarism died out and the militia principle flourished. Today it allows a military establishment with a regular nucleus of only 6,000 men to mobilize in an emergency a fully armed home defense force of 600,000 all in the space of 48 hours. Some of the mechanisms that permit this remarkable expansion are widely known: for example, every Swiss reservist keeps his military firearm at home and reports on mobilization to a unit that has its depot within his immediate neighborhood. But the difficult as well as easy features of Swiss militiadom are worth emphasizing. Military obligation, for example, persists through the Swiss male citizen's active life. Reserve training periods are long — several months a year during his early manhood. Those selected for command positions, a duty difficult to refuse, must serve perhaps twice as long as ordinary militiamen, and so on. The Swiss army, on its own ground, is judged to be formidable; but its effectiveness is purchased at a high cost in human commitment.

Moreover, the Swiss Constitution firmly limits its respect for the liberty of the subject when a conflict with military duty arises. Swiss male citizens living abroad must pay a tax in lieu of performing military duty. The right to vote was until recently restricted to those who bore arms, or had done so, a provision which excluded female suffrage. And the state recognizes no right of conscientious objection. Pacifists can be and are imprisoned if they persist in their principles. Domestic critics of the milita system voice their own reservations about its nature. For all the emphasis officially laid on its egalitarian character, they say, comparison of the rank lists of a canton with a directory of those holding professional and managerial positions there in civil life shows a high degree of overlap. Military and civilian elites, in short, are formed from the same body of citizens, thereby giving the lie to the militia's representation of itself as a social order in which promotion is determined by military competence alone. These, however, are perhaps quibbles with what may be judged one of the most successful army-state relationships in Europe. If there are objective hesitations about the wider applicability of the Swiss system, they have to do with Switzerland's enjoyment of an almost uniquely defensible national terrain and with the country's underinvestment in first-rate military technology, the result of its policy of neutrality, and of its overinvestment in human at the expense of material resources.

The same criticisms cannot be levelled at Switzerland's nearest military equivalent, Sweden. For the Swedish have made almost effective compromise between the militia and the regular principles, to raise, from a population scarcely larger than Switzerland's an army which is operationally formidable both on a day-to-day basis and, when fully mobilized, by the embodiment of its large reserves. The secret of its formula is twofold: Sweden's industrial base is larger and more sophisticated than Switzerland's, while the permanent complement of its armed forces is more numerous. Sweden's industry produces armored vehicles, artillery, and aircraft which, at least until the most recent technological leap by the superpowers' armaments factories, were the equal of anything in the world. Sweden's population, meanwhile, has been brought to accept that the nation's defense requires the dedication of extended periods of duty by its young conscripts to their initial military training. No Swiss conscript serves more than four months in any one period of induction. Swedish conscripts may serve as much as a year if called upon to do so; and the regular leadership that trains them is maintained at a much higher level of strength than its Swiss eqivalent. As Swedish terrain also presents formidable difficulties to any aggressor contemplating invasion, professional military judgement holds that such an aggressor may well feel himself deterred by the combination of material barricades and national capability with which he is confronted.

Among the other Scandinavian armies, two approximate in some degree the ethos and character of the Swedish, while the third does not. The Finnish army, subject to limitations in its size and quantity of equipment imposed by Finland's peace treaty with Russia, is animated by a fierce patriotism and by the legendary military qualities of the Finnish people. Politically non-aligned though the country is, its capacity for self-defense must be obvious enough to give pause even to so powerful a neighbor as the Soviet Union, were it to contemplate a reprise of its aggression of 1939–40. The Norwegian army, though a conscript force, also partakes of the militia spirit of the Swedish. Though very small — it fields only one active brigade — its personnel are distinguished by an individual hardihood that constantly astonishes the foreign NATO contingents which come to learn winter warfare skills at their side. The army, moreover, is reinforced by a large voluntary "Home Guard" whose purpose is to deny, at a local level, the opportunity to an invader to seize terrain by surprise attack as the Germans did in 1940.

A similar Home Guard, conceived for the same purpose, exists in Denmark. A force created by popular wish after the liberation of the country in 1945, it embodies what may be called the militarist obverse of the Danish attitude to national defense, the reverse of which is more strongly informed by that neutralist– pacifist outlook which finds so much support throughout Scandinavia. The Danish army suffers from heavy parliamentary support for that position. Starved of men and funds in a country which finances one of the most generous and comprehensive social security systems in Europe, its operational capacity is low enough to cause constant worry to NATO, and has prompted the Bundeswehr to detach one of its divisions to Schleswig-Holstein as prop to reinforce the five tiny Danish brigades stationed on the peninsula and in the islands.

NATO is also concerned by the lower than desirable operational capacity of the Belgian and Dutch armies, which take their place in NATO's order of battle in the Central Front. Both, again, suffer financially from the heavy commitments made by their governments to the countries' welfare systems. In the case of the Belgian, the military stringency manifests itself particularly in an inability to replace obsolete and obsolescent equipment; in the case of the Dutch, economies are achieved by stationing a large proportion of the army committed to NATO on Dutch instead of German soil. Although in theory it can move to its assigned battle zone in an emergency at high speed, its absence from its "forward defense" positions on a day-to-day basis causes understandable disquiet at NATO high command levels.

Socially and politically, however, both the Dutch and Belgian armies are models of conformity and acceptability. During the 1960s the Dutch army suffered from a degree of indiscipline among its conscripts, infected by the prevailing "youth culture" that found particularly strong expression in that country, but it has now subsided. Both armed forces, moreover, maintain elite units whose services are particularly valued within the NATO Alliance: the Dutch marines, who operate harmoniously and effectively with their British counterparts in exercises to reinforce north Norway in an emergency; and the Belgian para-commando regiment, which is reckoned one of the most effective special force organizations in the world.

Western Europe's other armies, the Irish and the Austrian, belong to non-aligned states and are too small to be of operational significance. The Austrian army, though a conscript force, has modelled its ethos on that of the neighboring militia of Switzerland, with some success; that ethos has spiritual roots in the popular *jäger* tradition of the Habsburg Tirol, and is validated militarily by the high defensibility of much of Austria's terrain. Politically the army is entirely uncontroversial. The Irish, by contrast, though militarily insignificant, is unwillingly enbroiled in the complex nationalism of its homeland. The descendant of the insurrectionary force that fought the British for independence in 1918–21, it is also the victor of the Civil War of 1921–22, from which the losers, today represented by the Irish Republican Army, withdrew into underground illegality. Nonetheless, the IRA continues to represent itself as a legitimate embodiment of the nationalist movement, and its armed units (in practice mere terrorist cells) as the official army of the Irish people, to which true nationalists owe loyalty. The labyrinthine complexities of Irish political feeling accord this extraordinary twist of argument a certain force in the domestic context. The result is that all Irish governments, since the emergence of nationalist violence in Northern Ireland in 1969, have taken care not to involve the army in internal security duty against the IRA, lest the preconditions for civil war are thereby somehow recreated. This disinvolvement has had the desired political effect, but at the expense of perpetuating the army's lack of credibility as an effective military force. The only satisfying role it had been able to find for itself by way of compensation is in United Nations peace-keeping duty, in Africa and the Middle East, where it frequently serves besides the armies of Europe's other non-aligned states, particularly those from Scandinavia.

The last element in the Western European military scene is supplied by an army from outside the continent, that of the United States. Not only is it the largest and most powerful of those hitherto reviewed, it is also the force whose presence on European soil lends ultimate point to the post-war effort made by the North European states to provide for their conventional territorial defense. Without the presence of the US Seventh Army in southern Germany, outnumbered though it is by the West German army itself, the credibility of all NATO's armies, in their current state of equipment and at their present manpower levels, would, confronted by the power of the Warsaw Pact, be almost totally deficient. Western Europe's post-war military begins, indeed, with the decision by the Truman government in the late 1940s to tranform the American army of occupation in Germany from a symbolic to an operational force. As Colonel Summers' chapter graphically reveals, the post-war army of occupation's operational capacity had declined at the time of the Berlin blockade to a pathetically inept level. It consisted of a single division, unequipped materially or morally to defend its zone, and therefore Western Europe itself, from a Russian incursion, should Stalin have chosen to risk such an adventure. During the fifties and sixties it was painfully rebuilt to a strength of five divisions, with a powerful tactical air force as a complement to its armored counter-attack capability. The commitment of the United States to the defense of the non-Communist government in South Vietnam then ushered in what proved to be a time of troubles of great severity for the United States army as a whole, ramifying throughout its widely scattered areas of deployment and extending even to the German-based Seventh Army. Though the army's political reliability was never cast into doubt by the incident, its social foundations were sorely shaken, as also was its relationship with American society at large.

The army of the United States is an intensely American institution, characterized by large size, institutional homogeneity, and a strong problem-solving ethos. Continental isolation encouraged a tradition of keeping the army small until after World War II; then America's rise to world power required that its permanent peacetime size should increase. It preserved, nevertheless, its image of itself as the nucleus for national mobilization in emergency — which had come in 1861, 1917, and 1941 — and a repository, therefore, of training and operational skills that were deployed when a crisis pressed.

Vietnam presented it with exactly such a crisis, and the army responded in a fashion that had become traditional. The selective draft — in effect a form of regular recruitment — was set aside, and universal conscription implemented initially with exemptions for those undergoing university education. Training facilities and officer-candidate selection systems were rapidly expanded. New formations were cultivated, existing formations brought up to new strength. Between 1965 and 1967 the army moved with great efficiency from a peace to a medium-sized war footing, and effectively engaged the Viet Cong and North Vietnamese army units on the territory of South Vietnam, which in 1964 had seemed doomed to fall to their attack.

Two phenomena then intruded to set back the army's successful conduct of the war. The first was organization: instead of activating the whole reserve system as was normal American practice in time of war, the administration had decided merely to enlarge the intake of draftees; but, to minimize parental anxieties, it had determined that service in Vietnam should last no longer than one year for each individual. The effect was to keep units in a state of turmoil, with untrained draftees arriving at the same rate as combat-experienced veterans were leaving, a state of affairs that made the conduct of operations fraught with difficulties. The second phenomenon was connected with the first: because the administration would not activate the reserves — a distinction connected with the legally ambiguous nature of the country's involvement in Vietnam — the population could not see the war as a national emergency of the type which had previously engaged its whole-hearted support, as in Korea. The onus of the draft thus became unpopular, first, because it exempted college students, then, as they too were drawn in, because it did not, since the parents of college students constitute a vocal and effective political lobby in the United States. Disaffection in the army from the war itself, fuelled by its confused and apparently interminable nature, was reinforced by discontent at home. Eventually, though the army came close to winning victory on the ground, the government conceded defeat because of the erosion of the army's, together with the country's, will to persist in the battle.

The side-effects of the Vietnam débâcle, manifested in extensive drug-taking, indiscipline, general disrespect for authority and sound military practice and by the outbreak of severe black–white hostilities — though blacks had contributed disproportionately to the combat effort, and perhaps because of that — spread from South-East Asia to units in the continental United States and as far away as the army in Germany. A genuine army "crisis" was perceived and was officially admitted, if only by the implication, heard as late as the mid-1970s, that "the trouble is bottoming out" or "the army has been turned round."

Today, the army has unquestionably been "turned round", thanks to two measures in particular. The first was the decision to abandon the draft and establish the "all volunteer force." Though volunteers of the right quality were lacking initially, enough have now been found, thanks in part to economic recession, to make the army an enthusiastic and efficient organization once again. The second was re-equipment, begun in the 1970s but funded most generously by the Reagan administrations. Some of the funding has been lavish, leading to investment in overcomplicated systems that have not worked. But the army's new tanks and helicopters in particular are of superlative quality, and the general level of technical well-being brought by the rearmament program of the last ten years has helped indirectly to revive the army's human qualities also. The Seventh Army is now widely regarded, with the Bundeswehr, as the best of those deployed on the Central Front.

The other West European NATO armies might well indeed emulate the West German or American examples, as they are frequently counselled to do, not least by the Supreme Allied Commander himself. His words have had some effect. Rumbles of isolationism from an American electorate, which wearies of doing for the Europeans what they will not do for themselves, prove even more persuasive. For all that, levels of effectiveness, actual or potential, remain far lower than they should. Money lacks, of course; but there is also a widespread European reluctance to pay the tax of longer periods of national service and reserve training liability — both comparatively cheap ways of enhancing efficiency — which might compensate for heavier spending.

The hope for a Europe capable of defending itself, so strong in NATO's early years and implicit in the "Lisbon goals" that set its long-term objectives, remains a chimaera. Europe without the physical presence of the Seventh Army and without the guarantee of US nuclear protection remains a sub-continent that an aggressive Soviet Union would have at its mercy, whether it operated against it by direct military action or merely by threat and blackmail.

And yet, looking back over forty years to 1946, the development of Western Europe's armies in that period constitutes a collection of episodes in which the citizens of the states involved may take a certain national and even collective pride. The domestic misbehavior of four armies — the French, Spanish, Greek, and Portuguese — led to no long-term constitutional damage and now seems firmly consigned to their past. The militarily most important and politically most suspect of the armies, the West German, has been reconstituted as the central prop of the European military system, without damage to the West German state, to its relations with its neighbors, or to the NATO Alliance. The British army, thanks to its eccentric national structure, has pulled through an era of potentially destructive decolonization without causing a moment's alarm either to the British state or people; and has maintained a remarkably effective contribution to the defense of the Central Front meanwhile. Italy's army, potentially a disruptive element in that ideologically divided society, has remained inert during a period of acute domestic readjustment and has now actually been set on course towards greater professional efficiency. NATO's smaller members, in Scandinavia and the Low Countries, have been raised from a condition of virtual non-existence to a level where each is able to make a respectable contribution to European defense, if not in some cases as large a one as might be desired. Europe's neutral states have pursued or enhanced their capability for self-defense. No country in Western Europe, the Greeks' brief descent into rule by their colonels apart, has fallen under military dictatorship. No country has abandoned altogether, under economic pressure or through collapse of will, the capacity to make some effort for its own conventional defense. No country has suffered divisive domestic conflict or fallen into civil war through the failure of its army's resolution to support legitimate authority and the cause of social harmony. It is a better record than can be read in the history of Europe between the wars. The standards of decency maintained and efficiency achieved by Western Europe's armies since 1945 are part of the record of the European renaissance. It is as honorable a part as any other, political, economic, social, or cultural. Europe's soldiers are entitled to the respect of those they defend.

2 THE BRITISH ARMED FORCES SINCE 1945

Roger Beaumont

Britain and the United States share a common heritage of culture and democracy. But they also differ in many ways, in their respective social systems, geographical context, economic resources, and the wider historical setting. In the military realm, congruence was greatest during World War II, in the realms of strategy and tactics. After 1945, however, Britain ceased to be a first-class power, a fact not at first readily accepted, or even perceived. In any event, since the end of World War II British defense policy has been shaped by a tug-of-war between deployment of forces in Western Europe, maintaining a small independent nuclear deterrent force, and meeting "out-of-area" commitments, punctuated by a few minor limited war campaigns — fought in times of financial malaise, dismantling of empire, and the abandonment of a far-flung naval presence.

Analyses of British defense matters are circumscribed by the Official Secrets Act, and informally by difficulties experienced by outsiders or perceived critics whom the authorities may attempt to steer or nudge in the right way.[1] Yet it was in Britain that war correspondents first became a power in the land; it was in Britain where the art of second-guessing the military first took root, and has continued, in the face of strong counter-currents.

The ethos of each of the services also poses a problem. Strong differences between service functions and outlooks shape style and attitudes in ways both generic and British. Perhaps the leap from the intense tribalism of the army to the upper tiers of bureaucracy may be somewhat greater in the British military system than other armed forces. Yet it is not always the army that is most insular or rigid in reflex. In any case, the unique socializing power of British military institutions, especially the army, is widely respected,[2] although how much they reflect atavism *versus* a core of strength — or both — is not clear.[3]

Imperial Retrenchment

As Robert Harkavy has noted, a major geostrategic change has been under way since 1945, the shrinking of the basing network which the

Anglo-American Allies used to wage global war in World War II. That withdrawal from empire has had, even to the present, a qualitative influence on the armed forces, and on the perceptions of the British public of them. The actual numbers of forces in imperial garrisons was never very large, and today historians are grappling with the problem of just why it was that, with fragile stirrups and thin reins, the imperial masters were able to stay in the saddle for so long. Beyond that lies an analogous paradox, the fact that successor states hung onto many of the martial trappings and mannerisms of the British. Sadly, that was often rather more the case than with the Mother Country's democratic institutions. A *Punch* cartoon in the early 1960s caught the irony, depicting two African officers on a reviewing stand in British tropical uniforms, one remarking, "And to think that I almost went to the London School of Economics."

While large parts of the empire became self-governing in the late nineteenth and early twentieth centuries, Britain's shedding of imperial holdings began in earnest after World War II as a new Labour government came to power on a high tide of hopes for Social Democracy. While Attlee and his Ministers proved more moderate on defense than the rhetoric of Marxist shop stewards and Aneurin Bevan had suggested, Attlee presided over the major retreat from empire. Burma, India, and Palestine were all given independence within three years of the war's end.[5]

In India, British commanders and officers played a major role in parcelling out resources in the partitioning of the subcontinent. As arbiters in communal wrangling and in security roles, they were often helpless as Muslims and Hindus massacred each other in the bloodiest religious strife in modern history. British forces were almost unscathed and the last marched out solemnly in 1948 through the gate of India at Bombay. British officers served in key positions for half a generation, as American and then Soviet influence replaced that of the Raj in India, and America and China in Pakistan.

Imperial divestiture[6] slowed briefly, but resumed after Ghana was created from the Gold Coast in the mid-1950s. As it progressed, the armed forces were involved in dozens of counterinsurgency operations. In the Middle East, Britain's imperial base was moved time after time, as it came under siege from insurgents in Palestine, 1946–48, to Egypt and on to Kenya in the mid-1950s, to Cyprus in the late 1950s and early 1960s, and finally, to Aden until final withdrawal form the Middle East in the late 1960s.

In Malaya, the "Emergency" began in 1948 and dragged on until

1962. Small campaigns were fought to protect Malaysia and Singapore against Indonesian incursions. Covering forces were positioned in Brunei and Sarawak until the mid-1960s, as commitments in the Far East, aside from the demi-division at Hong Kong, were cut to arms aid, advisors, and military training in the UK, and after fending off Indonesian incursions, small garrisons by invitation of local states. As defense of Western Europe became Britain's main priority, operations "out-of-area" were less and less imperial and growingly a product of Cold War dynamics.[7]

British forces also fought three major campaigns, none exceeding the scale of major colonial — imperial wars. In June 1950, Royal Navy and Commonwealth naval forces were first into Korean waters when the Korean People's Republic launched a Soviet-planned and -equipped assault on the Republic of South Korea. The RAF played a small role, while the Commonwealth Divison was the largest force other than Korean and American units to fight in a war that ended in a stalemate in July 1953. Anxiety in Europe over American diversion of forces weakening its commitment to the newborn NATO was matched by General MacArthur's suspicions of British leaks of secrets to the Soviet bloc. His suspicions were proved accurate — not, as he believed, through the Labour government, but through British "moles" in Washington working close to US intelligence agencies.

However stained the escutcheon of the Secret Services, the British army's gleamed brightly. In April 1951 limited UN operations in northern South Korea were hit by a major Chinese attack. The Gloucestershire Regiment was caught in a human flood, surrounded, and cut off from food and water, which rendered their water-cooled machine guns useless. US aircraft pounded the encircling Chinese as various UN forces tried vainly to break through. As the nearby Northumberland Fusiliers and Ulsters and a small Belgian unit were pushed back, the Glosters, cheering to the sounding of the "Long Reveille," fought on until their ammunition was gone and they were ordered to break out. Only 39 were able to walk into UN lines, but they had held a Chinese corps at bay for a week.[8]

The general experience of the Commonwealth Division was that of other UN ground forces in Korea, mainly static warfare on fixed lines, with occasional fighting retreats and limited attacks. British and other Commonwealth elements supplemented American naval and air forces and Royal Marine Commandos were involved in various special operations. After the war, British prisoners-of-war were deemed to have won a special kind of victory, as the stout resistance of British conscripts to their captors led to a debate in the US after the war, and the subsequent adoption by the US army of a "Combat Arms Regimental System" — an attempt to emulate the British system, with further attempts along that line after Vietnam.[9]

Britain's next major campaign was the invasion of Egypt, along with French and Israeli forces, in October 1956. The hastily planned operation was successful, but revealed major deterioration in interservice coordination, doctrine, and the state of training and communications. The US and USSR condemned the Anglo–French–Israeli enterprise while heated debates in Parliament raged about the humiliation and the mismanagement. Britain as a superpower was seen as a thing past in all quarters.[10]

After Eden was succeeded by Harold Macmillan, the Tories substantially reduced conventional forces, and increased reliance on a strengthened strategic deterrence, as increasing numbers of V-bombers came into service, missile and nuclear tests progressed in Australia, and a British H-bomb was tested in May 1957. Under Minister of Defence Duncan Sandys, conscription was ended and Britain began a measured withdrawal to a posture of a second-class world and a first-class European power.[11]

From the White Paper of 1958 on, British defense policy became further detached from the "special relationship,"[12] on the eve of Vietnam. Also fateful was the Tories' demise in the wake of a scandal linking the Secretary of State for War with a call girl. The new Labour Defence Minister, Denis Healey, imported American systems analysis techniques to aid in the pruning, ironically an approach to military problem-solving which had first been shaped by British operational researchers.[13] The Defence Operational Analysis Establishment, with service science and procurement links, was formed as an in-house think-tank. At the same time, the Wilson Labour government presided over the transition to Polaris as the British independent deterrent, the result of the accord reached between President Kennedy and Prime Minister Macmillan when the Americans cancelled Skybolt in 1962, making V-bomber modernization out of the question.[14]

The onset of détente in 1968 coincided with the final phase of British withdrawal from the Far and Middle East. De Gaulle's blocking of Britain from the Common Market and wrangles with Rhodesia were special problems for Britain, but both seemed small compared with American problems in Southeast Asia. In the early 1970s, Henry Kissinger often seemed to be treating Britain as a minor partner in the Western alliance as the Nixon administration sought to overcome the

Vietnam malaise and reassert America's role as a first-class power.

Concern over Britain's economic state mounted in the 1970s when Edward Heath was defeated in an election after losing a face-off against the miners' union. A government bail-out of Rolls-Royce added injury to insult. Throughout the 1970s the defense budget, pegged to declining increases in gross national product, fell below 5 per cent then 4 per cent and finally, by the early 1980s, to 3 per cent — all in the face of major inflationary pressures and spiralling personnel, development, maintenance, and procurement costs. In spite of such strain, however, Britain allocated a higher percentage of GNP to defense than other NATO members in Europe.

Conscription

Some people, like Corelli Barnett, foresaw the squeeze in the late 1960s, and called for Swiss-type universal service with tiny regular forces and large reserves. A more recent solution for the all-volunteer cost squeeze through conscription has been made by Ken Booth,[15] a proposal linked to the question of Britain's ability or will to maintain the broad spectrum of defense capacity that it had in the past, especially with regard to nuclear weapons.

The Conservatives had put an end to National Service less than a decade after B. H. Liddell Hart called for such a move in *The Defence of the West*.[16] He argued that technical changes in warfare ended the need for big battalions-in-being, and was also concerned about alienating youth. However valid the latter concerns, the Suez affair and a growing reliance on nuclear deterrence in the late 1950s ended what many saw as an unpopular and inefficient system.

In the 1968 Sandys White Paper, overseas commitments were honored, but Sandys noted a changing posture of the army in its Commonwealth-bolstering role, from that of neighbourhood beat-cop to "SWAT" team. Amassing adequate numbers of fast, modern air transports to carry the "SWAT" team became and remains a main concern in British defense planning.

The last National Serviceman was paid off in 1961, and Britain grappled with problems of recruiting and retention in the face of soaring civilian pay and rising procurement and maintenance costs. When, in 1967 de Gaulle took France out of NATO, the independent French deterrrent was a new stimulus, along with American slights since 1946, to maintain an independent British deterrent. CND — Committee for

Nuclear Disarmament — gained substantial publicity in the late 1950s, but crumbled away in the early 1960s as Polaris came into service and CND links to Soviet security elements became publicly known. Then, along with anti-nuclear movements across Europe, CND surged forward again in the late 1970s, and Carter and Reagan were both forced to cancel plans to deploy neutron bombs. After the deployment of American cruise and Pershing II tactical missiles began at the request of Western European governments, CND and other anti-nuclear movements in Western Europe lost visibility and influence outside their regions.

Retrenchment — and Déjà Vu in Ulster[17]

In 1967–68, as the Wilson government cut back and withdrew British forces from the Far East and Aden, social unrest mounted. Students at the Sorbonne clashed with the CRS as British counterparts assaulted the establishment at new British universities, and American-style civil rights marches began in Ulster. Catholic clashes with security forces dominated by Ulster Protestants pushed the province toward civil war in 1969, and almost a full division of troops was shunted from the Rhine to the Boyne to stand between the factions. A satire in *Punch* on British army officer selection testing included as a multiple-answer choice: "I want to go to Northern Ireland and keep Christians from murdering each other." But it was soon a matter beyond irony.

Initially, most Catholics welcomed the British troops as a buffer between them and their traditional foes, and British public opinion leaned in favour of the Catholics. The honeymoon ended, however, after "Bloody Sunday" in Londonderry in 1972, when British paratroops not trained in the subtleties of "low-intensity warfare" fired into a crowd and killed 13 people, later claiming terrorists who had opened fire were in the throng. Rekindling of old images of Black-and-Tans put the British force under siege.

Rather than a flash of fury from British authorities and security forces that seemed the goal of terrorists and the Catholic population to differing degrees, the reaction was a mix of apathy and irritation. As the Provisional Irish Republican Army and the Irish National Liberation Army emerged, with violent tactics and Marxist overtones, and faint traces of KGB and various European and Third World groups' support of Irish insurgents emerged, British forces maintained coolness and their proverbial sang-froid became a major asset. When British officers claimed that perhaps no other army could have maintained that coolness in such a setting, it seemed a more credible claim to many Americans than might have been the case before US involvement in Vietnam or the ghetto riots of 1965–68.

British troops developed elaborate procedures to protect themselves as adversaries — including women and children — beset them with an array of weapons, from rocks and Molotov cocktails to gigantic plastic explosive traps, along with sniping and psychological warfare. British security forces stopped using sensory deprivation techniques in the late 1960s and early 1970s, due to domestic pressure and to sensitivity regarding Ireland in the US, Canada and Australia, not to mention Britain itself, and among Britons resident in the Republic of Ireland — and the delvings of Amnesty International.

One side-effect was that British forces underwent a kind of combat conditioning, in a weak analogy to the old Northwest Frontier. Another was a refinement of low-intensity warfare techniques, including intelligence, liaison with internal security forces, psychological warfare, and handling of explosives, including chemical sensing and the use of robots. Another was a steady increase of aid from Irish Republic security elements.

A less visible British army role was the raising, training, and equipping of the Ulster Defence Regiment — the UDR — in numbers about half the size of, and a symbolic counterpart to, the Republic's small army. The UDR, seen by the terrorists as a surrogate to the ''B'' Specials, became a prime target of attacks, political and physical.[18]

By the 1980s, British counter-intelligence had infiltrated and forced a fragmentation upon the IRA *et al.* Violence had declined, as had British troop strength. Major Irish-American politicians had asked for an end to American financial aid to groups supporting terrorism, and President Reagan had extended the carrot of financial aid in prospect of an accord between North and South. Occasional sensational attacks became the mechanism of the violent factions, such as the attempted kidnapping of Princess Anne, bombing attacks on Earl Mountbatten, the Horse Guards at Hyde Park Corner and barracks, Mrs Thatcher at Brighton, and London park bandstands, and the mortar assault on the Newry police station in February 1985.

Little note was taken in the US of anti-Catholic support for the Ulster Defence Association and other Protestant militant elements.[19] Both sides seem locked in an embrace of grinding pathology, each enshrining all its own acts as noble or clever and its foes as evil incarnate. Thus while British forces in Northern Ireland are linked to past wrongs, whether they remain for ever more or leave soon, their[20] involvement since 1969 is far from the most sordid chapter in the record of the British military in Ireland. Only seers or fools would feel safe in claiming to see very far ahead into these mists.

The Ever-Curving Path: Britain and Nuclear Deterrence

In August 1945, in less than a week, Britain's power collapsed an order of magnitude below the US and the USSR. After Hiroshima, it would take but a handful rather than hundreds of thousands of high-explosive bombs to virtually wipe out smaller powers like Britain, France, Germany, Italy or Spain. That grim, simple fact of national identity and survival, while rarely articulated, weakened Britain's military posture after 1945, separate from the fatigue and bankruptcy brought about by the war. Yet the full effects were not immediately apparent in policy, and adjustments were often made reluctantly.[21]

In spite of a massive reduction in armaments along with other major powers after the war, Britain retained substantial military forces for just over a decade, a burden borne in spite of massive dislocation, privation, damage and obsolescence brought on by the war. It was also in spite of erosion of Britain's pre-war trade advantages,[22] and dependency first on US loans and then on a major share of Marshall Plan aid after 1947. Beyond personal privations in the austerity era under the Attlee Labour government, 1945-51, there were several reminders of the new order of things. The real muscle in Western military power lay in the possession, ability to make and to drop atomic bombs.

Contrary to promises made by Roosevelt to Churchill, the US Congress slammed the door on sharing nuclear energy and weapons secrets. While also on relatively lean defense spending, America made it clear from 1946 that it meant to be the senior partner in Western defense. The McMahon Act of 1946 sealed off American nuclear weapons from the world. British economies and withdrawal from Greece led President Truman, in 1947, to lay forth his doctrine of "containment." The Marshall Plan soon followed, to bolster war-shattered Western European nations' economies, and deny Communism the fertile compost heap of socioeconomic decay in which it flourished. Much of this aid was directed at Britain and, with its substantial military portion, became a kind of Cold War Lend-Lease.

In the late 1940s, America's defense superstructure was rebuilt, as Congress approved a command system which meshed military and intelligence, much like the British wartime hierarchy, but with new labels. When the Soviets closed Berlin's road and rail access routes in 1948, the Western powers mounted a 15-month airlift, mainly a US air force effort, but with support from the Royal Air Force as well, including Sunderland flying boats which landed on Berlin's lakes. That and a Communist *coup* in Czechoslovakia hastened the growth of a Western defense community, which metamorphosed into NATO — the North Atlantic Treaty Organization — in 1949, the year that Mao drove the nationalists to Formosa, and the USSR tested its first atomic bomb. In the early 1950s, Communist insurgencies in Greece, Indochina, Malaya, and the Philippines were overshadowed by the Korean War. Anti-western regimes appeared in various parts of the Third World, affecting British bases as already noted, especially in Egypt.

As Britain undertook its own nuclear weapons research, and the V-bomber strategic force went into production, the USAF's Strategic Air Command handed over B-29s over to the RAF to fill the gap, the main British strategic bomber being the lumbering Lincoln.[23] As SAC extended its bases round the rimlands of Eurasia, a close relationship developed between SAC and RAF Bomber Command, especially after the Eisenhower administration reduced the strictures of the McMahon Act, as the Kennedy administration would even further in the early 1960s.

The role of the V-bomber force was altered by the test-firing of a British hydrogen bomb in 1955. From that point, Britain targeted Soviet cities, its deterrent being by implication retaliatory,[24] and the technologies of accuracy rather too expensive to develop alone. It was also in conformity with the difficulties of target identification for V-bombers, and later for the Polaris submarine force — if it was not pre-empted at the outset of a conflict.[25]

The V-bombers' function in the equation of Western nuclear battle management was described as one of blasting on through Warsaw Pact Soviet defenses, opening a corridor for SAC. Such hints raised at least the possibility that leaks of RAF "city-busting" designs from the cryptic depths of British defense doctrine and policy might cover for another targeting plan aimed at blinding Soviet command-and-control and battle management along its shortest warning axis.

While Britain's war-worn and strained economy had some resurgence after 1945, it began to fall away from the pattern of upward curves seen in other industrial states.[26] As problems emerged pointing to what became known as the "English disease," both Tory and Labour government defense economies brought British conventional defense resources under close rein, and stabilized the British nuclear deterrent in a world of proliferation.

Indeed, over thirty projects had dead-ended by the late 1970s, most, like the TSR-2 aircraft[27] and "Blue Streak" missile, rather far from American public consciousness, but the cancellation of the "Skybolt" loft-bombing missile system by the Kennedy administration in 1962 made headlines on both sides of the Atlantic.[28] Thor medium-range ballistic missiles were given to Britain by the United States to augment the V-bomber deterrent until Polaris-type submarines came on station. The subsequent attempt to establish nuclear weapons-firing surface ships manned by mixed NATO crews, the so-called multilateral force, came to naught, and the decision mechanism in NATO for using nuclear weapons remains a cumbersome committee.

The relatively modest British deterrent was modernized in the 1980s as British-built Chevaline multiple warheads, whose development began under Wilson's government in the late 1960s, entered service. The first serious parliamentary debates on the deterrents came in 1980 and 1982, as Britain committed funds for a Trident-based force to be deployed in the 1990s. Choices were made from estimates which soon showed signs of large overruns, as the pound sagged and technical problems emerged, leading one analyst to suggest that Britain had been forced into "specialization by economic default".

The wider exchange between US and British nuclear weapons experts begun in the Eisenhower years continued. The Soviets have argued since SALT II that Britain's and France's deterrents be counted as theater nuclear weapons — thus also investing Western theater weapons with a strategic flavor.[29] The adoption by a weakened Labour Party of a unilateral nuclear disarmament stance during the brief surge of anti-nuclear agitation in the early 1980s as "Euromissiles" were deployed in England raised a prospect, however problematical, of Britain falling back to a much-reduced role in NATO, or in the European Defence Community, if not neutrality, and relying totally on conventional forces of various types — from a conscripted militia to highly refined elite-based regulars.[30] One theme that changed little, however, was the persisting view of the deterrent as a relatively fuzzy symbol of national sovereignty, rather than seeing it linked to any specific policy, or range of policies, relative to contingencies.[31]

Against these uncertainties regarding the logic of deterrence, the revolution in conventional warfare and the Falklands War have brought a focus back on the importance of human will, stamina, and skill. The complex, evolving interactions of policy, technology, and human dimensions of military organization must be kept in view in appraising approaching major decision-points in British defense policy and procurement, both in terms of what seems to be and what might be.

"Tommy This and Tommy That": the Army

The British army both shrank and changed in the aftermath of World War II, with a fitfulness matching Britain's searching for a new self-image while surrounded by symbols and remnants of lost glories. The Indian army went in 1947, and with it the Northwest Frontier school of arms in which several generations of British officers first tasted war. Imperial "small wars" were past — but something very like them lay ahead. About a thousand British soldiers have died since 1945 in seven sizeable counter-terror and guerilla campaigns — Palestine, Malaya, Kenya, Cyprus, Aden, Malaysia, and Ulster. The army also bore the brunt of the British commitment in Korea, 1950–53, of Suez, 1956, and the Falklands, 1982, with about 1,300 killed in all three. In addition, many dozens more were to die in garrison duties across the shrinking firmament of empire/commonwealth, as well as in over sixty minor operations.

The major foci of army concern and resource dispositions, however, remained at home and in Germany, as European defense took shape in stages from 1947 on. Against a background of oscillating, but always lean, resources, but bolstered by Marshall Plan aid in the late 1940s and early 1950s, the British Army of the Rhine took shape. As with the US army, it prepared for a "Theater War," a defensive battle against Soviet mega-blitzkrieg. Lying directly west of the Group of Soviet Forces Germany, the BAOR is the "lion in the way" on the North German plain — less a plain than a riverine-laced conurbation. British I Corps is under NORTHAG — Northern Army Group — with Dutch, Belgian, and German forces, on the left flank of CENTAG, the main American area of concentration. Its headquarters is at Bielfeld.

BAOR is comprised of essentially four divisions of armor, supported by an artillery division dispersed in long-range support roles, plus a small mobile reserve and reconnaissance element — the 5th Field Force. Corps support forces are under the British Logistical Support Command, mainly in the Rear Combat Zone — as are over 70,000 civilian dependants. Its equipment is variegated and complex, including over 40 different types of vehicles, 5 radar systems, over half a dozen

Table 2.1: British Forces Strength and Distribution, 1984

Overall Service Strength

	Active	Reserves
Army	161,539	219,642
Royal Navy–Royal Naval Air Service–Marines	71,281	37,000
Royal Air Force	93,089	29,893
All services	325,909	287,535

Schematic Representation of Distribution

Canada– Training-liaison	N. Ireland 9,400	Great Britain Strategic Forces 2,500 Reserves 220,000	Germany c. 56,000
	(Norlant)	Gibraltar Cyprus c. 2,000 4,800	Hong Kong c. 9,000
Belize 1,500			Brunei c. 2,000
		(Indian Ocean) Diego Garcia RN detachment Ascension RN/RAF detachments "Fortress Falklands" c. 4,000	

From *The Military Balance 1984–1985* (International Institute of Strategic Studies, London, 1984) and *Statement on the Defence Estimates 1984,* Command Paper 9227-1 and 2 (Her Majesty's Stationery Office, London, 1984).

major command and control nets, 11 types of artillery pieces of different sizes, 10 rocket systems, 6 types of aircraft, and over 20 small arms, mortars, and mine types. In addition, RAF Germany has 13 squadrons earmarked for support.

How would BOAR fill its role as a small "wedge" in the much larger NATO fan of forces from North Cape to the Armenian border? Given the many scenarios of Soviet pressure and attack, from small bounds and negotiations to a gigantic attack, it is easy enough to say that it depends on too many unforeseeable variables. Focusing on the most general stereotype of a Soviet juggernaut crashing into CENTAG, a role of reserve or flank attack would seem most likely. How would the complex fabric of BAOR — or other NATO forces — hold up in such a tumult? Given the demonstrated quality of the British infantry in the Falklands, and the respect evident among Britain's allies in Europe for her little army, in all likelihood it would do rather well.

There are many mechanical problems. Just as RAF Germany is

experiencing teething problems with adopting the Tornado for service, so BAOR is facing problems of transition of a number of systems, most critically the Challenger Chobham-armored tank in lieu of Chieftain. The latter had had a lot of bugs worked out, and was familiar. New electronic warfare and C_2 — command and control systems — also have many bugs to be worked out in peacetime, and other problems may not appear until the press of battle. British systems, the product of greater relative poverty than some of her allies, are not fully interoperable. (That is not fully a product of dearth of treasure.) In recent exercises, the flood of data flowing from US C^2 systems, for example, swamped the much smaller capacity of British computers and led to substantial dumping.

Most critical perhaps in a theater war would be losses also swamping the medical facilities. Projections are about 2,000 casualities a day, and the fairly rapid arrival of 50,000 reinforcements. Different lines on graph paper drawn a degree or two more than the former and less than the latter make the "half-life" of BAOR very short. The mobilization and training base, and reserves in existence in Britain, do not make British ground forces a significant element in theater war of any magnitude after about three weeks to a month — or less if nuclear weapons are used, and the British paid a special tribute by the controllers of the Russian god of battles.

Britain is meeting its commitments. Whether BAOR would play a synergistic role à la the "Old Contemptibles" of the British Expeditionary Force in 1914, or suffer the lot of Sir John Moore's little army, lies in the hands of fate. How much longer the commitment will be honored at this level is a question that may be left in abeyance, or paid for by lopping off another loop in Britain's nexus of defense. The draining off of a division to Ulster of the 55,000-man BAOR contingent and the maintenance of the 2nd Division as a reserve in the UK that can move either way has been matched by a shrinkage of British divisional strength to the lowest of any current major power.[32] At the same time, there is much about British methods and systems that is admired by various observers, e.g. the new Challenger tank and the Wavell-Ptarmigan command-and-control system.[33]

Beyond orders of battle and tables of equipment lie the nuances. The colorful imagery of the old Cardwellian regiments, a product of the 1860s, although expensive and frustrating in wartime, has lived on in essence. But the army has changed. Ironically, in the face of admiration in the US army for that system, some British defense analysts have called for a Corps of Infantry along the lines of the Royal Artillery or

Royal Armoured Corps,[34] to end for good the congruence between designation and actual areas of recruitment, a trend which has continued in some infantry units.

Neither is the larger structure of the army wholly rationalized at higher levels, nor the flow of authority within forces. Ten military districts and various commands overlie complex bureaucratic networks. Unlike the US, FRG, and USSR, where the division remained a main building-block, and chains of command are relatively clearly drawn, the British system is less sharply rationalized. The Army Board, for example, shares authority uncertainly with the military chain of command. It should also be noted that infantry regiments in the UK are assigned to two different types of divisions, one operational, the other administrative.

Six main administrative divisions encompass infantry regiments (i.e. US battilions) thus:

Household Divisions[36] — 8 regiments of Foot Guards — Grenadiers — Coldstream Guards — Scots Guards — Welsh Guards — Irish Guards; and two regiments of Household Cavalry, Life Guards and Royal Horse Guards (an anomaly)

Queen's Division — Regiments traditionally raised in South and Southeast

King's Division — regiments traditionally raised in the North and Northern Ireland

Prince of Wales' Division — regiments traditionally raised in the West Country and Wales

Light Division — old light infantry regiments

Scottish Division — Scottish infantry regiments

Outside this nexus lie the Royal Engineers, Royal Electrical and Mechanical Engineers, the Royal Artillery, Royal Army Ordnance Corps, Royal Signals, Woman's Royal Army Corps, Royal Army Medical Corps, Army Catering Corps, Royal Corps of Military Police, Royal Corps of Transport, Royal Armoured Corps and other ancillary elements — the "infrastructure," the support services — the "tail".

There are, beyond the Household Division, two *corps d'élite* in the army, the Special Air Service and the Parachute Brigade.

The Special Air Service (SAS),[37] is the descendant of one of many World War II "mobs for jobs," carefully selected, arduously trained, and very secret, recipients of decorations listed as "X" or "Y" in the *Army Gazette*, its handiwork visible in various operations, but under a cloak and darkly, e.g. Cyprus, Malaya, Aden, Kenya, Northern Ireland, and the Falklands. They have made international news from time to time, as when they aided the German GSG 9 at Mogadishu, in Northern Ireland when a group was arrested in the Irish Republic, in the Princess Gate affair when they broke into the Iranian Embassy, and in the Falklands. They have also had some influence on US Special Forces, as a model and in training.

The Parachute Brigade, its three batallions and support units a small vestige of the multi-divisional forces of World War II, has been visible in post-colonial skirmishes, and a model for many foreign forces. There is, as a result of promotion patterns, a sense that the Royal Green Jackets — the Rifle Brigade — are a kind of "Black Mafia" and an elite *sui generis*. Some also believe this is true of some Royal Artillery units. Indeed, many of the British army believe that their unit is an elite[38] — a strength of the system in respect of morale, if not cohesion and interchangeability in the larger sense, let alone tolerance for creativity.

In spite of all the badges, tartans, hackles and other appurtenances which mark the British army even in the field, and give it a faint flavor of the feudal, the reality is that the regionalism which such trappings once conveyed has largely fallen away. Overall, there is far less regionality in recruiting than was the case even in the 1960s, although in the infantry substantial pockets of regionalism can be found; e.g. the Devon and Dorsets, Irish Rangers and Sherwood Foresters all have over three-quarters of their strength raised from the locale designated in their title. The furor that arose when a Labour government disbanded the Argyll and Sutherland Highlanders in the 1960s may have been the last major spasm of regionality. Perhaps . . .

While Americans and others see the British system as stable, a close look at the history of British military organization shows much turbulence and a search for improvement through restructuring very like that which has been the norm in US forces since 1942.[39] Thus genealogies of British infantry and calvalry regiments reflect substantial restructuring and amalgamation since World War II, e.g. the 1966 merger of the Queen's Royal (West Surrey) Regiment, the Queen's Own Royal West Kent Regiment, the Buffs (Royal East Kent) Regiment, the Royal Sussex Regiment and the Middlesex (Duke of Cambrige's Own) Regiment into the Queen's Regiment. (Even the old Indian army was subjected to major shuffling and relabeling approximately every twenty years from the Mutiny of 1857–58 to independence in 1947.)

The oscillating "dialogue between harmony and invention" seen in the past seems unlikely to ease in the face of Britain's economic malaise. Beyond that, the expanding flow of complex military technology is more and more beyond the reach of all but the superpowers, and taxing even their capacity.[40] Yet the premium on dispersion, mobility, initiative, and stamina are much in line with the strong light infantry–*corps d'élite* ethos which exists across the British army.[41]

The Royal Air Force[42]

Sixty RAF squadrons are organized under three main headquarters: Strike Command, at RAF High Wycombe; Support Command, at RAF Brampton, and Royal Air Force Germany, at RAF Rheindalen. The latter is the main component force in NATO's 2nd Allied Tactical Air Force, commanded by the Commander-in-Chief, RAF Germany, close to the "cutting edge," in constant near-contact with major Warsaw Pact forces and sharing crowded air space and bases in the FRG with other NATO forces. At the present time, modernization is aimed at bringing the multinational Tornado on line, a process hampered by shortages of support personnel and spare parts.[43]

Strike Command is made up of three main groups. No. 1 has strike, reconnaissance, fixed wing and helicopter transports, and tanker aircraft. No. 11 Group's mission is all-weather air defense of Great Britain, and NATO defense zones on the western sectors of the Central and Northern regions, and the Atlantic. Its forces are continually in contact with Soviet aircraft flying close to British territory, and would be responsible for covering reinforcement and evacuation in a theater war. No 18's role is reconnaissance and maritime patrol.

Support Command oversees the substantial training network, including fighter training at RAF Valley, multi-engined, navigation, flight engineer and electronic air-crew training at RAF Finningly, helicopter pilot and instructor training at RAF Shawbry, the Royal Air Force Academy at Cranwell, the University Air Squadrons, and the Central Flying School at RAF Scampton, which trains instructors and houses the Red Arrow demonstration flying team. It also controls the training of various non-flying personnel, including the RAF Regiment, whose role is airfield defense, including the manning of Rapier close-range anti-aircraft missiles at various locations in the UK and Germany. Logistics, communications, medical support, catering, police, and education also comes under its purview.

The Royal Air Force's broad range of aircraft includes Jaguar and Tornado strike aircraft, products of multinational collaboration. Its US-built Phantoms have British engines, while British-produced aircraft include the Buccaneer, the Nimrod, the Harrier short and vertical take-off and landing aircraft also used by the US Marines, and the Hawk advanced jet trainer. RAF and Navy variants of the Harrier bore the brunt of operations in the Falklands, where its ability to land and take off from nearly any piece of ground proved vital in the absence of conventional aircraft carriers and runways. Its quick changes of course, hovering capacity and deceleration confounded Argentinian pilots.[44]

The war in the South Atlantic also made the need for in-flight refuelling apparent. The tanker fleet has been expanded and modernized, and steps taken to ensure that most aircraft can be refuelled in flight.[45] Transport lift has also been brought up to date.[46]

In the 1984 Defence Estimates, attempts to upgrade incrementally experienced a setback. Budgeting guidelines called for an increase of 15 percent in aircraft strength over the next decade, while holding manpower steady. One basic problem resulting from short resources over the years is the drying up of certain pockets of indigenous expertise and productive and maintenance capacity in British industry. Beyond that, it has hampered the development of the range of versatility, leading to gaps in the spectrum of capability, except what can be "bought in." The effects of the "brain drain" over the years, while real, cannot be easily measured.

While RAF fighter pilots have done well in the US Air Force's mock battle contests in Nevada, the RAF lacks the sophisticated airborne warning-and-control systems (AWACS) of the USAF, a gap that the Nimrod AEW-3 was designed to narrow, but technical problems and cost increases have delayed it for two years. At the same time, the RAF and other services have done far more in countering chemical–biological warfare. The US has studied RAF techniques; the RAF has a reputation for innovative ordnance design as well.

The RAF, like the Royal Navy and the USAF, has a major function in providing positive support in airlifting in disasters, including Ethiopia, and more specifically in aiding those in peril in various situations, having saved over 5,000 lives over the last decade. (The RAF maintains special mountain rescue teams.)

Senior, Silent, and Shrinking: the Royal Navy

The Senior — and Silent — Service has undergone the greatest relative shrinkage of the forces since 1945.[47] The umbrella of empire has been furled, and the navy's main role today is that of serving as the mainstay of NORLANT, NATO's eastern Atlantic command. Since 1945, except for China and Korea at the outset, Suez, and the Falklands, the navy has had far less a role to play in Cold War and Commonwealth operations than the other forces.[48] The Polaris force was, in fact, while manned by the navy, set off from the fleet more sharply than the US oceanic deterrent.

In the mid-1970s, the navy's involvement in the "Cod War"[49] (involving a fishery dispute with Iceland), the prospect of minor neo-gunboat diplomacy roles, and the overshadowing by the United States and Soviet fleets offered a somewhat Gilbert-and-Sullivan irony relative to the long heyday of British naval supremacy. The Royal Navy has boarded an average of just over a thousand fishing vessels a year over the last decade, its Fishery Protection Fleet serving on behalf of the Ministry of Agriculture, Fisheries and Food.

The threatened cuts of the Thatcher government in 1982 would have made Britain a third-class naval power. How much these proposals encouraged the Argentine junta to seize the Falklands is not clear, nor is what would have happened had the Argentines been a bit more patient. Carrier forces were slated for especially major surgery, and only one was on hand for the Task Force. Substantial improvisation and modification were undertaken even before the Task Force set out, and the effects of decisions on design driven by sharp economies over a generation came to light in the press of operations. Rapid conversion of merchant ships to auxiliary roles and the special reliance on Harrier VTOL aircraft in the absence of standard carriers were visible at the time, and such questions as weapons mixes, the lack of AWACS, and problems of ship materials and construction emerged later.

The Falklands also led to some new conclusions about the vulnerability of various ships, from sea-keeping to damage control, and the extent to which high technology creates problems as well as solves them.[50] While the pattern of cutbacks was reversed after the campaign, the Royal Navy, once numbered in dozens of capital ships and hundreds of cruisers, destroyers, frigates, and submarines, now weighs in at less than 60 major warships.

4 SSBN–Polaris submarines — strategic forces — 3 in service — 1

refitting
22 other submarines
4 ASW carriers and assault ships
1 ASW frigate
13 destroyers and cruisers
39 frigates
31 patrol vessels
34 anti-mine warfare vessels

c. 35 miscellaneous support ships and tankers

The patrol areas are no longer global, although Britain still claims a share of Western conventional deterrence in the form of presence and "rapid response" outside its NATO–UK regional focus.[51] The Fleet has five main bases: Rosyth, Devonport, Portland, Portsmouth, and the nuclear submarine base at Faslane in Scotland near the US counterpart at Holy Loch. The navy's main functions are surveillance of Soviet submarines, the ever-present fishing boats, protection of British offshore oil installations, and practicing wartime tasks like providing security for the shipping lanes supporting a theater war, as well as protecting the Polaris submarine deterrent force.

There is, of course, much to the Royal Navy beyond the ships. It includes a shore establishment, and its own *corps d'élite*, the Royal Marine Commandos, slightly over 7,000 men, and the naval variant of the SAS, the SBS — Special Boat Service, much smaller, but its numbers classified.[52] The Royal Navy's air elements number 20 squadrons, 4 fixed wing and 16 helicopter. Eight of them are training units, 6 anti-submarine and 2 reconnaissance–strike fighters.

How the "Lessons of the Falklands" and the decision to establish "Fortress Falklands" and strengthen conventional elements will affect the future is unclear. The navy Task Force suffered most in that operation, with over two-thirds of warships hit, and five sunk or gravely damaged. While the Thatcher government's naval cut proposals exceeded those of any Labour government, beyond those lay organizational problems, including poor links between designers and builders and the naval bureaucracy, inter-service battling, weak combined planning and strategy formulation, and the weakening of Britain's shipbuilding industry.[53]

The ill wind of the Falklands at least threw into relief many problems that stemmed from peacetime inertia. Beyond the individual problems, it was clear that spreading out lean resources or leaving them in a lump does not ultimately mask the fact that the larder is smaller, and that, to extend the metaphor, defeat takes the form of loss and humiliation. For the navy, the Falklands was, as Wellington said of Waterloo, a damned close-run thing.

On the brighter side of that campaign were the many instances of high performance by people of all services, troops ashore "yomping" and "humping" and winning in the face of substantial odds with light equipment, the performance of naval damage control teams, anti-aircraft missiles, the improvisational skills of logisticians underlining the importance of personnel quality and training — including the oft-ignored art of marching.

The Very Silent Service: Intelligence

A sense of fog and half-light pervades any consideration of the question of British intelligence. Like other nations' intelligence services, performance and effect can only be glimpsed, fleeting and out of focus. And like the intelligence structures of other nations, Britain's is divided into functions within and outside the military province. Seconding (cross-assignment), the use of cover, and anonymity make analysis difficult by intent to contemporaries — and to historians as well. The main Secret Service structures which are visible are: MI5 — counter-intelligence; MI6 — foreign intelligence; and MI9 — prisoner-of-war escape and evasion. Other mechanisms evident in World War II which one would assume have some function within current systems include SIGINT — Signals Intelligence; SOE — Special Operations Executive, sabotage and espionage in occupied Europe; London Control Section — the deception effort which masked the true time and place of invasions of the continent; and the efforts now deemed Enigma–Ultra, surrounding the decrypting of German high-level command radio messages.

In the formal military area lies the regular staff intelligence function, i.e. the maintenance of files, maps, and other data bases to aid commanders and staffs in planning and operations within each service, but most research and analysis have been focused on the glamorous realm of strategic and quasi-military intelligence.

While official histories and memoirs have lifted corners of the veil of secrecy, much remains fuzzy.[54] Sensationalism abounds in intelligence journalism,[55] and is shaped by special class tensions and treasured resentments.[56] Matters such as relationships with the military, the dynamics and processes, the structure, the carry-over of data and of rapport or hostility and rivalry from the days of empire, and the nature of links with the civil police and Special Branch are not even faintly traced in detail.

The most critical visible problems are those of competence and penetration. A great deal of the by-play in British intelligence has become popular fare, e.g. the exploits of Sidney Reilly in Czarist and Bolshevik Russia and the "Trust"; the "turning" of Philby, Burgess, and Maclean; the Blunt case; and the amassing of evidence in regard to Sir Roger Hollis.[57] While many shortfalls and failures are evident, the successes which came to light a generation after World War II raise a difficult question in regard to appraisal of current effectiveness and potential. Is the "Service" as bureaucratically hapless as depicted in, say, the novels of John Le Carré? How could it ever have been so adroit as to carry off such *coups* as the "Man Who Never Was?" Or the Double-Cross System?[58] Or the London Control Section?[59] Or the decrypting triumphs at Bletchley Park and the guarding of that great secret for over thirty years?

Given the many purported gaffes of other intelligence services, the apparent "turning" of Admiral Canaris, the selling of secrets by US naval officers between the wars, the work of the Rote Kapelle, the possible tricking of Stalin by the Germans into his blood purges, penetrations of the Bundesnachrichtendienst and so on — one can well ask what is a reasonable performance? Beyond that lie questions as to how one gains a clear enough view of the intelligence game to make a judgement — and how much of what one gets to see is the game or an intentionally warped version of it, since part of the game is to confuse the audience. Did British deception skills extend only to a certain point, short of the adroitness perceived by foes in the characterization of *Albion Perfide?* How much may evidence of floundering and old-boyism essentially be correct, and even short of full disclosure? Or is some portion of it the use of a facade of bumbling and muddling through to mask a greater degree of effectiveness? The virtual paralyzing of the IRA and the forcing of the Provos to a fragmented cellular structure raise interesting questions. Thus one can only be sure that one cannot be sure.

"Train Hard, Fight Easy": Training and Education

In a certain sense, everything peacetime forces do is training. Statistics regarding expenditures for training and enrollments do not include operational and unit training or maneuvers. However, about 10 percent of Britain's defense budget is earmarked for training, mostly for training specialists across the range of branches and services — the cost of training some specialists is 1,000 times that of infantrymen. Over 60,000 people are being trained or training outside units at any one time, with slightly over 42,000 at the service colleges:

Entry level institutions (approximate average student population):
    Royal Military Academy, Sandhurst   c. 600
    Britannia Royal Naval College, Dartmouth   c. 350
    RAF College, Cranwell   c. 450
Advanced level:
    Staff College, Camberley   c. 170
    Royal Naval College, Greenwich   c. 150
    RAF Staff College, Bracknell   c.85
Technical colleges:
    Royal Engineering College, Manadon   c. 425
    Royal Military College of Science, Shrivenham   c. 450
Joint service:
    Joint Services Staff College
    Royal College of Defence Studies   c. 75

The Royal Army Educational Corps was founded in 1920 as a successor to the Corps of Army Schoolmasters, and aimed at improving the quality of soldiery for both service and civilian life. It also had a special task: the shaping and passing on of doctrine. Over the years it drifted far from the latter purpose. Viewed by some officers as having been a bit too "Bolshie" in imbuing troops with a Labourite *Weltanschauung* during World War II, thus aiding in the defeat of Churchill in the 1945 election, the RAEC has no counterpart in the US army. Fairly pedestrian in mission, and rather less than an academic *corps d'élite*, it shrank substantially after National Service ended. Its main functions now are primary pre-entry recruit instruction, army instructor training, and preparing all ranks for promotion examinations. The Directorate of Army Training, a separate organization, oversees branch and technical training except for the RAEC's Army School of Languages.

The services also pay for pre- and post-entry degree and certificate programs, on a broad scale. They also maintain a system of 115 schools, 80 in Germany, enrolling slightly over 30,000 dependent children. Subsidies are also provided for officers and men whose children are enrolled in independent, mainly boarding, schools — public schools. A few fellowships for higher degree work in universities are also provided.

The British Home Command

There has not really been a British "high command" since 1945, and in the late 1970s analysts looking at Britain as a middle-tier power noted a "lack of any central organism for covering all questions of strategy . . . evolution of the modern British planning machinery has been erratic and incomplete."[60] This is not for lack of trying by some.[61] In the 1946 White Paper, the Minister of Defence was charged with coordinating the policies of the three service Ministers, and the principle was extended to the Commonwealth as well. But service integration remained elusive.[62]

Many chickens came home to roost in the Suez affair. Even before that débâcle Lord Louis Mountbatten, as First Sea Lord, had favored fusion of the services' planning and command-and-control. He was thwarted and arguments against such a model echoed those used against general staffs in the US and Britain half a century before, invoking fear of Prussian militarism and reduced "opportunities of access."[63]

Each service's wish to hold its own was hardly unique to the British system, as can be seen in America and elsewhere since 1945. However naïve reform advocates were in underestimating personalities and cliques, the Civil Service's power in the realm of defence was being eroded by the forces of science and technology on the one hand and the growing breadth of experience and sophistication of the professional military on the other, another parallel to the American pattern.[64]

The role of the Ministry of Defence as a central planning agency was strengthened by Earl Mountbatten as Chief of Defence Staff in the mid-1960s and in the late 1960s by Minister of Defence Denis Healey; one development was the creation of the National Defence College. The services' autonomy was steadily whittled away in the 1970s and early 1980s, when the Falklands threw up problems of a lack of effective central service integration. The main result was Command Paper 9315,[65] defining a new "fully unified defence policy and staff." The staffs of the individual service chiefs' staffs were halved with the declared goal a "fully unified Defence Policy and Operational Staff," with a four-star (full general, admiral or air marshal) Vice Chief of the Defence Staff overseeing four areas: Strategy and Policy; Programs and Personnel; Systems; and Commitments, the first headed by a Deputy Secretary, the others by three-star Deputy Chiefs of the Defence Staff. Each service chief remained responsible for fighting effectiveness, management, morale, and overall efficiency, while retraining access to the Prime Minister and the defence-related secretaries of state. As a bold step toward a *Grosse Generalstab*, its course will be watched, but even if successful by any clear standard short of war, a counterpart in the United States seems unlikely.

In a parallel vein, how far the highly confident march toward centralization and the introduction of a computer-based defense information system — MINIS (Management Information System for Ministers and Top Management)[66] — might go the way of McNamarian and Healeyan strategems is also problematical.

The issue of centralization in the context of command-and-control is emerging as complex weapons and $C^{2/3}$ make traditional forms costly and cumbersome operationally. The once dreaded and prohibited delegation of "fire-no-fire" authority to computer-controlled weapons was faced a generation ago. In spite of resentment among junior unit commanders in Vietnam and subsequent critiques of higher authority having violated the sanctity of the chair-of-command in instances like the Mayaguez incident and the abortive "Eagle Claw" raid in Iran, steady advances and frequent bounds in sophistication have made inter-branch fusion and centralization the rule. It appears that the Falklands Task Force commander had much latitude in his charge and command authority. But due to the murky circumstances surrounding the matter of the sinking of the *Belgrano*, when direct linkage with the Prime Minister and her approval became part of the debate over the rules of engagement, full judgement on that must be left to future historians.

Some Numerical Dimensions: Statistics on the Forces[67]

The general state of the forces shows both divergence from previous conditions and some patterns which might be seen as carryovers of previous forms. A very high percentage of officers are homeowners — 71 percent, almost a third of the enlisted force overall, and 66 percent of the navy's enlisted forces. A vestige remains, however, of an old unwritten dictum — "subalterns may not marry, captains may, majors should and colonels must." Just less than 10 percent of officers aged 17–24 are married, while 93 percent of those over 35 are. The pattern of "single men in barracks," however, has been eroded, with just over a quarter of enlisted personnel aged 17–24 being married.

Another tradition still evident is a substantial inflow of young service personnel, in the manner of the old apprentice system. Only 56 percent of recruits of all services are classified as adults, i.e. over the age of 17½. Substantial numbers, deemed apprentices, are under 17. The services vary widely in this practice; less than 40 percent of navy recruits are adults, while just over half of the army's are, and 76 percent of the RAF's. The system, based on a logic of bending proverbial twigs and competing for skilled labor in a world in which prolonging childhood through "adolescence" was not in vogue, has been modified from a system of 14-year-old entry used until well after World War II. The term "boys" has been dropped, the entry age having been raised as the age of adulthood was lowered to 18.

There is less advancement of women in the services in Britain than in the US, perhaps due to cultural and economic differences — and perhaps a less strident urgency of the feminist revolution in Europe. Servicewomen comprise about 4 percent of service strength, with 5 percent each in the Royal Navy and RAF, and 3 percent in the army. Numbers and outflow have both remained steady over the last few years, but recruitment nearly doubled in the wake of the Falklands War — as it also did for men. In 1983, the percentage of women entering the forces was almost half again as much as men, while "outflow" was slightly greater. A more notable trend, however, was the substantial decline in women who chose to exercise their right to give 18 months' notice in the enlisted force, even more so than male officers, and in marriage and pregnancy releases. Disciplinary releases declined from 431 in 1978–79 to 143 in 1983–84, another steady trend. Moreover, the quality of female personnel, especially officers, soared above the level of their male counterparts.

Some changes were shaped by forces moving in the parent society. Conscription is long behind, and British force structure has not suffered turbulence on the scale that wracked American forces in Korea and Vietnam or in mobilization augmentation surges in 1948 or in the Berlin call-up of 1961. Suez and the Falklands were far smaller, and Ulster has involved only about 8 percent of the army, and less than 5 percent of total service strength at peak to date.

Of 94,000 personnel overseas, just over three-quarters are in Europe, with 67,000 of those in Germany. Sixty-eight percent of the forces *in toto* are stationed in the United Kingdom, the bulk of them in the South — and over three-quarters in England. Perhaps the most dramatic benchmark of the decline of Britain's role as a major power is the bringing home of the Royal Navy. Over 90 percent are now at home bases versus half the army and just over 80 percent of the RAF.[68]

The stability of forces gained through more careful selection, education, and man-management is evident in various indicators relative to discipline. ("Man-management" refers not to personnel management but to the close-in leadership style based on rapport and close monitoring of personnel.) About 5 percent of the total strength now leave each year for various reasons, about half of these through choices allowed under regulations to recruits as well as those somewhat further along to opt out at scheduled intervals. Just under 7,000 leave under what are general equivalents to the American military's; "unfit/undesirable" categories.

It would not only be awkward stylistically, but also misleading, to end such an overview on a numerical note. There is a range of qualitative aspects that falls outside the strictly rationalistic realm with respect to any armed forces and their links to their parent society. However risky it may be to fall upon intuition and impression in this domain, there are some crucial questions deriving from the unique social system of Britain that have shaped, do shape, and will shape Britain's armed forces, especially since some anticipate an end to reliance on nuclear deterrence in a generation or less. Whether that means a return to big battalions or not, some of the "fuzzy" aspects are worthy of consideration.

The British Military Mystique

What of the state of the society from which the forces are raised? What of the variety of attitudes towards the nation, and toward military service? The British armed services have long been viewed far differently by various factions and classes, at least since Cromwell's New Model Army generated a proverbial concern about the dangers of military rule. Thus a recent shift in attitude in the working class toward nationalism stands in some contrast to traditional contempt for blacklegs. There has also been some modification of views among intellectuals, although since the late 1950s condemnation of the personal costs and agony of imperial–major power status has been played steadily on the stage, as in *Serjeant Musgrave's Dance* and *The Entertainer;* in fiction, e.g. Leslie Thomas' *Virgin Soldiers* series; in film, in *Bridge on the River Kwai, Yesterday's Enemy, Tunes of Glory,*

The Hill, A Bridge Too Far, and *Private's Progress;* and a darkling, post-Freudian view of empire can be seen in *The Jewel in the Crown, The Far Pavilions,* and *The Regiment* series. Academic history, often shaped on left-of-center premises in Britain as in the United States, has also tended either to avoid military matters and images, or to portray them in negative light. That, too, seems to be changing.[69]

Yet, at the same time, the symbols and cues of Britain's military past lie at every hand throughout the nation, in monuments and sculpture in churches, in museums and galleries, and in antique shops, book-sellers and pubs. In solemn ceremony, there is little apathy or derision, or the plastic, gaudy, or garish quality that characterizes much American patriotic ritual. The contrast of tone and proportion in joint ceremonies involving US and British or Commonwealth troops throws such differences into bold relief. Britain may not be militaristic — but martial it is.

One finds, for example, in the rooms of boarding schools, in homes, and in bookshops and newsellers a genus of the comic strip based on a distorted, but far more authentic, historically based view of modern war than the vividly sado-masochistic surrealism of American war comic books. Thus what playwrights, filmmakers, novelists and academics do on one level is offset by other forces in the popular culture, to degrees yet unmeasured in a social science sense. That was highly visible in the Mafeking-night-like explosion of martial enthusiasm seen in Britain in the Falklands campaign of 1982, a folk-mythic surge of patriotic and martial enthusiasm which erupted to the bemusement and consternation of many observers. It is that kind of social storage battery of martiality that has discharged from time to time which confounds precise quantification but which must be kept in view in considering British martial potential.

There is little disagreement that the British forces' recruiting has come a long way from days when the army was virtually a kind of sociological sump.[70] As technological skill has become a main shaper of recruiting, new opportunities in the job market have raised the price of labor. People costs are now half of the defense budget — in spite of dramatic increases in the cost of equipment and its maintenance. The various elaborate schemes for subsidizing education throughout the services, for identifying skills and moving recruits that are uninterested or untrainable out of the system would have bewildered Kipling's *Soldiers Three* or Gerald Kersh's *Sergeant Nelson of the Guards.*

However class-ridden British society may be, the services have gone several miles further down the road of careful "man-management" than the American services in general. The brutality and silliness of bull may not be wholly dead, but the residue is only a shadow of the past. The special premium put on *corps d'élite* in the Cold War and in post-imperial fire brigade roles has increased the demand for bright, able people at the "cutting edge". Especially harsh rites of passage and the demands of expensive technology have purged many chances to select and promote officers on social criteria — but not all.

There are special mechanisms for "getting acquainted" and the boys' and apprentice schemes of the feudal and mercantilist past have been retained and modernized. Army Cadet Force and pre-service encampments allow mutual appraisal, and assure a much higher average level of ability and purposefulness among those who pass through such screens.

Several patterns and trends are evident: more recruits coming from a broader geographic base, from higher levels of the working class and lower middle class, a higher retention rate, lower delinquency of the old hard-drinking, hard-fighting variety. One paradox is that the high demand for literacy in the Royal Military Police has given it the highest scorers of any corps' enlisted personnel.[71] Just as scientists sustantially undercut the position of the defense civil servants after 1945, increasingly expensive and complex technology has led to an upgrading of standards in the forces.

Changing trends in the social origins of the officer corps have been most marked in the army. Fewer officers enter precommission courses from public and grammar schools; more come from Catholic public schools. At the same time, the Household Brigade remains a bastion of class- and income-linked selectivity, free of women and non-white minorities. Scotland has become less a disproportionate source of officers and men than it once was, and the Ulster troubles have undercut recruitment from the Irish Republic, most notably in the Irish Guards, the "Micks." The Irish Guards still receive shamrocks from the Queen Mother on Saint Patrick's Day, but have fewer Catholic Irish now, recruiting mainly from the Irish in London or from the urban centers of the North, as well as from the Protestant Irish in Ulster.

Ultima Ratio Regis: the Question of Aid to the Civil

The ever-nagging problem of Northern Ireland, the rough-and-tumble of the coal miners' strike, the stridency of some political elements, including nationalists in various parts of Britain, can be seen as part of a general flickering malaise across Europe and much of the rest of the world. Pandemic terrorism has already affected the lives as well as the pocketbooks of the citizenry of the industrial democracies. The Maginotizing of embassies, security checks in airports, explosive sniffers in post offices are symptoms, and British daily life has been affected by terrorism more than most Western nations over the last generation, e.g. the signs in the London Underground and buses about unattended packages, bombings in London, and the search routines at various public facilities. How forces which are already stretched thinly would cope if they were summoned to play a major constabulary role as great or greater than Northern Ireland, or across a range of micro-conflicts on the domestic scene, is undoubtedly a matter of concern for British defense planners. The Territorial Army and Home Service Force were recently expanded with such duties in view. The synthesis of many lessons and principles by Brigadier Frank Kitson raised anxieties in certain circles in Britain about the role of the army in "aid to the civil" (authorities) in a domestic setting a decade ago.[72]

Britain's forces, then, while thin on the ground, are like dragon's teeth, in that the capacity to move quickly and to expand along various axes has been kept alive. In any conflict short of a major nuclear attack or a general uprising, the cadres could be watered and would bring forth something more substantial than warlike apparitions. The greatest tribute to that potential may have been paid by the Soviets, who are from time to time reported to station more agents in Britain than any other country.

Uncertain Reserves: British Inventiveness

During World War II Britain brought forth many clever weapons and stratagems, e.g. the initial development work on miniature radio-detonated proximity fuses, compressed-shell guns, nuclear weapons, and the cavity magnetron. The US army, air forces and navy adopted British techniques such as skip-bombing, fighter direction systems, and parachute harnesses, and hungered for the Mosquito bomber. The Rolls-Royce Merlin engine, which powered Spitfires, Mosquitoes and Lancasters, was produced in the US by Packard. Ultimately merged with a US-built airframe to make the hybrid P-51, it played a major role in defeating the Luftwaffe. British radar and navigation aids were adapted, and their Ultra–Enigma code-breaking and deception efforts and photo-interpretation techniques were passed to the Americans, along with substantial intelligence tradecraft, as were many military staff techniques and logistical methods.

After 1945, British industry continued to lead the way in a rather broader field of defense-related devices than is generally appreciated, including:

- anti-submarine warfare sonobuoy technology
- the angled-deck, steam catapult and landing-light systems adapted for use on US aircraft carriers
- the Harrier vertical takeoff and landing fighter adopted by the US Marine Corps
- Barnes-Wallis's swing-wing design, used in the US F-111 and variants
- the air-cushioned vehicle
- the Martin-Baker ejection seat
- the triple-spool quiet fan jet engine
- Chobham tank armor
- detection of nuclear weapons' transient radiation effects on electronic systems (TREE) and electro-magnetic pulse (EMP)
- the light-emitting diode
- anti-chemical-biological protective clothing

Any appraisal of Britain's military potential must keep that innovative potential in view. While at some point Britain might no longer be able or inclined to do it, such an assumption would be rather risky, for friends as for foes. The Falklands showed the lion still had teeth and claws and some canniness and in 1984 the Royal Air Force's 617 Squadron (the Dam Busters) dominated the USAF's Giant Voice bombing trophy series for the first time. Whether such triumphs, the post-Falkland surge of enthusiasm and recruiting and various attempts to salvage a faltering economy will prove to be dots on an upturning curve remains to be seen. Certainly some of the old well-springs are still there. Whatever the travails and the flaws, the armed forces of Britain have maintained a symbolic essence as well as some unique technical capacity. They have been more significant and effective when weighed in the balance than the British taxpayers or planners might have expected or intended — or, indeed, as they deserved. As a glance at Shakespeare or Kipling will suggest, it was not the first time. Nor is it likely to be the last.

Notes

1. Dan Smith, *Defense of the Realm in the 1980s* (Croom Helm, London, 1980), pp. 264–265.
2. Richard L. Hudson, "At Britain's Sandhurst, Military Leadership is the Name of the Game," *Wall Street Journal*, 24 December 1984, pp. 1 and 8.
3. John M. MacKenzie, *Propaganda and Empire: The Manipulation of British Public Opinion, 1880–1960* (Manchester University Press, Manchester, 1984).
4. Robert Harkavy, *Great Power Competition for Overseas Bases: The Geopolitics of Access Diplomacy* (Pergamon, New York, 1982).
5. E.g. James Morris' trilogy, *Pax Britannica* (Harcourt, Brace and World, New York, 1968); *Heaven's Command* (Harcourt Brace Jovanovich, New York, 1974; and *Farewell the Trumpets* (Faber, London, 1978).
6. Philip Darby, *British Defense Policy East of Suez, 1947–68* (Oxford University Press, London, 1973); and Julian Paget, *The Last Post, Aden, 1964–67* (Faber, London, 1969).
7. John Gallagher, *The Decline, Revival and Fall of the British Empire* (Cambridge University Press, Cambridge, 1982).
8. Eric Linklater, *Our Men in Korea* (Her Majesty's Stationery Office, London, 1952), pp. 53–61.
9. Eugene Kinkead, *In Every War But One* (W.W. Norton, New York, 1960); for a critical view see Albert Biderman, *The Road to Calumny* (Macmillan, New York, 1967).
10. Andre Beaufre, *The Suez Expedition, 1956* (Faber, London, 1969).
11. William P. Snyder, *The Politics of British Defense Policy, 1945–1962* (Ohio State University Press, Bowling Green, 1964).
12. Lawrence Freedman, *Britain and Nuclear Weapons* (Macmillan, London, 1980), pp. 4–22.
13. Laurence Martin (ed.), *The Management of Defense* (Macmillan, London, 1976), pp. 89–98.
14. Andrew J. Pierre, *Nuclear Politics: The British Experience with an Independent Strategic Force* (Oxford University Press, London, 1972); and Margaret Gowing, *Independence and Deterrence* (Macmillan, London, 1974).
15. Ken Booth, "Strategy and Concept" in John Baylis (ed.) *Alternative Approaches to British Defense Policy* (St Martins, New York, 1983), pp. 154–190.
16. B. H. Liddell Hart, *Defence of the West* (William Morrow, New York, 1950), pp. 118–134.
17. For a recent perspective, see Josephine Howie, "Britain's Irish Problem" in *Royal United Services Institute–Brassey's Yearbook 1984* (RUSI–Brassey's, London, 1984), pp. 75–87.
18. Jo Thomas, "Non-Violent Ulster Party Calls on Britain to Disband Local Regiment," *New York Times*, 27 January, 1985, p. 8.
19. E.g. Ivan Rowan, "Scots' Uneasy Eye on Ulster," *Sunday Telegraph*, 3 October, 1971, p. 21.
20. N.a., see poll results in n.a., "The Trouble with Ulster," *The Economist*, 2 June, 1984, pp. 50–52 and 57–59.
21. Lawrence Freedman, *The Evolution of Nuclear Strategy* (St Martin's, New York, 1981), pp. 310–311.
22. E.g. Frank Wesley Craven and James Lea Cate, vol. 5, *The U.S. Army Forces in World War II* (University of Chicago Press, Chicago, 1955), pp. 237–239; Warren F. Kimball, "Lend-lease and the Open Door: The Temptation of British Opulence, 1937–1942," *Political Science Quarterly*, no. 86 (1971), pp. 232–259; and James R. Leutze, "Technology and Bargaining in Anglo-American Naval Relations: 1938–1946," *United States Naval Institute Proceedings*, no. 103 (1977), pp. 50–61; Christopher

Thorne, *Allies of a Kind: British and the War against Japan, 1941-1945* (Hamilton, London, 1978).
23. Andrew Brookes, *V-Force: The History of Britain's Airborne Deterrent* (Jane's, London, 1982).
24. Lawrence Freedman, "The Rationale for Medium-Sized Deterrent Forces" in Christoph Bertram (ed.), *The Future of Strategic Deterrence Forces* (International Institute for Strategic Studies, London, 1980), p. 47.
25. For a sense of the logic of deterrence made public as Britain's deterrent took shape, see John Slessor, *Strategy for the West* (Cassell, London, 1954); *The Great Deterrent* (New York, Praeger, 1957); and *What Price Coexistence?* (Praeger, New York, 1961).
26. David Greenwood, "The Defense Policy of the United Kingdom" in Douglas J. Muncy and Paul R. Viotti (eds.), *The Defense Policies of Nations* (Johns Hopkins, Baltimore University Press, 1982), pp. 197-214.
27. S. Hastings, *Murder of the TSR-2* (Cassell, London, 1966).
28. David Bolton, "Setting the Scene" in *RUSI-Brassey's Yearbook 1984*, pp. xix-xx.
29. Differing recent analyses are: William Wallace, "European Defence Co-operation: The Reopening Debate," *Survival*, vol. 26, no. 6 (November-December 1984), pp. 260-261; and David M. Adamson, "U.K. and French Nuclear Forces Bearing on Arms Control," *National Defense* (January 1983), pp. 26-30.
30. For a review of options, see Peter Nailor and Jonathan Alford, *The Future of Britain's Nuclear Force*, Adelphi Paper No. 156 (International Institute for Strategic Studies, London, 1980); for a rejection of the independent deterrent, see Malcolm Chalmers, *Trident: Britain's Independent Arms Race* (CND Publications, London, 1984).
31. Kenneth Hunt, "Perspectives of the World Scene, 1983: The NATO Alliance II," *RUSI-Brassey's Yearbook 1983*, pp. 30-31.
32. N.a., *The Military Balance, 1984-1985* (International Institute for Strategic Studies, London, 1984), p. vii.
33. Robert Miller-Bakewell, "The Military Communications Market: A UK Viewpoint," *International Defence Review Special Electronics Issue*, no. 1 (1984), pp. 15-22; in the same issue also see Chris Warren, "The Ptarmigan Style," pp. 63-69.
34. Corelli Barnett, *Britain and her Army, 1509-1970* (Allen Lane, London, 1970), p. 489; Terry Gander, *Encyclopedia of the Modern British Army* (Nautical and American Publishing Company of America, Annapolis, Md., 1982), p. 15; Peter Young and J. P. Lawford (eds.), *History of the British Army* (G. P. Putnam's, New York, 1970).
35. The best recent survey is Henry Stanhope, *The Soldiers: An Anatomy of the British Army* (Hamish Hamilton, London, 1979).
36. Anthony and John de St Jorre, *The Guards* (Crown Publishers, London, 1981).
37. Tony Geraghty, *This is the SAS* (Arco Publishing, New York, 1984); for a recent overview of some British elite forces, see Max Walmer, *An Illustrated Guide to Modern Elite Forces* (Arco Publishing, New York, 1984), pp. 54-62.
38. Martin Edmonds, "Military Elites: Some Observations and Reflections in a Cultural Context: The United Kingdom," paper presented at Inter-University Seminar on Armed Forces and Society, 23-25 October 1980.
39. M. J. P. Chilcott, "Britisher Straightens the Record," *Army* (November 1984), pp. 16-17.
40. N.a., "Emerging Technologies: An Uncertain Factor," *Strategic Survey* (International Institute for Strategic Studies, London, 1984), pp. 12-17.
41. "Cormorant" (pseudonym), "Strategies of European Nations" in John C. Garnett, *The Defence of Western Europe* (Macmillan, London, 1974), pp. 109-133.
42. John W.R. Taylor, "How Good is the RAF?" *Air Force* (October 1984), pp. 24-27; for a recent survey, see Chaz Bowyer, *The Encyclopedia of British Military*

Aircraft (Bison Books, London, 1982).

43. Giovanni Briganti, "Royal Air Force Germany," *Armed Forces Journal International* (December 1984), pp. 56 and 60.

44. Jeffrey Ethell and Alfred Price, *Air War South Atlantic* (Macmillan, New York, 1983).

45. N.a., "RAF Expands Tanker Fleet," *Defense Attache*, no. 1 (1984), p. 26.

46. Graham Smith, "Army Delighted with Tri-Star," *Soldier*, 7 May 1984, pp. 30–31.

47. Desmond Wetten, *The Decline of British Seapower* (Jane's, London, 1982); for earlier perspectives, during Wilsonian reappraisals, see B.B. Schofield, *British Sea Power: Naval Policy in the Twentieth Century* (Batsford, London, 1967) and Lawrence W. Martin, *The Sea in Modern Strategy* (Chatto and Windus, London, 1967).

48. David Miller, *An Illustrated Guide to Modern Subhunters* (Arco Publishing, New York, 1984).

49. Erling Bjol, *Nordic Security*, Adelphi Paper No. 181 (International Institute for Strategic Studies, London, 1983), pp. 30–33.

50. Walter Pincus, "Diary of a War," *Houston Chronicle*, 13 January 1985, p. 31.

51. T. A. Boam, "Defending Western Interests outside NATO: The United Kingdom's Contribution," *Armed Forces Journal International* (October 1984), pp. 116–118 and 120; for an opposite view, see Malcolm Chalmers, *Paying for Defense: Military Spending and British Decline* (Pluto Press, London, 1985).

52. James, D. Ladd, *The Invisible Raiders: The History of the SBS from World War II to the Present* (Arms and Armor Press, London, 1983); and Philip Warner, *The SBS– Special Boat Squadron* (Sphere Books, London, 1983).

53. Bruce George and Michael Coughlin, "British Defense Policy after the Falklands," *Survival*, vol. 24, no. 5 (September-October 1982), pp. 201–210.

54. F. H. Hinsley, E. E. Thomas, C. F. G. Ransom, and R. C. Knight, *British Intelligence in the Second World War: Its Influence on Strategy and Operations* (Cambridge University Press, New York, 1979) and succeeding volumes.

55. Nigel West, *A Matter of Trust, MI5, 1945–72* (Weidenfeld and Nicholson, London, 1982); and *MI6* (Randon House, Garden City, 1984).

56. E.g. see Tony Bunyan, *The Political Police in Britain* (St Martin's, New York, 1976); and Jonathan Bloch, *British Intelligence and Covert Action* (Brandon Books, Dingle, Ireland, 1983).

57. Chapman Pincher, *Too Secret Too Long* (St Martin's, New York, 1984).

58. J. C. Masterman, *The Double-Cross System in the War of 1939 to 1945* (Yale University Press, New Haven, 1972); and William Stevenson, *A Man Called Intrepid* (Ballantine Books, New York, 1976).

59. George Cruickshank, *Deception in World War II* (Oxford Unversity Press, New York, 1980).

60. James Bellini and Geoffrey Pattie, *A New World Role for the Medium Powers: The British Opportunity* (Royal United Services Institute, London, 1977), p. 109.

61. Michael D. Hobkirk, *The Policies of Defense Budgeting: A Study of Organisation and Resource Allocation in the United Kingdom and the United States* (National Defense University Press, Washington, DC, 1983), esp. pp. 13–24, 47, 58, 68–70, and 77.

62. J. H. F. Eberle, "Defence Organisation: The Future" in Laurence W. Martin (ed.), *The Management of Defence* (Macmillan, London, 1976), pp. 105–123.

63. Richard Hough, *Mountbatten* (Random House, New York, 1981), p. 259; and T. D. Bridge, "UK Defence 1984/85," *Army Quarterly and Defence Journal*, no. 114 (1984), pp. 262–265.

64. Franklyn, A. Johnson, *Defense by Ministry: The British Ministry of Defence*, (Duckworth, London, 1980), p. 182.

65. Laurence Freedman, "Economy Rules at M.O.D.", *Defense Attache* (April 1984), pp. 13,14, and 17; and J. D. Lunt, "Heseltine with a Long Knife," *Army*

Quarterly and Defence Journal, no. 114 (1984), pp. 271–279.

66. Secretary of State for Defence, *Statement on the Defence Estimates 1984*, pt. 1 (Her Majesty's Stationery Office, London, 1984), p. 12.

67. Statistics in the following portion are drawn from the *1984 Statement on Defence Estimates* unless otherwise noted.

68. Wetten, *Decline of British Seapower*, pp. 5–9.

69. Michael Howard et al., "What is Military History?" *History Today* (December 1984), pp. 5–13.

70. J. F. C. Fuller, "The Soldier," Chapter 2 in *The Army in my Time* (Rich and Cowan, London, 1935), pp. 19–33.

71. Stanhope, *The Soldiers*, p. 55.

72. Frank Kitson, *Low Intensity Conflict: Subversion, Insurgency and Peacekeeping* (Archon, Hamden, Conn., 1971).

3 THE DANISH AND NORWEGIAN ARMED FORCES

Nigel de Lee

The Danish and Norwegian armed services constitute the majority of the resident forces available for the defense of the Northern Flank of Allied Command Europe. The responsibilities of the commander of AFNORTH extend an enormous distance, from the North Cape to the River Elbe, and cover a great diversity of terrain, threats, and resources.

Norway and Denmark have some political characteristics in common. Both are egalitarian liberal democracies, both have a past colored by pacifism and neutralism, and both are members of NATO on special terms. In other ways they are very distinct. Norway is huge in relation to its population, with rugged mountainous terrain and severe weather conditions. Denmark is densely populated in comparison, enjoys a gentle, fertile landscape, and temperate weather. Both are threatened by the Soviet Union's need to secure access to the oceans, protect its own bases, and give flank support to offensive operations in more important areas. It is held by those with experience of the northern flank that NATO could not win a war in Norway or Denmark but could lose one there.[1]

Danish Security Policy: the Armed Forces in Context

Denmark has been criticised for taking a measured approach in its commitment to NATO, and for maintaining a small defense establishment. But the Danes have a distinct national security policy, and a particular attitude to the uses of armed force, which derive from the history and the social, political, and economic characteristics of the kingdom.

Since 1864 Denmark has occupied a strategic position of great interest to powerful neighbors, but has lacked the economic and demographic resources necessary to raise armed forces strong enough to meet external threats. The Danes have had to choose one of three policies; accommodation to the wishes of a powerful neighbor; membership of an alliance to counter-balance strong neighbors; or disarmed, unobtrusive neutrality. Owing to the strength of anti-militarist and pacifist feeling, "harmless" neutrality would most satisfy the population, were it attainable.'

In 1864 Denmark was defeated by Prussia and Austria. From then until 1918 the policy was one of formal neutrality, but combined with accommodating German interests. After 1918, the Danes disarmed almost entirely, and put their faith in the League of Nations. In 1939 they hoped to escape direct involvement in war by declaring neutrality and making certain concessions to Germany, as they had in World War I. But the Nazis were not appeased, and occupied Denmark on 9 April 1940, crushing thoughts of opposition by brutal intimidation.

After the defeat of 1864, many Danes adopted an attitude to defense based on "What is the use?", thinking that their country was indefensible, and that resistance to external attack could only bring futile suffering. The bitter experience of German domination in World War II produced another slogan: "Never again a 9th of April," indicative of loss of faith in appeasement and grim determination to take all possible measures to save their country from invasion in the future. The product of these two coexisting attitudes is the policy of adherence to NATO on special terms.

In 1945 many Danes hoped that the UN might establish an effective system of collective security. They were disillusioned by the conduct of the Soviet Union, especially by the seizure of Czechoslovakia in 1948. At the same time, attempts to form a neutral bloc in Scandinavia failed. The only choice left was either to accomodate the USSR, or join the Atlantic Alliance. The Danes chose the Atlantic Alliance, but with considerable reservations, and without enthusiasm. The Alliance was and is considered the only realistic way of meeting the threat, but the Danes have always been concerned that their adherence must not appear threatening or provocative to the Soviet Union.[2] This concern accounts for Danish attempts to balance deterrence with reassurance.

Deterrence is served by membership of the Alliance; arrangements for receiving allied reinforcements; adaptation of Danish plans and forces to NATO strategy; and the forces' level of alert and preparedness.[3] The will to resist alone, until external reinforcements arrive, is signified by the Royal Decree of 1952, which requires the forces to mobilize and fight, without orders, in the event of an attack on the kingdom, and to ignore orders to cease resistance. It is supported by the Total Defense concept, which would coordinate military and civil measures to ensure swift and comprehensive mobilization of the entire nation for war. The large and enthusiastic Home Guard would play an important part in this process.

In pursuit of reassurance, Danish policy minimizes the role of the armed forces in maintaining security. The Danes hold that security can never be absolute, that some level of risk must be accepted, and that an excessive reliance on force can increase the risks of war. They consider that in the 1980s the risk of armed conflict is very low,[4] so a high level of military activity would be dangerous as well as unnecessarily expensive.

At the political level, the pursuit of reassurance is expressed as firm and vocal support for a policy of détente. Since the 1967 Harmel Report, the Danes have used NATO as an instrument of détente, with a particular emphasis on confidence-building with the Warsaw Pact.[5] This policy is maintained despite developments such as the Soviet invasion of Afghanistan.[6] The wish to make membership of NATO seem purely defensive gives rise to the restrictions imposed by Denmark; allied forces cannot be based in the kingdom in peacetime, exercises are carefully controlled, and only Danish troops are allowed on Bornholm. The complete ban on nuclear weapons arises largely from strong domestic pressures, but is held to contribute an extra dimension to reassurance.

The emphasis on détente, sustained by traditional anti-military sentiment and reluctance to increase spending on defense in an era when the cost of military equipment is growing at a disproportionate rate, accounts for the small size of the Danish effort. The size of the Danish forces may be intended to reassure the Soviet Union, but it must undermine credibility of the Danish commitment to reduce dependence on nuclear weapons.[7] It also makes Denmark more dependent on allied, particularly West German, assistance in case of emergency.[8]

Defense plans recognize the importance of Denmark to NATO and the Warsaw Pact. For NATO, control of Danish territory, waters, and airspace is of vital importance to the defense of southern Norway, northern Germany, and the United Kingdom.[9] The Soviet Union would regard control of Denmark of great value to support an offensive drive to the Channel ports, or to support more sustained operations against NATO sea lines of communications if the initial blitz failed.[10] The Soviets also see Denmark as a suitable base from which NATO could launch deep strikes into the heart of the Warsaw Pact.[11]

The main features of the defense plans are absolute dependence on external reinforcement, close integration of Danish and allied forces, and rapid mobilization.

The scale and timing of external reinforcement would depend partly on SACEUR's Common Reinforcement Plan, and partly on a decision by the Danish Folketing to invite reinforcement. In 1982 allied forces provisionally earmarked to reinforce Denmark included a British infantry brigade, two-thirds of an American Marine Corps corps, and an American infantry division, plus two British and five American squadrons of combat aircraft. These would provide substantial additional strength if they were requested in time and able to arrive safely.[12] Their safe arrival would depend almost entirely on the speed and efficiency of Danish mobilization, which is intended to hold the enemy and provide reception for allied forces. There is little doubt that the Soviets would attempt to pre-empt or disrupt this mobilization in the event of war; probably by a surprise amphibious attack on southern Jutland, and by small desants elsewhere. An attack on Zealand could be made as a distraction;[13] it would also weaken the SAM defenses of BALTAP.

There is no doubt that the Danish armed forces are well integrated at all levels, on a service and inter-allied basis.[14] In 1961 NATO set up COMBALTAP as a joint command to cover all forces in the Baltic Approaches. The Commander of COMBALTAP is always the Danish Commander Operational Forces Denmark, to ease the wartime transition of authority from national to NATO command. In the subordinate commands, WESTLAND, EASTLAND, NAVBALT, and AIRBALT, there are integrated staffs, with strong West German representation. In 1969 the Danish service staffs were merged into a single Defense Command.

At lower levels, there are frequent national and allied exercises to ensure smooth coordination of all forces in defense operations. Reinforcement reception and deployment are frequently practiced, as are defense of the national territory and closure of the straits.[15]

The success of all these complicated measures depends on early warning and timely decisions by political leaders. They believe that before there can be an attack, there must be economic, political, and military indications.[16] If this is so, then the success or failure of Danish plans would depend solely on political leaders' will to act in time.

The Danish Army

The Danish army is designed to provide minimum essential protection against a surprise attack in peacetime, and to generate adequate forces, in sufficient time, to guarantee the safe arrival of allied reinforcements, and make a substantial contribution to the defense of the national territory in wartime.[17] The Danes believe that their ground forces can help to deter attack without appearing to offer a threat to the potential enemy, but, if attacked, could moblize so quickly that the attacker would be confounded.

The army has a complicated structure, based on the principle of rapid mobilization of reserves and the assumptions of swift allied reinforcement. The mechanized formations in Jutland might be deployed, along with their Bundeswehr comrades, in an active forward defense of Schleswig-Holstein. In contrast, the role of the troops in the Danish Islands would be to act as the last line of defense against Warsaw Pact amphibious forces. A substantial element of the reserves would be deployed to protect the national territory from desants from the air. In this they would be supported by the volunteers of the Army Home Guard.

The terrain in most of Denmark does not favor defensive operations; it is open, undulating, and dotted with woods; very suited to mechanized advance. The forces in the Islands would be isolated from each other by perilous sea crossings, and have very little depth for defensive operations. Only in the south of the Jutland peninsula, in Holstein, does the ground offer major water obstacles that could provide good conditions for a sustained defense.

The structure of the army was decided by the 1973 Defense Act. This Act was intended to facilitate and expedite the process of mobilization, and increase the role of regular soldiers, to make the operational element of the peacetime army more efficient and alert, and reduce the burden of service on conscripts.

In peacetime, the army has a strength of 22,000, and four main components. The administration, about 7,000 strong, consists of the staffs of HQs, schools, and recruiting authorities. The Training Force, some 7,000, consists of the units engaged in training conscripts. There are 19 regiments: 8 infantry, 2 tank, 3 artillery, 2 engineer, 2 signals, and 2 logistic. These regiments produce trained companies of conscripts, which they would mobilize as formed sub-units in an emergency. The UN Force is about 500 men, and serves as part of UNFICYP in Cyprus. It is not funded from the defense budget, so it can be reinforced without affecting the financial basis of the defense effort.

The Standing Force consists of 8,500 regulars, organized as teeth-arms cadre units of five mechanized brigades and one regimental combat team. These units are at instant readiness to repel attack. They are the mainstay of the army Combat Force, whose other troops are conscripts who have completed their six months' basic training, organized as cadres of six regimental combat teams and eight battalions. In the event of an alert, the Standing Force could be reinforced, within a few hours, by the Augmentation Force, 4,500 recently discharged conscripts. They would fill out the order of battle of the mechanized brigades with additional companies of armored infantry. The reinforced Standing Force is known as the Covering Force, and its main initial task would be to ensure the safety of full mobilization, and of the reception facilities for allied reinforcements.

Full mobilization would bring 65,000 more reserves into the army. Some 41,000 would constitute the Field Army Reserve. Of these, 12,000 would join the Covering Force, adding more battalions to the mechanized brigades. The other 29,000 would fill out the Combat Force regimental combat teams and battalions of motorized infantry, and form an additional 14 battalions. The remaining 24,000 reserves would constitute the Local Defense Forces, organized as 21 battalions of infantry and 7 of artillery. The last reserve of all, but a most active and enthusiastic one, would be the Army Home Guard, which can muster 540 companies for neighborhood defense. It is claimed that the entire mobilization process could be completed within 24 hours. Denmark is well served by excellent communications, so no doubt this feat of logistics could be accomplished, provided the enemy did not interfere.

Once mobilized, the Danish army would probably be transferred to NATO Command. The Field Army formations would be controlled by the major HQs; WESTLAND, covering Jutland and Schleswig-Holstein, down to the River Elbe; and EASTLAND, consisting of the Danish Islands, including the isolated island of Bornholm. The seven Military Region HQs would control the Local Defense Forces, and, though the 37 District HQs, liaise with the Home Guard. The three mechanized brigades in WESTLAND would be formed into the Jutland Division. This formation would have a strength of 20,000, with 170 tanks, 230 guns and mortars, and 280 anti-tank weapons. A Field Army regimental combat team would consist of 5,000 men with 47 tanks, 150 APCs, 58 guns and mortars, and 78 anti-tank weapons. A Local Defense brigade would dispose of 6,000 men, 68 guns and mortars, and 80 anti-tank weapons.[18]

Two-thirds of the personnel in the peacetime army are regular, the remainder being conscripts under training or serving with the Alert Force. The reserves are nearly all former conscripts. The 1953 Constitution obliges all able-bodied men to contribute to the defense of the country, but this obligation was never fully enforced. Traditionally, military service has been unpopular. In the 1960s and 1970s some 15 percent of those chosen to serve objected on grounds of conscience, and were exempted. In 1973 the government decided to enhance the proportion of regular soldiers in order to reduce the burden of conscription. Since then, changes in social attitudes and a deterioration in the level of employment have greatly improved the recruiting situation — contrary to the expectations of the 1970s, in the 1980s there has been no shortage of suitable candidates for regular service. These soldiers serve initially for three years, and can extend their term by another three if they are satisfactory. After six years' service, a soldier may sign on for a full career, which can last until he is 60 years old. There are no longer any objections to conscript service; all conscript soldiers are in fact volunteers, attracted by a reasonable rate of pay and the opportunity to acquire useful skills. The 1985–87 Defense Agreement extended conscript service from nine months to a full year. Former conscripts are called up annually for refresher training whilst in the Mobilization Force.[19] The Army Home Guard is a purely voluntary part-time force. It has a strength of 60,000 or so, of whom some 8,000 are women. The turnover of personnel is about 10 percent per annum, and the average age of the volunteers has fallen in the 1980s.

The army has never had difficulty in attracting regular officers, and no longer lacks reserve officers. Candidates for regular commissions must complete basic conscript service, then train as sergeants, serve as sergeants for 18 months, and study for three years at the Military Academy. Once commissioned, officers are paid at the same rate as graduate civil servants, and enjoy a similar social prestige. They are commissioned into particular regiments, and can remain within them up to the rank of major, after which they are mobile. Postings generally last for three years, or two for command appointments, but are flexible. Reserve officers attend a series of training courses in special schools and are required to attend extended refresher training. The Home Guard provides its own officers, and trains them in weekend sessions in its own schools.

Women have not achieved equality, but their status is changing. They may train as officers at the Military Academy, but have been excluded from serving in combat units. In 1985, some were posted to armored car units, as an experiment.

The army is armed and equipped from a number of foreign sources, and scales of issue vary from formation to formation. The mechanized brigades of the Standing Force in Jutland have 120 Leopard I tanks, those in Zealand retain 88 Centurions. The Centurions were kept partly because replacement with Leopard II was delayed by financial difficulties, partly because a study of the 1973 war in the Middle East led to the conclusion that it would be more cost-effective to modernize and upgrade the Centurion. The mechanized infantry are carried in 650 M-113 APCs, supported by 68 M-106s with mortars. The artillery has 72 M-109 155 mm SP howitzers, and 276 towed guns, plus 81 mm and 120 mm mortars. There are 140 TOW launchers, 400 Carl Gustavs, plus LAWs and RCL weapons for anti-tank defense. Air defense weapons include 36 Bofors L-60 40 mm guns and the Redeye SAM. Army aviation consists of 16 Saab T-17 light aircraft and 12 Hughes helicopters.[20]

The 1985-87 Defense Agreement considered it a matter of urgent importance to improve short-range air defense and anti-tank capacity. Lesser priorities were to increase stocks of tank and artillery ammunition, provide modern CBW protective suits, modernize communications, and procure combat helicopters.[21]

Because the Danish army expects to fight in close cooperation with allied reinforcements, it has not developed a distinctive "national" style of tactics. Great emphasis has been placed on compatibility with allied forces, and the army has adapted itself accordingly. The Jutland Division is trained to use the same tactics as the Bundeswehr. In the Danish Islands, the army uses a more British style. Joint exercises with allied units reinforce and develop operational compatibility.

The main war roles of the army are to prevent a *fait accompli* by the enemy, to hold enemy attacks to provide time for the safe arrival of allied reinforcements, then to fight in close cooperation with allied forces to defend the national territory. It is likely that the WESTLAND and EASTLAND commands would have to fight distinct campaigns, because the means of transport between Jutland and the Islands would probably be destroyed by war action.[22]

In WESTLAND, the Jutland Division would probably move southeastwards into Germany, in conjunciton with the 6th Armored Infantry Division of the Bundeswehr, to counter Warsaw Pact forces advancing along the Baltic coast. They would be supported by the Bundeswehr Home Defense Group 13, a reserve brigade of mobile infantry. If pressed back, this integrated corps of NATO forces could take advantage of the woods and water obstacles in southern Jutland to seal off the peninsula.[23] The rest of the WESTLAND Field Army, a regimental combat team and 13 battalions, would act as a mobile force to cover the few practicable beaches on the east coast of Jutland, and protect reception facilities for allied reinforcements.

The Local Defense Forces, twelve battalions and seven companies, would provide less mobile defense against diversionary attack on key points and centres of population. They would act in close cooperation with the Home Guard, Civil Defense, and police. The Home Guard main role in WESTLAND and EASTLAND would be surveillance by intensive local patrolling. In the event of an enemy airborne or air mobile desant, the Home Guard would be expected to observe and report on enemy activity, and cooperate with Mobilization Force units in making counter-attacks. Some companies would be committed to guarding and carrying out demolitions, others to assisting in control and evacuation of the civil population.

The EASTLAND Command in war would dispose of two mechanized brigades, five regimental combat teams, and nine battalions of the Field Army supported by one battalion and nine companies of Local Defense Forces.[24] Their primary role would be defense of the vital islands from amphibious assault. It is assumed that these attacks would be accompanied by airborne or heliborne assaults, either in direct support, or as diversions. The main defense effort is concentrated on Zealand, the most important island, but there are significant forces on Funen, Lolland, and Falster.

The basic principle for defense against amphibious assaults is to prevent the enemy force from landing, or, if it does get ashore, to hold it on the beach, and counter-attack as soon as possible. In Zealand, there are only two or three vulnerable beaches, and they would be defended by four regimental combat teams deployed on the coast. The two mechanized brigades would be positioned a short distance inland, as a counter-attack force. Airborne and heliborne attacks would be regarded as a secondary threat, to be contained by less mobile forces until the amphibious forces had been repelled.[25]

The Danes have decided not to strengthen the defense of the beaches with permanent fortifications. Instead, they rely upon the combat teams arriving in time to dig in and prepare strong field works. They are considering the procurement of mobile batteries of missiles to improve their capacity to destroy ships and hovercraft. These plans all depend upon the early acquisition and assessment of accurate information of enemy activities and intentions. Some of the islands are only a few hours' sailing time from East Germany. The Soviets are very well aware of the critical importance of surprise and speed in the conduct of operations, but particularly for success of amphibious assaults. It is certain that if the Warsaw Pact forces did not achieve surprise, Danish and allied forces could make an attack very difficult. It is also obvious that the success of Danish plans depends on good surveillance and intelligence, leading to early warning.[26]

The garrison of Bornholm, the remote outpost, consists of a regular combat team. The island is not a suitable target for amphibious assault, and is of great value to NATO as a surveillance base. It must be assumed that the enemy would either destroy the surveillance facilities by air and naval bombardment, then ignore the island, or seek to take it by airborne desant. In either case it appears that the garrison would be overwhelmed or isolated within hours of the commencement of war.

The Danish Navy

The Royal Danish Navy is a predominantly regular force of mainly light units. It is designed to cooperate closely with other NATO air and naval forces in COMBALTAP in order to deny the enemy use of the Western Baltic and passage of the Danish Straits. By fulfilling these missions it will help to defend the Danish, West German, and Norwegian coasts from invasion, and secure reinforcement and resupply across the North Sea.[27] In peacetime, the navy maintains a high level of readiness and careful surveillance of Warsaw Pact activity. It also performs fishery protection duties around Greenland and the Faroes.

In the 1980s Warsaw Pact naval and amphibious forces in the Baltic have expanded to the extent that NATO naval units are outnumbered by a ratio of four to one, and the Pact maintains two divisions and a brigade of amphibious troops, of whom 5,000 could be landed as a first wave. Owing to financial pressures, the Danish navy has lost ships and manpower, and heavy units have been replaced by lighter ones.[28] This development will probably be persistent, with a shift from reliance on standing forces to one on reserves to provide the war strength.[29]

The operational elements of the navy are the Fighting Fleet, the Surveillance Force, Fishery Protection Squadrons, and the Land Force. The Fighting Fleet consists of 38 vessels organized in the Frigate, Submarine, Light Attack Craft, and Mine Warfare Squadrons. There are 5 frigates, 4 coastal submarines, 7 minelayers, 6 minesweepers, and 16 fast attack craft.[30] By 1987 the Fleet will be reduced to 35 units, gaining a submarine but losing an old cable minelayer and three minesweepers. The Surveillance Force disposes of 22 patrol craft and cutters; by 1987 it will be increased by one Standard Flex, a newly designed multi-purpose small vessel. The Fishery Protection Squadron has five ocean-going vessels, five cutters, and eight Lynx helicopters, four embarked. The Land Force consists of two coastal forts, at Stevns and south Langeland and the Frogmen's Corps. The Material Support

Command maintains three main bases, at Copenhagen, Frederickshagen, and Korsor, a mobile base, and three logistic vessels. The Operational Support Command maintains the Naval District HQs (Bornholm, the Sound, Langeland, Great Belt, and Kattegat), coastal radio stations and coastal radar.[31] On mobilization, the Fleet would be augmented by 37 coastal patrol boats from the Reserve.[32]

The 1985–87 Defense Agreement proposed to increase the combat effectiveness of the Fleet by modernizing the coastal radio network and purchasing more modern weapon systems for the ships. The three newer frigates, of the Niels Juel class, are to have more Harpoon, the upgraded Sea Sparrow SAM, and the Sea Gnat and RAM anti-surface-to-surface missile systems. The Lynx helicopters are to be adapted so they can spot targets for Harpoon. The submarines are to have an improved coil-guided torpedo. More controlled mines will be held in stock. There are no plans for any major building program, the only project in hand being for the construction of the Standard Flex class of vessel.[23] The two coastal forts are armed with 155 mm guns. They were intended to give direct support to naval activities, such as minelaying, but are now considered obsolete.[34]

The navy has a peace strength of 5,875 service personnel, including 1,215 conscripts, 1,380 officers, and 2,500 civilians. On mobilization, this would increase to 12,255 sailors and civilians. By 1987 it is planned to increase the war strength to 12,840, but this is to be accomplished by increasing the Reserves from 3,870 to 4,685. The officers, conscripts, and civilians in the peacetime navy are to be reduced in number; there is to be a small increase in the number of regular ratings.[35] By these shifts of emphasis the navy will become more professional, but also more dependent on the Reserves. The navy is supported by a Home Guard of some 5,800 engaged primarily in coastal watch and close harbor security activities.[36]

The main peacetime work of the navy is surveillance of Danish waters and of the Western and Central Baltic in general. This is done using observation posts, coastal radar and extensive patrols. Naval vessels also perform the full range of usual duties, enforcing sovereignty, fishery protection, Coast Guard policing, survey, and rescue.[37] In wartime, the navy would act in concert with other national and NATO forces, particularly the West German navy and Naval Air Wing. Early decisions to deploy and fight would be vital to the success of plans for naval defense.[38] Warsaw Pact naval and air bases are so close to Danish territory that warning of an impending attack, and the time to make a response, would be minimal.[39]

The first aim of NATO forces would be to deny the enemy control or use of the Western Baltic. The second, residual aim would be to continue to deny the enemy safe passage of the straits, even if the Western Baltic were under Warsaw Pact control.[40] Plans for naval action are based on aggressive tactics in support of a strategy of defense in depth, and this entails a forward defense. Swift deployment forward is essential for several reasons. From the political point of view it is necessary to cover the vulnerable centers of population on Zealand,[41] especially in view of the enemy's acquisition of long-range weapons. From the military angle, it is the only means by which the NATO forces can obtain space for maneuver, as the Baltic is so constricted.[42]

When action commenced, the plan would be to combine deep strikes into the full depth of the enemy position with barrier operations to protect Danish and German coasts from amphibious attacks. East of Bornholm, submarines and aircraft would engage in offensive mining along the Polish coast and in sea lanes, to reduce and inhibit the enemy logistic effort. Submarines would also make direct attacks on enemy shipping in deeper waters. All bases and other facilities along the East German and Polish coasts would be targets for air strikes.[43]

West of Bornholm, the full range of available forces would be employed, echeloned in depth, in small mobile groups, to reduce enemy amphibious forces and ships by successive and repeated attacks.[44] The barrier operations would take advantage of the constricted access, shallows, and variety of units available to present the army with a wide range of unpredictable threats, so he could not concentrate upon securing himself against any one in particular.[45]

Submarines and aircraft would act furthest forward, to conduct surveillance, combat reconnaissance, and opportunity attacks.[46] Closer in, fast attack craft, supported by frigates, would launch sudden missile attacks from concealed assembly areas, taking full advantage of their detailed knowledge of the local waters.[47] Approaches to possible landing beaches, shallow waters such as the Fehmarn Belt, and the entrances to the Straits would be denied to the enemy by extensive use of mines, both contact and controlled. Mines for the most important areas are kept ready for use at very short notice.[48]

The inner waterways of the archipelago would be patrolled and defended by vessels of the Surveillance Force and the older, smaller, torpedo-armed patrol craft. In due course, Standard Flex ships will replace them, and carry on mine clearance as well. If the enemy managed to secure a foothold on one of the islands, the navy would use all its means to isolate that particular piece of land by controlling or denying adjacent waters to the enemy.[49]

It seems that in the event of war there would be sudden and fierce naval action in the Western Baltic. The Warsaw Pact has a great superiority of numbers, but no room for dispersion or maneuver. If the NATO forces were deployed forward in time, and permitted to take offensive action, the small, mobile Danish forces could inflict great loss on the enemy. The question of time is the key, and this in turn depends greatly upon efficient intelligence and surveillance work in peace, to spot preparations for an attack. This task is much complicated by the increasingly high level of Warsaw Pact maritime, naval, and exercise activity in the Western Baltic. However, the Danes do possess a most valuable outpost on the island of Bornholm, which may be able to provide early warning of an attack.

The Danish navy is small and shrinking. But it is well suited to operating in the peculiar conditions of the Baltic, and has adapted to working closely with other NATO forces in the area. If it had sufficient warning, it could make a useful contribution to the defense of COMBALTAP.[50]

The Danish Air Force

Like the navy, the Royal Danish Air Force is a largely professional service, trained and equipped to operate in very close collaboration with allied forces. It is small, but due to the strategic location of Denmark, has to prepare to fight on several fronts, and to conduct all types of air operations, from air defense to deep penetration attacks.[51] Local flying conditions require all-weather aircraft and highly trained pilots.[52] In the early 1960s the air force had a strength of 160 jets in ten squadrons, but by 1984 it had been reduced to 96 combat aircraft in six squadrons. By 1987 there will be a further reduction to 84 first-line aircraft.[53]

The Tactical Air Command (TAC) deploys three squadrons of the F-16-A/B for fighter ground attack operations; a squadron of F-104-G for interception, and two squadrons of the F-35-XD Draken, one for reconnaissance, the other for maritime strike. All the squadrons have 16 first-line aircraft.[54] By 1987 the F-104-G will be phased out. By 1988 the TAC will have 57 F-16 and 32 F-35-XD.[55] The main flying stations are at Karup, Aalborg, Skrydstrup, and Verbese, but there are over 100 civil aerodromes that could be put to military use in emergency.[56]

Besides the combat aircraft, the air force has a Transport Squadron of three C-130 Hercules, and a number of fishery inspection and light communication aircraft.

The air force has been in control of land-based air defense units since 1962, when it took over the NIKE groups from the army.[57] There are six Area Air Defense units, each with six I-HAWK launchers, and it is planned to deploy two more units by 1987.[58] There are also six Short Range Air Defense Squadrons, armed primarily with radar-directed 20 mm and 40 mm automatic cannon. These guns are obsolescent, and short-range air defense is considered an area of serious weakness.[59]

The fighting elements are supported by an operational support structure of Command HQs, Air Stations, SAM Stations, and Control and Warning Stations. The Control and Warning Group is integrated into the NADGE system. The logistic support structure consists of the material command, main workshops, and supply depots.[60] The Air Home Guard, with a strength of 12,400, monitors airspace over the land territory up to an altitude of 6,000 feet. It operates a network of 400 observation towers with direct communication to the low-altitude warning centres of the Control and Warning Group.[61]

In peacetime the strength of the air force is 9,550, which includes 1,300 officers, 4,575 regular personnel, 1,230 conscripts, and 2,365 civilians. By 1987 the number of conscripts will be halved, and there will be small increase in the numbers of other categories, making the strength 9,125. The war reserve will remain at a strength of 10,000.[62]

Personnel in the fighting units are trained with an emphasis on cooperation with allied forces. Pilots learn to fly in Denmark, then go to the Eurotraining School in the USA for advanced training, before returning home to convert to their operational aircraft. There are plenty of coastal ranges with scope for live-firing, and many exercises are shared with 2nd ATAF from the Central Front. Each squadron has 22 pilots and 16 aircraft, so there is a reserve of 30 percent. The I-HAWK units regularly fire on the NATO ranges in Crete, and often take part in NATO exercises in Denmark.[63]

Since 1980, equipment policy has been dominated by procurement of the F-16 and I-HAWK. It was considered a matter of urgency to replace the F-104 and NIKE. The F-16 has been very well received by its pilots, but the program has been delayed by financial difficulties.[64] Two squadrons will have to retain the F-35-XD until the 1990s.

There are plans to buy new equipment for early warning, command and control, and local air defense. Radar stations at Skagen, Skrydstrup, Vedbaek, and Stensved provide cover which overlaps with the South Norway and Central Front networks. NATO has decided to fund certain new projects; there is to be a new chain of low altitude coastal radar to feed data directly into NADGE; a Marconi Martello radar is to be installed on Bornholm, and this will be able to see a long way into Polish airspace.[65] The Danes have always been pioneers in the technology of data handling for command, control, and communication (C_3). Now they are developing an advanced system at Skrydstrup, to transfer information from AEW direct to NADGE.[66] For short-range air defense the air force may acquire the German L-70 Superfledermaus System.[67]

The peacetime roles of the air force are surveillance, the repulse of violations of airspace, preparation for war, air reconnaissance, the early identification of aggressive moves, rescue, support of the North Atlantic Territories, and air transport.[68] The functions in support of North Atlantic Territories are primarily civil. The defense of Greenland is in the hands of the United States, in accordance with the Treaty of 1951. In the event of war the Faroes would come under the protection of the UK air defense scheme.[69]

In wartime, the main roles of the air force would be surveillance and warning, air defense, defense against invasion and support of naval and ground forces.[70] All operations would be conducted in close cooperation with allied air forces, particularly those of the UK and West Germany.[71] Surveillance and warning would be of vital importance to the protection of Denmark, as Warsaw Pact aircraft are based only two minutes' flying time away.[72] Early warning from Danish sources would also be of critical importance to the air defense of the UK and Southern Norway as Warsaw Pact aircraft could attempt to penetrate Danish airspace on their way to attack those areas. The Danish warning system would rely on NATO Airborne Early Warning and the new chain of low-level coastal radar.[73] The F-16s and F-104 squadrons are kept on constant high alert by frequent exercises, and by their peacetime duty of policing the national airspace.[74]

Air defense would involve the use of aircraft and SAMs. The aircraft would be employed in forward air defense, in offensive operations to strike enemy airfields, aircraft on the ground, missiles, and C3 installations.[75] Defense of Danish airspace would depend primarily on the I-HAWK units, with some interception by aircraft as a secondary measure. There are four I-HAWK units on Zealand. The gap between Zealand and North Germany used to be covered by CAPs, but is to be closed by installing two I-HAWK units on Funen. There are also to be I-HAWK units on the air bases at Skrydstrup and Karup, to improve the base security of the F-16 squadrons. These deployments should help in denying the enemy air superiority over invasion beaches on Zealand and Jutland, and the main reinforcement port at Ejsberg.[76]

Both aircraft and SAMs could be used in defense against invasion. The Draken reconnaissance squadron would be used to locate enemy amphibious forces by photo reconnaissance. The F-16s would be used to lay mines deep in the enemy rear areas, and to support naval surface operations.[77] The I-HAWK might be used directly against landing ships approaching assault beaches. In support of the navy, one of the Draken squadrons would be employed in anti-ship attacks.[78] In support of the army, the F-16s would probably concentrate on anti-tank work.[79]

The air crews train equally for air defense and for strike against maritime or land targets.[80] They are particularly trained in low-level all-weather attacks, night flying, and countering electronic warfare.[81]

The air force is small, but has good aircraft and SAMs. It has adequate training, and exercises regularly with allied forces. As with the navy, it could put up a good performance if given sufficient warning and mobilized in time.

Norwegian Security Policy: Détente from Strength

Norway achieved independence in 1905, after ninety years as a possession of the Swedish crown. The Norwegians were anxious to avoid foreign entanglements and followed a neutralist foreign policy. During World War I Norway was able to avoid involvement, being protected by the maritime predominance of the Royal Navy. Between the world wars, Norway supported the League of Nations. In 1939 the government declared a policy of neutrality, and hoped to avoid being drawn into the war. But since 1918 the strategic importance of Norway had been enhanced by developments in submarine and air warfare. Both Britain and Germany were aware of the value of the Norwegian coast. The Germans moved first, and invaded Norway, in April 1940, despite the presence of Royal Navy patrols on the approach routes. The Norwegians fought the invaders, and were hastily reinforced by improvised British and French expeditionary forces. But the German plans had been well prepared, and the Norwegian forces, enfeebled by years of neglect, were overwhelmed.

Immediately after 1945, the Norwegians hoped that the UN might succeed where the League of Nations had failed, but they were soon disappointed. They were skeptical of plans to form a neutral bloc in

Scandinavia, convinced that their future safety must depend upon close cooperation with the Atlantic powers. By 1949 they had to choose between isolated neutrality, a special relationship with the Soviet Union, or the Atlantic Alliance.[82] They decided to join the Atlantic Alliance as the basis of maintaining peace and democracy in Norway.[83]

Since 1949 membership of NATO has been the foundation of Norwegian security. The Alliance provides Norway with the political solidarity and military strength with which to deter aggression.[84] But the Norwegians are also concerned to reassure their neighbors that their membership of NATO is purely defensive in intent, and signifies no aggressive intentions.[85] Their aim is not only to achieve security from attack, but to do so at the lowest possible level of military participation,[86] and to maintain an atmosphere of tranquillity in the north.[87] The dual policy of deterrence and reassurance bears some resemblance to that of Denmark, but the Norwegians lay a stronger emphasis upon the absolute need to achieve effective deterrence before pursuing reassurance through active détente and its ramifications.[88]

In practical terms, the policy of reassurance is expressed in the ban on nuclear weapons and restrictions on the presence and activities of allied forces in peacetime. The ban on nuclear acquisition, use, or presence also conforms to popular demand. It is Norwegian policy to seek to reduce NATO's dependence on nuclear weapons, and discourage early use.[89] But the Norwegian government has made it clear that the ban is not unconditional, and has taken a skeptical view of proposals for the creation of a Nuclear Free Zone in Europe.[90] The restrictions on allied forces prohibit the permanent presence of foreign troops in peacetime, exclude them from areas of the national territory adjacent to the Soviet Union, and regulate exercises to make them appear non-threatening and predictable.[91] This concern to ensure that nothing Norway does to defend itself can be represented as a potential threat to the Soviet Union extends to the arrangement for pre-stocking material for the use of allied reinforcements.[92]

Deterrence and defense depend upon maximum use of Norway's own resources,[93] and making credible preparations for the swift, safe arrival and deployment of external reinforcements in an emergency.[94] The credibility of allied reinforcement is sustained by the pre-stocking program, to provide for their early arrival by air,[95] and the regular program of reinforcement and field service exercises involving NATO and Norwegian forces.[96] Norwegian resources are minute compared to those of the USSR, but the Norwegians are absolutely determined to strain every nerve to defend themselves and their interests. They believe that determination and ingenuity can overcome some of the disadvantages of numerical and material inferiority.[97] Public opinion is very strongly in favor of the official security policy,[98] and of the measures for a military defense.[99]

The overall defense policy is based on the Total Defense concept. This concept involves the mobilization of the whole society to protect itself and to generate the maximum military effort in order to hold the national territory until allied help becomes effective.[100] A Civil Defense and Emergency Planning Directorate coordinates schemes involving political management, economic defense, civil defense, police, public health and information services. The aims are to maintain the national will to resist, protect the civil population, repair war damage and support the armed forces.[101] The Civil Defence services can call on 75,800 trained personnel, 9,500 of them in 14 mobile columns, and they are active in the event of natural emergencies, such as flood or forest fires, as well as training for war.[102] There are measures to stockpile commodities for emergency use,[103] and to provide shelters and early warning of air raids. The war organization at central, regional and local levels is mobilized to take part in national and NATO military exercises to ensure proper coordination in wartime.[104]

Plans for military defense rely upon early detection of an attack, and for this reason the Norwegians are most concerned to maintain a close and continuous surveillance of their own territory and adjacent areas.[105] In the event of a warning of attack, the armed forces would mobilize quickly, with the process of forming and deploying the reserves being protected by the Home Guard. The bulk of the mobile forces would be sent to the north,[106] on the assumption that the Danish and German forces in BALTAP would defend approaches to south Norway, and the central regions would be screened by neutral Sweden.[107] The forces in the north would hold enemy attacks by land, sea, and air, whilst other forces secured the bases and lines of communications for allied reinforcements. Upon the arrival of the allied reinforcements, the Norwegian forces would act in conjunction with them to repulse the enemy.[108] In sum, in the south the Norwegians would rely upon a forward defense conducted by allies in BALTAP, and in the north they would rely upon their own national forces to delay and frustrate the enemy until allied forces arrived to reinforce.

The Norwegians recognize that, in the event of war, the consequences of their reassurance policy might make them vulnerable. Because of the ban on the basing of allied forces in Norway, they face a permanent local imbalance of forces in the north, and, if war were to break out, they would have to devote considerable effort to guarding reception facilities and lines of communication for external reinforcements. However, they recognize that the far north is of such strategic importance to the USSR that it is bound to maintain a military predominance in the area, and would do so even if north Norway were heavily garrisoned with NATO forces.[109] Indeed, the Soviets evidently fear that in wartime north Norway would be used by NATO as a base for massive attacks on their strategic facilities in the Kola peninsula.[110] NATO is acutely aware of the value which north Norwegian naval and air bases would have for the Soviets in protecting and supporting the Northern Fleet.[111] But the Norwegians believe that in view of their own state of alert and the nature of the terrain and conditions in the north, the Soviets would not be able to mount a successful offensive in that area with the forces they have in place in peace-time. Any large-scale reinforcement of the area could be taken as a warning, and provide time for NATO to take countervailing measures.[112]

The Norwegians regard their armed forces as an expression of the national will to maintain security and sovereignty. It is most important to them that the forces are seen as an integral part of society, and not as a separate institution.[113] It is for this reason, and to maximize the utilization of scarce manpower, that the forces are based on conscription. Most conscripts are content to serve, only some 1 percent requesting exemption.[114] The defense command has been careful to ensure that conditions in the forces are in step with those in civil life. Conscripts can make their views known through a machinery of democratic representation, which is considered most important in ensuring that they have an enthusiastic and positive attitude to their duty.[115] Women are not liable to conscription, but have been allowed to train as regular officers and NCOs for non-combatant functions only. Overall, recruiting for regular cadres is good.[116] The intimate connection between the armed forces and civilian society is reinforced by the Home Guard, a purely voluntary organization with a strength of 90,000.[117] Besides training for its mobilization role, the Home Guard maintains close liaison with the National Defense Association and the National Volunteer Riflemen's Association.[118] The Home Guard Youth Wing, with a strength of 2,000, is a fruitful source of cadets for the Military Academy.[119] These attitudes and institutions reflect the national determination that any agressor will be confronted with a nation in arms.

The Norwegian Army

The Norwegian army is the main arm of the defense forces.[120] It is a mobilization army, with its war strength based on a reserve of former conscripts.[121] It is lightly equipped, but effectively trained to fight in Norwegian conditions, taking advantage of the mountainous terrain and arctic climate of the north.[122] In the 1980s, senior officers have expressed concern that the imposition of financial strictures has delayed the purchase of new equipment and restricted training.[123] There is also some anxiety that in the future the effect of a falling birth rate will force a reduction in the size of the army. But the Norwegians have shown ingenuity in adapting and recycling old military equipment, and in any case their lack of material and reduced numbers may be countered by the improved prospect of allied reinforcement, and by their own high motivation and level of training.[124]

The basic operational unit of the army is the brigade. Studies have discovered that smaller formations lack adequate combat endurance.[125] There are plans to reorganize and reinforce the brigades to conform to a "Brigade 90" standard, with significant additions to anti-tank and anti-aircraft capability and better mobility. In suitable or strategically important areas, the Brigade 90 will be given an armoured battalion, and be known as the "Brigade 90 P-F."[126] These plans have been modified by financial considerations, but the government intends to raise three formations to Brigade 90 standard by 1988,[127] and to have ten at Brigade 90 by the late 1990s.[128]

In peacetime the army has a strength of about 20,000, of whom 12,000 are conscripts. There is the equivalent of two brigades in the Standing Force of regulars and trained conscripts; the Brigade North, in Troms; the two battalion groups on garrison duty in South Varanger and Porsanger, and a battalion group, including the Royal Guard, based in Oslo. In addition, there are armored sub-units guarding the main airfields.[129] Brigade North is to be the first Brigade 90 P-F.[130] There are 25 training and mobilization regiments, 14 infantry, 3 artillery, 3 rear services, 2 tank, and 1 each for engineers, transport, and signals. The Training Regiments' HQs are also Defense Region HQs, responsible for the local Home Guard. The Home Guard are organized in platoons and companies.[131] Norway is divided into two main commands, South and North. COMSONOR consists of four Military Districts, Trondelag, Serlandet, Ostlandet, and Vestlandet. COMNONOR maintains four Operational Commands, in Finnmark, Troms, Nord-Halogaland and South-Halogaland, with the HQ of the Sixth Division at Harstad acting as Military District HQ.[132]

On mobilization, the army would call up some 150,000 reservists, to form a Field Army of 13 brigades, supported by Local Defense Battalions operating within their own Districts, and some 72,500 Home Guards for neighborhood defense.[133] After mobilization, a Field Army Brigade would have a strength of 6,000 men, and be equipped with 27 tanks, 60 artillery pieces and heavy mortars, 24 anti-tank guns and recoilless rifles, six anti-tank guided weapons launchers, and 200 vehicles. The main units in the Brigade would consist of three battalions of infantry, one of artillery; an air defense battery; and reconnaissance, tank, mortar, anti-tank, engineer, and transport companies. This formation is regarded as being capable of sustained operations in all types of battle.[134] The infantry battalions and companies are organized on a quadratic basis, each unit being of three rifle and one support sub-unit.[135]

Arms and equipment have been acquired from a range of foreign sources, particularly the US, West Germany, and Sweden. The infantry have the German AG3 rifle and MG3 squad machine-gun, with the American M72 heavy machine-gun. There is a mixture of towed and self-propelled 105 mm and 155 mm howitzers, all of American manufacture, as are the heavy mortars. The armor is of mixed origin and age. There are 70 Leopard I and 70 NM-116 tank destroyers, these being old American M-24s upgraded and modernized; the infantry are carried in the M-113 APC. There is a great variety of anti-tank weapons; the 76 mm LAW and Carl Gustav from Sweden, the 106 mm RCL and the TOW ATGW system from the United States. Sweden supplies the special soft-skin tracked vehicles, the BV-202 and BV-206, for cross-country mobility in snow.[136] The lack of modern short-range air defense weapons was a serious cause of anxiety in the late 1970s,[137] but recently the army has acquired the RBS-70 light SAM to supplement the 20 mm and 40 mm gun systems.[138]

Conscripts are called up for service at the age of 19. Having completed a year's training, they are transferred to the reserve, being liable for service until age 44. After the age of 32 they are no longer eligible for service in the mobile brigades of the Field Army, and would most probably serve in the Local Defense Force.[139] The call-up takes place every four months. The conscripts are given four months of recruit training, one month common basic, and three months basic-to-arms in local centers. The next three months are devoted to advanced training, in special centers or with units. The last segment of service is spent in collective training, and in duty with the Standing Forces in the north or in Oslo. Reservists are called up for regular refresher training, which concentrates on personal skills, and on collective operational readiness, which is tested by short intensive exercises.[140]

It is regarded as important to make training as realistic as possible.[141] There is great emphasis on physical fitness, independent action without support by small sub-units, and coordination with friendly forces, whether native or foreign.[142] A majority of the soldiers are accustomed to mountainous areas and winter conditions, so the army can concentrate on tactical training.[143]

The corps of regular officers and NCOs amounts to some 12 percent of army war strength. There is no shortage of candidates for the military schools, and this has included a fair number of women since 1977.[144] However, there have been some difficulties with covering all the responsibilities of the regular cadre. Since 1979 financial limits and new laws on terms of employment have forced a reduction in the use of available resources.[145] There have also been difficulties in retaining officers and NCOs due to the disruption caused by the posting system.[146]

In peacetime, the army performs three main functions: surveillance of the frontier with the Soviet Union, which is done by the battalions in Finnmark; maintenance of a covering force against surprise attack, which is served by Brigade North; and training reserves for the Mobilization Force.

In the event of war, the first Norwegian troops to be fully ready for action would be the Home Guard, which would take post within a few hours, ready to repulse attacks by distraction forces, and to allow the Mobilization Forces to assemble and deploy in safety.[147]

The Local Defense Forces, older reservists, but with territorially based units and equipment in local stores, would also mobilize quickly. Their role would be to secure the lines of communication for the Field Army Brigades destined to go north, to cover vulnerable stretches of the coast, and provide cover against desants from the air. After the mobilization phase they would be employed for general rear area security purposes, with the active assistance of the Home Guard. In the event of an enemy penetration, they would conduct guerrilla attacks on his rear areas.[148]

The Norwegian strategy in the north is determined by the ground and the local correlation of resources. In Finnmark the terrain is mainly open tundra, good going for mechanized forces when dry or frozen, in summer and winter. But the next county, Troms, is extremely mountainous with summits well over 1,500 feet, access routes constricted, and cut by ridges, rivers and fjords.[149] Conditions in

Troms make rapid movement difficult, and concealment easy for static troops.[150] The forces in place on the Soviet side consist of two motor rifle divisions and a marine infantry brigade. They are faced by two battalions of the Norwegian army in South Varanger and Porsanger.

In the event of a Soviet offensive, it must be assumed that the attacking forces would be reinforced, and would be aiming to seize Norwegian territory as far south as the Lofoten Islands, in order to secure and ease the activities of the Northern Fleet. Given the benefits of some measure of surprise, they would be able to push through Finnmark.[151] The Norwegian response would be to refuse battle in Finnmark and draw back the South Varanger and Porsanger battalions.[152] Meanwhile, Mobilization Forces from South Norway would start to arrive by air, a redeployment exercised since 1978.[153] In less than a day, a battalion group would arrive. A full brigade would arrive, to take up pre-stocked material, in two to five days, and another in from four to seven days. Within a week there would be five brigades available to defend the north.[154] These brigades would take up defensive positions, some prepared, in the area between Bardufoss and Troms.[155] Here they could mount a defense based on holding strongpoints in key areas, primarily the summits and the sparse lines of communication.[156] The Soviet forces would be canalized and strung out by the terrain, unable to employ their standardised tactics of concentrating massive firepower to maximise shock effect.[157] By this stage of an advance, the Soviet ground forces would be suffering from logistic strain, having motored some 1,000 km from their bases.[158] Unless the Soviets could attack with strategic suprise, or intercept Norwegian reinforcements coming north, they would find it difficult to break through the mountain barrier before allied reinforcements started to arrive. It is estimated that, if ACEMF were deployed to Norway, it could arrive in six days. Moving by air, a US Marine Corps Marine Amphibious Brigade could reach Trondelag, where material is pre-stocked for it, within eight days. The UK–Netherlands Commando Brigade would arrive by sea within ten days. In 30 days the Canadian CAST Brigade Group would be in place. Of these reinforcements, only the UK-Netherlands Commandos and the Canadians would be fully trained in mountain and arctic warfare, but the others could be employed to reinforce strongpoints covering valley bottoms.[159]

In order to defeat the Norwegian defense of the north, the Soviets would have to outflank or envelop the Norwegian positions in the mountains. It would be very difficult to accomplish this by infiltration on the ground, because the Norwegian troops are all ski-mobile, and very skillful at small-scale patrol and ambush operations.[160] The Soviets would make extensive use of helicopters for troop carrying and assault operations, and could use them to achieve a vertical envelopment of the Norwegian positions.[161] The Norwegians cannot match the Soviet helicopter forces, having only 26 UH-1B utility helicopters.[162] However, they are ordering more of the RBS-70 system, which will make helicopter assaults on their positions very hazardous. The only other way of disrupting the Norwegian defense would be by an amphibious assault, with the marine infantry acting as a forward detachment of the ground forces advancing down the main axis. Such an assault would be of at least battalion group size, and would be strongly supported by naval and air forces.[163] The Norwegian response to this threat is primarily in the hands of the air force and navy, but a Soviet landing might have to be met by Local Defense battalions, or a brigade held in reserve for the purpose.

It has been suggested that the Soviets might seek to outflank the Norwegian army by attacking through Finnish and Swedish territory.[164] This seems unlikely in view of the distances to be covered on such a route, the difficulty in the event of Finnish and Swedish resistance, and the fact that such a maneuver could not outflank the main area of Norwegian resistance.[165]

In sum, any Soviet attack on north Norway would have a most uncertain result, and this is not a prospect that would appeal to the Soviet leadership. The possibility of Soviet ground force attacks on other areas of Norway seems remote for geographic reasons, unless Denmark is over-run by the enemy. If the southeast coast were to be threatened by sinister developments in BALTAP, the Norwegians could concentrate their remaining eight brigades to face the threat, leaving the protection of reinforcement facilities to the Local Defense Forces and Home Guard.

The Norwegian Navy

The Norwegian navy is the second largest in Scandinavia, and is a coastal defense force. It could not conduct independent blue-water operations, but could give valuable support to allied naval forces in the eastern Atlantic,[166] and protection to allied reinforcements approaching Norway by sea. A distinctive feature is the heavy dependence on coastal artillery as a means of countering the amphibious threat from the Soviet Union. Like the army, the navy concentrates its attention on protecting the north, and the lines of communications leading to the north.[167] Senior officers are content with the basic structure of the naval forces,[168] but they are worried by the effects of financial strictures: in particular by the failure to renovate old coastal forts or replace old ships[169] when the threat from the Soviet Northern Fleet and marine infantry is growing.[170] In 1983 is was necessary to lay up a frigate and a corvette in order to save money, despite evidence of Soviet submarine intrusions into the northern fjords.[171] There are plans to acquire new units and modernize old ones,[172] now that the financial pressure caused by acquisition of the F-16 has eased. But it seems likely that due to inflation and budgetary slippage many projects will be delayed. The net result will be that the navy will shrink slightly and become lighter.

The naval forces consist of the Fleet, Coast Artillery, Naval Home Guard, and Coast Guard. There are two major Operational Commands, North and South, and nine Coastal Region Commands. The main bases are at Haakonsvern, Olavsvern and Ramsund.[173] In peacetime, the strength is 7,500, of whom 1,000 are in the Coast Artillery, and 5,500 are conscripts.[174] The fleet is a balanced force of light units. There are two divisions of submarines, with a total strength of 14 small diesel boats. The two frigate division share five small frigates. The ASW division has two corvettes. The two Mine Warfare divisions have a total of twelve minelayers and minesweepers. The Amphibious Assault division deploys seven landing craft, each capable of carrying 7 AFVs and 100 men. The two flotillas of Fast Attack Craft have 38 missile boats. The two Coastal Defence divisions deploy a number of patrol boats and coastal transports.[175] The Coastal Artillery maintains 40 forts, 15 in the North and 25 in the south. In peacetime, 19 are active, with 21 in reserve.[176] The active forts maintain a high level of alert, and some would be prepared for action in less than an hour in an emergency.[177] The Naval Home Guard has a strength of 5,400, and in war would operate a number of auxiliary trawlers. Its duties are mainly surveillance and reporting.[178] The Coast Guard was formally constituted in 1977.[179] This body was raised to police the new sea territories of the Continental Shelf and Exclusive Economic Zone. The service has six patrol vessels, capable of carrying the Penguin II missile, seven fishery protection vessels, and six Lynx helicopters with an ASW capability.[180]

Like the army, the navy has suffered from a shortage of funds to pay for new ships, so has had to retain and refit old ones.[181] Most of the larger units now in service were constructed in the 1960s, with generous help from the US,[182] and the minesweepers are now thirty years old.[183] Major projects have commenced to upgrade the five frigates, some of the submarines, and some of the older Fast Attack craft.[184] Particular attention will be paid to improving anti-aircraft systems.[185] On the whole, the navy is content with its major weapons systems, the Penguin and Sea Sparrow, and radar systems, which work well in the peculiarly cluttered environment of Norwegian coastal waters.[186] Some new vessels are on order. Between 1989 and 1993 the navy will take delivery of six "Ula" class submarines from Thyssen, and may order two more.[187] It is intended to acquire more minehunting vessels, but no firm orders have yet been placed.[188]

The coastal artillery is also due for improvement. The forts are armed with torpedo batteries, and gun batteries with 75 mm, 105 mm, 127 mm, and 150 mm guns.[189] Some of these guns are old, and very worn.[190] The forts are protected by controlled and anchored mines, and light anti-aircraft guns for point defense.[191] There are plans to upgrade the offensive capabilities of some forts by installing new 120 mm guns,[192] 75 mm semi-automatic guns, and modern fire control gear with radar, laser and TV systems.[193] Air defense is to be strengthened by installing batteries of RBS-70 light SAMS.[194] An entirely new fort is to be built in Trondelag, in order to enhance the security of the reception area and pre-stocked stores for the American MAB.[195]

Conscripts entering the navy serve for 15 months. Their training is intensive, and concentrates on activities in the north.[196] Most serve in the coastal forts, and they are recalled for intensive refresher exercises after they have completed their military service.[197] The fleet is manned mainly by regulars. In the late 1970s and the 1980s, the navy has been able to recruit suitable officers and NCOs,[198] but has had difficulty in retaining them. Many retired early because pay was regarded as inadequate, and the posting system disrupted family life.[199] In the summer of 1983 the navy introduced a new posting system based on application rather than assignment in an attempt to solve this problem.[200]

Despite this discontent over terms and conditions of service, the navy believes that high standards of training have been maintained, due to a tradition of professionalism, and regular exercises with allied navies. Submarines go to the UK for training with the Royal Navy.[201] Frigates serve with STANAVFORLANT. The navy takes part in the NATO reinforcement and field service exercises.[202] Operational training, mainly in the north, concentrates on anti-invasion measures in close cooperation with friendly ground, air, and naval forces.[203]

In peacetime, the main tasks of the naval forces are to mark the sovereignty of Norway over the national territory; to maintain surveillance and an early warning capacity; and to be prepared to defend the coasts and waters against attack.[204] In wartime the primary tasks would be to defend the coasts against amphibious assault; to secure the coastal lines of communications within the coastal archipelago; to clear the sea lanes of enemy mines; and to provide mobility for the army in areas where land communications were bad or vulnerable.[205] The provision of early warning of a likely attack is considered to be particularly important and increasingly difficult, because the Soviets are stepping up routine naval activities and exercises, which could be used to mask an attack.[206]

The Norwegian coast is rugged, and the waters along it are difficult to navigate, which should give the defending forces a great advantage.[207] Defense against amphibious assault would involve submarines, FACs, minelayers and the coastal forts, in cooperation with the air force. All the main fjords, most suitable beaches, and centres of population are protected by forts. Their presence would force an enemy either to land on unsuitable stretches of the coast, or to spend time and accept losses in suppression operations. Such costly and tedious operations would provide time for defending forces to concentrate against the enemy. Besides denying or delaying access to desirable landing beaches, the forts would act as coordination centres for mobile units.[208] The submarines woud probably be employed directly against the amphibious forces[209] and their meager logistic supports.[210] Closer to the shore, the missile armed FACs would make direct attacks, seeking to evade the Soviet covering and support forces, to strike directly at the landing ships.[211] Immediately off the coast, offensive mining would be effective, as the Soviets have a limited mine clearance capacity.[212] The Soviet amphibious forces also suffer from poor air defense capability. This means they would have to attack with local air superiority,[213] or under cover of darkness. But the hours of darkness are very short for the summer months, and the Norwegian FAC are well suited to night attacks. The Soviets would undoubtedly support amphibious landings with airborne or air-mobile assaults.[214] The strengthening of the coastal forts' air defense systems, and the Norwegian and allied air forces, would be expected to repulse these attacks.

The navy would also have to protect the leads, the inner waterways of the coastal archipelago. These sea lanes would be vulnerable to penetration and attack by enemy fighter-bombers, submarines, and

FACs, using missiles, torpedoes, and mines to interdict reinforcement and resupply convoys moving north.[215] The coastal forts and minefields would close some of the vital chokepoints and exits to the enemy,[216] but it is inevitable that some would get into the lines of communication. The frigates and corvettes, with the helicopters of the Coast Guard, would conduct ASW operations to clear the leads for convoys going north.[217] The minesweepers and new minehunters would keep sea lanes and harbors clear, with help from the coastal protection patrol boats.[218] The main responsibility for dealing with large-scale air attacks would fall to the Norwegian and allied air forces, forewarned by Airborne Early Warning. Once equipped with Sea Sparrow and the RBS-70 on a proper scale, the frigates, corvettes, and FAC could probably deal with small-scale attacks on their own.[219] The navy has additional protection from air attack from the character of the coast, which provides many hardened shelters in caves and plenty of opportunity for dispersal and concealment.[220]

Beyond the coastal waters, the frigates and submarines might join in NATO barrier operations to close off the South Norwegian Sea, and protect reinforcement and resupply convoys going north. In such operations, the submarines could operate forward, with frigates standing back in support.[221] However, it is most likely that the Norwegian navy would be too busy covering the enormous length of the coast to take part in more distant operations.

The Norwegian Air Force

The Norwegian air force is small, with its main strength in fighters.[222] It is intended to make a contribution to the defense of Norway, but is too small to cover the airspace and meet the threat without substantial help from NATO reinforcements.[223] Training and exercises emphasize close cooperation with allied air forces, and also with naval and ground forces.[224] The Norwegians realize that they lack the resources to maintain a balanced force, and have decided, in consultation with allies, to concentrate on surveillance and early warning, air defense, and securing reception bases for allied reinforcements.[225] The air force is being re-equipped with the F-16, the Falcon, and the Orion, and is now considering the modernization of ground-based air defense systems,[226] which have been an area of weakness since the 1970s.[227] In peacetime the air force has a strength of 9,500, including 5,000 conscripts and 114 combat aircraft. There are four squadrons with 18 F-16s each, and one squadron of 35 F-5s.[228] A maritime patrol squadron of 7 Orion P-3B is based at Andoya.[229] An Airborne Early Warning Squadron, with the

E-3A AWACS, is to be based at Ørland, and will feed information directly into the NATO network.[230] This will replace the squadron of Falcons now based at Moss.[231] There are two transport squadrons, and two squadrons of utility helicopters.[232] The air force also operates Sea King helicopters for coastal search and rescue operations, and Lynx for the Coast Guard.[233] The F-16s are armed with Sidewinder and Bullpup air-to-air missiles, and are to be equipped with Penguin III for anti-ship operations.[234] They are based at Rygge and Bodo, with the F-35s at Ørland.[235] There are also main bases at Bardurfoss, Erlann, Sola, and Gardermoen, and in the north civil airfields are well adapted for military use in emergency.[236]

The Oslo area is protected by four batteries of NIKE Hercules SAMs, with 128 missiles in all.[237] There are 54 I-HAWK launchers on order, and these are to be deployed to cover airfields in the north and center of the country, thereby helping to secure reinforcement bases.[238] It is intended to keep the NIKES until 1990 at least.[239] Close air defense is primarily by the L-70 system, with some older L-60s still in use. In wartime, the influx of reserves would add seven extra light AA battalions to the four established in peace.[240] The authorities are considering the options for the future of close air defense, and will probably decide to combine guns with light SAMs.[241] The Air Home Guard, with a strength of 2,500, provides two battalions of AA troops equipped with a heavy machine-guns, and local ground defense, for air bases.[242] The air defense radar system is linked to NADGE, but is regarded as obsolete and vulnerable to electronic warfare.[243] The government is planning to modernize the whole system, and protect the radars by putting them into hardened silos.[244]

The air force has good new aircraft, but has had difficulty in retaining pilots to fly them and technicians to maintain them. There is no shortage of candidates for training, but social and economic reasons induce many of them to retire early.[245] Much of the flying and operational training is done with allies. The F-16 pilots are trained at Sheppard AFB in America.[246] The NIKE batteries regularly fire on the NATO ranges in Sardinia.[247] The air force always takes a full part in NATO exercises, to ensure that air reinforcements will become effective as soon as possible after their arrival.[248] Under NATO agreements and plans, there are eight airfields prepared to be Collocated Operating Bases, and to receive British, Canadian, and American aircraft in an emergency. They would also handle and support aircraft flown from USN carriers if necessary.[249]

In peacetime, the most important tasks of the air force are maritime and air surveillance, and air policing. It is Norwegian aircraft that would provide NATO with early warning of any threatening developments in the area of the Kola peninsula.[250] Alert fighters also have to intercept and turn back Soviet aircraft intruding into Norwegian airspace.[251]

In wartime, the first priority of the air force would be to protect the army in the north from Soviet air attacks. This would have to be done by interception attacks, closely coordinated with the Field Army's use of its SAMs. The second priority would be to cooperate with the navy, particularly the FACs, in striking enemy amphibious forces. The third priority would be to provide air defense over the leads and the lines of communication and reception areas for reinforcements. These tasks would all fall to the F-16 squadrons. The fourth priority, the protection of air bases, would be carried out primarily by the I-HAWK and Close Air Defense units.[252] More offensive air operations, such as interdiction and ground attack in support of the army would have to be left to allied air forces. The Norwegian air force is too small to sustain the levels of attrition that such operations would impose.[253] The air force is indeed equipped with ultra-modern aircraft, but so few of them that it faces a desperate struggle against the odds in the event of war.

Conclusion

The Danish and Norwegian armed forces present a series of parallels and paradoxes. Both sets of forces serve highly developed, democratic, pacific states. But in one there is a tendency to professionalization of the services, whilst in the other conscription is taken to be inevitable and beneficial. Norway is an area of primarily maritime and air interest to NATO and Warsaw Pact alike, but its defense is in the hands of an army of reservists, with the navy and air force playing an auxiliary role. Denmark is an area whose acquisition by the Warsaw Pact would have a profound effect upon land operations on the Central Front, but it is defended first by air and naval forces, with the army as a last resort. Norway produces a maximum national defense effort, but is of comparatively lesser interest to the Warsaw Pact. Denmark is of much greater interest to the potential enemy, and is less strongly defended. Given these considerations, and those of geography and the local correlation of forces in each area, Denmark seems much more vulnerable than Norway.

Notes

1. A. Farrar-Hockley, "Dynamic Defence: The Northern Flank," *RUSI Journal* (December 1983), p. 11.
2. Danish Government, *Denmark's Security Policy Situation in the 1980s* (unofficial translation), 29 November 1984, pp. 1, 25, 73.
3. Ibid., pp. 54–55.
4. Ibid., p. 4.
5. Ibid., pp. 7–8, 72–73.
6. Ibid., p. 27.
7. Ibid., pp. 43–47.
8. C. N. Donnelly, M. J. Orr, P. H. Vigor, Z. I. Chojecki, and S. P. Dalziel, *Soviet Amphibious Operations, Implications for the Security of NATO's Northern Flank*, CR-57 (Shape Technical Centre, The Hague, March 1985), p. 189.
9. O. K. Lind, "Defence and the Baltic: Forward Defence for the UK?" *RUSI Journal* (June 1985), p. 10.
10. Donnelly et al., *Soviet Amphibious Operations*, pp. 23–24.
11. Ibid., p. 189
12. Ibid., p. 56.
13. Ibid., pp. iii–vii, 47.
14. Lind, "Defence and the Baltic," p. 10.
15. Donnelly et al., *Soviet Amphibious Operations*, pp. 162, 185.
16. Lind, "Defence and the Baltic, p. 12.
17. *The Danish Defence Agreement 1985–87* (unauthorized partial translation), p. 1.
18. *Danish Defence Agreement*, pp. 1, 2, 8; Donnelly et al., *Soviet Amphibious Operations*, pp. 190–191.
19. Extract from *D.V. Report*, 1985.
20. International Institute for Strategic Studies (IISS), *The Military Balance 1984–1985*, (IISS, London, 1984).
21. *Danish Defence Agreement*, p. 2.
22. Donnelly et al. *Soviet Amphibious Operations*, pp. 46–47.
23. R. D. M. Furlong, "The Strategic Situation in Northern Europe, Improvements Vital for NATO," *International Defence Review* vol. 12, no. 6 (1979), p. 905.
24. Lind, "Defence and the Baltic," p. 10.
25. H. M. H. Boysen, "Denmark" in *NATO's 15 Nations*, Special No. 1 (1980), pp. 31–32, "Defence of the Islands and Coasts," in *NATO's 16 Nations*, Special No. 1 (1983), pp. 31–32.
26. Donnelly, et al., *Soviet Amphibious Operations*, p. 47.
27. N. F. Lange, "Naval Control of the Danish Straits" in *NATO's 15 Nations*, Special No. 2, (1982), pp. 38–39; A. Bethge "The Role of the German Navy in the Northern Flank Area" in *NATO's 15 Nations*, Special No. 2 (1982), pp. 20–21.
28. H. Kampe, "The Maritime Situation in the Baltic Approaches," *Naval Forces*, no. 1 (1985), pp. 28–9.
29. *Danish Defence Agreement*, Enclosure 2.
30. Lange, "Naval Control," p. 39.
31. *Danish Defence Agreement*, Enclosure 2.
32. IISS, *Military Balance 1984–1985*.
33. Ibid., *Danish Defence Agreement*, p. 3.
34. Extract from *D. V. Report*, 1985.
35. *Danish Defence Agreement*, Enclosure 2.
36. Donnelly et al., *Soviet Amphibious Operations*, pp. 187–188.
37. Lange, "Naval Control," pp. 38–39.
38. Ibid., p. 39.

39. Kampe, "The Maritime Situation," p. 29.
40. Boysen, "Defence of the Islands," p. 31.
41. Lind, "Defence and the Baltic," p. 12; Lange, "Naval Control," p. 39.
42. Kampe, "The Maritime Situation," p. 29.
43. Bethge, "The Role of the German Navy," p. 44.
44. Ibid., p. 44.
45. Kampe, "The Maritime Situation," p. 29.
46. Lind, "Defence and the Baltic," p. 10.
47. Lange, "Defence against Amphibious Attack" in *NATO's 16 Nations*, Special No. 1 (1984), pp. 34, 39.
48. Lind, "Defence and the Baltic," p. 10.
49. Boysen, "Defence of the Islands," p. 31.
50. Kampe, "The Maritime Situation," p. 29.
51. P. Thorsen, "Air Operations in the Baltic Approaches," in *NATO's 16 Nations*, Special No. 2 (1984), p. 33.
52. J. Brodersen, "Tactical Air Power; Considerations in the Northern Region" in *NATO's 15 Nations*, Special No. 2 (1979), p. 79.
53. *Danish Defence Agreement*, Enclosure 3.
54. IISS, *The Military Balance 1984-1985*.
55. *Danish Defence Agreement*, Enclosure 3, p. 4.
56. *Danish Defence Agreement*, p. 4; Donnelly et al., *Soviet Amphibious Operations*, pp. 187-189.
57. N. S. Holst-Sørensen, "The Royal Danish Air Force" in *NATO's 15 Nations*, Special No. 2 (1979), p. 46.
58. *Danish Defence Agreement*, Enclosure 3.
59. B. Wanstall, "Air Defence in the Baltic; Has the Tide Turned?" *Interavia* (December 1982), p. 1299.
60. *Danish Defence Agreement*, Enclosure 3.
61. Wanstall, "Air Defence in the Baltic," p. 1299.
62. *Danish Defence Agreement*, Enclosure 3.
63. Wanstall, "Air Defence in the Baltic," p. 1298.
64. Brodersen, "Tactical Air Power," pp. 25-27.
65. Wanstall, "Air Defence in the Baltic," p. 1298.
66. Thorsen, "Air Operations," p. 29.
67. Ibid., p. 30.
68. Ibid., p. 33.
69. Holst-Sørensen, "The Royal Danish Air Force," p. 49.
70. Thorsen, "Air Operations," p. 33.
71. Lind, "Defence and the Baltic," p. 10.
72. Thorsen, "Air Operations," pp. 10-12.
73. Lind, "Defence and the Baltic," pp. 10-12.
74. Thorsen, "Air Operations," p. 29.
75. Ibid., p. 30.
76. Wanstall, "Air Defence in the Baltic," p. 1299.
77. Thorsen, "Air Operations," p. 30.
78. Wanstall, "Air Defence in the Baltic," p. 1299.
79. Thorsen, "Air Operations," p. 33.
80. Wanstall, "Air Defence in the Baltic," p. 1298.
81. Donnelly et al. *Soviet Amphibious Operations*, p. 162
82. J. J. Holst, "Norwegian Security Policy for the 1980s," *Co-operation and Conflict*, vol. 17, no. 4 (1982), p. 208.
83. Royal Ministry of Defence, *Main Guidelines for the Defence Establishment during the Period 1984-1988* (Oslo, 1984), p. 31.
84. Ibid., p. 35.

85. Ibid., p. 37.
86. Holst, "Norwegian Security Policy," pp. 208, 211.
87. R. Hansen, "Our Defense Mission is to Secure Peace," *Norwegian Defense* (1978), p. 2.
88. Royal Ministry of Defence, *Main Guidelines*, p. 4.
89. Holst, "Norwegian Security Policy," pp. 223, 225, 228.
90. Royal Ministry of Defence, *Main Guidelines*, p. 43.
91. Ibid., pp. 23-24.
92. Press Department of Ministry of Defence, "Pre-Stocking of Allied Military Equipment," *Norwegian Defence Review* (1983-84), p. 27.
93. J. Nordhaug, "75,000 in Civil Defence 20% Increase is Sought," *Norwegian Defence* (1977), p. 25.
94. Royal Ministry of Defence, *Main Guidelines*, p. 32; Holst, "Norwegian Security Policy," p. 211.
95. Holst, "Norwegian Security Policy," p. 210.
96. Press Department, Ministry of Defence, "Exercises in Norway with Allied Participation," *Norwegian Defence Review* (1983-84), p. 24.
97. K. Frydenlund, "Security and Détente," *Norwegian Defence Review* (1981-82), p. 4.
98. Holst, "Norwegian Security Policy," p. 216.
99. T. Stoltenberg, "3 Per Cent Annual Growth Investments Must be Increased," *Norwegian Defence* (1979), p. 2.
100. S. Hamre, "Our Defence System Maximises the Whole Nation's Defence Capability," *Norwegian Defence* (1979), p. 7.
101. J. Nordhaug, "75,000 in Civil Defence," p. 26.
102. J. Nordhaug, "Norwegian Civil Defence Still in Development Phase," *Norwegian Defence* (1978), p. 23.
103. Ibid., p. 28.
104. T. R. Byrntesen, "Civil Emergency Planning Must be Geared to All Types of War Conditions," *Norwegian Defence Review* (1981-82), p. 28.
105. Royal Ministry of Defence, *Main Guidelines*, pp. 49-50.
106. Ibid., p. 30; K. Østbye, "Home Guard Well Suited to Take on First Wave of an Attack," *Norwegian Defence Review* (1981-82), p. 33.
107. S. Hamre, "Growing Power of Soviet SS-20s Most Serious Threat to NATO," *Norwegian Defence Review* (1981-82), p. 10.
108. Royal Ministry of Defence, *Main Guidelines*, p. 31.
109. Holst, "Norwegian Security Policy," p. 213.
110. Donnelly *et al.*, *Soviet Amphibious Operations*, pp. 158, 163.
111. Ibid., p. 21; P. Whiteley, "Norway in Context of European Defence," *Norwegian Defence* (1977), p. 6.
112. Royal Ministry of Defence, *Main Guidelines*, pp. 46, 47; Holst, "Norwegian Security," pp. 213, 215; R. Hansen, "Political Framework for Norway's Security," *Norwegian Defence* (1977), p. 3.
113. H. F. Zeiner Gundersen, "Soviet Power Build-up Decisive for US," *Norwegian Defence* (1977), p. 9.
114. Hamre, "Growing Power of Soviet SS-20s," p. 15.
115. Zeiner Gundersen, "Soviet Power Build-up," p. 11; Hamre, "Our Defence System," p. 10.
116. S. Hamre, "Good Year for the Armed Forces," *Norwegian Defence* (1978), p. 8.
117. O. Berg, "Home Guard Can Mobilize in Hours," *Norwegian Defence Review* (1983-84), p. 2.
118. H. Nygaard, "Home Guard Needs Officers and Better Weapons," *Norwegian Defence* (1977), p. 23.

119. Ostybe, "Home Guard Well Suited," p. 31.
120. Donnelly et al., *Soviet Amphibious Operations*, p. 69.
121. E. Ingebrigtsen, "Ground Defence of the North," in *NATO's 16 Nations*, Special No. 1 (1983), p. 69.
122. Donnelly et al., *Soviet Amphibious Operations*, p. 178; R. Eios, "Considerable Improvements in Army's Fighting Units," *Norwegian Defence Review* (1981–82), pp. 16–17.
123. Ingebrigtsen, "Ground Defence," p. 69; Royal Ministry of Defence, *Main Guidelines*, p. 28; S. Hauge, "Defence Probably Better than Ever but Weaker Relative to Threat," *Norwegian Defence Review* (1983–84), p. 1.
124. R. Lawson, "Norway's Contribution to NATO of Great Importance," *Norwegian Defence Review* (1983–84), p. 5; R. Eios, "Extensive Modernization of Army will have Priority," *Norwegian Defence* (1979), p. 14.
125. Royal Ministry of Defence, *Main Guidelines*, p. 59.
126. Eios, "Considerable Improvements," pp. 16–17.
127. Royal Ministry of Defence, *Main Guidelines*, p. 60.
128. Ibid., pp. 67–68.
129. IISS, *The Military Balance 1984–85* Donnelly et al., *Soviet Amphibious Operations*, p. 169.
130. E. Ingebrigtsen, "New Army Brigade Type Response to Threat," *Norwegian Defence Review* (1983–84), p. 14.
131. Donnelly et al., *Soviet Amphibious Operations*, pp. 170–72.
132. Ibid., p. 172.
133. IISS *The Military Balance 1984–1985;* Ingebrigtsen, "New Army Brigade," p. 14; Donnelly et al., *Soviet Amphibious Operations*, pp. 170–171.
134. Ibid., p. 172.
135. Ibid., p. 173.
136. Ibid., pp. 173–174.
137. O. J. Bangstad, "The Army Improves Education, Leadership," *Norwegian Defence* (1977), p. 11.
138. IISS, *The Military Balance 1984–1985;* Donnelly et al., *Soviet Amphibious Operations*, p. 174.
139. Donnelly et al., *Soviet Amphibious Operations*, p. 174.
140. R. Eios, "Norway" in *NATO's 15 Nations*, Special No. 1 (1980), pp. 81–82.
141. Eios, "Considerable Improvements," p. 18.
142. Donnelly et al., *Soviet Amphibious Operations*, pp. 174–175.
143. G. Schepe, *Mountain Warfare in Europe* (Queens University, Ontario, 1983), p. 27.
144. Bangstad, "The Army Improves," p. 13.
145. Eios, "Extensive Modernization of Army," p. 18.
146. Hauge, "Defence Probably Better than Ever," pp. 10–12.
147. Østbye, "Home Guard Well Suited to Take on First Wave of an Attack," *Norwegian Defence Review* (1981–82), pp. 31–33.
148. Donnelly et al., *Soviet Amphibious Operations*, pp. 170–171; Ingebrigtsen, "New Army Brigade," p. 14.
149. Schepe, *Mountain Warfare*, p. 43.
150. Donnelly et al., *Soviet Amphibious Operations*, pp. 32–34.
151. Ibid., p. 30.
152. Ibid., p. 41.
153. O. J. Bangstad, "Army Completing Equipment Procurement Programme," *Norwegian Defence* (1978), p. 10.
154. Schepe, *Mountain Warfare*, p. 45.
155. Donnelly et al., *Soviet Amphibious Operations*, p. 36.
156. Schepe, *Mountain Warfare*, p. 16.

157. Ingebrigtsen, "New Army Brigade," p. 14.
158. Donnelly et al., *Soviet Amphibious Operations*, p. 35.
159. Schepe, *Montain Warfare*, pp. 46–49.
160. Donnelly et al., *Soviet Amphibious Operations*, pp. 29–30, 166.
161. Ibid., p. 165.
162. IISS, *The Military Balance 1984–1985*.
163. Donnelly et al., *Soviet Amphibious Operations*, pp. 36, 63–64.
164. F. P. U. Croker, "The Defence of Northern Norway," *RUSI Journal* (December 1984), p. 29.
165. Donnelly et al., *Soviet Amphibious Operations*, pp. 40–42.
166. Ibid., p. 180.
167. Royal Ministry of Defence, *Main Guidelines*, pp. 61–62.
168. C. O. Herlofson, "Navy Must Adapt Equipment to Future Challenges," *Norwegian Defence* (1978), p. 12.
169. Royal Ministry of Defence, *Main Guidelines*, p. 68; Herlofson, "Navy must Adapt," p. 15.
170. R. Breivik, "Navy has Versatile Power to Resist Seaborne Innvasion," *Norwegian Review* (1981–82), pp. 20–21.
171. R. Breivik, "Replacement of Navy's Vessels Difficult Task," *Norwegian Defence Review*, (1983–84), p. 17.
172. Royal Ministry of Defence, *Main Guidelines*, pp. 68–69.
173. Donnelly et al., *Soviet Amphibious Operations*, pp. 177–179.
174. IISS, *The Military Balance 1984–1985*.
175. Ibid.; Donnelly et al., *Soviet Amphibious Operations*, pp. 177–178.
176. Donnelly et al., *Soviet Amphibious Operations*, p. 180.
177. Herlofson, "Coast Artillery Gets an Important Place in Navy," *Norwegian Defence* (1979), p. 16.
178. Ostbye, "Home Guard Well suited," p. 33.
179. S. Hamre, "Good Year for the Armed Forces," *Norwegian Defence* (1978), p. 7.
180. Herlofson, "Navy must Adapt," p. 14; IISS *The Military Balance 1984–1985*.
181. Royal Ministry of Defence, *Main Guidelines*, pp. 62–63.
182. Breivik, "Replacement of Navy's Vessels," p. 16.
183. Breivik, "Navy has Versatile Power," p. 23.
184. Royal Ministry of Defence, *Main Guidelines*, pp. 62–63.
185. Breivik, "Navy has Versatile Power," p. 23.
186. Breivik, "Assuring the Security of Reinforcements to Norway," in *NATO's 15 Nations*, Special No. 2 (1982), p. 68.
187. Breivik, "Replacement of Navy's Vessels," p. 16.
188. Royal Ministry of Defence, *Main Guidelines*, p. 63.
189. Herlofson, "Coast Artillery," p. 18.
190. Breivik, "Navy has Versatile Power," p. 23.
191. Herlofson, "Coast Artillery," p. 18.
192. Royal Ministry of Defence, *Main Guidelines*, p. 62.
193. Herlofson, "Navy must Adapt," p. 14.
194. Breivik, "Navy has Versatile Power," p. 23.
195. Royal Ministry of Defence, *Main Guidelines*, p. 62.
196. Herlofson, "Navy must Adapt," p. 13.
197. Herlofson, "Coast Artillery," p. 16.
198. Herlofson, "Improved Ships' Manning High Naval Priority," *Norwegian Defence* (1977), p. 17.
199. Breivik, "Navy has Versatile Power," p. 24.
200. Breivik, "Replacement of Navy's Vessels," p. 17.
201. Herlofson, "Navy must Adapt," p. 14.

202. Herlofson, "Improved Ships' Manning," pp. 16–17.
203. Donnelly et al., Soviet Amphibious Operations, p. 180.
204. Breivik, "Navy has Versatile Power," pp. 20–21.
205. Royal Ministry of Defence, Main Guidelines, pp. 61–62.
206. Breivik, "Navy has Versatile Power," p. 21.
207. Breivik, "Replacement of Navy's Vessels," p. 16.
208. Herlofson, "Coast Artillery," pp. 17–18.
209. Breivik, "Navy has Versatile Power," p. 21.
210. Donnelly et al., Soviet Amphibious Operations, p. 89.
211. Herlofson "Navy must Adapt," p. 12.
212. Donnelly et al., Soviet Amphibious Operations, p. 77.
213. Ibid., p. 75.
214. Ibid., pp. 94–95.
215. Breivik, "Assuring Security of Reinforcements," p. 68.
216. B. M. Grimsvedt, "Norway's Coastal Defence — Fast Moving Vessels in Narrow Waters," in NATO's 16 Nations, Special No. 1 (1984), p. 78.
217. Breivik, "Assuring Security of Reinforcements," p. 68.
218. Breivik, "Navy has Versatile Power," p. 22.
219. Breivik, "Assuring Security of Reinforcements," p. 68.
220. Donnelly et al., Soviet Amphibious Operations, p. 179.
221. Bethge, "Role of the German Navy," p. 44–46.
222. M. T. Sørensen, "Conventional Air Defence of Europe," in NATO's 15 Nations, Special No. 1 (1982) p. 36.
223. Holst, "Norwegian Security," p. 219.
224. Donnelly et al., Soviet Amphibious Operations, p. 162.
225. Sørensen, "Conventional Air Defence," p. 36.
226. Royal Ministry of Defence, Main Guidelines, pp. 65, 70.
227. H. F. Zeiner Gundersen, "Soviet Power Build-up Decisive for US," Norwegian Defence (1977), p. 10.
228. IISS, The Military Balance 1984–1985.
229. Sørensen, "Conventional Air Defence," p. 62.
230. M T. Sorensen, "Many Applications for Admission to the Air Force," Norwegian Defence Review (1983–84), p. 19.
231. Sørensen, "Conventional Air Defence," p. 62.
232. IISS, The Military Balance 1984–85.
233. I. T. Narvhus, "The Royal Norwegian Air Force," in NATO's 15 Nations, Special No. 2 (1979), p. 74.
234. Breivik, "Assuring Security of Reinforcements," p. 69.
235. I. T. Narvhus, "Air Force Takes Delivery of First F-16 Early in 1980," Norwegian Defence (1979), p. 20; M. T. Sørensen, "The Norwegian Air Force is Modern, but Lacks Airfield Defence," Norwegian Defence Review (1981–82), p. 26.
236. Donnelly et al., Soviet Amphibious Operations, p. 160.
237. Ibid., p. 160.
238. Sørensen, "Many Applications for Admission," p. 19.
239. Sørensen, "The Norwegian Air Force is Modern," p. 29.
240. IISS, The Military Balance 1984–1985.
241. Royal Ministry of Defence, Main Guidelines, p. 64.
242. Ibid., p. 66; Ostbye, "Home Guard Well Suited," p. 33.
243. Sørensen, "Many Applications for Admission," p. 18.
244. Royal Ministry of Defence, Main Guidelines, p. 65.
245. Sørensen, "Many Applications for Admission," p. 19.
246. Ibid., p. 18.
247. N. W. Arveshoug, "Airforce Improving Equipment and Training," Norwegian Defence (1977), p. 21.

248. Donnelly *et al.*, *Soviet Amphibious Operations*, pp. 161–162.
249. Holst, "Norwegian Security Policy," p. 219.
250. Lawson, "Norway's Contribution to NATO," p. 4.
251. Holst, "Norwegian Security Policy," p. 211.
252. Royal Ministry of Defence, *Main Guidelines*, p. 64.
253. Holst, "Norwegian Security Policy," p. 233.

4 AUSTRIA AND SWITZERLAND: THE DEFENSE SYSTEMS OF TWO MINOR POWERS

H. R. Fuhrer*

Austria and Switzerland are two neutral states in the center of Europe. Both of them attract countless tourists; yet foreigners know surprisingly little about these countries. All too many American school leavers imagine that the Swiss earn their living by making cuckoo clocks, or by providing numbered bank accounts to international jet setters and gangsters. Austria, for many, is a fairy tale land where peasants yodel in the mountains and townsmen waltz in Old Vienna. Even the Austrians and Swiss are not well informed about their next door neighbors. Their countries adjoin; they share a common culture; they profess the same religion. Yet the Swiss and the Austrians are strangers to one another. Their history books have little to say about the respective neighbor. The public continues to hold many stereotypes: Eastern Europe begins at Arlberg; modern Austria is identical with the Habsburg monarchy whose mounted knights were defeated many centuries ago by the Swiss at Morgarten and Sempach; the Swiss are alpine shepherds who make milk, cheese, and chocolate; alternatively, the Swiss are money-grubbing bankers and tradesmen. Admittedly, these clichés of late have lost some of their former force. Nevertheless, Austrians and Swiss as yet know all too little about one another, and this essay — among other things — seeks to play a modest part in improving this state of affairs.

Fortunately, contacts have improved over the last forty years between Berne and Vienna. Diplomatic and — to a lesser extent — military exchanges of views and friendly cooperation have increased. The foreign policy of the two countries entails constant contact and discussions. For instance, a newly appointed Foreign Minister makes his first trip abroad to Vienna or Berne. Personal relations are commonly of the most amicable. Both countries abide by the same principle of armed neutrality, and now collaborate in a manner that would have appeared unthinkable even during the first ten years following World War II.

---

*Translated by L. H. Gann

Both states are situated along sensitive zones of the European power system. Switzerland lies between France and Germany, the hereditary enemies of yesteryear; Austria between the Warsaw Pact and NATO. The two countries have a similar stake in the principle of neutrality; and yet have developed different concepts to assure its maintenance. The Swiss traditionally have traded with the world at large; yet they unreservedly regard themselves as Westerners; Austria, by contrast, has had to learn how to adopt a Western viewpoint. Relations with the US have never been so close as they are now. Yet Austrian foreign policy is based on the principle of equidistance between East and West; hence "Ostpolitik" remains tremendously important to Austria. Whereas the Swiss commonly have little comprehension of the Eastern viewpoint, the Austrians are better informed about the East than any other Western Europeans, having learned from their own traditions and history how to understand the mind and actions of the Eastern European nations. The Austrians worry much less than the Swiss about the threat from the Warsaw Pact countries. To the Austrians, Eastern Europe has always formed part of their living space. The Swiss, by contrast, are aware of, and apt to criticize the fact that, Austria's defense effort is smaller than Switzerland's.[1]

The two countries also differ in lesser matters. In Austria, the Habsburg heritage still echoes in the realm of diplomacy and in public life, as the Austrians have stuck to the imperial protocol and a love of splendid titles; Swiss diplomacy, and much of the Swiss public, by contrast retain their accustomed love of economy and simplicity. Similarly, party affiliation plays a very different role in Austria and Switzerland. In Austria, official appointments require the sanction of political parties. In Switzerland, cantonal and religious affiliation play a much greater part. These differences are reflected also in defense policies.

Nevertheless, Switzerland and Austria share common problems. From the geostrategic standpoint alone, it is obvious that Austria, since 1955, has served as an outer defensive bastion of great importance, especially as regards air defense. Even if Austria were to be only partially occupied by potentially hostile forces (as was the case between 1945 and 1955), the threat to the Swiss Confederation would dramatically increase. This essay cannot attempt to elucidate in full all the security problems faced by the two countries under consideration; the present analysis must of necessity bear a controversial, at times a subjective, character. It will, however, attempt to provide a general introduction to the most salient issues bearing on a problem not widely discussed in Anglophone literature.

The Neutrality Policy of Two Minor European Powers

Introduction

When coalitions are hard to form, when the protection offered by a coalition appears inadequate or overly costly, neutrality appears as a convenient alternative to the search for security supplied by an alliance.[2]

Daniel Frei, Professor of Political Science at the University of Zürich, thus outlines the general problem under discussion. The call for neutrality as an alternative peace policy has been heard wistfully in the Federal German Republic, the Netherlands, Norway, and Denmark; but neutralism has not affected the defense policies of these countries. In current discussions, Switzerland and Sweden are often mentioned as examples of countries that survived the conflagration of World War II with little damage to themselves. The fate of Switzerland and Sweden strikingly contrasted with the experiences in World War II of Holland, Belgium, Denmark, and Norway, all of which failed to find security through neutrality. Neutrality, the point bears repeating, is not in and of itself identical with security. Neutrality may be an alternative to membership of an alliance, but a neutral power must still be willing to defend its independence. Neutrality does not mean defense on the cheap, provided the neutral power is truly willing to defend its freedom and its independence. Those who ignore this elementary truth are apt to think in a selfish or an unrealistic fashion, and ignore today's realities of power.

What does it mean to be "neutral"? According to the Hague Convention of 1907, neutrality entails non-participation in the wars of other powers.[3] Neutral states enjoy certain privileges and in turn take on specific obligations.[4] A neutral power may not provide assistance to a belligerent by furnishing troops or military intelligence, and must prevent military action within its territory or airspace. It must treat all belligerents equally, and must also abide by specific obligations in peacetime. A neutral power may not commit aggressive acts, conclude alliances, or provide military bases to other powers. In case of necessity, however, it must maintain its military defense in order to be able to defend its neutral status. Each neutral state must maintain its neutral status in its own way, and policies suitable for one neutral power may not suit another. Neutrality is not an article for export — a maxim particularly applicable to Austria and Switzerland. A neutral state also enjoys specific privileges, for example, the right to territorial integrity and the right to maintain pacific relations with all belligerents.[5]

International law, by contrast, does not require of the neutral power neutrality in economic relations or neutrality of opinion. The neutral power is entitled to make known its views regarding the rights or wrongs of an ongoing conflict, or to abstain from doing so. This applies both to the government of a neutral state and to its citizens. If a neutral government accepts certain restrictions in this respect, or imposes restrictions on its media, it does so of its own sovereign volition.

A neutral power thus faces complex problems, some of which can be illustrated by the historical experiences of Switzerland and Austria. Switzerland has been a *de facto* neutral power since 1815, but it was only in 1915 that Swiss neutrality obtained *de jure* recognition as a neutral power.[6] Swiss neutrality has resulted from centuries of trial and error. The Swiss Confederation learned from long experience that intervention in foreign conflicts would have mortally threatened its internal stability, given Switzerland's heterogeneous composition (with four separate languages and cultures, full autonomy for the cantons, etc.). Articles 453 of the Versailles Treaty, 1919, once more confirmed Swiss neutality. On 14 May 1938 Switzerland was freed also from the obligation to participate in economic sanctions, and thereby returned to what is known as "integral neutrality," a status it has maintained ever since.[7]

Swiss neutrality has been affected radically by the conclusion of the Austrian State Treaty (Östereichische Staatsvertrag) of 15 May 1955. The treaty profoundly changed Switzerland's strategic position by creating an 800 km long wedge between NATO's northern and southern segments, and also a partial territorial barrier between NATO and the Warsaw Pact. In exchange for creating a neutral thorn in NATO's flesh, the USSR agreed to relinquish its hold on Austria. In the Moscow memorandum of 15 April 1955, the Austrian delegates assured the USSR that a declaration would accompany the State Treaty whereby Austria would perpetually maintain its neutrality "in the manner followed by Switzerland." The State Treaty itself made no mention of neutrality, but the Austrian Federal Law (Bundesverfassungsgesetz) of 26 October 1955 stated that Austria would voluntarily abide by perpetual neutrality, and that Austria would defend its neutrality by all means at its command.[8] This law obtained formal recognition or implicit consent on the part of all states maintaining diplomatic relations with Austria; no power, however, has proffered a guarantee.[9]

The Austrian and Swiss experience has thus considerably diverged. Switzerland has been neutral for over 170 years; Swiss neutrality is firmly rooted in Swiss national consciousness, and has even become a national myth. Austrian neutrality has lasted for only 40 years; Austrian neutrality came suddenly. After a period of constant change, from monarchy to the First Republic, and then to the occupational regime, Austrian neutrality formed part of a third attempt in the twentieth century at finding a new national identity. Whereas Swiss neutrality has been guaranteed by the great powers, Austrian neutrality lacks such international guarantees. Switzerland, as a sovereign power, enjoys the right to conclude foreign alliances (embodied in Article 8 of the Federal Constitution), but Austria is constitutionally prevented from concluding a military alliance. While Swiss neutrality is internationally taken for granted, Austria feels forever obliged to reiterate the reasons for its neutrality. Switzerland takes pride in a strong conventional defense of its territory; Austria spends much less on military forces designed to assure that total defense of its territory. (Estimate defense expenditure in 1983 amounted to US$2,055 billion for Switzerland, as against only $US826,365 million for Austria.) Whereas Switzerland has refrained from joining the United Nations (UN), Austria became a member in 1955, and provided troops to the UN for peacekeeping missions.

Austria and Switzerland, on the other hand, share many common features in the pursuit of neutrality. Both enjoy an international status of neutrality; occupy a strategically important position; and are committed to armed neutrality. Both countries try to avoid excessive economic dependency while favoring attempts at integration. They provide international services in representing the interests of individuals and of other states; and both provide international aid within the framework of international organizations. International contacts and pacific negotiations are assisted by both countries by their providing facilities to the UN in Geneva and Vienna respectively. A liberal policy in granting political asylum is pursued by the two countries, and they collaborate, or work separately, in conferences designed to assure peace. The Austrian model of defense policy resembles the Swiss version in that they must seek to avoid a "preventive occupation" of their respective territory on the part of either one or the other of the two contending military alliances. The neutral powers can carry out this assignment by threatening the flank of the potential opponent's main line of assault, and especially by safeguarding their own airspace to such effect that a detour through neutral territory becomes too costly, and that a potential aggressor will thereby be deterred from violating the neutral power's territorial integrity.

Previous Experience with the Concept of Armed Neutrality

The preventive success attained by the Swiss army in World War II is well known. Recent research has not diminished this achievement. My own book, *Espionage against Switzerland: the German Secret Service and Switzerland in World War II*,[10] shows that Switzerland managed to avoid an enemy occupation through a favorable constellation of many factors. The German leadership long believed the informants of the SS SD (the SS Security Service) who believed that Switzerland would ultimately be persuaded to join the Greater German economic sphere by dint of economic and military threats. The Swiss internal power of resistance against the Nazi temptations, however, turned out to be greater than expected. Hitler's strategic aims moreover did not center on Switzerland. Geography and Swiss defensive capability combined, in 1940, to dissuade the Germans from outflanking the Maginot line by way of Switzerland; the Germans knew that they would have an easier task by invading the Netherlands, Belgium, and Luxembourg. Later on, Hitler first considered an invasion of Great Britain; in 1941 he decided to attack the USSR. Once Germany's military fortunes began to wane, and the Allies had occupied France, the Germans relied for the protection of their Alpine flank on Switzerland's willingness to defend its territory against any aggressor whatsoever. In any case, the Germans no longer had sufficient troops to think of occupying Switzerland. The Germans left Switzerland alone because they had a high opinion of the Swiss army and the Swiss national will to resist. They also understood the geographical obstacles involved in a prospective attack on Switzerland, the likelihood that war would destroy the Swiss communications system, and the need to preserve Switzerland as a center for espionage and as a source of hard currency. Had the Germans won the war, they could in any case have obtained control over Switzerland, "the little hedgehog". In addition, Switzerland had a number of friends in the German Abwehr (the counter-intelligence service of the armed forces) and in the ranks of the German Resistance, friends whose efforts should not be underestimated.

Switzerland's defensive preparations before World War II had been strikingly superior to those of other neutral countries such as Norway and Denmark. Having mobilized its armed forces on 1 September 1939, Switzerland deployed an army of 400,000 men, organized in nine divisions, six brigades, and a substantial number of frontier defense formations. During the six years preceding World War II, Switzerland had spent something like 830 million francs (15 billion in present currency).[11] Norway and Denmark had neglected their defensive preparations and could mobilize no more than 30,000 and 13,000 men respectively. They were also psychologically ill prepared for war. Operation Weserübung, the German occupation of Denmark and Norway in World War II, provided a fatal example.[12] Though individual units fought bravely, Denmark and Norway had neglected their defensive preparations to such an extent that their strategy of deterrence had turned into a "strategy of invitation." The Swiss record in this respect was not of course beyond criticism. In 1939, Switzerland resolved to defend its airspace against foreign overflights.[13] But the Swiss air force at the time possessed no more than 86 combat planes. During the entire war, Switzerland experienced 6,501 violations of its airspace, on average three a day. The Swiss succeeded in shooting down only 16 foreign planes and in forcing 186 to make forced landings.[14] Nevertheless, Swiss resolution did succeed overall in protecting its neutrality.

After World War II, Switzerland no longer faced an immediate threat. The task of defending its neutrality, wedged between two hostile powers, passed to Austria; in this sense the history of Austria's armed neutrality constitutes the continuation of Switzerland's. It was only in 1955 that Austria regained its sovereignty after ten years' occupation. In 1956, only a year after the conclusion of the Austrian State Treaty, the Hungarian rising shook the stability of the young Republic when 160,000 refugees, including 7,000 servicemen, sought asylum in Austria.[15] The Austrian government had at its disposal no more than ten battalions, including one mechanized battalion. Only 5,000 men and 50 armored vehicles could be deployed at the frontier to guard Austria's neutrality. There was no Austrian air force. The Austrian effort was no more than a gesture, but at least they showed their goodwill in attempting to take seriously the provisions of the Moscow memorandum. Austrian rearmament thereafter proceeded, but slowly. The defense effort received an impetus in 1958 during the Lebanon crisis when the US sent an entire division by air across Austria to the Middle East; the Austrians had no means of preventing this violation of their neutrality. It is doubtful whether the resultant gain in a speedy troop deployment justified the harm done to the principle of Austrian neutrality by the Western superpower.

Austria's willingness to defend its neutrality was again tested in August 1968 during the Czech crisis. Austria's political and military leaders had correctly interpreted the events leading up to the crisis; Austria did not mobilize its armed forces, and relied on those formations that were at the military leadership's immediate disposal. Subsequent events justified this caution. Nevertheless, the preparations made were quite inadequate to deal with crises of such a kind, especially as regards the defense of Austria's airspace. This time Austria had to cope with 140,000 refugees. All the same, it would have been able to mobilize a total of 120,000 men organized in ten brigades, and a substantial number of territorial frontier defense (Grenzschutz) and reserve (Landwehr) formations. According to General Emil Spannocchi, Austria would have been capable of a linear conventional defense by this time. Armaments had improved and the first fortifications designed to safeguard strategic frontier positions had been made ready.[16] The army thereafter confined its preparations to a conventional defense in depth. In addition, Austria continues to give asylum to large numbers of refugees from the East, and spends vast sums for that purpose. Following the last war between Israel and Syria, Austria had soldiers stationed on the Golan Heights and over 30,000 Austrian conscripts have performed peacekeeping services for the UN. Both Israel and Syria recognize and respect the value of these soldiers.

Service under the UN helps to provide Austrians with a sense of identity, as Austrian UN soldiers, wedged between two hostile powers, seem to play a role similar to Austria, caught between two hostile alliances. Unfortunately, Austria's ability to defend its neutrality still leaves much to be desired — especially as regards the defense of Austria's airspace. (The USSR's decision in 1983 to shoot down an unarmed South Korean airliner over Soviet territory highlighted this latter problem.) In 1985 the Austrian air force numbered no more than 32 Saab and 105 combat planes; Austria was therefore in no condition effectively to defend its airspace. The Swiss air force is considerably stronger, though the Swiss also have their problems. Switzerland at any rate is resolved to defend its airspace as an integral part of its general defense as an independent and neutral country. The Swiss believe that the World War II experience clearly proved that states unable or unwilling to do so simply invite aggression.[17]

Elements of Security Policy

Effective defense entails more than merely the maintenance of an army; defense requires a wider strategic concept, one that must adjust to ever-changing realities. The Swiss concept of total defense of the homeland found its most recent formulation in 1973.[18] In 1975 the

Austrian Parliament embodied the Austrian concept of comprehensive territorial defense (*Umfassende Landesverteidigung*) in the Austrian constitution; ten years later Austria had finalized its defense plan.[19] Both countries thereby have chosen a strategy that required neither the militarization of policy nor of public life as a whole,[20] but one that seeks to adjust locally available means to such threats that arise in future.[21] Figure 4.1 attempts to illustrate the operation of the Swiss concept of comprehensive territorial defense in a schematic form.

Figure 4.1: The Swiss Territorial Defense Concept

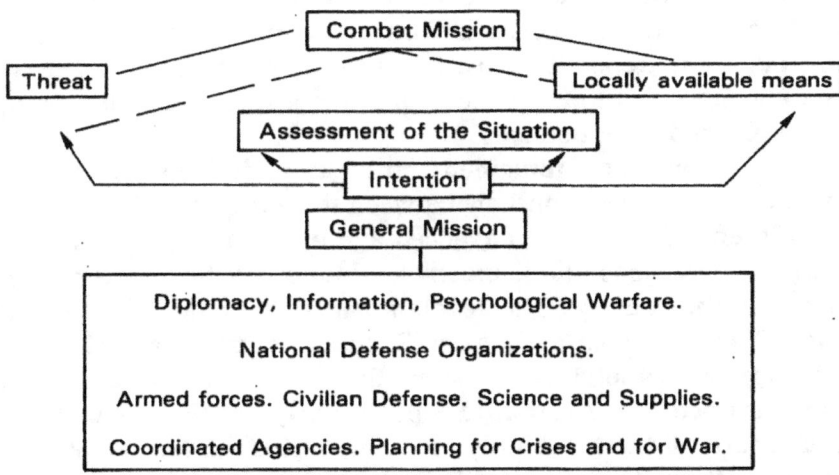

To sum up, both Switzerland and Austria are resolved to defend their independence and their spiritual and cultural values. Their armed forces are not the only means available for this purpose, but they form the only instrument available for the purpose of repelling a military invasion. Existing international law indeed prescribes such defense, and excludes all forms of total disarmament, of passive defense, or of social defense (entailing only resistance against an enemy occupation). The subsequent sections seek to show how far Austria and Switzerland have respectively succeeded in this purpose.

Austria's Defense Policy

The Background

In 1945, the Allies liberated Austria from Nazi rule. For the next ten years Austria remained an occupied country, a country nevertheless influenced profoundly by its previous history. The imperial tradition, entailing the subject's respect for the sovereign, has by no means entirely died out. The bureaucracy has remained a powerful force; so have the parties with their centralized power structure. But Austria has also experienced many changes.[22] In 1938 a great majority of Austrians had welcomed the Germans; thereafter, however, Nazi attempts to destroy Austria's national consciousness led to a revival of long standing conflicts between Austrians and Prussians, and also to some attempts at resistance. After the liberation in 1945, Austrian policy-makers — many of them members of the underground — endeavored to wipe out those organizations and political notions derived both from the Nazis and from the corporate state established during the First Republic. Austria's new rulers resolved to build a democratic state and to effect economic reconstructions with the help of allied aid and investments.

Austria, however, remained politically divided. The Social Democrats experienced conflicts between the émigrés of 1934 vintage, many of them of somewhat advanced age by the time of their return, and the younger generation, mostly revolutionary Socialists who had remained in the country. The revolutionary forces gained control and characteristically styled their party Socialist Party of Austria (SPÖ). The bourgeois Catholic camp, strengthened by the accession of the liberals, formed the Austrian People's Party (ÖVP). (The liberals formed a party of their own only in 1956.) The Communists rebuilt the Communist Party of Austria (KPÖ), but failed to make any political headway. The Nazis were excluded from political life. The initial elections, sanctioned by the Allies in 1945, gave 85 seats to the ÖVP, 76 to the SPÖ, and 4 to the KPÖ. Nevertheless, the occupation era witnessed a striking growth in state enterprise. (Between 1946 and 1947 basic industries and heavy industries, energy supplies, banks, and all federal enterprises were placed directly under the state.) The new *Gemeinwirtschaft* that emphasized the public sector left a powerful role for the parties in directing the economy. In 1955 Austria regained its sovereignty, asserted its international neutrality, and joined the UN. Initially, the new Republic emphasized non-involvement in international questions. From the 1960s, Austria increasingly sought links with other European organizations, at the same time continuing to stress its neutrality.

Austrian domestic politics came to rest on an electoral system that had perfected proportional representation and that exalted the power of political parties — so much so that a candidate's party affiliation, either as "red" (Social Democrat) or as "black" (Austrian People's Party) plays a major role for promotion in important posts in the military, in public enterprises, and in education. At the same time the Austrian economy developed in a striking fashion — so much so that Austrians could justly speak of their own "Austrian economic miracle." In 1950, the Swiss average per capita income was three times as large as the Austrian average per capita income. By 1970, the Swiss average per capita income only exceeded its Austrian equivalent by two-thirds. Austria, in making this progress, owed a good deal to US aid. Austria moreover incurred heavy budgetary deficits — much more so than Switzerland, a country firmly wedded to private enterprise. Nevertheless, Austria's gross national product has shown a striking overall increase since the end of World War II.

The development of Austria's defensive potential by no means matched the growth of its economy. From 1955 onward, the Austrians began slowly to rebuild their military; in doing so they built alike on the traditions of the former Bundesheer (the army of the First Republic), and they also used those military cadres formerly employed in the Wehrmacht. They studied the Swiss example of armed neutrality without, however, copying it. The Austrians fixed the conscript's length of service in a manner that constituted a typically Austrian compromise (nine months — as against the twelve months demanded by the ÖVP and six months requested by the SPÖ).

From the start, the Austrians faced grave obstacles. They failed to appreciate the expense involved in rearmament and, from the beginning, spent too little on the military. The rearmament program aroused doubts as to its need and efficacy. Austria, moreover, had to contend with serious restrictions imposed by Articles 13 and 14 of the Austrian State Treaty. These stipulations prohibited the ownership, manufacture, or even the testing of specialised offensive arms. These included nuclear arms, weapons of mass destruction, chemical and biological weapons, self-guided or guided missiles, and artillery pieces with a radius exceeding 30 kilometers. Whereas other neutral states, such as Finland, have succeeded in getting such agreements altered in their favor, Austria remains subject to these conditions to this day. But without guided surface-to-air missiles, the armed forces cannot adequately defend their airspace; the army is at a similar disadvantage as regards defense against armored fighting vehicles. Surprisingly enough, however, the Austrians have as yet failed to do everything in their power to get rid of restrictions that impair Austria's duty to maintain a state of armed neutrality, while stressing the defensive character of their military preparations. The Austrians might well point to the examples of Finland, Bulgaria, and Yugoslavia, all of which have succeeded in revising erstwhile restrictions placed on their respective defensive capabilities. Courteous enquires in Moscow to this effect have, however, as yet merely elicited a Soviet "Nyet." It would be extremely dangerous for Austria in future to continue the present policy of military inadequacy, using Moscow's negative attitude as an excuse.

Comprehensive Territorial Defense (Umfassende Landesverteidigung)

The concept of comprehensive territorial defense (CTL) found its first embodiment in an Austrian White Book issued in 1971.[23] By this time serious deficiencies had become apparent in the Austrian military; a new defense law, promulgated in 1971, to some extent imitated the Swiss militia model by imposing on the conscripts a six-month service period, supplemented by 60 days devoted to brief military manoeuvres. In 1973 the task of elaborating a new defense doctrine was transferred from the Ministry of Defense and the Ministry of the Interior to the Federal Chancellor's Office. In 1975 the concept of Comprehensive Territorial Defense found embodiment in the Federal Defense Law (Bundesverteidigungsgesetz). This doctrine substantially resembled the Swiss model and, after lengthy study, was finalized in the Territorial Defense Plan (*Landesverteidigungsplan*) of 1985.

The Plan posits three possible major emergencies. In the event of an international crisis, Austria will make defensive preparations, using active formations, frontier defense forces, and territorial security forces from violating Austrian neutrality. Should any of Austria's neighbors become involved in war, Austria will employ active formulations and mobilize reserves to prevent foreign forces from violating Austrian neutrality. Should foreign forces actually launch an attack on Austria, Austria will defend its frontiers, mobilize all its forces as soon as possible, and attempt to recapture any territory that may have been lost.

The new strategy aims at total defense. This includes what is known as "spiritual defense," preparations designed to convince both the Austrian and foreign nations that Austria is determined at all costs to defend its territorial integrity, unity, sovereignty, freedom, and democratic order. The Austrian Defense Plan therefore envisages also civil and economic defense, including preparations designed to assure the management of economic crises by means of planning production, assuring food supplies, raw materials, communications, employment, the care of refugees, and so forth. Figure 4.2 represents the new strategy in graphic form, in the shape of parallel pillars.

Figure 4.2: The Austrian Strategic Defense Concept

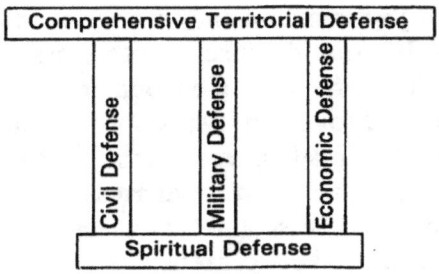

Figure 4.3: Potential Invasion Routes into Western Europe.

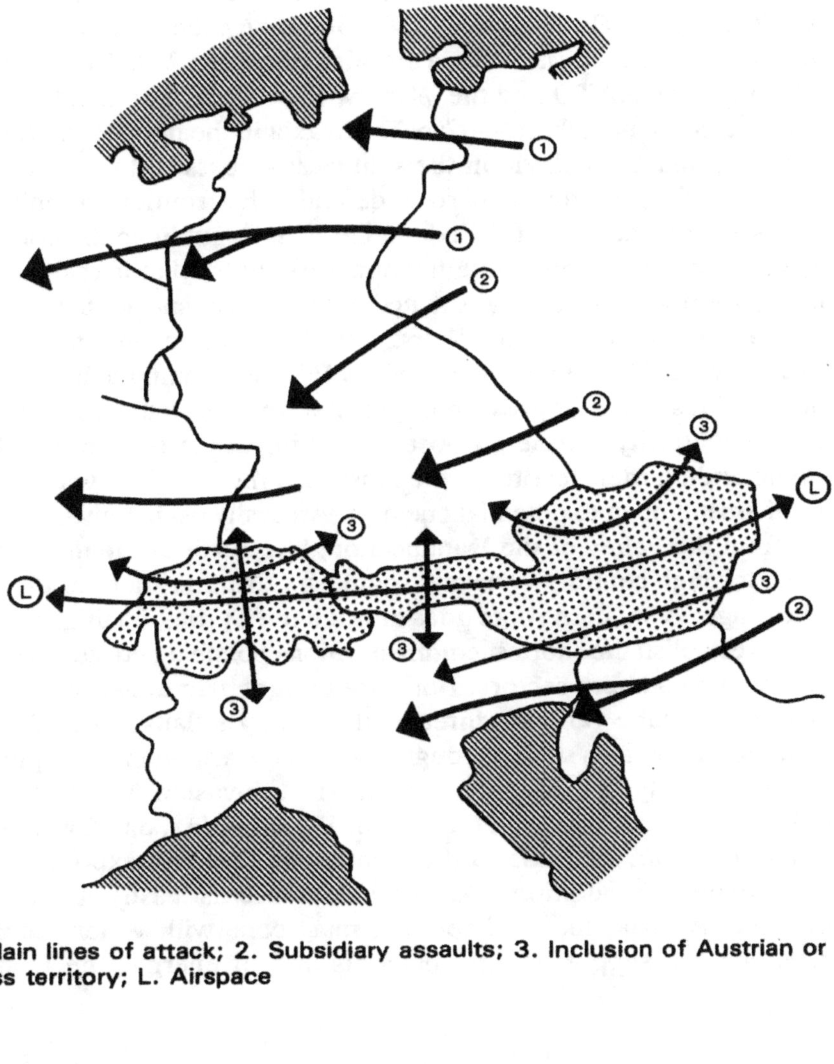

1. Main lines of attack; 2. Subsidiary assaults; 3. Inclusion of Austrian or Swiss territory; L. Airspace

The concept can work only if the Austrian nation maintains the will to defend its independence. Planners must therefore succeed in convincing the public through the media and through political education in the schools and public life that defense is both workable and worthwhile. Ongoing efforts to this effect have encountered opposition on the part of the so-called Peace Movement whose proponents do not accept that peace is best served by an adequate defense, and who misrepresent the Austrian defense plan as a design for aggression. Austria's willingness to defend itself is, however, essential for its security, and forms an assignment worthy of Austria's best citizens.

Austria's Strategic and Defense Doctrine

Austria is a democratic state with a federal constitution comprising nine states (*Bundesländer*). Something like 7.5 million people live in a country embracing 83,850 sq.km. with a frontier of nearly 2,000 km. Austria lies between the NATO and the Warsaw Pact blocs. The frontier along Austria's eastern neighbors — Czechoslovakia in the northeast, Hungary in the east, and Yugoslavia in the southeast — passes through hilly or flat terrain of a kind that is hard to defend. The frontier adjoining the two western neighbors — the Federal German Republic in the north and Italy in the south — goes through mountain country that is easily defensible. Strategically, Austria is situated in the central and southern region that separates NATO from the Warsaw Pact. It does not adjoin the northern sector where NATO and the Warsaw Pact both maintain heavy troop concentrations.[24] An aggressor might therefore be tempted to violate Austrian neutrality for the purpose of striking at the opponent's flank.

In defending their territory, the Austrians must reckon with several lines of assault open to potential enemies. An easily usable invasion route leads from the valley of the Danube along the north of the main alpine ranges, through central Styria and southern Carinthia south of the main alpine range. A western route goes through the Tyrole, enabling NATO forces to establish the shortest communications possible between NATO's northern and southern sectors. Both sides might plan to use the western part of the Danube valley to threaten the enemy's flanks. The Warsaw Pact forces might also strike through Styria and Carinthia for the purpose of entering Italy by way of the classical invasion routes via the Talgliamento, the Piave, and the Adige. Vienna, Linz, and Graz, major cities all of them, lie close to the frontier and thereby expose Austria to blackmail. In addition, Austria's airspace is easily threatened. Moreover, Austria, like Switzerland, must cope with wider problems concerning the supply of raw materials and of energy, the relations

Figure 4.4: Potential Invasion Routes into Austria and Switzerland.

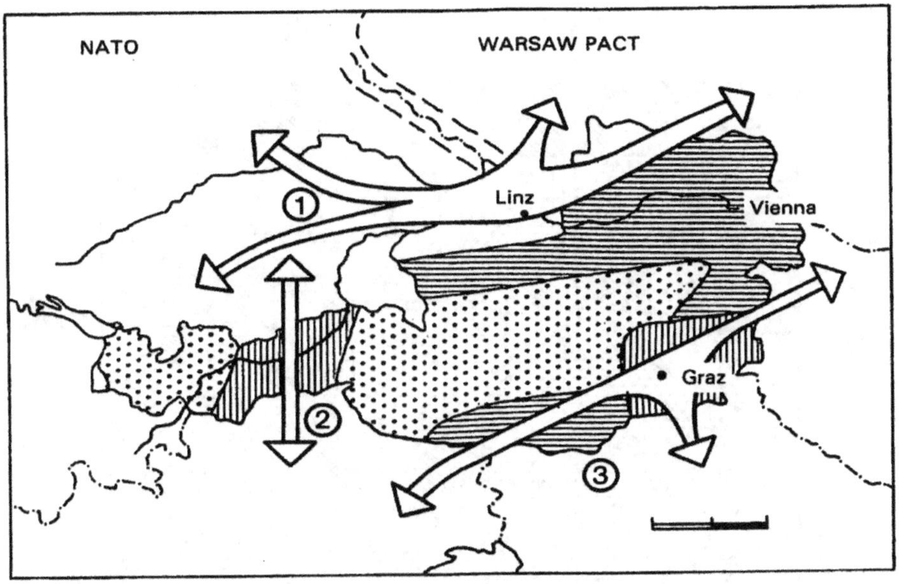

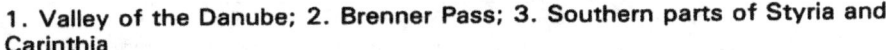

1. Valley of the Danube; 2. Brenner Pass; 3. Southern parts of Styria and Carinthia

▦ Main operational theaters for aggression

▤ Subsidiary operational theaters

▨ Areas without value for an aggressor

Sources: Stutz, *Raumverteidigung;* Freistetter, "Die strategische Lage Oesterreichs."

between the industrialized and the developing world, as well as threats that might derive from areas peripheral to Europe, including the Middle East.

Principles of Combat in Defensive Operations

Austria's principles of total territorial defense (*Raumverteidigung*) find no parallels in the NATO countries and therefore deserve some extended comment. The concept primarily derives from the studies of General Emil Spannocchi (retired since 1981).[25] Austrian planners have divided the entire country into "key zones" (*Schlüsselzonen*), and defense regions (*Raumsicherungszonen*). The defense of the key zones is designed to impede the enemy's advance and weaken his forces. The defense rests on key areas and defensive positions. In order to delay and destroy the enemy, the defenders will launch mechanized counter-

110 *Austria and Switzerland*

Figure 4.5: Principles of Territorial Defense

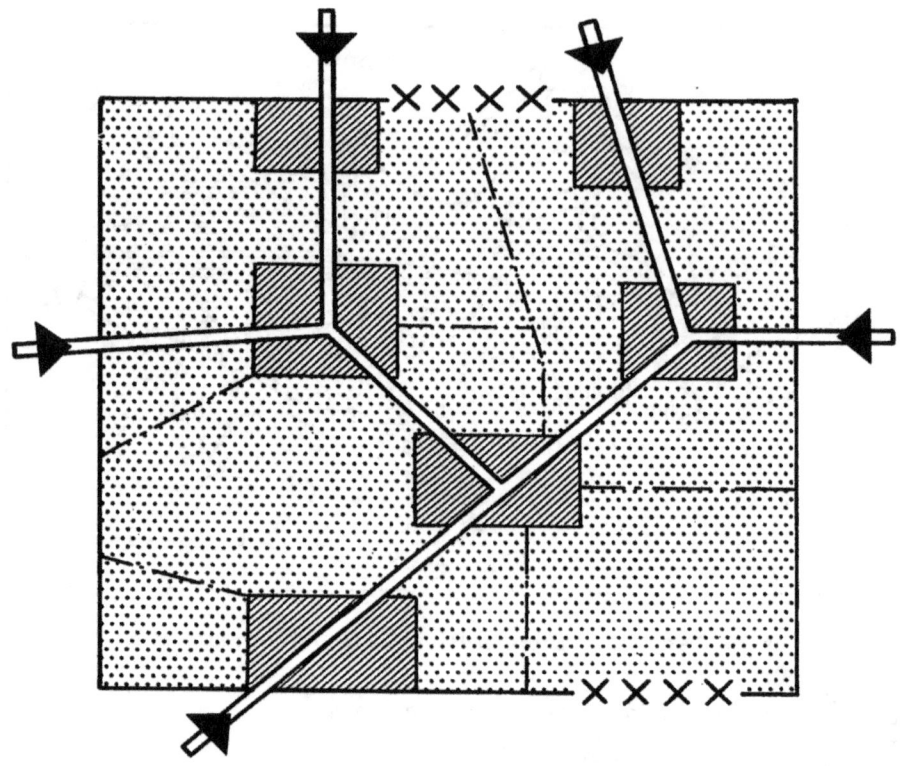

 Key zones: "cover important lines of operations as a cork closes a bottle"

 Regional defense zones: "mobile actions, based on the principles of guerilla warfare"

⇨ Main operational lines serving the aggressor

attacks, reinforced, where needed, by mobile light infantry (*Jagdkampfkräfte*). The key zones are designed to impede the enemy assaults, and canalize them in such a manner as ultimately to bring them to a halt. Between the "key zones" lie the "defense regions," where combat is designed further to delay and weaken the enemy. Along the frontier zones operations are carried out by frontier defense formations; in the remainder of Austria's territory operations are conducted by light infantry battalions that use delaying tactics, ambushes, and sudden assaults. In addition, this defensive concept aims at safeguarding Austria against airborne attacks and fifth column activities. The Austrians are determined to avoid major battles, and to seek success through minor operations. The Austrian defense concept largely excludes the possibility of nuclear conflict.

From 1975 onward, the Austrian armed forces have practiced the total territorial defence concept in successive maneuvers. The so-called "Spannochi doctrine," however, has been widely misunderstood. In Austria, the concept was often discredited as a Socialist solution designed to assure defense on the cheap. Critics abroad misinterpreted the concept as a form of partisan warfare or even as a "strategy of invitation." The major territorial defense maneuvers of 1979 and 1982 clearly indicated, however, that the territorial defense concept does not simply entail guerrilla warfare, but contains several operational components. Territorial defense is a form of warfare designed for the weaker contenders; it accepts the handicap involved in turning Austria into a theater of war, and in refraining from carrying war into the enemy country. The greatest weakness inherent in the concept lies in the inadequacy of Austria's air force; this is in no position to safeguard the mobilization of the armed forces or to protect the movement of mechanized forces or to assist in the defense of protected zones. As long as Austria accepts the present restrictions on its armaments, the Austrian air force cannot carry out its allotted mission.

The Organization and Armaments of the Austrian Armed Forces

Austrian defense is the responsibility of the Federal Ministry for Defense. Subordinate to the ministry are associated agencies and army command. The army command in turn controls the field army, the territorial defense formations, and the military academies. The army relies for recruitment mainly on conscription. Draftees serve for a period of six months, and in addition must spend a total of 60 days for the purpose of military exercises. The cadres must serve for additional periods of 30 to 90 days. Each year 40,000 conscripts are called to the colors. In addition, there are 70,000 to 80,000 soldiers who must fulfill their obligation to attend military exercises.

Austria does not simply rely on militia, but on a mixed system. The Bereitschaftstruppen (the Standing Alert Force) comprises one mechanized division, three light infantry battalions, and various corps troops. This force can move into action within 20 hours. The remaining land and air forces are ready for action only after mobilization. The militia formations embrace the Landwehr (manned by conscripts supported by permanent cadres) and local defense formations. Territorial defense is organized on a regional basis with one military commander for each of the nine *Bundesländer*. The military commanders control the alpine units (which form part of the Permanent Alert Force in peacetime), and the Landwehrstammregimenter (training units). The military commanders take charge of the mobile Landwehr units and the regional defense formations. The mobile Landwehr is organized into light infantry brigades and mechanized brigades. Each mechanized brigade contains 51 medium sized tanks. The Austrian forces include more than 200 SK-105 Kürassier tanks — destroyers locally produced by Steyr-Daimler-Puch. The mechanized artillery battalions contain 38,155 armored howitzers, make M-109. The staff and mechanized infantry battalions are equipped with Saurer armored personnel carriers. In addition, US M-60 tanks are in service. Austrian defense preparations against enemy armored assaults at any rate seem "workable."[26] Austria moreover is engaged in further strengthening its defense. By 1986, it hopes to have completed the intermediate stage of the Territorial Defense Plan. The army will by then consist of: the Permanent Alert Force, comprising one mechanized infantry division (15,000 men); 8 light infantry brigades of the mobile Landwehr with 45,000 men; and 33 local defense formations of the militia with 75,000 men; as well as specialist units, supply units, guard units (10,000 men), and 28,000 reservists. When the plan is complete, the Austrian army will be able to mobilize a total of 300,000 men.

The air force and the anti-aircraft defenses, by contrast, are in worse shape. The Austrian air force forms part of the army. It is divided into military aviation (three air regiments) and three air defense battalions. Existing restrictions on Austrian armaments have serious effects on air defense. Effective anti-aircraft formations ought to contain both guns and guided rockets; aircraft should be equipped with both ordinary weapons carried on board and rockets. The mechanized infantry brigades contain Bofors M-42 air defense armored vehicles with 40 mm guns. The remaining units are equipped with M-58 20 mm Oerlikon guns. The air defense battalions possess M-65 35 mm Oerlikon guns, and also "Sky Guard" or Superfledermaus radar equipment. The air force is weak. It is equipped with aging Saab 105-OE fighter-bombers, supplemented by 24 new Draken planes. In addition, the Austrian forces are able to deploy numerous helicopters which are, however, difficult to employ effectively without guided missile support. On the other hand, Austria has what is perhaps the most modern of all early warning systems; the Goldhaube radar system. At the very least, Austria's military hardware needs to be supplemented by the purchase of new planes and air defense weapons.

Swiss Defense Policy

During World War II Switzerland experienced a far-reaching degree of political isolation. Thereafter, the country increasingly adopted an outward-looking policy, one that attempted to link neutrality with global cooperation (expressed in the formula "solidarité, neutralité, universalité").[27] The Federal Council (Bundesrat) did not succeed in its original design of joining the UN; but Switzerland thereafter took an increasing share in the specialized work of the UN regarding economic, cultural, technical, and humanitarian issues.[28] The Swiss participated in numerous peacekeeping missions.[29] The possibility of joining the UN continued to remain under discussion, even though the Swiss electorate would probably not at present approve such a move.[30] Switzerland joined a variety of international organizations, for example the European Organization for Economic Cooperation and, later, the European Free Trade Association (EFTA). It also established an association with the European Community, resumed diplomatic relations with the USSR, and later took an increasing share in economic development and aid for the Third World.

This outward looking policy during the 1950s and 1960s went with economic prosperity, economic growth, the expansion of the welfare state, and the immigration of foreign workers, and was accompanied by a general mood of optimism. From the end of the 1960s, however, the national consensus came under serious attack for the first time, both from left-wing critics who called for fundamental social changes, and from right-wingers who feared that Switzerland stood in peril of losing its national identity, At the same time Switzerland experienced a serious economic recession. From the beginning of the 1980s the Swiss economy began to recover; but the optimism of former days had waned, as Switzerland now confronted a variety of new problems — alienation among many of its young, including drug use and growing hostility toward military service. In addition, Switzerland had to deal with many other predicaments familiar to the Western world — financial problems, ecological questions, unemployment, and such like. Nevertheless, Switzerland remained one of the world's most stable and prosperous countries, committed to a policy of armed neutrality and to a military system woven into the very fabric of national life.

General Aspects

The Swiss are probably the least militaristic and most military people in the world. The mere ownership of an automatic firearm forms an indictable offense in most parts of the globe; in Switzerland, on the other hand, there is nothing remarkable in seeing an ordinary citizen cycling along the road with his submachine gun slung across his back. The terms "citizen" and "soldier" are almost synonymous; yet Switzerland is a most pacific country.

Switzerland's security policy rests on the concept of *Gesamtverteidigung* (total defense), elaborated in its most recent form in 1973. *Gesamtverteidigung* embraces not merely the army, but the nation as a whole. The Swiss concept considers the following emergencies arranged in an ascending scale of gravity. Peace may be threatened by large-scale attempts at terrorism, by threats to essential supplies (oil, for instance). Such threats will be countered by diplomatic means and other suitable counter-measures. The next scenario entails war involving neighboring states and possible violations of the Swiss frontier. Switzerland, in such an event, would mobilize its armed forces as a means of deterring invasion. If an enemy should invade Switzerland, the Swiss will defend their security, their nation, and their country. In the event of nuclear attack, or of major natural catastrophes, or of catastrophes involving nuclear power plants, the Swiss will endeavor to help the civil population in as efficient a manner as possible. The most desperate scenario involves enemy occupation of large parts of the country. Even in such an eventuality, the Swiss will continue fighting with their remaining forces in such parts of the country where conditions are favorable. Such a protracted struggle is seen as essential both as a means of national survival, and as an instrument for maintaining the legitimacy of the state; long-lasting resistance moreover may well achieve ultimate success. These scenarios are not all mutually exclusive, but all of them involve Swiss resistance to possible blackmail.

The defense of Switzerland has many aspects: an effective foreign policy;[31] protection of the state against internal subversion; civil defense (centering on the local communes, with shelter space now available for 85 percent of the Swiss population); the provision of food and raw materials (essential in a country that imports 100 percent of its raw materials, 45 percent of its food, and 75 percent of its energy); and the maintenance of adequate armed forces.

The armed forces serve solely for the defense of Swiss soil. In peacetime, the Swiss armed forces cannot cooperate with those of other countries; it is only in wartime that such collaboration may be considered. In the event of hostilities, the armed forces will defend the country's frontiers, prevent the enemy from securing his main objectives, and — if the worst should come to the worst — make sure that at least a part of the country effectively remains under Swiss sovereignty.

In addition, the armed forces are charged with the task of helping the civilian population in the event of major catastrophes and of preventing serious breaches of public order. (Swiss militia men have thus taken part in assuring airport security and in guarding participants in international conferences — assignments that have mistakenly led a German journalist to conclude that the army has functioned more often as an instrument for maintaining order at home than as a means for deterring aggression from abroad.[32]

The Swiss are a nation in arms. The Swiss army comprises no more than about 3,000 permanent cadres; the rest are part-time soldiers. In 1983, the total number of active militia men (*Wehrmänner*) and members of the voluntary women's service amounted to 420,000. Very few Swiss refuse to do their military service. (In 1983, only 745 refused to do so, and thereby incurred punishment.) Deliberate abstention from military service remains an indictable offense, though discussion is under way concerning the treatment of those who refuse to render military service, and the institution of labor service for conscientious objectors. An ordinary soldier at present must spend 392 days in uniform (up to the age of 50); a corporal 511 days; a captain 1,174; a major 1,343; and a colonel 1,513. (These figures do not include voluntary service.) Having spent 118 days in basic training, a Swiss soldier must serve eight times 20 days in repeater courses in the Auszug (21–32 years); three times 13 days in supplementary training in the Landwehr (33–42 years); and twice six days in the Landsturm (43–50 years). Switzerland, not surprisingly, has therefore developed a striking *esprit militaire* and a strong sense of patriotism. As Machiavelli said centuries ago, "The Swiss have no army, they are an army."

Switzerland's Strategic Position and Defense Concept

The Swiss Confederation lies in the heart of Europe and occupies a geostrategic position similar to Austria's. In the event of a major attack from the east, directed at Central Europe between the Baltic and the Alps, Switzerland would only be a secondary theater of war. Nevertheless, an opponent — the Warsaw Pact or even NATO — might choose to embark on "preventive action" to secure Swiss air bases or important road communications by means of sudden assaults carried out by airborne forces. By doing so, an enemy might seriously interrupt Swiss mobilization plans, and even aim at forcing the Swiss government to capitulate. Enemy assaults by land from southern Germany and Austria would face a number of geographical obstacles, illustrated in Figure 4.6.

Figure 4.6: The Central Mountain Barriers

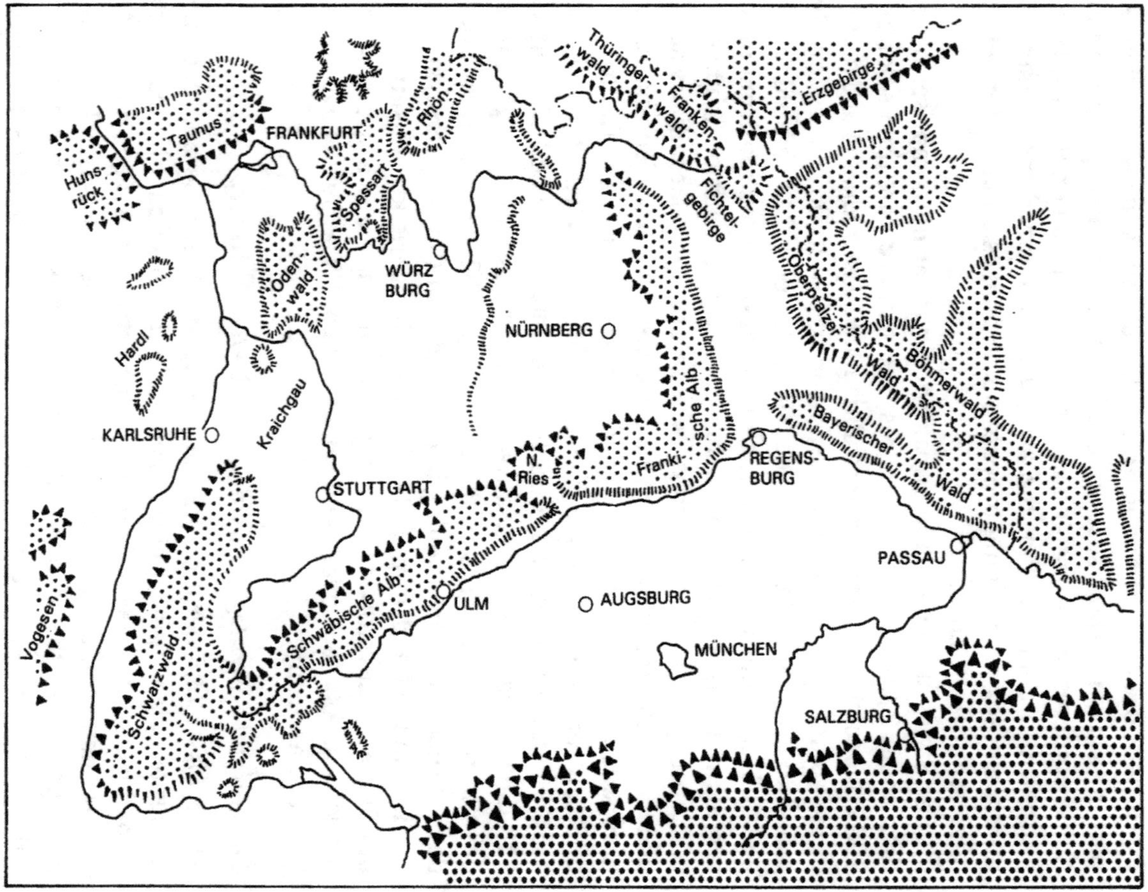

Franco recognized that the support of his generals might be negated by dissent from middle-ranking or junior officers. Since he could not offer many financial inducements beyond the fact of employment to the junior officers, he maintained their loyalty by ideological persuasion, constantly reaffirming the traditional and authoritarian values to which they were wedded. Ironically the very processes Franco used to maintain support impoverished the army, both in terms of the reactionary values it espoused and the equally outmoded equipment it possessed.

Manpower and Recruitment

The Spanish armed forces are composed of approximately 116,000 regular servicemen together with some 214,000 conscripts (1984). Until recently, compulsory military service was for 15 months, but this is to be reduced to 12 months and greater emphasis is to be placed on voluntary short service engagements of three to four years following the success of the air force in this approach. (Fifty percent of their manpower consists of short service enlisted men and 50 percent regular.)

At present the size of the individual services is as follows: army 240,000 including 170,000 conscripts; navy 57,000 (of which 12,000 are marines), including 44,000 conscripts; and air force 33,000. There are over 1 million reserves, although most receive little or no training. In addition there are some 63,500 members of the Guardia Civil, and 47,000 in the Policia Nacional, both paramilitary forces and organized, if not deployed, largely on infantry lines.

In the spring of 1984 the Cortes passed a bill which for the first time since the Napoleonic Wars seems likely to reform and thus reduce the manpower of the Spanish armed forces and in particular the army officer corps. During the Civil War more than 22,000 Provisionales (Provisional Ensigns) were appointed, nearly half of whom were retained at the end of the conflict. Despite this the Military Academy contrived to produce nearly 400 officers a year and by the 1980s the problem of overmanning was widely acknowledged to be acute. In 1973 there were 28,045 officers (of whom over 800 were generals or admirals) in the three services, out of a total manpower of 293,000. By 1976–78, 61.8 percent of military expenditure went on salaries (a proportion 50% higher than in West Germany or Great Britain), but so low were these salaries that 64 percent of officers had to supplement their pay by taking second jobs.[6] The situation was exacerbated further during the 1970s and early 1980s by the enhanced opportunities offered to non-commissioned officers (NCOs) to be commissioned. Inevitably a top-heavy structure such as this produced further rigidities,

Figure 4.7: Openings into Switzerland and Main Roads in South Germany

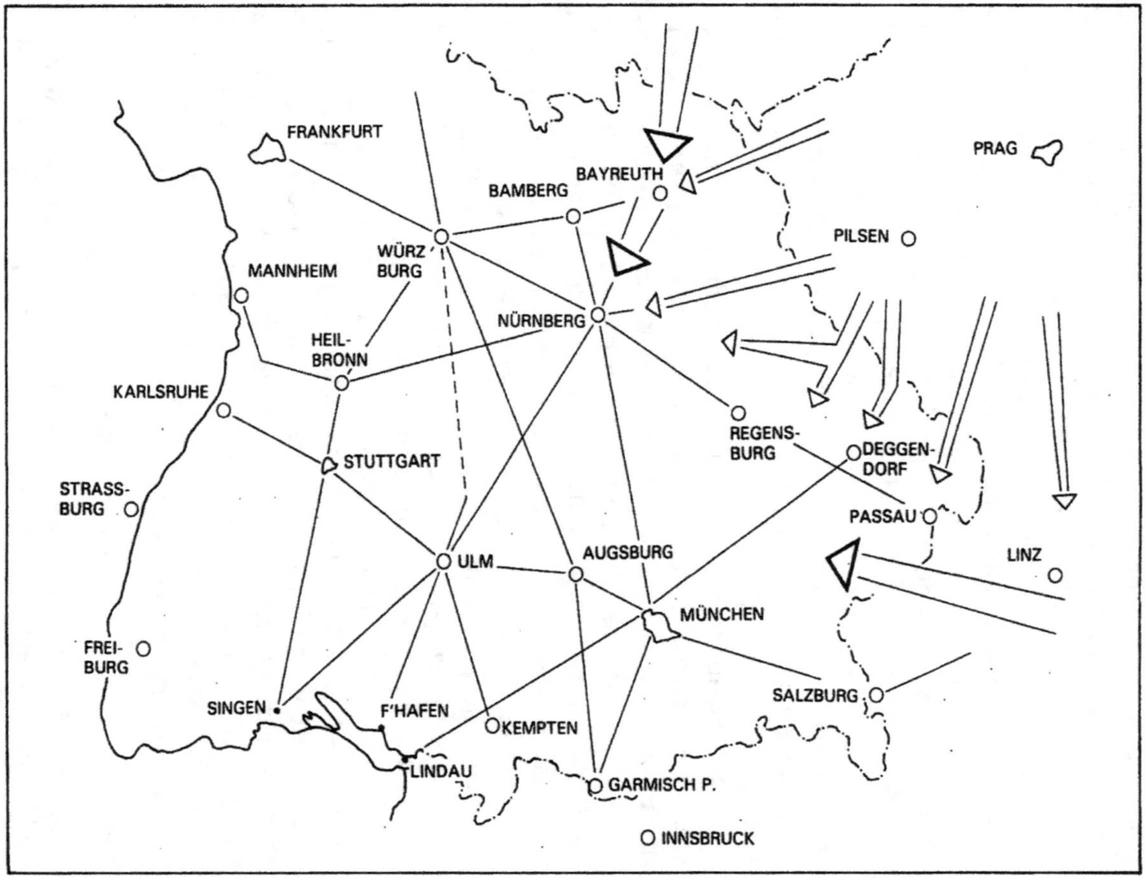

The principal invasion routes from southern Germany include the *Autobahn* route Leipzig–Bayreuth–Nürnberg along the northeast, and the southeast flank along the lower course of Salzach–Inn, bordered by Upper Austria, an entirely uncovered area (Figure 4.7).[33] Given Austria's importance for an invasion from the northeast, Switzerland would do well to familiarize itself with Austrian conditions.

To cope with such threats, the Swiss army has elaborated its own concept of spatial defense (*Raumverteidigung*), formalized in a decree dated 6 June 1966. This concept combines defense and counter-attack for the purpose of safeguarding particular regions. The Swiss army bases its defense on prepared bases (*Stützpunkte*) and barriers designed to halt or break up enemy assaults. In addition, infantry and mechanized forces stand ready for offensive action.[34] The general disposition of the Swiss army corresponds to the country's topographical structure, as illustrated in Figures 4.8 a and b.

According to the Swiss defense concept, the field army corps (FAK) will prevent enemy penetration of the respective corps areas, cover areas of particular strategic or operational importance, and engage enemy land and airborne forces. The field army corps will cooperate closely with the frontier brigades. Armored units of the mechanized divisions will carry out counter-attacks in order to destroy enemy forces that have broken through. The mountain army corps (Geb. AK) will prevent enemy advances into the alpine region, and will cover the flanks and rear of the field army corps. The mountain army corps will at least defend a part of the alpine region for a protracted period.

The air corps and anti-aircraft formations will impede the enemy air squadrons engaged in attacking important objectives. The air corps and anti-aircraft formations will assist the army by reconnaissance in the enemy's rear, by providing air cover, and by attacking objectives outside the reach of other arms. In addition, the air corps and anti-aircraft formations will cooperate with territorial organizations to warn the army and civilians of impending air attacks.

Organization and Armament of the Swiss Army

The combination of universal military service and the militia system enable Switzerland rapidly to mobilize an army of more than 600,000 — an extraordinary achievement, given the small size of the Swiss population (6.5 million) and of Switzerland's area (41,293 square kilometers, with a population density of about 150 inhabitants per square kilometer).

The Swiss armed forces comprise a small air corps, containing one air defense brigade, an airfield brigade, a small parachute unit, and one

Austria and Switzerland 119

Figure 4.8 a: Switzerland's Topographic Structure

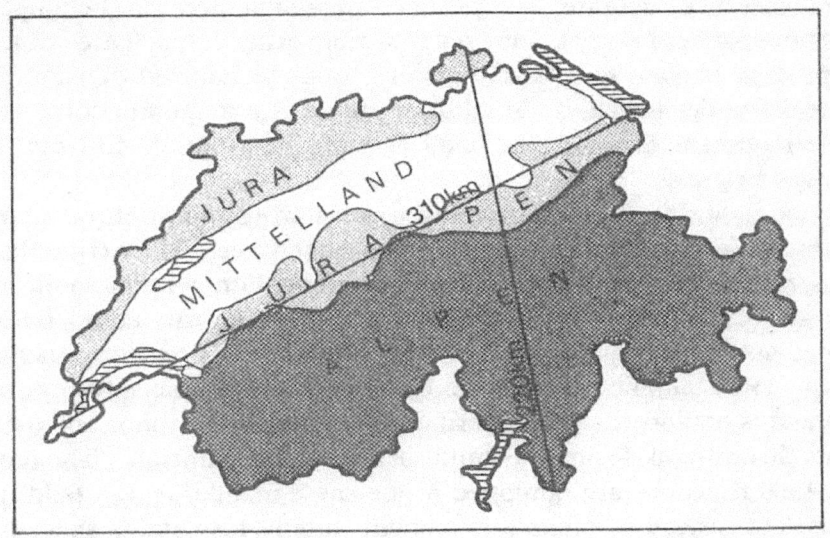

Figure 4.8 b: Disposition of the Swiss Army

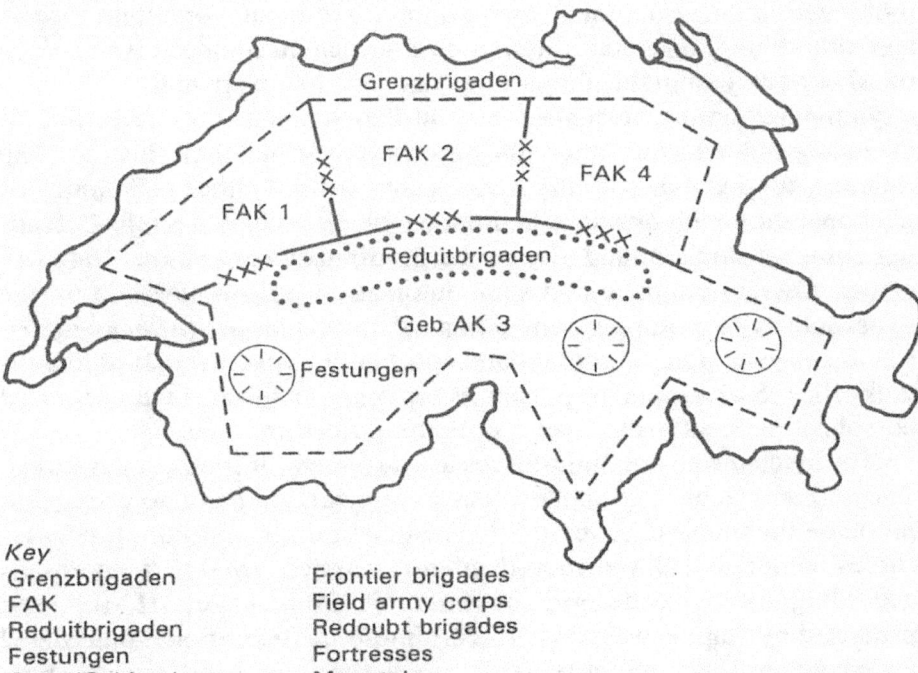

Key
Grenzbrigaden   Frontier brigades
FAK   Field army corps
Reduitbrigaden   Redoubt brigades
Festungen   Fortresses
Geb. (Gebirge)   Mountain.

flying brigade. Between them, these units dispose of 1,800 anti-aircraft guns (many of them of the most modern kind), 300 combat aircraft for reconnaissance, defense, and ground operations, and 100 helicopters.

The main field army comprises four field army corps. Three of these corps each contain two field divisions, one mechanized division, and several frontier brigades. In addition, there is a mountain corps, with three mountain divisions, as well as separate frontier, fortress, and redoubt brigades.

Each field division in turn comprises a staff battalion, three infantry regiments (each with one infantry support and three fusilier (rifle) battalions, one artillery regiment, one engineer battalion, a light mobile anti-aircraft unit, a communications unit, and one company equipped with guided anti-tank missiles. Since 1981, all field divisions have included two armored battalions. Of these, one serves as a counter-attack formation and is equipped with modern 61/68 vehicles; the other operates as a mobile anti-tank formation and is armed with Centurions. The mountain field divisions are equipped in the same manner as the field divisions, but instead of tanks they contain supply formations specialized for work in mountain country.

The mechanized division, the counter-attack formation *par excellence* at the corps commander's disposal, consists of a staff battalion, one motorized infantry regiment, two armored regiments, one light mobile anti-aircraft unit, one mobile anti-aircraft formation equipped with guided missiles, one communications unit, and one engineer unit.

Individual combat brigades vary in their composition according to the nature of the terrain where they are employed and their mission. The infantry, the main arm of the Swiss army, is used either as infantry or in cooperation with armor. The infantry blocks enemy assaults defending bases or barriers; and also serves in offensive operations. Infantry is armed with automatic and semi-automatic weapons; in addition the Swiss infantry is equipped with a total of 3,000 mortars (*Minenwerfer*), 1,340 anti-tank guns, 2,400 guided anti-tank missiles, and 20,000 anti-tank rifles. Switzerland at present is equipping its forces with armored personnel carriers armed with anti-tank guided missiles.

The mechanized and light forces are designed for mobile operations. They possess about 840 modern tanks; Switzerland has also decided to purchase the modern Leopard 2 (11) battle tank. In addition, the Swiss forces comprise 1,350 armored infantry carriers, M-113 modernized according to a Swiss design, supported by 290 howitzers H-109, and protected by Rapier weapons. According to the operational plan dated 9 September 1982, the tank — in cooperation with artillery, aircraft, and combat helicopters — will dominate the battlefield until at least the year 2,000 and beyond. Switzerland therefore continues to adhere to the defense plan adopted on 6 June 1966, in which the infantry's ability to repel tanks continues to play a major part. The Swiss try to improve existing methods in a variety of ways, for instance through attempts on the part of the Gruppe für den Rüstungsdienst to provide more effective ammunition.[35] Swiss armament suffers from a variety of weaknesses — most weapon systems as yet have inadequate night vision; Switzerland as yet possesses no anti-tank helicopters or one-man anti-aircraft (helicopter) rockets, although work is under way to improve the penetrative power of existing anti-tank projectiles. Lack of financial resources and the expense incurred by the purchase of the new Leopard 2 battle tank has restricted progress.

These deficiencies, however, should not be overestimated. Switzerland — the point bears repeating — remains a nation in arms, able and willing to mobilize something like 625,000 men, an impressive total given the small size of its population. The Swiss arsenal needs improvement. But given the limits of their resources, the Swiss have made a major arms effort. (In 1984 they maintained a total of 840 tanks, as opposed to 1,810 for Italy, and only 170 for Austria.) The Swiss officer corps is of high quality, drawn from citizens of good education. The officers in no wise form a part of a "free masonry" or a social elite; on the contrary, promotion to a high rank is open to citizens of humble birth. Foreign misconceptions to the contrary notwithstanding, the Swiss are prepared to defend their territory as a whole; they do not plan to retreat to an alpine redoubt. (Should the field army corps fail in their alloted tasks, the troops will continue hostilities in the form of guerilla operations.) Despite existing weaknesses, Switzerland understands the wisdom in the Roman injunction *si vis pacem, para bellum* (if you want peace, prepare for war).

Conclusion

Switzerland and Austria both try to maintain their neutrality between two competing power blocs; both have put their trust in a militia system and similar concepts of spatial defense. But there are differences. Owing to its exposed position, Austria also maintains a small standing force, a mechanized infantry division; but it is doubtful whether this is adequate for the country's needs. There are striking differences in the Austrian and Swiss air defense systems. Austria's Goldhaube provides the country with a modern early warning system and should be able to serve as a guidance system for fighter planes; but Austria lacks the required fighters. The Austrian State Treaty moreover prohibits guided anti-aircraft missiles. This prohibition places Austria in a Catch 22 situation, as the same State Treaty imposes an obligation on the country to defend its neutrality effectively, including its airspace.[36]

Austria's defense system has other weaknesses. The Austrians try to buy security on the cheap. They seem convinced that a pacific foreign policy and Vienna's position as a UN city will buy better protection than the relatively expensive Bundesheer. Austria's policy must unhappily remind an observer of Norway's in 1940. Austria's two-party system creates additional difficulties, as the opposition inevitably criticizes the government on every contentious issue. Austria must contend with a broad alliance that rejects defense — Greens, Young Socialists, some ÖVP members, and peace marchers of every conceivable persuasion have joined in attacks against the Austrian military. Switzerland's "consensual democracy" is less vulnerable in this regard, but even the Swiss have had to cope with attacks from those who oppose the defense establishment for whatever political reason.

The Austrian and Swiss concepts of "spatial defense" are hard to compare. Both are adjusted to their respective countries' limited means, to particular missions and terrain, pursuing modest aims at weakening the opponent by defense in depth, and by assuring — at best — the retention of a part of the national territory. This imposes a heavy burden on their own military and civil population by confining military operations to the home territory. As they are neutral powers, their defense policy is of a purely reactive kind. Austria had the opportunity of making an entirely new start, but arrived at a solution similar to Switzerland's, possibly for military reasons, possibly also because no other solution would have been acceptable in a political sense.[37]

Austria and Switzerland alike moreover face a grave long-term problem — steeply rising defense costs, a desperately difficult matter for minor states in particular. In 1960 Switzerland had spent 945 million francs, and in 1984 an estimated 4,248,000 francs. This steep rise in military expenditure is not surprising, given the worldwide cost explosion for military equipment. (In 1950, a Vampire combat plane cost 430,000 francs; a generation later, a Tiger combat plane cost 10,000,000 francs.) Yet during the same period, the share of the Swiss gross national product devoted to defense declined (from 2.4 percent in 1960 to 1.9 percent in 1981). Switzerland continued to lead in Europe as regards the percentage of the population serving in the army (10.0 percent in Switzerland and Israel, 2.2 percent in Austria; 1.4 percent in the USSR.;

0.9 percent in the US and France; 0.8 percent in the Federal German Republic; 0.7 percent in the Netherlands). But in terms of defense expenditure, Switzerland in 1981 compared poorly with most other major countries (8.4 percent to 15 percent in the USSR, 6.1 percent in the US, 4.3 percent in the Federal German Republic, 3.4 percent in the Netherlands, 3.1 percent in Sweden). Only Austria spent even less (1.2 percent) in proportion than Switzerland.

Swiss and Austrian planners alike must also face the more fundamental question of whether they are spending their money wisely, or whether they are merely preparing for the last war. This author has himself discovered in the Bundesarchiv/Militärarchiv in Freiburg (Federal German Republic) a secret defense plan worked out by General Weygand in 1940, at a time when advanced German armored forces had already penetrated to the Loire river.[38] Weygand's plan strikingly resembled present-day Austrian and Swiss spatial defense concepts, a fateful parallel that might induce present-day planners to re-examine existing assumptions.[39] Whatever designs, however, the future may see, defense requires firm national commitment, determined resistance to pacifist temptations, and the unswerving conviction that vigilance is the eternal price for liberty.

Notes

1. Inge Santer, "Oestlich der Schweiz ist kein militärisches Loch," *Die Weltwoche* (Zurich), 8 April 1981; Erich Gysling, Marcel H. Kieser and Inge Santer, "Die Schweiz grenzt nicht an Russland," *Die Weltwoche* (Zurich), 23 July 1980; Josef Feldmann, "Schwächen sind erkennbar," *Wochenpresse*, 9 September 1981; Emil Spannocchi, "Unsere Schweizer Freunde können beruhigt sein," *Schweizer Soldat*, no. 3 (1978), pp. 6–7.

2. Daniel Frei, "Kriegsverhütung durch Neutralität," *Beiträge zur Konfliktforschung*, no. 4 (1981), pp. 37–55; see Rudolf L. Bindschedler, "Neutralitätspolitik und Sicherheitspolitik," *Österreichische Zeitschrift für Aussenpolitik*, no. 6 (1976), pp. 339–354.

3. Agreement dated 18 October 1907, Second Peace Conference at The Hague.

4. The Austrian ratification document was deposited at The Hague on 27 November 1909 and has been recognized by the Austrian Republic. Austria's perpetual neutrality was recognized by Belgium, Bolivia, Brazil, Chinese People's Republic, Cuba, Denmark, Ethiopia, Federal German Republic, Finland, France, Guatemala, Haiti, Japan, Laos, Liberia, Luxembourg, Mexico, Netherlands, Nicaragua, Norway, Panama, Phillipines, Poland, Portugal, Romania, Salvador, Spain, Sweden, Switzerland, Thailand, US, USSR. This agreement is not subject to alteration; neither are the obligations assumed by the neutral state. A state is recognized as neutral only if it abides by the obligations laid down in this agreement.

5. Wilhelm Kuntner, "Militär-und Sicherheitspolitik neutraler Staaten — Ein österreichischer Beitrag" in Dieter Lutz and Annemarie Grosse-Jütte (eds.), *Neutralität — Eine Alternative?, Zur Militär- und Sicherheitspolitik neutraler Staaten in Europa* (Nomos Verlagsgesellschaft, Baden-Baden, 1981), p. 77. See also Rudolf L. Bindschedler, "Neutralitätspolitik und Sicherheitspolitik," *Oesterreichische Zeitschrift für Aussenpolitik*, no. 6 (1976), 339–354.

6. For the French text of the key passage see Edgar Bonjour, "Oestereichische und schweizerische Neutralität," *Schweizer Monatshefte*, no. 10 (1980), pp. 829–839.

7. See Edgar Bonjour, *Geschichte der schweizerischen Neutralität* (Helbing und Lichtenhahn, Basle, 1970–76), vols. 1–9.

8. See "Bundesverfassungsgesetz vom 26 Oktober 1955 über die Neutralität Oesterreichs," *Bundesgesetzblatt für die Republik Oesterreich, Jg. 1955*, 4 November 1955, p. 1151.

9. See note 4.

10. Hans-Rudolf Fuhrer, *Spionage gegen die Schweiz* (Huber, Frauenfeld, 1982).

11. "Neutrale Kleinstaaten im Zweiten Weltkrieg" in *Schriften der Schweizerischen Vereinigung für Militärgeschichte und Militärwissenschaften*, 10 vols, (Münsingen, 1973), vol. 1, p. 33; Emil Spannocchi, "Gegenüberstellung der Handhabung der militärischen Neutralität in Oesterreich und der Schweiz," Vortrag vor der Oesterreichisch–Schweizerischen Gesellschaft vom 11.3.1975, *Oesterreichische Zeitschrift für Aussenpolitik*, no. 3 (1975), p. 134.

12. See Walter Hubatsch, *Weserübung* (Musterschmidtverlag, Göttingen, 1960).

13. The full sovereignty of a state extends over its airspace, as well as its land territory, a point elaborated in the Chicago Agreement–ICAO Agreement, 1944; see Landesverteidigungsplan (Bundeskanzleramt, Vienna, 1985), p. 56, and note 17.

14. Bericht des Kommandanten der Flieger- und Fliegerabwehr-ruppen an den Oberbefehlshaber der Armee über den Aktivdienst 1939–1945, p. 16. Beilage II zum Bericht General Guisans an die Bundesversammlung über den Aktivdienst 1939 1945 (Berne, 1946).

15. Spannocchi, "Gegenüberstellung," p. 136 (see note 11).

16. Ibid., p. 138.

17. See also Beate Schär, "Durchsetzung der Souveränität im Schweizerischen Luftraum," *Neue Zürcher Zeitung*, 21 March 1985, p. 35.

18. See "Konzeption der Gesamtverteidigung," Bericht des Bundesrates vom 27 June 1973; Zwischenbericht zur Sicherheitspolitik vom 3 Dezember 1979; Zentralstelle für Gesamtverteidigung (ed.), *Einführung in die Gesamtverteidigung* (Berne, 1984); Lutz and Grosse-Jutte, *Neutralität;* Paul Stähly (ed.), *Wirtschaftliche Landesvorsorge im Rahmen der Sicherheitspolitik* (Haupt, Berne, 1983); Grundlagen einer strategischen Konzeption der Schweiz, Bericht der Studienkommission für strategische Fragen, *Schriften des SAD*, no. 11 (1971); Alfed Aebi, "Der Beitrag neutraler Staaten zur Friedenssicherung," *Schriften des SAD*, . 14 (1976); Gesamtverteidigung und Armee (ed.), *Sicherheitspolitik und Armee* (Huber, Frauenfeld, 1976); (ed.), *Handbuch der geistigen Landesverteidigung* (Vienna, Bundesministerium für Unterricht und Kunst n.d.).

19. Bundeskanzleramt (ed.), *Landesverteidigungsplan* (Vienna, 1985); Wolfgang Danspeckhuber, "Militärische Landesverteidigung Oesterreichs," *Internationale Wehrrevue*, no. 6 (1984), 721–731; Lothar Brosch-Fohraheim, "Die militärische Landesverteidigung. Der oesterreichische Weg und seine Entwicklung," *Oesterreichische Militärische Zeitschrift*, no. 2 (1983), pp. 101–108; Rudolf Striedinger, "Organisationsaufbau und Gliederung des österreichischen Bundesheeres," *Allgemeine Schweizerische Militärzeitschrift*, no. 5 pp. 259–263; Bundeskanzleramt, *Informationen zur Umfassenden Landesverteidigung* (Vienna, 1982).

20. See Bundeskanzleramt, *Landesverteidigungsplan*, n. 19 above.

21. Alois Riklin *et al.*, "Sicherheitspolitische Konzepte im internationalen Vergleich," *Beiträge und Berichte der Forschungsstelle für Politikwissenschaft an der Hochschule St. Gallen* (St. Gallen, 1976).

22. Andreas Baryli und Martin Neubau, "Der osterreichische Staatsvertrag von 1955," *Geschichte Historisches Magazin* (March/April 1985), pp. 12–19.

23. See Bundeskanzleramt (ed.), *Informationen zur umfassenden Landesverteidigung* (Vienna, 1982); Heirich Neisser and Fritz Windhager (eds.), "Wie sicher ist Oesterreich?" *Schriftenreihe Sicherheit und Demokratie* (Oesterreichische Verlagsanstalt,

Vienna, 1982), vol. 2.

24. Franz Freistetter, "Die strategische Lage Oesterreichs," (May 1983), pp. 237–242; Wolfgang Danspeckhuber, "Militärische Landesverteidigung Oesterreichs," *International Wehrrevue*, no. 6 (1984), pp. 721–731; Alfred Stutz, *Raumverteidigung — Utopisch oder Alternative?* (Verlag Neue Zürcher Zeitung, Zürich, 1982).

25. Emil Spannochi, born 1916, headed the Austrian Defense Academy 1963–72; from 1973 to 1981 he served as General of the Army.

26. Danspeckhuber "Militärische Landesverteidigung," p. 730.

27. See Wilhelm Mark, "Die Sicherheitspolitik der Schweiz" in Lutz and Grosse-Jütte, *Neutralität* pp. 43–71; Stähly, *Wirtschaftliche Landesvorsorge;* Gustav Daeniker, "Die Armee des neutralen Kleinstates als friedenssichernde Kraft," *Oesterreichische Militärische Zeitschrift*, no. 1 (1983), pp. 19–26; Josef M. Marolz, "Neutralität in Europa im Spannungsfeld zwischen Ost und West" in Buchbender, Beuhl and Quaden, *Sicherheit und Frieden* (Mittler und Sohn, Hereford, 1983); Jürg Späni, *Die Interpretation der dauernden Neutralität durch das schweizerische und das österreichische Parlament* (Haupt, Berne, 1983); Bruno Kreisky, "Hat Neutralität noch einen Sinn?," *Schriftenreihe der Europa-Union Schweiz*, vol. B, no. 4 (Berne, 1983); Stab GGST, *Ausgaben für die militärische Landesverteidigung im internationalen Vergleich (1965–1980)* (Berne, 1981), pp. 11–21; Josef Feldmann, "Demain il nous faudra arrêter l'ennemi hors de Suisse," *Le Temps Stratégique*, out of series (1984), pp. 25–36; Daniel Frei, "Kriegsverhütung durch Neutralität?" *Beiträge zur Konfliktforschung*, no. 4 (1981), pp. 37–55; Edgar Bonjour, "Oesterreichische und schweizerische Neutralität," *Schweizer Monatshefte*, no. 10 (1980), pp. 829–839; Kurt Furgler, Alois Riklin et al., *Wende in unserer Sicherheitspolitik?* (Athenäum, Lugano, 1978); *Referate Oesterreichisch–schweizerisches Seminar für vergleichende Zeitgeschichte ab 1945 vom 21–26 April 1985* in Linz, especially the paper by Peter Hablützel, "Die Schweiz seit 1945"; Hans Senn, *Friede in Unabhängigkeit* (Huber, Frauenfeld, 1984); Chance Schweiz (ed.), *Die Herausforderung der Zukunft* (Basileus, Basle, 1984).

28. See Späni, *Interpretation*, p. 28.

29. Archiv für Zeitgeschichte ETH Zürich (ed.), *30 Jahre Schweizerische Korea-Mission 1953–1983* (Zürich, 1983).

30. *Bundesblatt*, no. 1, p. 497.

31. See Zentralstelle für Gesamtverteidigung (ed.), *Einführung in die Gesamtverteidigung* (Bundeskanzlei, Berne, 1984).

32. Peter-Matthias Gaede, "Der wachsame Friede der Schweiz," *GEO-Magazin* (Hamburg), no. 4 (1985), p. 72.

33. Jakob Forster, "Die operative Bedeutung des Süddeutschen Raumes," supplement to *Allgemeine Schweizerische Militärzeitschrift*, no. 1 (Frauenfeld, 1983).

34. Bericht des Bundesrates vom 6 June 1966 über die Konzeption der militärischen Landesverteidigung (Berne, 1966).

35. Charles Grossenbacher, "Rüstungpolitik," *Allgemeine Schweizerische Militärzeitschrift*, no. 6 (1985), pp. 323–328.

36. See Inge Santer, "Eine unheilige Allianz kämpft gegen die 'Horror-Vögel'," *Die Weltwoche* (Zürich), 13 June 1985, p. 11.

37. Feldmann, "Demain," pp. 25–26.

38. Maxime Weygand, Befehl des französischen Oberkommandos vom 1 Juni 1940. Bundesarchiv/Militärarchiv, Freiburg i. Br., RH 19 II/291. Also see F. O. Mischke, *Vom Kriegsbild* (Stuttgart, 1976), pp. 264–65.

39. See Alfred Ernst, *Die Konzeption der schweizerischen Landesverteidigung* (Huber, Frauenfeld(Stuttgart, 1971), p. 398. For general accounts of the Swiss defense system in English, see John Keegan, "Switzerland" in *World Armies*, 2nd edn (Gale Research Company, Detroit, 1983), pp. 554–60 (on Austria, John Keegan, "Austria" in *World Armies*, pp. 30–34). For a book length study in English, see John McPhee, *The Swiss Army: La Place de la Concorde Suisse* (Faber, London, 1984), to be used with caution.

5 THE SPANISH AND PORTUGESE DEFENSE FORCES

Matthew Midlane

Spain and Portugal were both the least significant and most enduring of the European Fascist dictatorships which had their origins in the interwar years. Not until 1974 in Portugal and 1975 in Spain were these regimes tranformed, both in time to parliamentary democracy, although by startlingly different routes. Portugal developed via a revolutionary, but bloodless, military *coup*; which heralded a period of radical ideological fervor and chronic institutional instability, but culminated in the subordination of the military to left of centre and centrist civilian political parties. After the death of General Francisco Franco, Spain took the path of a return to hereditary monarchy coupled with political democracy, but not without evoking profound disquiet in its deeply conservative army and at least three (some would say five) attempts to overthrow constitutional authority by armed force. Nevertheless, despite weak economies and fragile institutions, both democracies remain intact, and gradually militarism has been superseded by the legitimacy of civil authority.[1]

The peoples of Spain and Portugal share a Latin heritage, some past history, relative economic poverty, and a geographic position largely isolated from European culture by the Pyrenees but strategically important to the defense of the West. They also exhibit many differences and share a reserve and at times enmity for one another which cannot be ignored in NATO's planning of Western defense.

Spain

The Historical Legacy

The Spanish armed forces, and in particular the army, appear, as one commentator has put it, "the real center of power in Spain . . . the key to political change in Spanish politics."[2] However, although the military have had an overwhelming presence in Spanish life, especially during the era of Franco (1936–75), the power has never been absolute and for much of the time has been more apparent than real. Indeed despite the military posturing of recent years and the numerous overt interventions in the political process, Spanish democracy remains alive and the military have acceded, however unwillingly, to the principles of civilian supremacy. Nevertheless the history of the nineteenth and twentieth centuries amply indicates how important the military have been in the development of the modern state.

From the time of the Napoleonic Wars until the present Spanish officers have involved themselves in politics. Before the restoration of the Bourbons in 1875 political conflict within the army was rife, liberal officers being as responsible as conservative for the *pronunciamentos* (statement of military demands) of the period. After 1875 the officer corps became deeply conservative, espousing the sacred unity of the nation, the defense of public order, the repression of progressive social movements and the maintenance of the colonial empire. With the exception of the last, these themes remain dominant in the minds of the more conservative of contemporary officers. The officer corps developed an enormous self-esteem and, whilst isolating itself from much of society, at the same time regarded itself as personifying the higher values of that society. In addition, and with serious long-term consequences for its own efficiency and professionalism, the numerical strength of the officer corps has always been vastly overinflated.[3]

After 1923 the *pronunciamento* period gave way to a more overt form of military intervention, the *coup d'état*. Social and regional unrest internally, and military defeat in Morocco, resulted in Spain's first military dictatorship, that of Primo de Rivera (1923–30). De Rivera fell because the military removed their support from his ineffectual regime, a fact which in itself fuelled the army's belief in its own importance.

The ensuing period of republican government did much to alienate the military. In particular there was a largely abortive attempt to reform the army by halving its divisions (from twenty to eight), by reducing its officer corps from 22,000 to 11,000, and by removing the legal jurisdiction of the army over civilians in security matters. Although nominally accepted, the reforms were insufficient to emasculate the political ambitions of many officers, which resulted in an unsuccessful *coup* in 1932. Continued civil and political unrest culminated in the election of a Popular Front government in 1936 which, in the perception of conservative officers, would lead inevitably to social and political upheaval, the destruction of traditional Spanish values and the political disintegration of a unified state. In July 1936 Franco was one of the three senior generals who took up arms against the government, the result of which was the catastrophic Civil War of 1936–39 and the emergence of Franco as the Caudillo (leader) of Spain for nearly forty years.[4]

During World War II, Spain remained neutral, although the government sympathized with the Axis powers. Between 1941 and 1943, 19,000 Spaniards served in the volunteer "Blue Division" against the Russians on the Eastern Front. In the post-war years, the influence of the Blue Division generals was primarily symbolic; their conduct exemplified a military view which rejected any concessions to the vanquished in the Civil War. When Franco revived the office of Vice President in 1962 its first incumbent (1962–67) was his old friend, the former leader of the Blue Division, Captain-General Muñoz Grandes. The two most senior figures in the abortive anti-democratic *coup* of February 1981, Generals Del Bosch and Armada, were also veterans of the Russian campaign.

The choice, by his fellow generals, of Franco as both Head of State and Commander-in-Chief was because of his political inexperience, not in spite of it. Nevertheless he soon mastered the art of balancing the various power groups in Spanish society and, although he leaned on the army as the ultimate guarantor of his regime, he was never wholly dominated by it. He used patronage with consummate skill; he maintained the swollen officer corps and thus bought the loyalty of its members; he granted enormous status to the senior generals and revived the ancient title of Captain-General and with it the position of military governor of the individual provinces. During his regime large numbers of officers served in government:

> 35% of Franco's ministers were military officers and almost 50% occupied civilian ministries. In 1974 there were three generals and an admiral in the cabinet, thirty-two in the Cortes (Parliament), four in the Council of State, two in the Regency Council . . . Seventy three per cent of these officers formerly in the cabinet sat on the boards of directors of major state enterprises.[5]

However, despite these imposing statistics, they were primarily positions of sinecure, not power; generals and admirals were never authoritative enough even to fund their own services adequately. Indeed it was because the officer corps was so large, and so impoverished, that Franco was able to exercise power through patronage. Nor did he allow it to build up a rival power base, regularly moving officials from one military region to another.

As an experienced soldier and an increasingly astute politician, particularly in terms of the promotion structures. Legislation in 1981 lowered the retirement age in all ranks, and thereafter generals were required to retire at the age of 64 and could not remain more than twelve years in that rank. To ease the transition the law enabled officers to transfer to a state of "active reserve" and to maintain many of the military benefits of their rank. Further reforms in 1983 introduced promotion by merit rather than seniority, but it remains the case that Spanish officers remain in rank years after contemporaries in other countries have been promoted. Indeed it is a measure of the intractability of the problem that reforms announced in 1983 will only reduce the number of army officers from 22,974 in 1983 to 17,743 in 1990. The largest percentage reductions will be felt in the most senior ranks: staff generals falling from 19 to 10, divisional generals from 51 to 35, and brigadier-generals from 130 to 98. Overall army manpower will reduce by 45,000 to 195,000 by 1985. Smaller cuts are required in the navy and air force, where the numbers of regulars will reduce by 800 and 1,000 respectively.[7]

The Social Structure and Attitudes of the Military

If the Franco era witnessed the further isolation of Spain from European society, its psychological impact on the officer corps was even more pronounced. Shorn of the influence of liberal officers, without any serious commitment to the values of civil supremacy, and with official support from the Head of State, Spanish officers developed not merely conservative attitudes but often deeply reactionary ones. This process was facilitated by their physical isolation in barracks and the very marked pattern of internal self-recruitment and recruitment from the more conservative regions of Spain. By the 1960s "79.6% of army officers, 65.8% of naval officers and 65.2% of air force officers came from military families." In addition nearly half of all officers married into military families.[8]

However the officer corps is less socially homogeneous and elitist than these statistics suggest, for increasingly in the last thirty years new officers have been the sons, not of the old landed interests, but of the Alfereces Provisionales and of NCOs. Whereas these developments did little to moderate the officers' reactionary political views, and may have exacerbated them, they did have important economic and social repercussions in providing an avenue of social mobility into a secure, if poorly paid, occupation. Nevertheless, at the same time, the diminution of the aristocratic component in the officer corps lowered the overall social status of the profession.[9]

The Spanish army was drawn exclusively from the victorious side in a civil war, a conflict which had been as divisive as any in modern times. Its principal occupation, both before and after the war, was not that of defense against external aggression, but of maintaining internal security, a role explicitly acknowledged in Article 37 of the Organic Law of the State (now repealed). In such circumstances it is hardly surprising that the army, together with the other arms of the security forces, was regarded by large sections of the population as alien, partisan, and repressive; and that civil–military relations often reflected these hostile attitudes.

Unusually, the military were also participants in the judicial process, terrorism, anarchism, and separatism all being crimes punishable by military rather than civil courts. Consequently, when controversial penalties were imposed, as with the death sentences for murder inflicted on five left-wing revolutionaries in 1975, much of the odium fell on the army. Nor were the privileges and powers of the military restricted to the security sphere; the Minister of the Interior had the power to "militarize" workers, which he did in 1976 when railwaymen, postmen, and firemen were conscripted during an industrial dispute.

Although the formal legal and constitutional relationships between the army, the state, and society have now altered, the attitudes of the military will inevitably take longer to adjust to change.

Civil–Military Relations in Contemporary Spain

On the death of Franco in November 1975, Spain reverted, as planned, to the Bourbon monarchy. The succession of Juan Carlos as King and Head of State was immediate and peaceful, his background under the tutelage of Franco, and as an army officer, reassuring those who wished to maintain the political status quo. However, after a brief period of continuity under Franco's last Premier, Carlos Aries Novarro, the King moved, with considerable political dexterity, towards the introduction of parliamentary democracy. But although institutional change was gradual and largely undemonstrative, it caused growing concern in military circles.

In February 1976 military jurisdiction over civilians in terrorist trials was abolished; simultaneously violence in the Basque provinces was on the increase, resulting in the death of nine senior officers in 18 months. In September 1976, a moderate, General Manuel Mellado, became Deputy Prime Minister, and from his earliest statements antagonized his erstwhile colleagues. Mellado emphasized the doctrine of civil supremacy and reminded the army that it had no role to play in the transition to democracy. Turning to the organization of the forces themselves, he expressed his intention of refashioning the army to emulate their more professional and efficient counterparts in Western Europe.

The first free elections to the Cortes for forty years took place in June 1977, and were preceded by the legalization of the Spanish Communist Party, a decision which provoked the resignation of the Navy Minister, Admiral Pita de Veiga, and of two generals in the retiring (nominated) Cortes. Nor were military anxieties calmed by the post-election abolition of the separate ministries of the navy, army, and air force, posts which had always been held by officers, or by the retention of Mellado as Deputy Prime Minister and his appointment to the newly created post of Minister of Defense.

Sporadic but regular incidents in the late 1970s indicate how tense civil–military relations had become. In March 1978 four actors received a two-year term of imprisonment each for insulting the armed forces in their mime routine. In December that year an army officer belonging to the liberal Democratic Military Union (UMD) was sentenced to nine years' imprisonment for sedition. By contrast, in 1980, two officers convicted of a right-wing plot (Operation Galaxia) to overthrow the government were sentenced to seven and six months imprisonment respectively. Both remained serving officers and the more senior, Lt.-Col. António Tejero of the Guardia Civil, was later to spear-head the attempted *coup* in 1981. In an equally bizarre manner Captain Juan Milans del Bosch, son of the Captain-General of Valencia later implicated in the 1981 plot, was sentenced to one month's imprisonment for calling the King a "useless pig." On the other hand a liberal officer, Colonel Graino, was awarded two months' close arrest for having written in a newspaper that there were officers of extreme right-wing views.[10]

In January 1979 there were demonstrations by officers and soldiers at the funeral of the assassinated Military Governor of Madrid and unrest in the armed forces continued throughout the year. There were repeated criticisms of the new Constitution as anti-clerical and separatist (in fact it was neutral as far as religion was concerned and regionalist rather than separatist), and concern was regularly expressed at attempts to professionalize the officer corps. In the wake of general elections in March, the Prime Minister, Sr. Adolfo Suarez, appointed the first civilian Defense Minister since the Civil War, whilst the widely disliked General Mellado retained an overall coordinating role in national security and defense.

However, by far the most potent threat to Spain's fledgling democracy took place on 23 February 1981. On that day the Cortes was full for a crucial vote on a successor to Sr. Suarez as Prime Minister when Lt.-Col. Tejero stormed into the building with 300 troops from the Guardia Civil and took all members of the Assembly, including the entire government, hostage. Despite the brilliance of the *coup's* timing little else went right for the conspirators. Within the building even right-wing political leaders condemned the attack as an assault on democracy, and outside the Cortes was sealed off by loyal members of the paramilitary National Police. A key supporter of the insurrection, General Milans del Bosch, put Valencia under military command, whilst further support in Madrid came under General Armada Comyn, Deputy Chief of Staff of the army and for twenty years tutor and confidant to the young Juan Carlos. Both claimed to act in the name of the King, but in doing so they made a fatal miscalculation. From the outset the King was adamantly opposed to the revolt and was able to neutralize any possible bandwagon of support for it by demanding loyalty to the Constitution and to himself in his dual role of King and Captain-General of the armed forces. Although a small part of the elite Brunete armored division joined the rebellion and briefly took control of the television station, it returned to barracks when confronted by loyal troops.

The King rallied the nation with an inspiring television speech and to Milans del Bosch he telexed an order to withdraw, adding:

> I vow that I shall never abdicate nor abandon Spain. Anyone who rebels will be in the position of provoking and will be responsible for provoking, a new civil war. I have no doubt of my generals' love for Spain. For Spain above all, and then for the sake of the Crown, I order you to do exactly as I have told you.[11]

By early morning del Bosch had withdrawn and after protracted negotiations Tejero surrendered at midday on 24 February. Despite the ability of sections of the army to mount such an attempt the *coup* had failed and ten of the other military regions had refused to support it. The King's position as a constitutional, but powerful, monarch had been made abundantly clear. As Vilanova has argued, "on 23 February, some generals used the king's name to convince the undecided, the next time he will be the first target. The next coup will be against the king."[12] In the aftermath of the attempted *coup* the leaders of all political parties led a demonstration of a million people through the streets of Madrid in support of "liberty, democracy and the constitution."

It took nearly a year before 33 alleged conspirators (32 military and 1 civilian) were brought to trial for their participation in the attempt to seize the Cortes and overthrow the government. Prior to the trial, 100 officers and men from units in Madrid issued a manifesto opposing the Constitution, the alleged bias of the media against the military, and the professionalization of the armed services. Implicitly, the document provided support for those awaiting trial. In court General del Bosch and Lt.-Col. Tejero attempted to implicate the King in the *coup*, an accusation denied by General Armada. Del Bosch and Tejero were both sentenced to 30 years' imprisonment for military rebellion and Armada to 6 years for conspiracy to military rebellion.

No further military intervention has been as dramatic as that of 23 February 1981, although the ensuing period has been littered with regular acts of insubordination and allegations of plots. On 3 October 1982, less than a month before a general election which returned, as expected, a Socialist government (Spanish Socialist Workers Party, PSOE) three senior officers were detained in connection with an alleged plan to halt the election and impose a government dominated by the military. At the same time General del Bosch and Lt.-Col. Tejero were moved from prison in Madrid to more isolated parts of the country and a number of right-wing officers were moved to posts in areas less politically sensitive than the capital.

The period from 1978 to 1982 was one of great tension and change in Spain. An autocratic era had given way, however uncertainly, to one of democracy. Initially acquiescent to the new monarchy, the deeply conservative and insular Spanish military displayed increasing concern at the direction and pace of political development. Socially and physically isolated from much of Spanish society, they had failed to recognize the strength of industrial and economic change which had brought with it a revolution in the social and political attitudes of much of the population.

Organization

The death of Franco was an obvious watershed for Spanish society and its armed forces. Not only would it necessitate some change in political structure, but it enabled the Spanish people at large to recognize the profound social and economic changes which had already tranformed much of Spain into an increasingly modern, urban, and industrial society. However, as described above, the armed forces were ill prepared to accept the "inevitability" of change, or to come to terms with the new role expected of them in a democratic era. Their history, social structure, ideological persuasion, and apparent economic self-interest made them highly resistant to reform. Nevertheless, since 1975 successive Spanish governments have been committed to the modernization, professionalization, and depoliticization of the forces, although all have also recognized that change should be incremental and its pace modest.

The process of reform has taken a variety of routes. The privileged position of the Spanish forces under the Constitution has been removed, as has their jurisdiction over civilians in the judicial process. The retirement age for officers was lowered in 1981, which will both help to reduce the numbers of generals and more rapidly remove those most closely associated with the Franco era. Promotion is now to be on the basis of merit rather than seniority and, although political allegiance will not debar an officer from advancement, it has been noticeable that since 1975 and even more particularly in the wake of the 1981 *coup* attempt, key commands have tended to go to moderate officers who have shown themselves committed to democracy and the Constitution. The thorny problem of the size of the officer corps has been broached, although the full implementation of manpower reductions will not take place until 1990. If more radical pruning is devised, it may take even longer.

Reform has also taken place in the organizational structure of the Spanish defense forces. The separate ministries of army, navy, and air force were disbanded in 1977 and replaced by a triservice committee, and for the first time since the Civil War a united Ministry of Defense. Although the early Ministers remained generals, further reform in July 1980 made one important psychological change in requiring the Minister and his immediate subordinate to be civilians.[13]

In late 1983 the Socialist Minister of Defense, Sr. Narcis Serra, introduced a new bill containing fundamental reforms of the armed services. Political control was to be even more firmly established. Henceforth the armed forces were placed under the control of the Prime Minister, and the holder of the newly created post of Chief of the Defense Staff would be directly responsible to the Minister of Defense.[14] In future the role of the Chiefs of Staff was to be merely advisory. The legislation, which came into effect in January 1984, lays great emphasis on the authority held by the responsible civilian politicians and on the subordinate position of military commanders. With the final abolition of the legal and constitutional autonomy of the army, civilian supremacy has been achieved.

Concomitant with the move towards a professional officer corps and a modern and democratically accountable decision-making structure has been a recognition of the need to alter the fundamental role of the Spanish army. During the Franco era its role had been seen in terms of maintenance of internal order; hence the army's organization and deployment were tailored to fit this task and, in particular, units were concentrated near Madrid and in those regions where domestic disorder might be expected to occur. However, the new defense doctrine gives much greater priority to Spain's role in NATO (see below) and within the army to the defense of the Pyrenees and the southeastern flank. Consequently the territorial organization of the forces has been altered and continental Spain will now consist of six rather than nine military regions (plus the Canary Islands and the Balearic Islands).

The army is divided into two main segments, the Forces of Immediate Intervention (FII) and the Forces for the Operational Defense of the Territory (DOT). The numerical strength of the DOT is being reduced as part of the overall process of modernization. In future the principal units in the army order of battle will be as follows:

A. *The Forces for Immediate Intervention*
   (1) The First Brunete Armored Division (Madrid). One armored and one mechanized brigade.
   (2) The Second Mechanized Division, Guzman el Bueno (Seville). One mechanized and one motorized brigade.
   (3) The Third Motorized Division, Maestrazgo (Valencia). Two motorized brigades.
   (4) One cavalry brigade.
   (5) One parachute brigade.
   (6) One airportable brigade.
B. *Forces for the Operational Defense of the Territory*
   (1) Nine infantry brigades (being reduced, perhaps, to one)
   (2) Two mountain divisions. In future these will consist of two brigades.
   (3) One alpine brigade.
   (4) One artillery brigade.
   (5) Various regiments of anti-aircraft and coastal artillery.

There are two garrisons on the Canary Islands with one brigade each and one brigade in the Balearic Islands. Approximately 19,000 troops are stationed in the North African enclaves of Ceuta and Melilla.

The main focus of the administrative changes in the early 1980s has been the army. The navy and air force have fewer manpower structural problems and were reorganized on more modern lines in 1970 and 1977 respectively. Their primary concern is with the modernization of their equipment and their role within NATO, issues which are bedevilled by financial constraint and political uncertainty (see pp. 140–142).

The main elements of the Spanish fleet are as follows: eight submarines, one aircraft carrier, eleven destroyers, eleven frigates, four corvettes, and a large number of patrol craft. Although the fleet is comparatively large, it is very aged, with over half of the vessels more than 25 years old. Currently it is being augmented with more modern vessels (see p. 142).

The air force is divided into four groups. Air Combat Command (MACOM) has 24 Mirage III-E, 46 Mirage F-1, 35 Phantom F-4C, and 4 Phantom RF-4C. The Air Tactical Command (MATAC) has 19F-5A/B, 14 RF-5A, and 6 P-3A Orion. Air Transport Command (MATRA) has 11 C-130 Hercules, 30 HC-4 Caribou and 23 CASA 212. Air Command of the Canary Islands (MACAN) has 24 Mirage F-1 and 11 CASA 212.[15]

Spain and its Allies

The influence exerted by the armed forces on political life has been the dominant feature of modern Spanish military history. Whilst Franco lived, memories of the Civil War and of the Caudillo's addiction to Fascism created an environment in which Spain was unacceptable as a member of NATO, based as it is on the principles of democracy, individual liberty, and the rule of law. Ostracized as it was from the Atlantic Alliance, Spain found uneasy solace in its relations with Latin America, Portugal, and the United States. Whereas Spain's relationship with Latin America and Portugal was not of serious military or strategic significance, that with the United States provided the basis for the gradual but very tentative modernization of the Spanish armed forces.[16] The first bilateral defense treaty was signed in 1953 and was renewed in 1970, 1976, and 1982. Under the latest agreement, the Treaty of Friendship, Defense, and Mutual Cooperation, the United States retains the use of four air and naval bases and may station up to 12,500 military personnel in Spain. It may not, however, maintain nuclear weapons on Spanish soil. The USAF stations three tactical fighter squadrons at Torrejon near Madrid, an important tactical fighter training facility at Zaragoza, and a small base at Moron, which could be rapidly reinforced if necessary. At Rota, near Cadiz, a major naval and air base provides the primary supply and repair facilities for the US Sixth Fleet. In return Spain has received financial aid, training places for military personnel in the United States, and the provision of military equipment. Prior to Spain's accession to NATO in 1982 it also received the important psychological boost of the friendship of a superpower and some limited participation in US military exercises. Specifically the 1982 Treaty provides for: a grant to Spain of $400m a year for five years; the purchase of 72 F-18A Hornets; and further help in the naval rebuilding program. Significantly the primary beneficiaries of the American link have been the navy and air force, and until recently the army received little by way of modern equipment or the professional training of officers.

Spain became the sixteenth member of NATO and the first new entrant since the Federal Republic of Germany when it joined the Alliance in May 1982. After the years of enforced isolation membership of NATO (and potentially the European Economic Community) had become a policy option open to Spain after the death of Franco. Initially it was only the political right who advocated entry, but by the early 1980s they had been joined by the then dominant Union of the Democratic Center (UCD). Since the increasingly powerful Socialist Party had shown itself hostile to NATO, Sr. Calvo Sotelo, the UCD Prime Minister, hurried through Spain's application for membership prior to a general election in October 1982. Somewhat pre-empted by this maneuver the new Socialist administration of Snr. Felipe Gonzalez began to waver in its attitude to continued membership of NATO. A referendum on the issue was promised and by the time it took place on 12 March 1986 Sr. Gonzalez supported the status quo. To the surprise of most commentators the Spanish people supported their Prime Minister and by a vote of 52.5 percent to 40 percent chose to remain in the Alliance.

The impact of Spain's entry into NATO has been the subject of widespread controversy.[17] At the political level any newcomer provides a psychological boost, suggesting as it does that, whatever its difficulties, NATO membership is attractive to outsiders. For Spain the attraction is that membership confers some legitimacy, and helps bolster its newly created democratic political institutions. By contrast, however, if Spanish democracy were compromised by domestic military intervention, NATO would find itself severely embarrassed. Similarly, morale in NATO countries might well have been adversely affected if the Socialist government had withdrawn Spain from the

Alliance. Indeed any such action could have stimulated the much-feared process of unravelling, whereby successive governments limit their contribution or commitment to NATO. Almost inevitably the Soviet Union reacted to Spain's decision to join NATO with the accusation that the addition of new members proved that the Alliance is both expansionist and aggressive in intent. In strategic terms the Soviet Union declared that Spain imperilled Soviet interests in the Mediterranean.

At the military level, Spanish participation in NATO is clearly beneficial, although its importance should not be overestimated. The Spanish army has least to gain and least to offer from membership. Despite its considerable size and the recent program of reform and re-equipment, the army remains insufficiently modern to make any serious contribution to the military balance on the Central Front. Although some impact might be made to the ACE mobile force, and certainly a number of Spanish army officers see this as a future development, the primary role of the Spanish army is likely to remain the defense of its own territorial base.

The addition of the extensive landmass of Spain does provide NATO with some geographical depth and the potential for launching (American) reinforcements into the Central area in time of prolonged crisis. However, such a capacity was probably available under the pre-existing agreements between Spain and the United States. More important in terms of Spain's geostrategic positition are the maritime benefits accruing to the Alliance. Both countries of the Iberian Peninsula are now member states and together they dominate the Atlantic approaches to the Mediterranean, and, in consort with the United Kingdom, the crucial choke point of the Straits of Gibraltar. Further benefit is certainly derived from the strategic position of the Spanish Canary Islands and the role they play in maintaining trade routes and in providing a potential staging post for the United States reinforcement of Europe or more controversially in the context of a crisis in the Middle East. Nor should the Spanish navy itself be ignored. Although still in the process of modernization and certainly in need of enhanced funding, the navy does consist of eight submarines, one aircraft carrier, eleven destroyers, eleven frigates, and four corvettes. However modest these resources in global terms, they do provide a most useful enhancement to NATO's Mediterranean forces.

Almost inevitably the facts of military life are clouded by political uncertainties. Iberia may now be united in NATO but Portugal remains uneasy about the implications of Spanish entry and would certainly be resentful were this to lead to Spanish military domination of the region. In much the same way Spain has not yet resolved its historic dispute with Britain over the sovereignty of Gibraltar and there is no doubt that Britain was angered by Spanish support for Argentina during the Falklands conflict. Subsequently relations have improved and the border between Spain and Gibraltar was opened in February 1985.

These political difficulties together with Spain's ambivalent view about its own future membership have frozen the process of full integration into the NATO command structure. Since Spain is now to remain a member it will not only have to decide whether to join the integrated military structure but also to clarify its future relations with Portugal. A unified Iberian Command under Spain would antagonize Portugal, which is jealous of its position in the existing IBERLANT (Iberian Atlantic Command).

At present IBERLANT is part of the overall responsibility of SACLANT (Supreme Allied Commander Atlantic) in Norfolk, Virginia, whereas Spain is directly attached to SACEUR (Supreme Allied Commander Europe). In all probability new structures will have to be devised to take account of new relationships in the area.

Budget, Equipment, and Arms Industry

The treaties between the United States and Spain and more recently accession to NATO provided an important stimulus to the comprehensive and long-term plan to modernize the armed forces. Even more important, however, has been the perspective of successive governments in the post-Franco era. All have wished to develop smaller, more professional, and efficient forces provided with modern doctrine and equipment Although that process has been under way for some time (see "Organization"), it is inevitably hampered by financial restraint. Spain, with a population of 38 million, has suffered severely from inflation and unemployment (16 percent and 18 percent respectively in 1983). Thus, whereas the Spanish armed forces remain comparatively large, budgetary provision for them has always been both modest and heavily biased towards both manpower and the army.

However, as part of the process of modernization Spain committed itself in 1982 to spend 2.04 percent of GDP until 1990 on investment in military equipment, and during the period 1978–82 overall defense expenditure rose at an annual rate of 4.7 percent (in real terms) — one of the fastest in Europe.

Spain's relative industrial backwardness has also meant that it has not, as yet, been able to devote sufficient resources to research and

Table 5.1: The 1977 Spanish Defense Budget

	% of Total	% Personnel	% Operations	% Material
Army	55.3	70	10	20
Navy	22.6	44	15	41
Airforce	22.1	47	16	37

Source: Colonel Francisco L. de Sepulveda, "Restructuring Spain's Defense Organisation," *International Defense Review*, vol. 17, no. 10 (1984), p. 1435.

development and the acquisition of technology to create a sophisticated arms industry capable of satisfying its domestic needs. In similar manner to its new European partners, though to a greater degree, Spain has become dependent for equipment upon others, particularly the United States. In the 1970s some attempt was made to diversify supplies and a range of equipment was purchased from France.[18] But despite this development the government in Madrid remains seriously concerned by the problem of dependence and has said that in future foreign purchases and production under licence must be accompanied by offset agreements to purchase products from Spain or to transfer technological expertise to Spain.

Table 5.2: Spanish Defense Budget (Selected Years)

	$m	% Government Spending	% GNP
1972	860	13.0	1.8
1975	1,701	14.5	1.8
1978	3,208	15.0	2.2
1982	4,529	14.3	2.5

Source: *Military Balance* (International Institute for Strategic Studies, London, various years).

The Spanish arms industry employs some 56,000 people and is the twelfth largest in the world.[19] Exports amount to 30 percent of production and are particularly successful in Latin America. It has built the AMX-30 main battle tank under licence from France and is to build an armored car based on German Leopard technology. In conjunction with West Germany Spain has produced over 1,000 BMR-600 armored infantry vehicles. Five hundred of these, together with 300 trucks and 200 buses, have been sold to Egypt as part of a $1,000m deal, the largest in Spanish history. For domestic use Spain is to produce a new main battle tank based on either the German Leopard II or the French AMX-32, although it is expected to have major modifications of Spanish design.

Spanish aircraft production is fairly modest, but it has had success with the STOL (short take off and landing) C-212 Aviocor, of which over 300 have been sold as a general cargo and troop carrier. Great hopes are expected for a larger transport aircraft, the CN-235. Advanced jet trainers are also being built and 88 have been sold to the Spanish air force. The most important program is the assembly in Spain of the 72 F-18A Hornet aircraft purchased from McDonnell Douglas in the United States.

Naval shipbuilding takes place in various parts of Spain and production ranges from small aircraft carriers (such as the *Príncipe de Asturias*) to coastal ships. The Baleares class of missile frigate has been adopted from the American Knox class and smaller corvettes and coastal craft have been sold to Mexico, Argentina, and the Congo. Recently the Ministry of Defense has approved the construction of 5 FFG-7 anti-submarine guided missile frigates by 1991.

Nevertheless these are all fairly modest programs in comparison with advanced industrial nations.

Portugal

The Historical Background

Twentieth-century Portugal, like its neighbor Spain, experienced a long period of Fascist government, which culminated with the overthrow of Premier Marcello Caetano by *coup d'état* on 25 April 1974. Although the era of Portuguese dictatorship is less well known than that of Franco, it was of even greater longevity, having its origins in an earlier *coup* of 1926, which brought to an end 16 years of economic and political chaos. Unlike Spain, the man to head the new regime was not a soldier, but a dry and wholly unflamboyant economics professor, Dr António de Oliveira Salazar, who became Prime Minister and *de facto* Premier in 1928.[20]

Salazar constructed elaborate institutions of corporatism, but the power brokers in Portuguese society remained the church, the financial interests, and the army, all three being interlocked by strong family relationships. Salazar's contacts with the highly conservative Catholic church and with the economic elite were good; but with the military he was less at ease. He recognized the importance of their support and as an arch-traditionalist he could extol their virtues. However, he was also a retiring intellectual and, as such, had little in common with them. Indeed Mario Soares, an opponent of Salazar and later to become Prime Minister himself, believed that Salazar despised soldiers. Certainly he was temperamentally unable to develop those ties of affection and loyalty, as well as ideology, by which Franco bound the army to his regime.[21] Salazar was never the creature nor the figurehead of the military; it was he who offered them patronage: not the contrary.[22] For example, the largely titular role of President of the Republic was always held by an admiral or a general and, although formally elective, the winner was always the nominee of the National Union, an institution wholly controlled by Salazar.[23]

A positive indication of the uneasy pattern of civil–military relations in the Salazar and Caetano eras can be seen in the frequency of military revolts and attempted *coups*. These were common in nineteenth- and early twentieth-century Portugal and remained so after 1926 despite the apparent support of the armed forces for the corporate state. Between 1926 and 1974 there were at least a dozen unsuccessful military plots against the government.[24] Although many were hesitant, tentative affairs with little chance, or even intention, of overthrowing the regime, they became a common feature of military life. Government response was minimal, most plotters retained their rank and many their posts; few were imprisoned and none executed. Whereas in Spain such leniency can be attributed primarily to fear of the military, this seems less evident in Portugal. Insofar as military opposition to Salazar was political, it came mainly from those with liberal or left of centre viewpoints and, as such, it was always more than balanced by conservative officers. The first example of more broadly based criticism came in the wake of the loss of the Portugese colony on Goa. Goa, an indefensible enclave in India, was overrun in December 1961 after vigorous but limited military resistance. The hapless Portuguese commander, General Vassalo e Silva, returned to a public rebuke from Salazar, a professional humiliation for which many officers never forgave the Prime Minister.

More important, however, was the long-term socializing effect of the colonial wars in Africa, which began in Angola in 1961. These were to sap both the Portuguese economy and the will of the military to prosecute a guerrilla war which seemed beyond their power and, for some, their will to win.

The Social Structure and Attitudes of the Military

During most of his period of office Salazar pursued staunchly conservative monetarist economic policies. However, by the 1960s he and his successor, Caetano, allowed more rapid economic growth, stimulated by foreign investment and the onset of the wars in Africa. As a result, and in further response to international influences, the 1970s saw a rapid rise in inflation. At the same time greater urbanization and some promise of modest political reform under Caetano created the environment for the growth of more radical political and social ideas, especially amongst Portuguese youth.

However, none of this would have been sufficient to provoke revolution had not corresponding changes been taking place within the armed forces, particularly the army. Although the Portuguese officer corps exhibited some limited political heterogeneity, prior to 1958 it was almost exclusively drawn from a restricted social and economic elite, or from those whose loyalty to Salazar was personal. Links between civil and military life were reinforced, since many officers retained civilian employment during their military careers.[25] Thus it was common for officers in technical corps to carry out consultancy work, sometimes for the army itself, even when on operational tours of duty in Africa. In the higher ranks some officers sat on the boards of companies and took extensive leave from their military careers to work in industry or commerce. Given the relative social exclusiveness of army officers and the conservatism of Portugal, it is probably not surprising that black soldiers were ineligible for commissioned rank. Furthermore officers were required to marry in church and their prospective wives had to provide a dowry or possess a university degree.

However, social and economic change began to limit the number of officer candidates and in 1958 Salazar abolished tuition fees at the Military Academy and provided the cadets with a salary. Inevitably the officer corps became less exclusive. The onset of the African wars brought further, complex changes. For some officers, though probably few private soldiers, the war had a radicalizing effect. The syllabus at the Military Academy began to include works on revolutionary and guerrilla warfare and experience, for the first time, of conditions in the colonies raised in some minds the legitimacy of war itself. At the same time a number of domestic and professional grievances began to emerge which were to have their impact on a much wider group of soldiers. Service in the colonies was arduous and, especially for regular officers in both the army and air force, exceedingly lengthy, as they tended to be cross-posted from Mozambique to Angola and to

Guinea-Bissau. It also became policy to retain whole units in one locality, so as to build up their detailed knowledge of the region. As the war became ever more protracted, and its final outcome uncertain, the strain on family life became intense. Nor was the morale of junior officers aided by the more comfortable lifestyle of staff officers, secure in regional or national headquarters. Inevitably the colonial conflict also demanded a much larger army and, despite the earlier reforms, the Military Academy was unable to provide sufficient officers.[26] Consequently large numbers of university students were conscripted and commissioned. In order to attract them to a long-term career, Decree Law 353 of 1973 allowed them to convert to regular commissions. The Act enabled such officers to retain their conscript rank and exempted them from the four-year training period for regular officers. Not unnaturally, the regular officers who had pursued a conventional career regarded this as a further erosion of their professional status. Meetings were called and protests sent to the government. When rebuffed by Caetano, dissent became more widespread. The narrowly based professional complaints also became more overtly political and began to attract not only those who had long opposed the regime but also others who had been radicalized by the wars in Portuguese Guinea, Angola, and Mozambique. This signalled the birth of the "Captains' Movement," later known as the Movimento das Forças Armadas (MFA).[27]

At the same time the stability of the government was eroded by the disaffection of more conservative figures. In December 1973 the extreme right wing, under former Commander-in-Chief of Mozambique, General Kaulza de Arriaga, planned a *coup*, and such was the ideological confusion of the early MFA that it was thought he might receive their support. More important opposition came from the conservative, but individualist, Deputy Chief of Staff, General António de Spínola, whose book *Portugal and the Future* attacked traditional colonial policy. The impact of the book was considerable. Caetano wrote, "when I closed the book I had understood that the military coup which I could sense had been coming was now inevitable."[28]

In a last effort to forestall military intervention, Caetano ordered senior officers to attend a ceremony at the Presidential Palace to endorse overseas policy. The Chief of Staff, General Costa Gomes, and his deputy, General Spínola, refused to attend. Six weeks later, with Spínola as its figurehead, the MFA overthrew the Caetano government in a peaceful *coup d'état*, popularly known as the Revolution of Carnations.

Civil–Military Relations

The *coup* of 25 April 1974 was bloodless, popular, and largely unexpected. From the outset the new government was headed by the reassuring and conservative figure of General Spínola, who became President. Nor was the initial program of the MFA particularly radical. It promised the removal of the more repressive institutions and personnel of the previous regime; it guaranteed the creation of wide-ranging civil liberties, including freedom of speech, association, and the press; it promised a more equitable distribution of the wealth of the society; and the election, within twelve months, by universal suffrage, of a Constituent Assembly. On external matters the program committed Portugal to previously negotiated international treaties and to the peaceful solution of the overseas wars. In the manner which now seems obligatory for military governments, the MFA promised to return to barracks after the election of the Assembly. The document did not mention Socialism and did not promise sovereign independence to the colonies.[29]

Nevertheless the program ushered in 18 months of intense, and at times revolutionary, political activity, during which time the MFA splintered into a variety of factions, each expressing a different philosophy. Political views differed amongst individuals, from unit to unit, and between the three services; the air force being regarded as the most conservative, the navy the most radical. Despite Spínola's seniority he had little authority or influence. Within three months he was defeated by those who wished to grant full independence to the colonies; and in July he was forced to accept Colonel Vasco Gonzales, a long-time radical and allegedly a Communist sympathiser, as Prime Minister. In September 1974 Spínola resigned, having failed to rally support from the population at large.

Two main questions dominated the MFA during the next year: what role would the armed forces have in the future development of Portuguese society and what ideological framework was the most appropriate for that development? Despite the MFA promise to return to their traditional role of defense against external attack, many officers believed that without military participation the impact of 25 April might be diminished or even reversed. This view was given greater substance in March 1975 when conservative supporters of Spínola mounted an abortive counter-*coup*. In the wake of this event MFA set up a Supreme Revolutionary Council (later restyled the Council of the Revolution, CR) with the objective of institutionalizing a military presence in political life. In early April 1975 the CR forced the political parties to sign a pact which guaranteed both military control of the presidency and ultimate military control, via a veto, of the legislative process. As an indication of their developing radicalism, the CR required any new constitution to be based on socialism.

Although the MFA had moved decisively to strengthen its position, elections to a Constituent Assembly took place, as planned, on 25 April 1975. Described by an MFA spokesman as "a pedagogic exercise," the elections resulted in an enormous popular mandate for the moderate Socialist Party and the centrist Popular Democratic Party. Despite its influence with the Gonzales faction in the MFA, the Portuguese Communist Party (PCP) fared badly at the polls.[30] In the months before and after the election the divisions in the MFA became ever more apparent, although the exact ideological positions of the protagonists were at times blurred in the frenzy of rhetoric and action. Four principal groupings emerged. Prime Minister Gonzales, with the support of Dr Alvaro Cunhal and the PCP, advocated an East-European-style state centralist approach to politics. With the help of the Fifth Division of the General Staff, who dominated the media, he attempted to radicalize the traditional northern peasantry through a program known as "Cultural Dynamization." A second faction led by Major Melo Antunes was closer to the Socialist Party. Their policies veered between those of West European Social Democratic parties and Third World non-aligned states. Even more heterogeneous were the views of the far left, which within the military came to be associated with COPCON (Operational Command of the Continent). COPCON, formed after 25 April, saw itself as the vanguard of the revolutionary process, and from its inception to its dissolution, in November 1975, played an ever-increasing role in political life. It was led by Brigadier Otelo Saraiva de Carvalho, a flamboyant extrovert figure who, as a major, had planned the original *coup*. His personal politics moved steadily leftward, but in the period of his greatest influence he was the proponent of a Cuban solution for Portugal. Finally there were those, known later as the "operationals," who viewed with alarm the increasing military experimentation and participation in active politics.

Throughout 1975 the authority of successive governments was in the process of disintegration and by the autumn the current administration was neither in control of the country nor the armed forces. In the north of Portugal the activities of the Fifth Division and the Communist Party antagonized the deeply conservative peasantry, resulting in numerous arson attacks on Communist Party offices. Within the armed forces the "operationals" decided that the time had come to end the near anarchy and to reassert more traditional military values.

The "operationals" main complaint, beyond their general concern at the chaos in society at large, was the growing indiscipline in the Portuguese armed forces. Fed with the rhetoric of revolution, and with the unusual experience of active and daily participation in political events, the conventional military command structure broke down. Indiscipline was rife and minor mutinies not unknown. Exercising their new-found "rights" some soldiers formed SUV (United Soldiers Will Win), an organization dedicated to the maintenance of the revolution. In an environment where, on some occasions, an officer's command became the basis for democratic discussion, the "operationals" felt that continued political activity, on a scale existing at that time, was incompatible with the survival of the armed forces as a structured, disciplined, and credible entity. On 25 November 1975, in circumstances never adequately explained, they outmaneuvered left-wing units in Lisbon and took full control. COPCON was soon disbanded, Carvalho demoted, and other radical officers eased out of positions of influence. General Ramallio Eanes became Army Chief of Staff, and in June 1976 was elected President, easily defeating left-wing opponents. Since late 1975 the direct role of the armed forces in politics has been progressively reduced, although for some time their formal position remained important. In February 1976 a new pact was signed between the MFA and the political parties. The CR retained its power to veto legislation (on constitutional grounds) but confirmed the return to civilian rule. In August 1976 Eanes announced that membership of the CR was not in future compatible with holding a regional command. Henceforth officers had to decide whether to pursue a political or a military career. During the following six years the residual powers of the CR chaired by President Eanes, were exercised in a manner which caused frequent conflict with elected governments. On a few occasions between 1980 and 1982 the CR vetoed legislation to denationalize banks and insurance companies. Nevertheless the momentum towards depoliticized armed forces continued. In March 1981 the role of President was separated from that of Chief of Staff of the armed forces; and in July 1982 constitutional reform abolished the Council of the Revolution. Finally in November 1982 the Assembly passed the National Defense Law, which stressed that the role of the armed forces was to defend Portugal against external aggressors and that in future senior military appointments were to be in the gift of the Minister of Defense, not the President.[31]

Presidential elections took place in Portugal on 16 February 1986 in which General Eanes was debarred from running for a third term in office. He was succeeded by the veteran Socialist and former Prime Minister, Mario Soares, who became the first civilian President and Head of State since 1926.

Inevitably not all soldiers relish the return to barracks and the abrogation of a political role. A "25 April Association" exists to propagate the values of the revolution and is claimed to have a membership of over 2,000 officers, spread between the three services.[32] A separate, shadowy, and wholly unconstitutional organization, the Popular Forces of April 25 (FP25) has claimed responsibility for a dozen murders and other terrorist activities.

Organization and Manpower

Since April 1974 the size of the Portuguese forces has shrunk from over 200,000 to a total of 63,500 in 1985. At the same time, the role of the largest service, the army, has altered fundamentally. In 1974 the vast majority of the army was fighting a seemingly endless counterinsurgency war in Africa, a role which ended abruptly with independence in Mozambique in 1974 and Angola in 1975. Today a much smaller army has as its role the defense of metropolitan Portugal and the provision of a modest contingency reserve for NATO. Inevitably changes of this magnitude produced serious structural problems and imbalances which are exacerbated by Portugal's parlous economic position.

In 1975 the six Portuguese metropolitan military regions were abolished and replaced by three: North, South, and Central, each commanded by a senior MFA officer. In turn, these have been regrouped into four military regions having their headquarters in Coimbra, Oporto, Evora, and Lisbon. There are also two island commands in the Azores and Madeira. The principal concern of the army today is the modernization of its equipment, which became obsolescent during the guerilla wars in Africa.

After 1975 regiments were renamed after their local recruitment catchment area, thus formalizing a pattern of regional recruitment which had long existed. During the heady days of 1974–76 the geographic origins of a unit were often as important as the political affiliations of its officers. For instance, regiments in the north tended to be conservative, in keeping with political attitudes in that area.

The rapid decline in the total manpower of the army has not been fully matched by a decline in the number of officers. In 1980 an army of under 40,000 still retained 3,000 captains and majors (many impatient for promotion), 800 Lieutenant-colonels and 60 generals. Conscription remains, although the period of service for the army was reduced from 24 months in 1974 to 16 months a decade later. Conscripts can become junior NCOs but more senior non-commissioned ranks are dominated by volunteers. Officers are trained at the Military Academy in Lisbon and are recruited in three main ways. Most come direct from high school, but some are former NCOs or conscripts who have passed the conscript officer course and remain eligible to transfer to regular commissions.

The army has a strength of 39,000 (1985) of whom 30,000 are conscripts. The principal fighting unit is a 4,500-man NATO brigade also known as the First Composite Brigade. Initially formed in 1976, its creation was seen as a major organizational step in the process of modernizing and depoliticizing the army. Technically it forms part of the reserve of AFSOUTH designated for possible use in the northeast of Italy.

Apart from the NATO brigade, the Portuguese army has the task of the territorial defense of Portugal, the Azores, and Madeira. Despite economic restrictions the long-term intention is to raise the level of the whole army to that of the First Composite Brigade and specifically to create a similar brigade in each of the three military regions together with a Special Forces Brigade and supporting arms such as army aviation (see "Budget, Equipment, and Arms Industry").

The Portuguese navy and air force are both small and much in need of modern equipment. The navy has 12,500 men, including 3,200 conscripts who serve for 24 months. In addition there is a marine contingent of 2,500. The Portuguese fleet has 3 Daphne class submarines, 17 frigates, 4 minesweepers, and a variety of patrol craft. The air force has 9,500 men, a figure which includes a parachute group of 1,800 and some 3,500 conscripts. Its aircraft include three fighter/ground attack squadrons whose primary aircraft are 40 elderly Fiat G-91 and 20 A-7P, a small recce squadron with 4 C-212B, and two transport squadrons with 5 C-130 Hercules and 12 C-212.[33]

Portugal and its Allies

Portugal's oldest ally, dating from a treaty of 1373, is the United Kingdom. Today, however, its most important military relationships are with the United States and as a member of NATO.

Portugal, unlike Spain, was invited to join NATO when it was formed in 1949. However, its economic and political isolation from the rest of Europe during most of the Salazar years, together with a preference for stronger ties with its overseas colonies, meant that its contribution to the Alliance had some strategic and symbolic importance but little direct military impact.[34] More important were its bilateral relations with the United States and in particular the agreement to allow American use of the strategically important Lajes base, in the Azores, 950 miles into the Atlantic. British and American use of the naval and air facilities at Lajes had first been agreed in 1943 and renegotiated in 1962, three times in the 1970s, and most recently in 1983. The latest agreement allows United States use of Lajes for seven years until 1991 in return for a package of military and economic aid. In the 1984 fiscal year Portugal was to receive $90m of military aid and grants followed by $105m in 1985 and further sums in succeeding years, primarily for the modernization of the armed forces.[35] The naval facilities at Lajes are used to monitor Soviet maritime and in particular submarine movements in the Atlantic and to give logistic support to the US Sixth Fleet. The air base provides a valuable and convenient refuelling stop for American aircraft en route to Europe. It was used for this purpose during the US airlift of military supplies to Israel during the 1973 Yom Kippur War when similar facilities were denied in Spain. In March 1984 Portugal agreed to allow the United States to construct a satellite tracking station in southern mainland Portugal. However, in a similar manner to Spain, Portugal has prohibited the installation of nuclear weapons on its territory.

In the early years after 1974 Portugal's membership of NATO came under severe strain. For a brief period in 1975 it was by no means clear whether the left-wing government of Vasco Gonzales would wish to remain in NATO or whether its ideology was compatible with that of the Alliance. In particular, the United States was deeply concerned at the degree of Soviet influence in Lisbon. Perhaps wisely, Portugal temporarily absented itself from those NATO committees where highly classified material was discussed.[36] With the reversion to more moderate governments Portugal gradually returned to full participation in NATO affairs rejoining the Nuclear Planning Group in 1980 and in the same year taking part in NATO exercises for the first time since 1974.

Excluding the Azores, Portugal's main contribution to NATO lies, not in the strength of its armed forces, but in its geostrategic position on the western tip of Europe, astride the important Atlantic approaches to the continent and the Mediterranean. The Deputy Prime Minister and Defense Minister (1983–85) Sr. Carlos da Mota Pinto has described Portugal as an area of "geostrategic sensitivity" and a potential international "shockpoint." Spokesmen in Lisbon regularly stress the importance of the Portuguese strategic triangle, formed by the Azores, Madeira, and metropolitan Portugal itself. This is seen as a unique strategic region, unaffected by Spain's entry into NATO. The main military role of Portugal in NATO, through the IBERLANT command, is to counter enemy maritime penetration of the area, to help keep open the narrow straits of Gibraltar and to provide protection of that area during rapid reinforcement, in times of increasing tension or open warfare. It seems doubtful, however, whether the Portuguese navy can make a major contribution in this role until the process of modernization has proceeded further.

In September 1982, a Portuguese naval officer, Vice Admiral Ilidio da Costa Pon, became the first Commander-in-Chief of IBERLANT. Although he is still subordinate to SACLANT, the creation of the post is regarded as establishing the importance and enhanced status of the region.[37] As yet, the Commander-in-Chief, IBERLANT, has no permanently assigned combat forces under his direct operational control. The command plans and conducts exercises in preparation for upgrading in time of war. IBERLANT's area of responsibility is from the north of Portugal to the Tropic of Cancer in the south, and eastwards to the Spanish border. Unusually for a maritime command, it includes the landmass of Portugal itself. It also incorporates within its area the Spanish Canary Islands, thus re-emphasizing the uncertain relationship between the Iberian neighbors and the unresolved issue of future NATO command structures in the region (see "Spain and its Allies").

Budget, Equipment, and Arms Industry

The constant warfare experienced by Portugal in its African colonies between 1961 and 1974 resulted in an enormous increase in the size of its armed forces and in the defense budget. During this era the primary role of the forces was that of counter-insurgency and their equipment and organization reflected this emphasis. Today there is an urgent need to complete the process of reorganization and even more importantly to re-equip the three services with modern, advanced weapons and communication systems. But, as is regularly asserted, the domestic economy is too weak to carry out this task without significant aid from Portugal's allies. Table 5.3 shows how the percentage of GNP committed to defense has been reduced since 1975.

Although Portugal recognizes that such modest expenditure is insufficient to acquire the resources necessary to perform its mission

Table 5.3: Portuguese Defense Budget (Selected Years)

	$m	% Government	% GNP
1975	1,088	35.2	6.0
1980	868	9.2	3.5
1982	803	8.9	n.a.
1983	713	8.9	3.5

Sources: *The Military Balance, 1981-1982* (International Institute for Strategic Studies, London, 1981); *The Military Balance, 1985-1986* (International Institute for Strategic Studies, London, 1985).

in NATO, the Lisbon government is unwilling to accept a role limited to the provision of bases and facilities in an area of acknowledged geostrategic importance. The equipment modernization program is dependent on further aid from the United States and other allies such as West Germany and the United Kingdom.

Within the army, the NATO brigade is now operational and most of its equipment is up to date. However, modernization of one element of the army has drawn scarce resources from the remainder. As the Chief of Staff of the Portuguese army, General A. Garcia dos Santos, has remarked:

> the majority of other units continue to be under-equipped for the completion of their missions or the adequate training of their personnel. The existence of the Brigade, which initially functioned as a stimulus, thus becomes a contradiction in as much as it accentuates the need to re-equip the entire Army.[38]

Similar problems exist for the air force and navy. By 1975 the air force was large, obsolete, and unprepared for European warfare. Despite some modernization the major role of air defense is still performed by elderly aircraft (Fiat G-91 and A-7P) from attack squadrons. There is urgent need for interceptor aircraft, surface-to-air missiles, and an adequate short-range air defense system, as well as more comprehensive communications facilities.

The Portuguese maritime tradition can be traced to the development of trade and a colonial empire in the fifteenth century and its legacy is still felt keenly in Lisbon. In the period after 1974 the navy suffered almost as great an upheaval as the army and is only now recovering. There remains an acute shortage of modern vessels, although a program exists to recreate an anti-submarine warfare capacity and to provide a more sophisticated minehunter and a minesweeper capability.

Portugal's defense industries reflect the modest size of its forces and the weakness and lack of sophistication of its economy. Although some increase in arms manufacture took place during the 1960s and 1970s, most production was of light arms appropriate for a guerrilla war. These industries are in the process of contraction despite some diversification towards the export market. Clearly Portugal is quite unable to compete with more affluent countries in this sphere and, given increasing technologies and ever-more expensive R and D, may fall further behind.

Conclusion

An any analysis of the defense forces and policies of Spain and Portugal it is tempting to conclude by drawing a range of comparisons between the two countries. Certainly a number of parallel themes emerge. Both have new democratic governments which have had to cope with armies prone to intervene in domestic affairs. Both have armed forces which are being modernized in an attempt to cope with the imperatives of defense within the framework of NATO. Neither country has the economic resources to fulfill this task without considerable financial and training aid from its Alliance partners. Even if forthcoming, each presumes that aid to the one might diminish aid to the other. Both Spain and Portugal emphasize the geostrategic importance of their mainland and island territories and the significance of the maritime regions with which they are linked. But these important, yet at times superficial, similarities obscure significant differences both within and between the neighboring states.

In the aftermath of the referendum Spain's future in NATO now seems more certain. However, important decisions remain. Will Spain join the integrated military structure and what arrangements will be made for the organization and command systems for the Iberian Peninsula, the Mediterranean and the Atlantic approaches to the southern part of Europe? Although both Spain and Portugal emphasize their geostrategic importance, Portugal is extremely wary of any "Iberian" solution which might imply Spanish domination of the region. It may be that an uneasy compromise will have to be maintained where the Spanish maritime effort is concentrated in the Straits of Gibraltar and west into the Mediterranean, whereas Portugal will look east into the Atlantic. The decision of Spain to remain in NATO means that it will certainly remain within the Western sphere of influence. This is important in both a military and political context. In simple military terms the Spanish armed forces are a useful, if marginal, addition to NATO's order of battle. Politically, Spain was and is an important addition to NATO, and accession has undoubtedly helped underpin Spanish democracy. Membership of NATO helps reduce the isolationist tendencies within Spain and in particular creates a focus of attention for the army, apart from any role in internal security and domestic politics. The Socialist government, once so emphatic in its desire to leave NATO, is now more supportive, believing that the modernization and democratization of the armed forces can only proceed safely within an Alliance framework.

By contrast, Portuguese commitment to NATO is longer standing and more profound than that of Spain, despite the uncertainties of 1974–76. As one of the poorer and smaller members of NATO, it seems unlikely that Portugal could ever sustain technologically advanced forces of sufficient size to add very much to the military strength of the Alliance. Nevertheless, the modernization of the air force and navy, and the creation of the NATO brigade, can, quite legitmately, be seen as an important sign of Portugal's intent to play as full a role as possible in NATO. In so doing the Portuguese armed forces can reaffirm that henceforth their role lies in the defense of the state from external aggression rather than in participation in internal politics.

Spain and Portugal are both allies and competitors, a relationship with which NATO must soon grapple. Whatever their strategic significance to the Alliance, and it is considerable, NATO will wish to maintain their membership as a sign of the political unity of the Western democracies.

Notes

1. The classic analysis of the relationship between a state's level of political culture and the propensity of the armed forces to intervene is S. E. Finer, *The Man on Horseback* (Pall Mall Press, London, 1962).
2. Juan Pablo Fusi, "Spain: The Fragile Democracy," *Journal of West European Politics,* vol. 5, no. 3 (July 1982), p. 234.
3. See (i) Stanley G. Payne, *Politics and the Military in Modern Spain* (Oxford University Press, Oxford, 1967); (ii) Adrian Schubert, "The Military Threat to Spanish Democracy," *Armed Forces and Society,* vol. 10, no. 4 (Summer 1984), pp. 529–542.
4. See Hugh Thomas, *The Spanish Civil War* (Penguin Books, Harmondsworth, 1965).
5. Schubert, "The Military Threat," p. 533. See also Charles Esdaile, "The Spanish Army 1939–1983," *Military History* (November 1983), p. 511. Esdaile cites 40 of 114

ministers as drawn from the military.

6. Colonel Francisco L. de Sepulveda, "Restructuring Spain's Defense Organisation," *International Defense Review*, vol. 17, no. 10 (1984), pp. 1431–1437.

7. Ibid., p. 1436.

8. Schubert, "The Military Threat," p. 536.

9. Kenneth Medhurst, "The Military and the Prospects for Spanish Democracy," *West European Politics*, vol. 1, no. 1 (1978), pp. 53–55.

10. Pedro Vilanova, "Spain: The Army and the Transition" in David S. Bell (ed.), *Democratic Politics in Spain* (Francis Pinter, London, 1983), p. 158. After widespread protests the sentences were later reviewed and each man was detained for two months and one day.

11. Telegram sent on the night of 23–24 February 1981. Text issued in Madrid on 18 March 1981.

12. Vilanova, "Spain: the Army and the Transition," p. 161. Vilanova alleges that the King estimated that 80 percent of the officers believed the rebels to be "patriots and men of honour." It was merely their timing and methods which were at fault.

13. In practice the change to civilian control had taken place a year earlier when Sr. Suaraz appointed a civilian, Sr. Sahagun, as Defense Minister. However, General Mellado retained overall responsibility for coordinating security and national defense.

14. The constitutional position of the King as Supreme Commander and Captain-General of the armed forces was not altered.

15. (i) Christian Muller, "Spain as a NATO Member Nation," *Armada International* (May-June 1983), pp. 84–93; (ii) de Sepulveda, "Restructuring Spain's Defense Organisation," p. 1434; (iii) Lieutenant General Ramon De Ascanioy Togores, "The Spanish Army: Modernisation and Transformation," *NATO's Sixteen Nations*, vol. 28, no. 5 (Special No. 1, 1983), pp. 77–81; (iv) Lieutenant General José Santos Peralba, "The Spanish Air Force in the 1980s and Beyond," *NATO's Sixteen Nations*, vol. 29, no. 4 (Special No. 2, 1984), pp. 74–78.

16. Spain signed the Iberian Pact with Portugal in 1939 and this was renewed in November 1977 as the Treaty of Friendship and Cooperation. It will last for ten years.

17. For the most succinct yet persuasive analysis see Colonel Jonathan Alford, "Spain and NATO," *International Defense Review*, no. 4 (1982), pp. 385–386.

18. Eight submarines, 30 Mirage III, 72 Mirage F-1 and approximately 25 helicopters, together with 300 AMX-30 tanks (very largely manufactured in Spain), 140 Panhard armored cars and the Roland surface-to-air missile system.

19. See Julio Leal, "The Spanish Defense Industry," *Nato's Sixteen Nations* vol. 28, no. 6 (Special No. 2, 1983), pp. 58–69; Robert A. C. Richards, "Spain and NATO, its Effects on the Spanish Defense Industry," *Defense* (April 1982), pp. 166–172.

20. Salazar formally took the office of Prime Minister in 1932.

21. Mario Soares, *Portugal's Struggle for Liberty* (Allen and Unwin, London, 1975), p. 114.

22. For a different view see Neil Bruce, *Portugal: The Last Empire* (David and Charles, Newton Abbot, Devon, 1975).

23. Between 1974 to 1986 all post-*coup* presidents were military figures. This altered in March 1986 with the election of Mario Soares as President to succeed General Eanes. The Portuguese Constitution prevented Eanes from running for a third term in office.

24. Many opposition figures during the Salazar era were military men. General Delgado ran for the presidency in 1958 and captured 25 percent of the vote in what were widely assumed to have been rigged elections. He was murdered in Spain in 1965, allegedly by agents of the Portuguese secret police, PIDE. Another dissident, Captain Galvão, received worldwide attention in 1961 when he captured the Portuguese cruise liner, *Santa Maria*. See Phillipe C. Schmitter, "Liberation by Golpe: Retrospective Thoughts on the Demise of Authoritarian Rule in Portugal," *Armed Forces and Society*, no. 2 (Fall 1975), pp. 5–33.

25. For instance, General António de Spínola, the first President in the post-coup period, was chief administrator of a steel company from 1955 to 1964.

26. Admissions to the Military Academy had fallen dramatically. In 1961–62 there were 257, but in 1971–72 only 72. At the time of the *coup* over 400 places were unfilled. Robin Blackburn, "The Test in Portugal," *New Left Review*, nos. 87–88 (September-December 1974), p. 11.

27. See John L. Hammond, "The Armed Forces Movement and the Portuguese Revolution: Two Steps Forward, One Step Back," *Journal of Political and Military Sociology*, no. 10 (Spring 1982), pp. 71–161; *Insight on Portugal, The Year of the Captains* (André Deutsch, London, 1975).

28. *Insight on Portugal*, p. 42.

29. The program is quoted in full in *Keesings Contemporary Archives*, 26 August-1 September 1974, pp. 26688-26689.

30. Socialist Party 38 percent, Popular Democratic Party 26 percent, Communist Party 12.5 percent.

31. This last provision has not been fully implemented. In practice the government and President have agreed to cooperate on the appointment and dismissal of senior officers.

32. "Down Freedom Way," *The Economist*, 30 June 1984, p. 7.

33. *The Military Balance, 1984–1985* (International Institute for Strategic Studies, London, 1984).

34. Between 1953 and 1961 Portugal trained and equipped a division, held as a reserve for Allied Forces Central Europe. This was only activated for exercise purposes for one month a year and by 1963 was largely defunct as Portugal became enmeshed in the African wars.

35. The US is to provide a total of $1.3 billion in credits over the seven years.

36. Lieutenant Commander James John Tritten, US Navy, "The Portugal Revolution," *Military Review* (August 1979), pp. 57–67.

37. Rear Admiral Louis A. Williams, US Navy, "The Atlantic Connection — IBERLANT," *NATO's Sixteen Nations*, vol. 28, no. 6 (Special No. 2, 1983), pp. 31–38.

38. General A. Garcia Dos Santos, "A New Army for Portugal," *NATO's Sixteen Nations*, vol. 16, no. 5 (Special No. 1, 1983), p. 73.

6 THE ITALIAN ARMED FORCES

Vittorfranco S. Pisano

When Italy emerged from World War II, its armed forces were in a parlous state. Defeat had inflicted serious material and psychological losses on the country; defeat had also seriously shaken the prestige of the armed forces. These blows were all the more serious, given the cleavage that had traditionally existed between the armed forces and the rest of Italian society. Ever since Italy had become a sovereign state in 1861, the military had insisted on non-interference in, and aloofness from, politics in particular and society in general. To a large degree, the armed forces have remained a closed society, if not a caste.

The Armed Forces and Society

The armed forces have always remained aloof from Italian society. Nevertheless, they have been consistently loyal to the state — regardless of its form of government or political philosophy; hence soldiers and sailors have served without apparent restlessness or ideological malaise under the monarchy, the Fascist regime, and finally the Republic.[1] Because of their apolitical posture coupled with their commitment to national institutions, the armed forces were repeatedly used to quell rebellions and restore order during civil disturbances, another factor that did not contribute to positive interaction between the military and society.

Moreover, the proverbial low priority given by the civil authorities to military policies capable of improving the institutional efficiency of the armed forces has been responsible for the perpetuation of bureaucratic and caste-oriented military structures developed by the military establishment itself.[2]

The fall of Fascism and the proclamation of the Republic gave way to the drafting of a new Italian Constitution aimed at the democratization of the various sectors of Italian society, including the armed forces,[3] and the repudiation of war as an instrument of foreign policy.[4]

According to the Republican Constitution of 1948, "Italy rejects war as an instrument of aggression against the liberties of other peoples and as a means of settling international disputes."[5] It further states: "Defense of the country is a sacred duty of every citizen. Military service is compulsory within the limits and the manner laid down by law . . . The organization of the Armed Forces is based on the democratic principles of the Republic."[6] Still according to the Constitution, "Limitations to the right of registering as members of political parties may be laid down by law for . . . career [regular] members of the Armed Forces while in service."[7]

The manifest purpose of these constitutional provisions is the amalgamation of the armed forces into Italian society, the prevention of aggressive militarism, and the foreclosure of any anti-democratic developments within the military establishment. At the same time, the Constitution appears to attribute limited importance to the military contribution as reflected by the exclusion of the military from honorary — as opposed to elective — membership in the Senate of the Republic. In fact, in the language of the Constitution, "the President of the Republic may appoint as Senators for life five citizens who have brought honor to the country through their exceptional merits in social, scientific, artistic, and literary fields."[8] Military merits are clearly not taken into account in that context.

In 1978, a law titled "Basic Provisions on Military Discipline" ("Norme di Principio sulla Disciplina Militare") was passed.[9] Ostensibly, its principal purpose is to afford, in accordance with the spirit of the Constitution, elective representation to the various categories of military personnel, including regular servicemen and conscripts. The new law has provided a structure through which the servicemen can voice aspirations and concerns and formulate proposals and recommendations pertinent to their military status, as opposed — naturally enough — to the institutional/operational aspects of the armed forces.[10]

But several other matters fall under the purview of this law. It specifically calls for military assistance during public calamities.[11] It sanctions the refusal to obey unlawful orders.[12] The law facilitates individual participation in social and other organizations (restrictions include prohibition of wearing military uniform and using military premises in connection therewith).[13] It renders the imposition of disciplinary measures at the unit level (adminstrative punishment) more difficult and it has even provided for the remission of such measures until 30 November 1977.[14]

To be sure, while in some ways the passage of this legislation is in keeping with the less rigorous spirit of current times, the motivation behind it was not only socio-functional, but political as well. The Basic

Provisions on Military Discipline constitute one of the many compromises peculiar to Italy's intrinsically discordant multi-party coalitions in Parliament and government.[15]

Although compulsory military service generally continues to be regarded *a priori* as a burden without reward and the armed forces are tendentially viewed as anachronistic or unnecessary on account of Italian peaceful intentions or because of the existence of an incorrectly perceived Western protective umbrella, the relationship between the military and society appears, on the whole, to be improving. In addition to the developments outlined above, contributory factors include the fact that career personnel are increasingly representative of a broad cross-section of Italian society, and a number of technical skills, with non-military applicability, can now be acquired in the armed forces by conscripts and short-term volunteers.

Domestic as well as international developments over recent years have moreover afforded the Italian armed forces a degree of visibility without precedent since the dramatic conclusion of World War II. Relief missions are performed by military units within Italy at times of natural catastrophe. International developments encompass Italian military participation in multination peace-keeping forces, as part of treaties with other nations and/or resolutions of the United Nations.

In fact, Italian contingents have taken part in the United Nations Interim Forces in Lebanon (UNIFIL) since 26 July 1979; in the multinational peacekeeping forces in Lebanon from 26 August to 12 September 1982, and from 26 September 1982 to 26 February 1984; in the Multinational Force and Observers (MFO) — whose administrative headquarters are Rome-based — in the Sinai since 25 April 1982; and in the multinational minesweeping operations in the Red Sea from 22 August to 7 October 1984.

To these peacekeeping and security endeavors should be added the Treaty of 15 September 1980 between Italy and Malta, in which Italy committed itself to protect Malta's neutrality, and Italy's support for the NATO decision of 12 December 1979 to modernize the European theater nuclear force (TNF) in response to the deployment of Soviet SS-20 missiles. TNF modernization entails, *inter alia*, the deployment of 112 cruise missiles in Italy. The selection of the Sicilian town of Comiso as the missile site was made by the Italian government on 7 August 1981.

These developments have produced two basic effects. On one hand, they have aroused various forms of protest within the pacifist/anti-nuclear/ecological camp, which is largely politicized, as evidenced by the militancy of party-connected groups such as Communists, Radicals, and "Demoproletarians" and the availability of party structures to the protesters. On the other hand, the same developments have engendered, both inside and outside military circles, a perception of increased usefulness with respect to the mission of the Italian armed forces.

Military Developments since 1945

The current organization of the Italian armed forces was adopted in the mid-1970s. Italian military history since 1945 encompasses reconstruction, reorganization, and slow modernization. Italian participation in World War II, initially on the side of the Axis and, after the armistice of 1943, on the side of the Allies, was catastrophic for the Italian armed forces, whose limited material assets had already been worn down by the colonial campaign in Ethiopia and the intervention in the Spanish Civil War in the mid- to late 1930s. The naval and air forces, in particular, were destroyed or rendered inoperative by the overall negative conduct of operations during World War II. Moreover, according to the terms of the peace treaty, the more effective surviving naval craft had to be ceded to the smaller allied powers.

At the end of the war, the remnants of the Italian army, exclusive of the Carabinieri (military police), totalled 320,000 men. Approximately 50,000 of them made up five combat groups equipped with British issue. Another 200,000 men were organized into five divisions and minor units, all tasked primarily with logistical duties within the 5th US army and 8th British army. Their equipment was provided by the Allies. The remainder of the land forces were under the direct control of the Italian Ministry of War, a predecessor of today's Ministry of Defense. Their equipment was exclusively Italian and obsolescent, while their duties entailed security operations in the islands of Sardinia and Sicily, the latter of which was experiencing incipient guerrilla activity by separatist groups. Since the vast majority of these troops were reservists, they had to be discharged as rapidly as possible.

In August of 1945, the Allied Military Commission — whose powers derived from the terms of the armistice between Italy and the Allies — limited the strength of the Italian army to 140,000 men, exclusive of the Carabinieri, whose authorized strength was set at 65,000. This first reorganization addressed territorial structure, training centers, and internal security duties.

After March 1946, the Italian army slowly began to acquire an operational structure. Five infantry divisions were authorized, each consisting of two infantry regiments, one artillery regiment, and one engineer/signal battalion. These divisions, plus ten non-divisional infantry regiments, were set up to augment the three internal security divisions previously activated.

By the time the peace treaty — The Treaty of Paris of February 1947 — was signed, the table of organization and equipment of the infantry divisions had been enhanced to include a headquarters element, two infantry regiments, two field artillery regiments, one anti-tank artillery regiment, one air defense artillery regiment, one engineer battalion, and one signal battalion. In October of the same year, divisional combat service support units were also formed and deployed.

At the end of 1948, besides the above-described five infantry divisions, the land forces comprised two infantry divisions having the more modern triangular structure, which was to become the standard model; five armored cavalry troops; one armored brigade; ten non-divisional infantry regiments, including three mountain regiments and one assault regiment; two mountain artillery battalions; two field artillery battalions; and two air defense artillery battalions.

In 1949, Italy became one of the twelve original signatories of the North Atlantic Treaty, which gave birth to NATO. At this point, thanks to increased defense spending and US military assistance — also in the form of arms orders to Italy's mechanical industries for utilization by the Italian and allied armed forces — Italian armament and equipment started to come into line with the defense posture of its Western partners. At the same time, the restrictions placed on the table of organization and equipment of the Italian armed forces — army, navy, and air force — by the peace treaty were largely superseded by Italy's commitment to, and participation in, NATO.

Except for a small number of career soldiers of aristocratic origin or otherwise close to the crown, the great majority remained in the armed forces after World War II, and swore allegiance to the Republic. Until Italy joined NATO, the Italian armed forces were influenced primarily by the British model, and thereafter by the American model. Political, technological, and strategic developments following the formation of NATO twice thereafter necessitated the restructuring of the Italian armed forces. Procedures generally entailed reduction in personnel, reorganization of combat units along more functional lines, modifications in the deployment of troops and matériel, greater coordination, and continual modernization with respect to mobility, mechanization, and firepower.[16]

Government Control

In keeping with Western democratic principles, the Italian armed forces are subordinate to civil authority. In fact, the security and defense policies are subject to the control of Parliament,[17] which, being the central legislative body, is further empowered by the Constitution to declare a state of war and confer the necessary powers on the government.

Moreover, command of the armed forces is constitutionally vested in the President of the Republic, whose official acts, however, must bear the pertinent ministerial countersignature, since he is the chief of state, but not the head of government or chief executive officer.[18] Consequently, the government — Italy's central executive organ technically called the Council of Ministers and chaired by the President of the Council of Ministers, a constitutionally prescribed office separate and distinct from that of the President of the Republic — is collegially responsible for the nation's security and defense policies.[19] The President of the Republic therefore remains the nominal supreme commander of the armed forces.

At the ministerial or departmental level, the Minister of Defense asssumed specific political and technical subject-matter responsibility for national defense and may delegate part of his authority to one or more Under-secretaries of State.[20]

The Defense Establishment

In his dual capacity, the Minister of Defense heads the military establishment, which is functionally subdivided into two sectors. The first, whose scope is operational, is supervised by the Chief of Staff of Defense (Capo di Stato Maggiore della Difesa, a position comparable but not equivalent to that of the Chairman of the Joint Chiefs of Staff in the US defense establishment) and the individual Chiefs of Staff of the three services: army, navy, and air force. The second sector, whose scope is technical/administrative, is in turn coordinated by the Secretary-General of Defense, who is also the National Director of Armaments. His hierarchical position is inferior to that of the Chief of Staff of Defense.

As the ranking general/flag officer of the Italian armed forces, the Chief of Staff of Defense coordinates their organization, training, and employment. At the same time, he serves as chief military/technical advisor to the Minister of Defense, as well as statutory member of the Supreme Defense Council, a national defense forum chaired by the President of the Republic. He imparts upon the Secretary-General of Defense and the Chiefs of Staff of the three services the pertinent technical instructions for the execution of programs approved by the Minister of Defense. Moreover, he chairs the Committee of the Chiefs of Staff, which consists of the Chiefs of Staff of the three services and the Secretary-General of Defense. This Committee meets for purposes of planning and coordination.

The Chief of Staff of Defense is assisted by a Vice Chief of Staff of Defense, who oversees and coordinates the activities of the individual departments of the Defense General Staff that have subject-matter responsibility for personnel, operations, logistics, finance, and electronics, respectively. The Chief and Vice Chief of Staff of Defense may not belong to the same service. In fact, these positions are rotated among the senior ranking general/flag officers of the three services.

Notwithstanding the above-outlined attributes, the position or status of the Chief of Staff of Defense is one of pre-eminence rather than clear-cut and full hierarchical authority, a problem for which the Ministry of Defense is currently studying a solution in the interest of a more functional chain of command and more effective joint operations.

The Army

The army is headed by the Chief of Staff of the army, who is assissted by a Vice Chief of Staff. The General Staff of the army encompasses six departments responsible for personnel, intelligence, operations, logistics, general affairs, and financial planning, respectively. These departments are identified by a progressive Roman numeral from I to VI in the sequence above. No department (Reparto) has a specific denomination, even though departmental subject-matter responsibility corresponds to one of the categories indicated above. Placed within the General Staff structure, but separate from the "numbered" departments, are the inspectorates and other offices for the combat arms and the technical, logistical, and medical services or branches of the army. There is no General Staff branch or corps. Officers who are graduates of the Army War College qualify for General Staff Service (Servizio di Stato Maggiore). These officers normally rotate between General Staff Service and command assignments.

Italy's land forces, all subordinate to the Chief of Staff of the army, are organized into three corps and seven Military Regions, the tactical mission of the latter being area defense oriented, as opposed to the more dynamically operational mission of the former.

There is no standardized corps structure in the Italian army. Subordinate units are assigned to a corps headquarters primarily in consideration of mission and terrain. On the other hand, the divisions and the brigades, which, when assigned, constitute the two major combat units subordinate to a corps headquarters, have a standardized structure or table of organization and equipment. While the corps are given a numerical designation, the divisions and brigades bear names related to Italian military history.

There are at present two types of divisions: mechanized and armored. Mechanized divisions consist of three maneuver brigades: two mechanized and one armored. Conversely, armored divisions consist of two armored brigades and one mechanized brigade. All other organic units — combat, combat support, and combat service support — are the same in both types of divisions. These organic units include one armored cavalry squadron, divisional artillery (field and air defense, consisting of four battalions), one light aviation battalion, one engineer battalion, one signal battalion, one logistical battalion, and one military police company.

The brigade, which constitutes the fundamental self-sustaining combat unit of the Italian army, is either organic to a mechanized or armored division or is a separate unit under the command of a corps headquarters, a Military Region headquarters, or other military authority. There are five standard types of brigades. In all cases their basic table of organization and equipment is intended to provide combined arms capability, maneuverability, and tactical and logistical autonomy. All brigades, regardless of type, include organic command and signal of battalion size, one anti-tank company, one or two artillery battalions, one engineer company, one logistical battalion, and one medical battalion. The specific nature and size of these organic combat support and combat service support elements as well as the number and type of organic maneuver battalions subordinate to brigade headquarters depend upon the type of brigade. The nature of Italian terrain and potential enemy capabilities have led to the formation of the five types of standard brigades: mechanized, armored, alpine (mountain), motorized, and airborne.

The mechanized brigade is the most flexible for the conduct of defensive operations. Assigned personnel can operate either aboard organic combat vehicles or on foot, depending upon the mission or terrain conditions, without downgrading combat capability. The mechanized brigade is capable of operating on flat terrain (plains), on rolling ground (hills), or built-up (urban) areas. Its maneuver force comprises three mechanized battalions and one tank battalion. Elements of organic artillery are self-propelled.

The armored brigade is characterized by the preponderance of assigned tanks. It is intended to counteract similar enemy formations and is conditioned by terrain limitations. Its maneuver force consists of two tank battalions and one mechanized battalion. Elements of organic artillery are self-propelled.

The alpine brigade is the most typically Italian combat unit, as one-third of Italy's territory is mountainous, the two principal mountain ranges being the Alps and the Apennines. The maneuver battalions of the alpine brigades vary from three to five. Organic artillery includes two battalions and is packed.

The motorized brigade exploits the element of speed and its capability for prolonged land travel, as its vehicles are mostly wheeled. Its maneuver force consists of three motorized battalions and one tank battalion. Organic artillery is towed.

As opposed to the multiplicity of the other four standard types of brigades, there is only one airborne brigade currently in service to the Italian army. Its mobility enables it to operate anywhere inside or outside the national territory, subject to airlift limitations. It consists of three airborne battalions. Organic artillery is parachutable. Carriers include Hercules C-130s, Fiat G-222s, and Chinook helicopters. The airborne brigade is under the direct control of the Chief of Staff of the army.

The maneuver battalions organic to the mechanized, alpine, motorized, and airborne brigades normally consist of one headquarters and services company, three infantry companies of corresponding nature to the type of brigade, and one mortar battery. The maneuver battalions of the armored brigades differ from the others because of their composite organization: they include two tank companies and one mechanized infantry company. All companies usually comprise three line platoons plus one or more support platoons. Consequently, divisions, brigades, battalions, and companies have a similar triangular structure.

Apart from the brigades and their subordinate elements, a variety of army units are trained, equipped, and tasked for special missions. They include one missile brigade, one airborne assault battalion, one amphibious battalion, various electronic warfare battalions, and barrier (area defense) infantry battalions. Their deployment as well as that of the corps and standard divisions and brigades will be discussed in conjunction with current Italian defense doctrine.

The territorial structure of Italy's land forces is based upon the geographical subdivisions of the country into seven Military Regions,[21] each under a separate commander, but all subordinate to the Chief of Staff of the army. The Military Regions are: North Western, North Eastern, Tuscan–Emilian, Central, Southern, Sicilian (insular), and Sardinian (insular). All Military Regions are further subdivided into a varying number of Military Zones with subordinate Military Districts. Included in the Military Regions are varying numbers of signal battalions, maintenance facilities, motor pools, and military hospitals. The mission of the Military Regions combines territorial defense with administrative duties. Combat units stationed in a given Military Region and not assigned to one of the corps or under the direct control of the Chief of Staff of the army are subordinate to the respective Military Region commander.[22]

From the standpont of their specific military competence, the Italian land forces correspond to different branches: "arms" and "services." There are six arms: Carabinieri, infantry, cavalry, artillery, engineer, and signal. The services perform technical, logistical, and medical functions. Because of tradition, branch insignia are either representative of the branch itself, the speciality within the branch, or the historical regiment, a now nearly extinct unit of the Italian army. A few clarifications should be made with respect to two of the arms in particular.

The Carabinieri arm, a military police corps vested with military and civil jurisdiction, is often referred to in non-Italian publications as a para-military force. In effect, the Carabinieri hold the status of the "first arm of the Army." With respect to military employment, the table of organization and equipment, depending on the type of Carabinieri unit, corresponds to that of infantry or armored troops. For law enforcement duties entailing civil jurisdiction, the Carabinieri are subordinate to the Ministry of the Interior, while in all other cases they are part of the defense establishment.

The Carabinieri structure follows territorial and operational criteria, in that order of numerical importance. During peacetime, the territorial organization is primarily concerned with law enforcement. In time of war, it also performs defense duties. The territorial organization substantially consists of a general headquarters and three divisions, each having, in turn, subordinate brigades, legions (regimental equivalents), groups (battalion equivalents), companies, occasional lieutenancies, and stations.[23] The operational organization is also subordinate to the general headquarters and is structured in accordance with the brigade–battalion–company chain of command concept. When assigned to other military units, Carabinieri generally constitute the organic military police element.

By law, the commanding general of the Carabinieri is selected from one of the other combat arms of the army as an out-of-branch assignment.

The infantry encompasses several specialities, part of which have historical origins that predate the unification of Italy as a sovereign state. The oldest surviving specialities are the *granatieri* (grenadiers), traditionally selected because of their height, as their name implies; the *bersaglieri* (sharpshooters), who were originally organized and deployed as an assault light infantry; and the *alpini*, whose basic mountain-troop mission has not changed, as they constitute the infantry element of the standard alpine brigade. On the other hand, the contemporary role of the *granatieri* and the *bersaglieri* is that of infantry troops assigned to mechanized units. To add a touch of color: the headress of the *alpini* has a lateral eagle feather, as opposed to the flowing plumes of the *bersaglieri* headgear.

More recent are the other infantry specialities: armor (as opposed to cavalry, which is classified as the arm separate from the infantry), airborne, and *lagunari* (amphibious commando- type troops, whose name is taken after the lagoon of Venice).

The armament, vehicles, and equipment of Italy's land forces are in most cases of Italian (domestic or licenced production), US, German, or French make. Combat vehicles, tanks, and artillery include M-113 and AMX-VCI armored personnel carriers; M-47, M-60AI, and Leopard tanks; M-107 175 mm self-propelled guns; 105 mm model 56 packed, FH-70 155 mm towed, M-109E 155 mm self-propelled, and 203 mm howitzers; 81 mm and 120 mm mortars; 57 mm and 106 mm recoilless anti-tank weapons; Cobra, SS-11, TOW, and Milan anti-tank guided weapons; 20 mm and 40 mm air defense guns; and Lance surface-to-surface missiles and improved Hawk surface-to-air missiles.[24]

The Navy

The naval forces are headed by the Chief of Staff of the navy, who is assisted by a Vice Chief of Staff. As in the case of the army, the General Staff consists of six numbered departments with responsibility for personnel, intelligence, operations, logistics, material structures, and the naval helicopter organization respectively. A number of inspectorates and offices are also placed within the General Staff structure. Similarly to the army, the Italian navy has an operational and a territorial structure, both subordinate to the Chief of Staff of the navy.

The operational organization, referred to as the Naval Squadron and headed by a squadron command, is subdivided into four naval divisions — numbered I through IV — and one submarine headquarters, each having subordinate squadrons or groups identified by a numerical designator. The surface fleet, which is the substantive component of the operational structure, is organized to include, besides other functional formations, two principal combat formations, each comprising at least one cruiser, two to three destroyers, approximately five to six frigates, and support craft.

The territorial organization encompasses five Military Maritime Departments (Dipartimento Militare Marittimo) and two separate maritime headquarters. The departments correspond to geographical criteria. They are the Upper Tyrrhenian (Sea), the Lower Tyrrhenian (Sea), Adriatic (Sea) the Ionian (Sea) and Otranto Channel, Sardinia (insular), and Sicily (insular). The territorial organization is tasked with administrative and logistical functions and with coastal patrol/defense responsiblities. Anti-submarine aircraft is organic to the air force, but is under the operational control of the navy.

In addition to line personnel and to technical, logistical, and medical services, the Italian navy includes one battalion of marine infantry, which is part of the operational organization, and a special forces group consisting of underwater specialists and commandos. The special forces are under the direct control of the Chief of Staff of the navy. The mission of the navy will be examined in conjunction with the discussion of current defense doctrine.[25]

The principal surface combatants, submarines, and coastal patrol ships are generally of Italian construction. They include, in addition to support craft, 3 cruisers, 4 destroyers, 16 frigates, 8 corvettes, 10 submarines, 7 hydrofoils, 30 minesweepers, 2 landing ships, and 2 replenishment tankers.[26]

The Air Force

In consonance with the other two services, the air force is headed by the Chief of Staff of the air force, who is assisted by a Vice Chief of Staff. The General Staff consists of six numbered departments, I through V being responsible for the same matters of the corresponding Army General Staff departments and Department VI for telecommunications and flight assistance. Inspectorates and other offices likewise fall within the General Staff structure.[27]

But, as opposed to the army and navy, the Italian air force tends to merge operational and territorial functions. It is organized into three Air Regions, numbered I through III. Assigned to the Air Regions are wings — consisting of one or two groups — and air brigades — consisting of two or three groups. Specific unit responsibilities include reconnaissance, interception, electronic warfare, anti-submarine warfare, and transportation. The air force mission will be discussed in conjunction with defense doctrine.

In addition to pilots and flight personnel, the air force includes technical, logistical, and medical services comparable to those of the army and navy.

Organic aircraft and missiles are in most cases of US or Italian make and include Aeritalia (Lockheed licenced) F-104-Ss, Fiat-Aeritalia G-91-Ys, Tornado MRCAs, Macchi MB-339-As, Fiat G-91-R/RIAs, Lockheed F/RF-104-Gs, Aeritalia G-222-VSs, Piaggio (Douglas licenced) PD-808s, Lockheed TF-104-Gs, Lockheed C-130-Hs, Piaggio P-166-Ms, SIAI Marchetti S-208-Ms, Macchi MB-326-Es, Agusta (Sikorski licenced) SH-3D-T/Ss, Agusta (Sikorski licenced) AB-204-Bs, Agusta (Bell licenced) AB-212s, and NIKE Hercules missiles.[28]

Personnel: Conscription, Cadres and Reserves/Mobilization

In accordance with national tradition, domestic socio-economic considerations, and the provisions of the Constitution of 1948, recruitment in Italy is based primarily on the draft system. All male citizens are registered automatically for the draft at age 17. The following year they are subject to physical and aptitude tests. Those who are fit and not entitled to dispensation or deferment for family, academic, or other reasons are inducted at age 19 into the army or air force for a 12-month period, unless drafted into the navy, in which case they serve for 18 months.[29] A legislative bill about to be introduced before Parliament contemplates the recruitment of women on a voluntary basis in the technical, logistical, and medical services to the exclusion of the combat arms.

For purposes of continuity and in order to meet long-range defense requirements, the draft/national service system is complemented by smaller career/regular cadres. All regular officers — 37 percent of whom are graduates of the army, navy, or air force academies — are recruited through a public competitive examination for admission into the respective military academies or appointment after other appropriate training. There is no equivalent of the university-connected Reserve Officers' Training Corps (ROTC) established in the United States. There are, however, officer candidate schools for both conscripts and career personnel. Regular non-commissioned officers are likewise recruited through a public competitive examination. These examinations may be taken before, during, or after mandatory national service.

Personnel strength needs are also met, as they arise, by allowing qualified draftees to extend their service at their request for specified periods of time. As a rule, extended active duty is applicable to draftees serving as reserve officers or reserve non-commissioned officers. Qualified draftees who apply for and pass the competitive examination to serve as reserve officers in conjunction with national service remain on active duty for three additional months to undergo officer training.

Individuals not interested in performing national service as ordinary draftees may apply for "auxiliary" service in the Carabinieri, the State Police, the Custodial Agents Corps (warden service), or the Firefighters Corps. Selection criteria are based on qualifications and law enforcement/fire prevention needs. Military service may also be substituted with "alternative" service for the duration of at least two years in a developing country. Finally, recognized conscientious objectors are entitled to perform specifically prescribed forms of social service.

The personnel strength of Italian armed forces in December 1984[30] was as follows: army — 260,000, including 189,000 conscripts; navy — 44,500, including 29,590 conscripts; and air force — 70,600, including 28,300 conscripts. To these statistics should be added the personal strength of the Carabinieri, the Finance Guard (Guardia di Finanza) and the State Police (Polizia di Stato, demilitarized in 1981 when its former name, Pubblica Sicurezza — Public Security — was modified to its present name). The first two possess military capabilities, while the third possesses paramilitary capabilities. Pertinent personnel strength is as follows: Carabinieri 90,000, Finance Guard 48,691, State Police 67,927. The Italian reserve system is in no way comparable either to that of the United States, which is largely based on voluntary reserve duty, or to that of Switzerland, where reserve duty is mandatory. Except for comparatively few individuals possessing highly critical military occupational specialties there is no reserve active duty for training. However, all former servicemen are subject to recall in case of a national emergency until age 45. It is therefore estimated that Italy's current reserve pool consists of approximately 5 million male citizens.

For immediate needs, the Italian reserve system is based upon recall to active duty of the most recently discharged draft contingents in order to meet the authorized personnel strength of existing units and to activate other units for which equipment has already been allocated and stored. Discharged personnel are advised on discharge from the armed forces where to report in case of an announced emergency entailing recall to active duty.

According to current estimates, the reserve pool of recently trained personnel available for immediate or short-term mobilization is as follows: army 250,000 to 550,000, navy 221,000, and air force 28,000.

The Intelligence Organization

The Italian intelligence system was totally restructured in 1977 with the passage of a new law titled "Formation and Organization of the Intelligence and Security Services and the Regulation of the State Secret."[31] Among other factors that led to the intelligence reform, particularly influential were the actual or alleged abuses by the former intelligence services, the judicially held unconstitutionality of certain provisions relative to state secrecy, the increase of subversive and terrorist groups, the escalation of political violence, and concern about foreign links to domestic terrorism.

Between the end of World War II and the enactment of the intelligence reform law, two services had succeeded each other in the performance of intelligence duties under the direction of the Defense General Staff: the Armed Forces Intelligence Service (Servizio Informazioni Forze Armate — SIFAR) from 1949 to 1965 and the Defense Intelligence Service (Servizio Informazioni Difesa, SID) from 1965 to

1977. Both operated as a militarily organized service responsible for all intelligence functions. However, three additional and smaller intelligence services — each called Operational Service for Intelligence and Analysis (Servizio Informazioni Operativo Situazione — SIOS) and connected first to SIFAR and later to SID — were instituted within the army, navy, and air force for the collection and analysis of intelligence of specific operational interest to each component of the armed forces.

The 1977 reform law introduced five major innovations: (1) intelligence surveillance by both government and Parliament; (2) removal of the central intelligence responsibility from the Ministry of Defense and, in particular, from the Defense General Staff; (3) attribution of the intelligence/security function to two services, one military and one civilian, while retaining the three respective SIOSs for the army, navy, and air force; (4) separation of the intelligence/security function from police powers; and (5) new regulations governing state secrecy.[32]

Pursuant to the 1977 law, all intelligence and security functions pertaining to Italian military defense are currently assigned to the Service for Intelligence and Military Security (Servizio per le Informazioni e la Sicurezza Militare — SISMI), created by said law. SISMI, however, is neither subordinate to the Chief of Staff of defense nor is it a department of the Defense General Staff. SISMI is subordinate to the Minister of Defense, who is responsible for structuring this service and supervising its operations in consonance with the directives of the President of the Council of Ministers. The director of SISMI is appointed by the Minister of Defense, subject to the concurrence of the Interministerial Committee on Intelligence and Security (Comitato Interministeriale per le Informazioni e la Sicurezza — CIIS), also instituted by the reform law. CIIS is chaired by the President of the Council of Ministers and its statutory members are the Ministers of Foreign Affairs, the Interior, Justice, Defense, Industry, and Finance.

Intelligence information and analyses as well as operations must be reported by SISMI not only to the Minister of Defense, but also to the Executive Committee for the Intelligence and Security Services (Comitato Esecutivo per i Servizi di Informazioni e Sicurezza — CESIS), yet another organ created by the reform law. CESIS is under the direct authority of the President of the Council of Ministers, who chairs it or delegates this task to an Under-secretary of State. The purpose of CESIS is to provide to the President of the Council of Ministers all data needed to coordinate SISMI and the other intelligence services set up by the reform law: Service for Intelligence and

Democratic Security (Servizio Informazioni per le Informazioni e la Sicurezza Democratica — SISDE), responsible for all intelligence and security functions pertaining to the defense of democracy and of the institutions established by the Constitution of 1948. CESIS also processes and analyzes intelligence information collected by SISMI and SISDE. The directors of both intelligence services are statutory members of CESIS.

With respect to the structure and operations of SISMI in particular, extremely limited information is available from official sources in the public domain. It was officially announced, however, that two decrees issued by the President of the Council of Ministers gave SISMI first a provisional structure and than a definitive one in order to implement the reform law. Moreover, journalistic sources claim that SISMI is largely patterned on its predecessor — the above mentioned SID — though there have been terminological changes. Reportedly, the SISMI divisions are six. The first is concerned with military security and counterespionage and coordinates the peripheral centers located in major urban areas throughout the country. The second division is tasked with both overt and covert collection abroad and maintains liaison with the intelligence services of allied and friendly countries. The third division is responsible for intelligence analysis and its dissemination through appropriate channels. The remaining three divisions presumably carry out electronic, technical, and administrative functions. Also according to press sources, SISMI's authorized strength amounts to approximately 2,500 persons.[33]

By law, recruitment of personnel assigned to SISMI, SISDE, or CESIS takes place with its consent inside the armed forces and the civil service or through direct hiring outside government. Presumably, SISMI draws the vast majority of its personnel from the Carabinieri and the armed forces in general. During periods of employment by the intelligence services, military personnel are civilianized. Oddly this rule also applies to SISMI personnel. Despite their potential value to intelligence activities, certain categories of individuals may not be employed by the intelligence services either permanently or occasionally. They are members of Parliament; regional, provincial, and municipal councillors; magistrates (judges and prosecutors); clergymen; professional journalists; and persons whose record does not guarantee fidelity to democratic and constitutional principles.

According to the reform law, the three SIOS of the army, navy, and air force must operate in strict liaison with SISMI. Their mission, which is not defined in detail in open sources, is presumably narrower than the one carried out by the military intelligence branches organic to the armed forces of the United States. Moreover, SISMI itself does not appear to be the strict equivalent of the US Defense Intelligence Agency. Likewise, SISDE cannot be readily compared to either the Central Intelligence Agency or the Federal Bureau of Investigation.

Apart from the overall cumbersome structure of the Italian intelligence community, the intelligence needs of the Italian defense establishment are hampered by the fact that the Chief of Staff of defense and the Defense General Staff lack an organic intelligence system. This concern has been voiced not only by private observers,[34] but also by the Ministry of Defense itself, in the 1985 edition of the *Defense White Book*.[35]

Doctrine and Operations

The operational employment of the Italian armed forces largely coincides with their NATO mission. In keeping with constitutional dictates and political rhetoric peculiar to the above-referred multi-party coalition system, Italian military doctrine is exclusively defense-oriented at both national and NATO levels. In point of fact, Italy is a signatory of the Nuclear Non-Proliferation Agreement of January 1969, ratified by Parliament in April 1975. Likewise, Italy has renounced all resort to chemical and biological weapons. Moreover, the national defense budget has consistently been one of the lowest in the Atlantic Alliance.

Italy's defense doctrine is conditioned by its geography and is predicated upon its political and military participation in NATO and its commitment to the fundamental principles of dissuasion, détente, and balance of forces. Moreover, ostensible geostrategic, economic, and commercial factors cause Italy to be particularly concerned with West European security, stability in the Mediterranean region, and the enhancement of North–South dialogue.

For strategic defense purposes Italy is divided into three geographical/functional sectors. The northeastern zone of operations requires primarily land/air defense capabilities. The southern zone of operations requires primarily naval/air defense capabilities. The remaining sector substantially constitutes an internal communications zone, requiring land/naval/air defense and logistical capabilities. In all cases, given the configuration of Italian territory, the principle of forward defense is applicable.

Current doctrine and plans assign to the Italian armed forces five missions, all requiring, to varying degrees, joint operations: (1) defense of the northeastern frontier; (2) defense of the southern air and maritime frontiers and sea communications; (3) air defense; (4) territorial defense; and (5) peacekeeping, security, and civil protection operations.

(1) Defense of the Northeastern Frontier. The northeastern sector is particularly sensitive, as a potential attack against Italy or NATO's southern flank by the Warsaw Pact forces would assign priority to this area. NATO estimates calculate that ten Soviet and Hungarian divisions, including over 2,340 tanks and 1,560 artillery pieces, are earmarked for employment against Italy's northeastern frontier. According to the same estimates, those divisions could be reinforced by seven divisions, including 2,000 tanks and 1,300 artillery pieces, currently stationed in the Kiev Military District.

The northeastern sector is geographically heterogeneous. It is characterized by high mountain ranges in the north and a vast plain in the south bound, in turn, by varying relief to the east and intersected by several rivers. Moreover, the northeastern sector borders with neutral countries whose territory would have to be overrun or simply crossed by the Soviet attacking forces. The reactive capability of these neutral countries would greatly influence the Italian defense posture with respect to the time factor.

Limited maneuver space and the proximity of critical industrial/urban centers to the northeastern frontier make forward defense indispensable. This necessitates, in the first place, the detection, slowing-down, and wearing out of the aggressor's maneuver before its forces can reach the defensive positions in the sector. Tasked with this mission are the reconnaissance and interdiction elements of the air force and the long-range artillery systems. Secondly, it would be necessary to contain enemy penetration efforts along the naturally and artificially fortified frontier areas by committing the mechanized and alpine units and by employing air, artillery, and anti-tank fire. Thirdly, contingency planning includes counter-attack by the armored units, supported by artillery, anti-tank, and air fire, in order to restore the forward defense line. Lastly, control must be maintained over the flank, the sea, and the rear areas to prevent enemy surprise actions.

Italian land forces already stationed and/or deployable in this sector are the 3rd Corps, headquartered in Milan; the 4th Corps, headquartered in Bolzano; and the 5th Corps, headquarted in Vittorio

Veneto. The 4th and 5th Corps are deployed on the front line whereas the 3rd Corps is in reserve. These three corps together comprise 19 maneuver brigades, one missile brigade, and support troops.

The 4th Corps is in essence the mountain corps, since its subordinate maneuver units are Italy's five alpine brigades: "Tridentina," headquartered in Bressanone; "Orobica," headquartered in Merano; "Cadore," headquartered in Belluno; "Julia," headquartered in Udine; and "Taurinense," headquartered in Torino. Assigned to the 4th Corps is also the 7th Carabinieri Battalion. The 4th Corps is deployed along the mountain ranges of the northeastern sector.

The 5th Corps comprises two mechanized divisions, one armored division, one missile brigade, and the Trieste Troops. Mechanized division "Mantova" is headquartered in Udine. Its subordinate brigades are mechanized brigade "Isonzo," headquartered in Cividade; mechanized brigade "Brescia," headquartered in Brescia; and armored brigade "Pozzuolo del Friuli," headquartered in Palmanova. Mechanized division "Folgore" is headquartered in Treviso and its subordinate brigades are mechanized brigade "Trieste," headquartered in Bologna; mechanized brigade "Gorizia," headquartered in Gorizia; and armored brigade "Vittorio Veneto," headquartered in Trieste. Armored division "Ariete" is headquartered in Pordenone and its subordinate brigades are armored brigade "Mameli," headquartered in Tauriano; armored brigade "Manin," headquartered in Aviano; and mechanized brigade "Garibaldi," headquartered in Pordenone. The missile brigade possesses both a numerical and historical denominator, 3rd Missile Brigade "Aquileia," even though it is the only such brigade in the Italian army. It is headquartered in Pordenone. The Trieste Troops are stationed in the Trieste area and constitute the equivalent of a motorized brigade. Also assigned to the 5th Corps are two amphibious battalions (*lagunari*) and the 13th Carabinieri Battalion. The 5th Corps is deployed in the Po-Friuli Valley.

The 3rd Corps comprises one mechanized division and one separate brigade. Mechanized division "Centauro" is headquartered in Novara. Its subordinate brigades are mechanized brigade "Goito," headquartered in Milan; mechanized brigade "Legnano," headquartered in Bergamo; and armored brigade "Curtatone," headquartered in Bellinzago. The separate brigade is motorized brigade "Cremona," headquartered in Turin. As indicated above, the 3rd Corps constitutes the land forces reserve in the sector.

Responsibility for logistical support to the land forces operating in the northeastern sector is assigned to the Northeastern Military Region.

Air forces committed to this sector include four fighter-bomber groups, two fighter-reconnaissance groups, and three light fighter-bomber groups, all based in Northern Italy — Veneto, Friuli, Romagna, and Lombardia.

Naval support for the sector includes coastal radar installations that monitor a large portion of the north Adriatic Sea, light gunboats and missile-equipped hydrofoils, missile-equipped helicopters, and anti-landing minefields.

(2) Defense of the Southern Air and Maritime Frontiers and Sea Lane System. The importance of the southern sector derives from Italy's peninsular position with a coastline of over 8,000 km. and to its dependence upon maritime traffic for the supply of needed raw materials. The mission of the Italian armed forces, which in this sector is primarily a naval/air responsibility, is to keep open the sea lanes, to control and protect the merchant-marine traffic, and to defend the coast from enemy sea landings and airborne operations.

The air forces available for this mission are based in southern Italy and in the islands of Sicily and Sardinia, but are reinforceable by units based in central and northern Italy. The southern-based air-force units include two fighter-bomber groups, two interceptor groups, one fighter-bomber-interceptor group, two anti-submarine patrol groups, one electronic warfare group, and one helicopter air rescue group.

The naval forces are drawn from the Naval Squadron and from the Military Maritime Departments. Departmental elements are responsible for mine counter-measures. Committed to the defense of the southern sector is also the marine infantry battalion "San Marco." The deployment of the underwater specialists and commando unit is likewise part of the defense plans.

Available land forces for this mission are drawn from the army's territorial organization in the sector and from units to be activated upon mobilization. Their role entails both area and mobile defense.

(3) Air Defense. The conduct of all military operations — land, naval, and air — is predicated upon air superiority, albeit limited in time and space. Italian air defense doctrine calls for air defense in the strict sense, i.e., neutralization of enemy aircraft while in flight before they reach military, industrial, or government objectives in Italy, and counter-air, i.e., neutralization of enemy aircraft before takeoff. In case of conflict, air force interceptors and part of the available fighter-bombers would conduct air defense in the strict sense, while the

remaining fighter-bombers would be committed to the counter-air role. Air defense would also be conducted with missile systems organic to the air force and those organic to the army but under the operational control of the air force. Also part of the air defense system is the land and naval artillery. The radar system, both national and NATO, is tasked with detection.

(4) Territorial Defense. This mission entails the defense of all national peninsular and insular territory with the exception of the above-discussed northeastern sector. This area generally coincides with the communications zone, which, in case of war, would be responsible for the support to the Italian armed forces operating in the northeastern and southern sectors and in the Mediterranean Sea. Moreover, this area could be the objective of limited actions during conflicts in the Mediterranean region not directly involving Italy.

The army is the service principally charged with the mission, but it also draws on the assets of the navy and air force as well as on those of the other security organizations with military and paramilitary capabilities. Each Military Region has territorial defense responsibilities within its boundaries. Infantry brigades already constituted for this purpose and under the control of Military Regions are the motorized brigade "Friuli," headquartered in Florence; mechanized brigade "Granatieri di Sardegna," headquartered in Rome; motorized brigade "Acqui," headquartered in L'Aquila; mechanized brigade "Pinerolo," headquartered in Bari; and motorized brigade "Aosta," headquartered in Messina. These brigades are assigned mobile defense operations, including the neutralization of enemy beach heads.

Smaller units to be activated upon mobilization are the security companies — 25 percent of authorized personnel being Carabinieri — for the static (fixed) defense of installations or otherwise sensitive sites; infantry battalions to be deployed as a reserve or to protect economic/strategic sites; artillery battalions for fire support; and engineer battalions to insure the viability of the main supply routes and to install artificial barriers.

Also assigned to the territorial defense mission, but initially held in reserve, is the airborne brigade, headquartered in Pisa, though under the direct control of the Chief of Staff of the army. The entire Carabinieri territorial organization likewise contributes to this mission, together with the Carabinieri XI Brigade, which coordinates its mobile battalions, and with the Carabinieri airborne battalion. The XI Brigade and the airborne battalion are especially trained in counter-airborne, counter-airlanding, and counter-guerrilla operations. Carabinieri forces not available until mobilization include the mobile nuclei, with functions analogous to those of the XI Brigade and airborne battalion.

With respect to territorial defense, the navy is assigned two functions. The first falls within general duties encompassing surveillance and interdiction normally carried out by the surface and patrol ships. The second entails specific territorial defense functions, including underwater screening, coast patrol, anti-intrusion systems, and intelligence-oriented special surveillance operations.

The territorial defense role performed by the air force is substantially the same it carries out in the northeastern sector.

(5) Peacekeeping, Security, and Civil Protection Operations. The type of international peacekeeping and security operations in which Italy has participated and can be expected to participate in the future have already been identified in the introductory section. To those can be added — although more defense-oriented — its participation in NATO's standing Allied Mobile Force (AMF) and Naval on Call Force Mediterranean (NAVOCFORMED).

With respect to civil protection, legislative enactments dating back to 1960 and elaborated upon in 1981 call for the employment of the armed forces during the organizational and execution phases of relief operations. Responsible for operational coordination are the Minister of Defense and the Minister for the Coordination of Civil Protection. For major emergencies, such as earthquakes and floods, a Rapid Intervention Force (Forza di Pronto Intervento — FOPI) has been instituted by earmarking specifically equipped units of the three services. FOPI is expected to be ready for deployment within 16 hours and to be in place within 24 hours.[36]

Relations with NATO

Since the creation of the North Atlantic Alliance, Italy has uninterruptedly participated in both the civil and military structures of NATO, including the Defense Planning Committee and the Nuclear Planning Group. The availability of Italian territory for NATO contingency planning, the establishment of major NATO headquarters, installations, organizations, and agencies on the peninsula and islands, the assignment or earmarking of a substantive part of the Italian armed forces to NATO commands, and their participation in NATO training exercises constitute Italy's military contribution to the Alliance.

Because of Italy's geographical location, the availability of its territory to the Alliance is strategically relevant. A US Senate report has defined Italy as "essential to military control of the Mediterranean."[37] In fact, Italy is the only nation in the central Mediterranean currently committed to Western defense. Moreover, the entire Mediterranean region can be covered from air bases located on Italian soil. An analysis prepared by a senior staff member of the US Defense Intelligence Agency addresses the continuing strategic importance of the Mediterranean in these terms:

> it remains the most traversed maritime area of the world. It flanks the European land mass at the south. It provides access to the shortest water route from Europe to the Persian Gulf and beyond. It forms the bridge between three continents; and via the Black Sea it probes into the southern heartland of Eurasia.[38]

At the same time, control of the Mediterranean Sea lends continuity to NATO's southern flank, which is not contiguous by land. In addition to its Mediterranean projection, Italian territory provides a backup area, as well as dispersal sites for tactical air power, for the Central European region.

Another US Senate report attests to the network of NATO/US installations and facilities in Italy:

> The major military installations provided by Italy to the United States and to NATO include the naval complex located at Naples, naval facilities at Sigonella, Sicily, and La Maddalena, Sardinia. Air Force facilities are located at Aviano Air Base [Friuli] . . . and at the San Vito Air Station [Puglia]. The U.S. Army utilizes facilities at Camp Darby, near Livorno . . . and installations at Camp Ederle located at Vicenza. Other smaller installations and facilities throughout Italy are associated with those installations. Ten separate NATO NADGE [NATO Air Defense Ground Environment] early-warning sites are also located in strategic places throughout the country . . . Details regarding the storage of nuclear weapons in Italy are classified.[39]

Of the NATO headquarters located in Italy, the highest military body is the Allied Forces Southern Europe command (AFSOUTH). It is located in Naples and exercises command functions over the allied forces in the central and eastern Mediterranean region, namely, Greece, Italy, and Turkey. Lower NATO headquarters subordinate to it include the allied land Forces Southern Europe Command (LANDSOUTH) in Verona, the allied Naval Forces Southern Europe Command (NAVASOUTH) in Naples, and the allied Air Forces Southern Europe Command (AIRSOUTH), also in Naples. Other Italian-based organizations and agencies — outside the operational structure — are the NATO Defense College in Rome and the Supreme Allied Command Atlantic (SACLANT) Anti-Submarine Warfare Research Center in La Spezia.

Since the defense of Italy's territory and the protection of its access to air and maritime communications coincides with the defense of NATO's southern flank, the NATO/Italian chain of command has been integrated for the execution of the wartime missions discussed above.

The Italian army, air force, and navy units assigned to the northeastern sector are subordinate to the commanders of LANDSOUTH, 5th Allied Tactical Air Force (FIVEATAF, headquartered in Vicenza and subordinate to AIRSOUTH), and Upper Adriatic Maritime Department, respectively. In case of aggression against the northeastern frontier initially involving Italy alone, each of those three commanders — all of whom are Italian general/flag officers — would remain under the command of the Chief of Staff of his specific service and to the Chief of Staff of defense. But, in case of aggression involving the entire Alliance, those three commanders are subordinate — directly or through intermediate commands — to the Commander-in-Chief of AFSOUTH.

Likewise, in case of a conflict involving initially Italy alone, the naval, air, and land forces committed to the defense of the southern sector of the peninsula would be subordinate to the commander of Italy's Naval Squadron (which coincides with MEDCENT — Central Mediterranean Area — an intermediate NATO command), the Chief of Staff of the Air Force, and the Chief of Staff of the Army, respectively. However, were the entire Alliance involved, the Italian forces assigned to this mission would be subordinate to the Commander-in-Chief of AFSOUTH through intermediate NATO commands.

With respect to air defense, Italian and NATO structures once again largely coincide. In the first of the above-discussed contingencies, the commander of FIVEATAF — an Italian general officer, as stated above — reports to the Chief of Staff of the Air Force. In the second contingency he reports to the commander of AIRSOUTH and, through him, to the Commander-in-Chief of AFSOUTH.

In essence, the Italian army and air force units assigned to the defense of the northeastern frontier of the peninsula concurrently defend NATO's southern flank and indirectly protect the rear of NATO's central region. The Italian navy, on the other hand, contributes to the protection of the Mediterranean communication routes for the NATO Alliance and provides anti-submarine and anti-air warfare capabilities in the territorial waters and straits.

Assessment and Outlook

While there can be little doubt as to the importance of Italy's contribution to Western defense, several factors that condition the effectiveness of the Italian armed forces should also be noted.

The parliamentary system of government set up by the Republican Constitution and characterized by the weakness of the executive branch creates cumbersome procedures that adversely affect the preparedness of the armed forces during peacetime and hinder their efficient deployment in case of war. This basic problem is intensified by the multi-party tradition rooted in Italian politics, whose mechanics practically foreclose the formation of a homogeneous parliamentary coalition, not to speak of the emergence of an absolute majority party.[40]

Moreover, the presence in Italy of the world's largest non-ruling Communist Party is a cause for concern. Although ambiguous statements made in recent years by the leadership of the Italian Communist Party (PCI) on foreign affairs and national defense matters have engendered a perception of pro-Western commitment, a relevant percentage of the PCI's rank and file cherishes pro-Moscow sentiments or supports a dubious neutrality stance frequently disguised under a pacifist garb.[41]

These governmental, political, and ideological factors are accompanied by organizational, technical, and logistical drawbacks. After basic and advanced individual training, draftees, other than those serving in highly specialized branches or units, tend to be assigned to garrison or office duties unrelated to military service in the strict sense of the term. In some cases, the geographical distribution of military personnel does not follow functional criteria. A frequently cited example refers to the fact that the military presence is greater in Latium — the region around Rome — than in Friuli, the anticipated principal zone of operations in case of war.

At present it is not difficult to satisfy the peacetime 300,000-man force aggregately required for the three services, but Italian demographic trends will cause a shortage of draftable personnel in the 1990s. In the absence of measures directed at increasing the length of national service —

attracting short-term volunteers, utilizing women for non-combat duties, or possibly assigning an active role to the reserve — defense capabilities will be downgraded. On the positive side, statistics for the years 1974–83 reflect a steady increase in the number of applications for admission to the military academies and for appointment as regular non-commissioned officers.

Of particular concern to the Ministry of Defense is the obsolescence and the insufficiency of certain types of armaments and equipment. As regards the matériel assigned to the northeastern sector, the following official observations are pertinent: 30 percent of the M-47 tanks are no longer reliable; 20 percent of the M-60 tanks are close to the end of their life cycle; a considerable number of 155 mm howitzers and 175 mm guns are "old generation"; part of the anti-tank weaponry, particularly recoilless rifles and bazookas, is antiquated; automatic data processing systems need to be installed; radar stations covering the Upper Adriatic Sea are insufficient; the number of assigned missile-equipped hydrofoils and helicopters and conventional gunboats is inadequate; and the F-104-G and Fiat G-91-Y aircraft urgently need replacement.

Similar problems are present in the southern sector: anti-submarine capability is insufficient; the same hold true in relation to air defense; the number of available destroyers, frigates, and minesweepers needs to be increased; corvettes and light ships require modernization; coastal radar systems are pending completion; long-range air reconnaissance must be enhanced; and more modern weapon systems must be acquired.

With respect to the overall air defense mission, the F-104-S interceptor aircraft is nearing the end of its life cycle. Army and air force anti-aircraft artillery is deemed insufficient. Radar systems require enhancement. In relation to the territorial defense mission, there is a requirement for the activation of a readily deployable reaction force. Finally, in case of full mobilization of the reserves, there would be shortages of equipment in various areas.

While plans are under way to replace obsolescent matériel — including joint production projects with other NATO countries — and fill required stocks, more serious problems exist with respect to military operations in case of prolonged conflict.

The Italian armed forces assigned to the defense of the northeastern frontier have the capability to withstand initially a minor or secondary attack from the Warsaw Pact countries, but would subsequently require external reinforcements, national and allied. Reinforcement by national troops raises a further problem, particularly in case of concurrent military operations in the southern sector of the peninsula and islands, since the forces stationed in that area during peacetime would have to be augmented through the mobilization of the reserves or even be supported by troops deployed in the north. Therefore, a conflict encompassing the entire national territory would inevitably require allied assistance.

In essence, Italy's resources — natural, industrial, and military — do not suffice to withstand alone the brunt of a major attack by the Soviet Union and its satellites. Nevertheless, its geostrategic position and military contribution in terms of peacetime deterrent and wartime operations greatly enhance the Western defense posture. Moreover, despite internal political and ideological dissidence, Italy has an unbroken record of commitment to the Atlantic Alliance, actively displayed, as late as 1984, with the initial deployment of cruise missiles as part of the West's response to Soviet intimidation. The Italian arms industry has substantially increased its output and the quality of its products, an achievement that parallels Italy's advances in peacetime industries. A final cause for optimism is Italy's willingness in recent years to participate in international peacekeeping missions, an important development that upgrades the operational preparedness of the Italian armed forces.

Notes

1. The Kingdom of Italy, founded in 1861, is regarded as the political continuation and the geographical expansion of the Kingdom of Sardinia under the dynasty of Savoy. The Italian unification process, the Risorgimento, was carried out by the liberal elite, the military establishment, and Giuseppe Garibaldi's irregulars. It was not a mass popular movement. The Fascist regime, which did not abolish the monarchy, took over governmental power with the assent of the crown from 1922 to 1943. It exalted the role of the armed forces, but, as a rule, drew their patriotic rather than their ideological/political commitment. The Republic was proclaimed on 2 June 1946, following a popular referendum. A small percentage of regular military officers, who felt that their allegiance was due to the person of the King, resigned from service without resorting to force.

2. A detailed assessment of the historical relationship between the military and Italian society appears in a series of articles published in *Politica Militare* (Turin) (April-May 1982). An English summary accompanies each article, written by Domenico Bartoli, Pietro Vasani, and Virginio Ilari.

3. The Constitution of the Republic of Italy was drafted by the Constitutional Assembly of 1946-47 and went into effect on 1 January 1948. It is substantially a compromise document produced by diverse and often adversary forces: Christian Democrats, Socialists, Communists, Liberals (nineteenth-century meaning of the term), Republicans, monarchists, and other minor political/ideological formations. Their only common denominator was their joint struggle against Fascism, particularly during the period 1943-45 when the Italian Social Republic was set up in northern Italy as a *pro forma* state controlled by Nazi Germany, and their intention of preventing the recurrence of Fascism or even a system of government characterized by a strong executive branch. Consequently, democracy and anti-Fascism became "catch-all" terms to express substantially different and clashing aims.

4. Prior to the Proclamation of the Republic, the Kingdom of Sardinia/Kingdom of Italy had waged a number of wars for unification, colonial, or other political purposes.

They include the First War of Independence (1848–49), the Crimean War (1855), the Second War of Independence (1859–61), colonial campaigns in Eritrea, Somaliland, and Libya (1870–1912), World War I (1915–1918), the Ethopian War (1935–36), intervention in the Spanish Civil War (1936–38), and World War II (1940–45). Those that occurred during the Fascist regime have been regarded since 1943 as Fascist wars of aggression. The second part of World War II (1943–45), thereafter celebrated as the War of Resistance, was in part a liberation movement against Nazi occupation — subsequent to Italy's surrender to the Allies in 1943 — and partially a civil war between those who remained faithful to Benito Mussolini, the founding father of Italian Facism, and the anti-Fascists. The anti-Fascist camp included reconstituted elements of the regular army and partisan formations of the various ideologies reported in note 3 above. The majority of the population, as had been the case during Risorgimento, were not active participants.

5. Article 11.
6. Article 52.
7. Article 98.
8. Article 59.
9. Law No. 382 of 11 July 1978.
10. Articles 18, 19, and 20.
11. Article 1.
12. Article 4.
13. Articles 5, 6, 7, and 9.
14. Articles 13, 14, 15, 16, and 21.
15. Coalition formulas since 1948 may be summarized as follows: centrist (Christian Democrats, Liberals, Social Democrats, and Republicans) from 1948 to 1962; center-left (Christian Democrats, Socialists, Social Democrats, and Republicans) from 1962 to 1972; brief return to the centrist formula in 1972–73; resumption of the center-left formula from 1973 to 1976; indirect/direct Communist support short of participation in the government from 1976 to 1979; and various nuanced formulas generally entailing a pentagonal Christian Democratic, Socialist, Social Democratic, Republican, and Liberal coalition since 1979. The last formula has seen the return of the Communist Party to its traditional opposition role, broken from time to time for the limited purpose of voting in favor of certain legislation after barter or compromise with the ruling coalition.
16. For a detailed historical overview with special reference to the land forces, see Stato Maggiore dell'Esercito, Ufficio Storico, *L'Esercito Italiano* (Rome, 1982).
17. The Parliament is a two-chamber legislative body elected directly by the people. It comprises the Chamber of Deputies and the Senate of the Republic, each of which has an Armed Forces or Defense Committee. Joint meetings of the two chambers take place in a very limited number of cases specified by the Constitution. None of them is applicable to defense matters.
18. In the constitutional scheme, the President of the Republic stands apart from the three traditional branches of government. Legal doctrine views this office as a constitutional organ created in the interest of constitutional legitimacy and observance. Because of this role as a "guardian" of the Constitution, his powers are frequently classified as "notarial."
19. Italy's system of government is a parliamentary system. In order to stay in office, the Council of Ministers (Government) must enjoy the confidence of Parliament. Its collegial nature causes decision-making, as well as political responsibility *vis-à-vis* Parliament, to be collective.
20. Ministers, except those "without portfolio," are members of the Council of Ministers and at the same time titular heads of the specific ministry assigned to them. Their responsibility is therefore twofold.
21. The Military Region should not be confused with the regional bodies of government. Italy is a unitary state subdivided into 20 regions, 96 provinces, and several thousand municipalities having derivative and limited powers specifically listed in the Constitution.
22. The operational and territorial structures reported above are drawn from the 1985 edition of the *Defense White Book:* Ministero della Difesa, *La Difesa: Libro Bianco 1985*

(Rome). Where comparable units are designated by different nomenclature, US military terminology is used in this chapter.

23. There are 11 brigades (9 of which are assigned territorial/law enforcement duties), 24 legions, 100 groups, 499 companies and lieutenancies, and 4,619 stations. The structure of the Carabinieri's territorial organization is generally patterned after the subdivision of Italy into regions, provinces, and municipalities reported in note 21 above. In fact, there is normally one legion in each region, one group in each province, and one station in most municipalities. The larger regions may have two legions, the larger provinces two or more groups, and the principal urban centers (municipalities such as Rome and Milan) several stations.

24. Assigned armaments listed in *Air Force Magazine* (December 1984).
25. Same source and terminological criteria as in note 22 above.
26. Ships listed in Stato Maggiore della Marina, Ufficio Documentazione, *Le Unità della Marina Militare* (Rome, 1984).
27. Same source and terminological criterion as in note 22 above.
28. Same source as note 24 above.
29. Reduction of naval service to 12 months is currently under consideration.
30. Same source as note 24 above.
31. Law no. 801 of 24 October 1977.
32. For a more detailed description and analysis in English of the Italian intelligence community before and after the 1977 reform law, see Vittorfranco S. Pisano, *A Study of the Restructured Italian Intelligence and Security Services* (Library of Congress, Washington DC, 1978), and same author, Chapter 4, "The Intelligence Reform of 1977," *Contemporary Italian Terrorism: Analysis and Countermeasures* (Library of Congress, Washington, DC, 1979).
33. Most journalistic reports concur with the foregoing description. For a particularly detailed report on the entire intelligence community, see *Panorama*, (Milan), May 8 1979, pp. 64–74.
34. See, for example, Piero Ostellino and Luigi Calligaris, *I Nuovi Militari* (Mondadori, Milan, 1983), pp. 183 and 192. Ostellino is a journalist, and Calligaris is a retired army general.
35. Ministero della Difesa, *La Difesa: Libro Bianco 1985*, Appendice Documentata, p. 47.
36. The five missions of the Italian armed forces as well as their disposition are drawn from the 1985 *Defense White Book*, notes 22 and 35 above. Additional data pertaining to the composition of the Italian armed forces are drawn from a highly polemical but detailed work prepared by Italy's Radical Party, *Quello che i Russi Sanno e gli Italiani non Devono Sapere* (IRDISP, Rome, 1983).
37. *Italy at a Critical Crossroads in her history*, a report by Senator Clairborne Pell to the Committees on Foreign Relations, United States Senate, on his trip to Italy, November 1976.
38. Winfred Joshua, "The Mediterranean and Italy: Global Context of a Local Problem" in *The Political Stability of Italy*, The Center for Strategic and International Studies, Georgetown University, Washington, D.C., 1976, p. 25.
39. *United States Military Installations and Objectives in the Mediterranean*, Report Prepared for the Committee on International Relations by the Foreign Affairs and National Defense Division, Congressional Research Service, Library of Congress, Washington, D.C., 1977, p. 26.
40. After the Constitution went into effect, only once have electoral returns given an Italian Political Party absolute majority status in the Parliament. It happened to the Christian Democratic Party in 1948. A contributory factor was the fear of a Communist victory: one of the aims of the Communist partisans during the War of Resistance (1943–45) had been to set up the "Italian Soviet Republic," as many electors remembered.
41. Since 1948 the PCI has consistently been the second largest party in Italy and since the 1976 parliamentary elections it has drawn between 30 and 34 per cent of the national vote.

7 FRENCH DEFENSE AND THE GAULLIST LEGACY

Douglas Porch

For nearly a half century now, France has appeared to be Europe's and the West's odd man out. A difficult ally at the best of times, it has tried the patience of its partners at least since the débâcle of May-June 1940 threw up two governments, each of which claimed to speak for France. In the post-war era, France tenaciously held to its colonies at a time of imperial disinvestment elsewhere. Hardly had the colonial wars ended and France re-directed its defense efforts to Europe, than de Gaulle put NATO on notice that France intended to script its own military policies, which it has continued to do ever since. Indeed, when attempting to analyze French behavior since 1945 pundits do not know whether to turn to history, to political science, or to Freud.

The Historical Background

If an examination of French defense policy often resembles an excursion into the intricacies popularly ascribed to the Oriental mind, this is in part because the heavy legacy of history and the divisions of French society have encouraged governments to adopt policies which have turned the most lucidly Cartesian of nations into a case study of "le paradoxe." France emerged from World War II a bitter and divided society. The right had been largely discredited because of its wartime collaboration with the Germans, and with it large sections of the armed forces, in particular the French navy — so influential had the navy become under the Vichy regime, that the Bishop of Lille was heard to express the fear that Marshal Pétain might replace him with an admiral.

When Charles de Gaulle resigned the presidency in 1946 to make way for the "régime des partis" which he so detested, the largely left-dominated Fourth Republic sought to settle old scores with its enemies in uniform. Between 1946 and 1948, over 13,000 "incorrigible Vichyite" officers were purged or forcibly retired from the French army, to be replaced in part by men who had (or perhaps had not) distinguished themselves in the Resistance. At the same time, military pay was slashed,[1] both to punish the forces for their anti-republican attitudes and to encourage a more "democratic" recruitment of officers. The results of these policies were not difficult to predict. As the purges had fallen most heavily on graduates of Saint-Cyr and the Ecole polytechnique, the intellectual level of the forces dropped and many good potential officers undoubtedly looked elsewhere for a career — by the mid-1950s, only 28.5 percent of new officers were being trained at Saint-Cyr, the rest coming up through the ranks. Also, the hoped for "democratization" of the officer corps fell short of the aspirations of the left. Rather than "democratize" recruitment (which, by the way, was already democratic), the Fourth Republic's policies accentuated a trend toward "internalization." The number of Saint-Cyr cadets from military families increased, so that by the mid-1950s, fully 58 percent of cadets counted a father or grandfather who was a career soldier. Even among officers trained at the Ecole spéciale militaire inter-armes (ESMIA), which prepares NCOs for commissions, 50.5 percent were sons of soldiers. The left did suceed in "democratizing" recruitment of the army in so far as many of the newly commissioned officers were now sons of NCOs rather than of officers. However, they soon discovered that "democratization," especially when linked to "internalization," forged a sword with the proverbial two edges. Many of these new men had sought commissions as a means of social advancement, and were disappointed, not to say embittered, by the official devaluation of the career of arms in the eyes of the nation in the form of low pay, sub-standard housing, slow promotion, and onerous duty.

Ever faithful to the paradox, however, the Fourth Republic pursued a series of bloody colonial conflicts abroad at the same time that it sapped the morale of its soldiers at home. Why France opted to battle it out in the colonies at a time when Woodrow Wilson's principle of "self determination of peoples" was elsewhere being extended to the imperium is a complex question, but can probably best be understood as a mixture of motives — the desire to recoup prestige forfeited in the collapse of 1940, an inability to separate French world influence and its traditional "civilizing mission" from the idea of an imperial domain, and, lastly, confusion and division at home which served to make the Third Republic appear a model of stability and statesmanlike example by comparison with its immediate successors.

The post-1945 colonial wars put one in mind of French Marshal Patrice MacMahon who, when visiting a fever hospital in Algeria, is alleged to have told a sick soldier, "Ah, typhoid. I've had that. Either it kills or it leaves you an idiot." For the Republic, these wars proved to be a terminal disease, while they left the army, and especially the colonial portion of it, in a dangerous state of psychosis. Relations between the French army and the Republic had been deteriorating steadily at least since the Dreyfus affair of 1894. After 1918, as the initial euphoria of victory quickly gave way to gloom as the costs, especially in lives, came to be counted, the generals were blamed for offering up a generation of Frenchmen, sacrifices to vanity and "esprit militaire." Nor did the political turbulence of the inter-war years leave the forces unscathed — the Socialists ritualistically voted against the defense budget, while some officers fraternized with sinister, conspiratorial elements on the right. The German invasion of 1940 touched off a bitter war of recrimination between politicians and the forces over who was to blame. The soldiers won the argument in the short term — Vichy laid responsibility for the defeat squarely at the feet of a decadent and divisive Republic.

However, Vichy did not have the final word. The French army had never presented a solid front. The least conformist sections of it — portions of the Foreign Legion, the *armée coloniale* and other dissident officers who had reached London — rallied to de Gaulle's appeal to fight on. Their numbers grew substantially from November 1942, when Operation Torch incorporated the *armée d'Afrique* into "La France combattante." In many respects, for French soldiers abroad, the liberation of France was a dream come true. The dissarray and instability of the Third Republic had served to convince influential sections of the colonial army, led by men like Gallieni and Lyautey, that Frenchmen lacked a nationalistic vision. For these men on the outside looking in, only the open air life of the colonies and the virile and constructive tasks of empire building offered an alternative to the self-consuming political divisions and quest for a risk-free existence which diminished the greatness of France. For them, 1944 offered the irrefutable proof, the positive confirmation, of the value of the French empire — the colonies had returned to save France.

Alas, the role of the colonial army in the liberation of France was barely acknowledged, credit going to the Americans, the Russians, and the Resistance. Hardly was the ink dry on Germany's capitulation than the colonial soldiers were marched off to their outposts of empire. The war in Indochina which sputtered to life in 1946 deepened their sense of isolation. Many of the native troops who had fought so loyally in Italy, France, and Germany now began to demonstrate a listlessness in combat which betrayed the first signs of doubt in the indestructibility of empire. France seemed at best indifferent, at worst hostile, to the sacrifices of its soldiers fighting over a vast and impossible terrain against what they saw as "la guerre révolutionnaire" directed from the Kremlin and the Forbidden City. When, in 1954, this struggle was adjourned to Algeria, the soldiers were in a foul mood. The reasons for the military revolt of 1958 which toppled the Fourth Republic and that of 1961 which sent a *frisson* of uncertainty through de Gaulle's young regime are too complex to be dealt with here. In general, they can be seen as the culmination of the army's attachment to its colonial mission, its frustration over its lack of victory since 1918, and, lastly, as the consequence of almost a century of steadily deteriorating relations between the army and the Republic.

The Gaullist era offered a renaissance for France, and nowhere was this more obvious than in defense policy. De Gaulle based his appeal on economic prosperity and political stability at home, while restoring the tarnished prestige of France abroad. The independence of France, and eventually of Europe, from the tutelage of the two power blocks formed his long-term goal. Defense was the first, and the essential, area in which Franch would make obvious its new direction in foreign policy. It was a bold new departure for France and one which broke with almost a century of tradition in foreign relations. Since its shattering defeat at the hands of the Prussians in 1870–71, France realized that it was a power in relative decline *vis-à-vis* its European neighbors. This produced varied reactions. Imperial conquest was one, an attempt to recoup in Africa the prestige which it had forfeited in Europe. A search for allies was a second — the breakdown of the Bismarckian order after 1890 allowed France to find friends in Russia in 1894 and Britain in 1904 to offset German advantages. Although France had resisted bravely in World War I it could be under no illusion that without the allies it would have succumbed to the Schlieffen Plan. As Hitler's power grew in the 1930s, France scurried to rebuild its alliance system. The defection of Italy to Hitler came as a great disappointment, for it made the "Petite Entente," the system of alliances with the fragments of the old Austro-Hungarian Empire, largely a nonsense. The apparent defection of Britain at Dunkirk followed by the British assault on the French fleet at Oran seemed to many French officers a fitting end to a frustrating attempt to cobble together a defense with a collection of slippery allies.

When, in 1962, de Gaulle finally liquidated the colonial wars and turned his attention to France's place in Europe, he launched what has been seen as a radical departure in defense policy. De Gaulle had been a late convert to the anti-imperialist camp, but by 1958, if not before, he had realized, as he put it, that, "L'Afrique est foutue et l'Algérie avec." France's prestige was no longer to be measured in the number of square kilometers of bush and desert which its troops occupied in Africa, but by the influence it could command in Europe. However, influence required military muscle. The colonial wars had retarded the modernization of the French forces because they required a preponderance of infantrymen at a time when European warfare had moved into the age of air power, missiles, and high technology. Until France could modernize its forces, it must remain one of NATO's second-class citizens shorn of influence, and, consequently, of prestige. His political enemies gasped with incredulity as the General withdrew France from NATO's integrated command in 1966 and announced the creation of a nuclear deterrent independent of the United States. De Gaulle merely predicted that, within a few years, all Frenchmen would be Gaullists. The truth of this statement has been cited as an example of de Gaulle's prescience. Today even the Parti socialiste has accepted the tenets of de Gaulle's master plan for defense. (The Communists accepted it almost immediately.)

In another sense, however, France was already Gaullist even before de Gaulle. Even as it searched for allies in the nineteenth and twentieth centuries, France was afflicted by a "Middle Kingdom complex." In the original Chines version, the Middle Kingdom was characterized by a general indifference to the doings of the barbarians beyond its borders and an acute sense of superiority of the Middle Kingdom and an acute sensitivity to any slight on its prestige.[2] This combination of attitudes was prominent in the Third Republic. The foreign policy issue most discussed in the two decades before 1914 was relations with the Vatican, which was tied to the issue of separation of church and state. Likewise, even before 1939, burning foreign policy issues like the question of intervention in the Spanish Civil War served more to define domestic political alignments than focus concern on the outside world. With the defeat of 1940, France withdrew almost completely from world politics, its leaders adopting the position that World War II was no longer France's concern.

France's intense nationalism and its frustrating experiences with alliance politics in the past helped to make de Gaulle's "independent deterrent" a readily acceptable alternative to reliance upon NATO in the minds of many Frenchmen who believed that France could somehow, for the first time in a century, escape the immutable laws of alliance politics and become a special case in European defense. For them, de Gaulle offered a Vichy regime without the occupation.

Gaullist attitudes to the outside world appear to be more a collection of traditional French fears and concerns, part of the old quest for prestige and discontent with the vagaries of coalition politics, than a new political philosophy. Likewise, when de Gaulle's defense policies are closely examined, they appear to be a less than radical departure from the past. True, the Third and Fourth Republics had sought security within the framework of alliance systems. But the "independence" of France's defense policy under the Fifth Republic does not really live up to its press notices, for, as several observers have noted, it relies on a credible American guarantee.[3] Alone, without the American nuclear umbrella, France would be as independent as a mollusk surrounded by a flock of seagulls.

When President François Mitterand and his Parti socialiste were voted to power in 1981, people expected, if not a "Night of the Long Knives," at least an important rearangment of personnel in the forces. However, it quickly became apparent that "la lutte finale" simply offered up more of "la même chose." As if to emphasize that he planned no abrupt changes in defense policy, Mitterand retained the Giscard-appointed Commander-in-Chief, General Jeannou Lascaze. Son of a colonial gendarme, paratrooper, Legionnaire, a much-decorated veteran of the "imperialist" wars in Indochina and Algeria, and former director of the French secret service SEDECE (whose Alice-in-Wonderland antics made those of the CIA and KGB combined appear positively rational by comparison), most Socialists must have believed that anything short of the guillotine was a less than fitting reward for Lascaze's services to the state.

The Socialist decision to retain many defense personnel has demonstrated that they intend to be very cautious about tampering with French defense policy. Observers have spoken of the new "realism" of Socialists in defense matters.[4] However, this realism has been the result of a gradual evolution of Socialist attitudes to France's role in Europe, and to the Gaullist legacy. Traditionally, the Socialists possess two characteristics which make it extremely difficult for them to reach decisions on defense questions — firstly, a very loose party discipline, and, secondly, an ambivalent, not to say hostile, attitude towards the forces. The first has been necessary to accomodate the great range of left-wing opinions and regional interests which congregate in the Socialist Party, and which set it apart from the rigidly disciplined Communists. In such a broad church, every man becomes his own theologian, and small seminaries form around influential spokesmen. It is difficult for a party leader to make the smack of firm direction felt among the power groups and independent personalities within the party. Therefore, he has two choices in the formulation of policy. He can wait for a consensus to emerge from the committees and party conferences. Or, he can, like the Socialist leader of the Popular Front government of 1936, Léon Blum, simply act in defense questions by executive fiat. Mitterand has done both.

The second charcteristic of the Socialists — hostility to the forces — is part the product of personal tastes, part of historical memory. Traditionally, the Socialist left has been far more interested in the political role of the army within the state than in questions of national defense. While eager to denounce the use of force in domestic politics, they proved reluctant in the past to think through the problems posed by the use of force in international affairs. Even though Léon Blum launched a massive rearmament program in 1936, the official line of the party maintained that national defense was not possible "en régime capitaliste." While the menace of Hitler grew ever larger, they continued to play *Versaillais* and *communards.* Only 35 Socialist deputies refused to vote "full powers" to Marshal Pétain in 1940.

After 1945, the Socialist Party (SFIO) became strongly Atlanticist, both because they recognized that France could no longer provide for its own defense, and because they saw a strong American presence in Europe as the best guarantee against a resurrection of the Wehrmacht. However, party opinion on defense questions — the European Defense Community debates of 1950–54, the militarization of the French nuclear program in 1956 — was divided. Like Blum before him, Guy Mollet, the SFIO leader, preferred to keep peace in the party by avoiding issues which were certain to cause ructions. During the Algerian War, the SFIO pushed their ambivalence to the point of total paralysis, allowing generals and *colons* to pursue an elusive "victory" while wringing their hands over the costs of war to France, both in human terms and in the price of tarnished international prestige. The party did unite against de Gaulle's explosion of the French bomb in 1960, his withdrawal from NATO's integrated command in 1966, and his *force de frappe,* arguing rather lamely that France could not afford the bomb and, secondly, that de Gaulle's policies would lead to a "confrontation of national forces."[5] But the SFIO, now in the final stages of decomposition, had little concrete to put in the place of de Gaulle's "new" vision.

The resurrection of the Socialist Party dates in part from 1969, when Mitterand realized that the General had succeeded in his threat to make all Frenchmen into Gaullists. Mitterand's brain trust in defense matters, Charles Hernu, set out to construct a coherent defense policy for the newly formed (in 1971) Parti socialiste, which would combine the traditional Socialist security solutions with the new reality of a national consensus behind de Gaulle's "independent" stance.

Hernu's has not been an easy task for, quite apart from anything else, the Socialists and Gaullists have in the past held quite different, even opposing, views on how armies should be organized. The left has taken its inspiration from Jean Jaurès' now classic *Armée nouvelle*, written in 1910. Jaurès' concerns were essentially two: firstly, he sought to open the officer corps to democratic influences and prevent the formation of a conservative, militarized leadership caste in the forces. Secondly, he wanted to create a broadly based army of conscripts, trained for six months followed by short periods of reserve mobilization, ready, in case of attack, to take up "the gun behind the cabin door." Jaurès argued that such an army would be close to the people and could not become a tool of domestic repression in the hands of the bourgeoisie. Nor was it capable of offensive action, so that, with such an army, France could not initiate a war of aggression. At the same time, hunkered down in its trenches and fortresses bristling like a hedgehog with bayonets, it would offer a formidable obstacle to any aggressor. The disastrous French offensives of the opening weeks of World War I, and the subsequent mobilization of virtually every fit Frenchman, seemed to lend credence in the interwar years to Jaurès foresight.[6]

The Social Context

While Jaurès' major concerns were political, de Gaulle began with the premise that advances in military technology had made forces of short-service conscripts obsolete. Armies required technicians, professionals capable of mastering gadgetry and managing an increasingly complicated military organization. Time has been on de Gaulle's side. Increasingly, conscript armies appear, in a military sense, to be dinosaurs in an age of advanced technology. Hernu's problem has been to re-edit *L'armée nouvelle* so that it reads more like *Vers l'armée de métier*.

In winning the Socialists over to more flexible and realistic military policies, Hernu has been aided by an evolution of attitudes and changes which have affected the two areas which most concerned Jaurès — recruitment of cadres, especially officers, and conscription. On the face of it, Socialists should be concerned about the officer corps for, if anything, it has become more narrowly recruited than even before. French lycées have a poor record in preparing their students for Saint-Cyr, so that places there go almost by default to sons of officers and NCOs trained in military preparatory schools — in 1972, 77.3 percent of Saint-Cyr cadets were trained in preparatory schools run by the army, and, in 1975, 88 percent of cadets were soldiers' sons. So successful is the socialization process at these preparatory schools that boys who fail to gain entrance to Saint-Cyr often enlist rather than seek a career in civilian life.[7] NCOs have been drawn traditionally from the "demographic surplus" of rural areas. A significant number of them are from disturbed or unstable family backgrounds — 22 percent list parents who are divorced, dead, or unknown.[8] Many volunteers come from "marginal social groups."[9]

This does not necessarily mean that the French army's efficiency has been compromised by its narrow recruitment base. French officers especially see the army as a vocation. They are well trained, dedicated, and resilient. Nor does the fact that roughly 80 percent of the 900 or so second lieutenants commissioned each year are drawn from the NCO corps lower officer standards. While the entrance requirements at Saint-Cyr are certainly less rigorous than in other French *grandes écoles*, they are still stringent and places there are at a premium. Therefore, it is fairly common for young men of good family to enlist in the hope of rapid promotion through the ranks, often with the support of influential officers in the regiment. Nevertheless, Saint-Cyr graduates still monopolize the higher ranks, in part because they are commissioned at a younger age than their ex-NCO contemporaries who are often eliminated by age requirements in the middle ranks.

The group most affected by this system is the NCO corps. The French raid their NCO ranks for officers to a greater extent than do most other Western armies. The reasons for this are historical and can be traced to the Napoleonic tradition of a "career open to talents," and to the fact that, since the *ancien régime*, there has been no group in French society which has traditionally furnished officers for the army, like, for instance, the Junkers in Prussia. Consequently, there is no stable NCO "class" in France. Rather, there is a constant hemorrhage of many of the best sergeants into the officer corps. The problem is probably less severe in elite units like the marines, paratroops, or Foreign Legion where unit loyalty, lower career expectations, insufficient command of the French language or of French military practices, and possibly even peer pressure, work to content men with sergeants' stripes. These units also attract high-quality recruits — the

Foreign Legion, for example, accepts only one applicant in six.

While Socialists are concerned by this high degree of self-recruitment, most explain it as the result of the falling prestige of the forces. That they no longer fear the military, however, has far more to do with their own perception of themselves rather than to any trends in officer recruitment. The Socialists now feel "legitimized," an integral part of French political life, and possess more confidence in their own staying power and support than in the past. They see themselves as the natural channel of protest and as an organization geared to redressing grievances. Hernu's contacts with officers exposed early on a seam of discontent in the forces waiting to be mined. He established a journal which he called (without much imagination) *L'Armée Nouvelle* to print complaints from NCOs about poor pay and conditions of service, and from officers who castigated the "asphixie intéllectuelle" of the forces. When the conscript discontent of 1974 erupted into demonstrations in several garrisons, Hernu was careful to disassociate the PS from the anti-militarists, supporting better conditions for conscripts but avoiding anything which might challenge the military hierarchy — he called the demands for the unionization of the forces "a nonsense."[10] Hernu has repeated that a professional force need not be a praetorian one, citing the Portuguese revolution of 1974 as evidence that professional soldiers can be sensitive to the needs of the country.[11] The responsibility for internal order which, in Jaurès day, resided ultimately with the army, is now the province of special police formations — the CRS and the Garde Mobile. While the government has expressed concern about the narrowness of Saint-Cyr recruitment, and about the social values and hazing which discourage the more "scientific" applicants,[12] their concerns seem to be to raise the calibre of professional soldiers rather than to create an army which is "closer to the people."

The attitudes towards defense and the United States held by many of the intellectuals and professional people who make up the Socialist Party has also evolved in the past three decades. In the 1950s, French intellectual circles were, generally speaking, pro-Soviet, at a time when the rest of Europe looked to America for aid and protection. Since 1958, France has lived under a regime whose elite was more or less hostile to the United States. Therefore, the opposition did not confront a government which was perceived as too dependent on America for inspiration and support. The bitter rivalry between Socialists and Communists in France, a rivalry which reaches back to the Tours Congress of 1920, did little to make the Eastern European example an attractive alternative for much of the French left. The Stalinism and organized cynicism of the French Communist Party, the speed with which it rushes to justify the most brutal and arbitrary acts of the Soviet Union, make America appear the more attractive option. Even if the Socialist left does not always agree with the policies of the United States, it regards itself as being firmly in the Western camp, and is almost pro-American by default.[13]

The attitude of the left to conscription has also evolved over the past decade. One of the fundamental reforms of the French Revolution, conscription has been supported by the left as a guarantee against class exploitation and military adventurism.[14] However, the reduced need for conscripts in the increasingly professionalized forces has meant that conscription has tended to fall especially heavily on those without the education or influence to escape it, like sons of immigrants. Nor do the forces seem to be able to employ conscripts profitably — half or more end up in overstaffed, non-military assignments which lower efficiency.[15] It is still argued that conscription is important in the socialization process, that it is a recognition of one's acceptance in the national community. But its rather arbitrary application and the general feeling among young men that it is a waste of time, even a handicap, has added force to the arguments of those who call for conscription to be evaluated in a rational, and not in an ideological context.

This view has been strengthened by the actions of conscripts themselves. Until quite recently, one of the major arguments in favor of conscription was that it provided large numbers of soldiers very cheaply. The argument was especially convincing as the long colonial wars had delayed modernization of the French forces, which required rather more riflemen than electronic experts. Conscripts served for little more than a few packets of "Gaulois" each month, topped up by family allowances. The fact that the French standard of living, especially in rural areas, remained relatively low until the economic upturn of the 1960s allowed conscripts to be housed in minimum comfort. In September 1974, conscript discontent over low pay, poor conditions in the barracks, and restrictions like the prohibition of certain periodicals and a parsimonious leave policy exploded with a demonstration of 200 conscripts in Draguignan, followed by others in Karlsruhe, Verdun, Nancy, and Lunéville. Soldiers' committees materialized in many garrison and demanded to negotiate with the military hierarchy. Giscard quieted the situation by raising pay, liberalizing leave policies, granting free trips on public transport to conscripts, and allowing a greater range of newspapers in the barracks.

Since then, Mitterand has increased pay yet again, so that a conscript army is no longer the cheap option it once was. Indeed, in terms of efficiency, it may now be more expensive than an all-professional force.

This is not to say that conscription will soon be abandoned. It is still very much part of the political culture of the nation, and most Frenchmen favor it — albeit in a shortened version. The Socialists have admitted that conscription is totally obsolete, but that it still has political life in it. Ironically, the strongest support for conscription comes from the army itself — 72 percent of officers in a recent poll supported continued conscription, while only 19 percent favored its abolition. For the army especially, conscription is seen as a "symbolic involvement" of the nation in its defense, an institution which guarantees an "intimate relationship" between the army and France. It prevents the social isolation of the forces by assigning to them a central civic role to play in the education of French youth, and one which limits the alienating effects of increasing technology and the bureaucratization of the forces.[16]

How have the Socialists, then, effected the marriage between Jaurès and de Gaulle? Elected on a promise to reduce military service to six months, the climbing unemployment rate caused them to delay reform until the summer of 1984, when conscription was set at nine months. To make up the shortfall in manpower, they have instituted a supplementary voluntary enlistment program (VSL) which allows conscripts to re-enlist at higher pay with choice of garrison and job assignment for a period of four to twelve months. Hernu has called for 20,000 VSLs, but at last report the results have been disappointing, due, it is hinted, to the hostility of the regular cadre.[17]

If the force structure which emerges from Hernu's program looks like an odd hybrid when viewed in the historical context of French defense — a hedgehog of French conscript reservists behind a "fer de lance" of tough professionals — it is in part because in their attempt both to leave the Gaullist consensus unruffled and to honor their own Socialist traditions, they have sewn confusion. However, confusion or, to put it more kindly, ambiguity is a necessary component of the French defense equation.

Nuclear versus Conventional Strategies

French "dissuasion" has two separate components — nuclear, both strategic and tactical, and conventional forces, whose job is to be prepared to fight in Europe as well as keep the peace in France's ex-colonies. The strategic forces are composed of a triad of weapon systems under each of the three services: the army controls the 18 IRBMs each with 1 megaton warhead located amidst the lavender fields of the Haute Provence on the Plateau d'Albion. The air force possesses 30 odd Mirage IV-A bombers which deliver an AN-22 gravity bomb with a 70 kiloton warhead. Sixteen Mirage 200-N aircraft designed for nuclear penetration have also been ordered by the air force.[18] The navy will soon have seven nuclear submarines, fitted with the new M4 missile. While this looks impressive on paper, many of these weapon systems, especially those of the air force, are desperately in need of modernization.[19]

The "tactical" arsenal (which the French now call "pre-strategic") is composed of five regiments armed with Pluton missiles with a range of 60 miles. Not unnaturally, the Germans are worried that the short range of the Pluton means that, if fired from France, they would fall to earth inside the Federal Republic. Therefore, the Pluton are soon to be replaced by the Hades, whose somewhat longer range means that, if fired from Strasbourg, they might just reach Poland. The air force's contribution to the "pre-strategic" arsenal consists of two squadrons of Mirage III-Es and three squadrons of Jaguars armed with nuclear gravity bombs (the AN-52) with a 20 kiloton warhead. The navy has flotilla of Superétendard aircraft which fly off the carriers Foch or Clemenceau.

The conventional forces, and particularly the army, have suffered most in the nuclear buildup. The long colonial wars delayed modernization, as did the division of labor within NATO which required that the French contribute infantry rather than technical expertise to the defense of Europe. De Gaulle's decision to break with NATO and go nuclear was an expensive decision for the army — first the air force, then, from 1972, the navy received the lion's share of funds for research and development of nuclear armaments. French nuclear doctrine, which treats strategic and tactical nuclear weapons *en bloc* rather than as separate categories, delays, if it does not eliminate altogether, a whole dimension of battlefield capabilities. The decision to raise conscript pay has eroded still further the cash available for modernization — by 1980, 75 percent of the defense budget was put toward pay and pensions.[20] While the French armaments industry has expanded and proves capable of manufacturing class equipment (much of it, critics claim, designed to fetch Arab oil money rather than fight in Europe), the army has too little of it. Much of the army's equipment is extremely good, some of it the best in the world — the 5.56 mm Fama rifle, the newly developed AUF-1 155 mm self-propelled gun, the Rita automatic-switching communications system, and the AMX-10RC armored car. While the regular army is fairly well equipped, budget cuts may mean that the army may in future find it difficult to replace and renew equipment.

The army is deficient in some areas, however. The lack of a main battle tank is probably the most notable defect. The recent decision to modernize the AMX-30 tank, which is considered too light and poorly armed, rather than develop a new tank plated with laminated-composite armor and equipped with a heavy gun as are the tanks of the NATO countries, was much criticized. France plans to collaborate with West Germany in the production of a new tank which, it is hoped, will be available in the early 1990s. "Until then," in the words of *The Economist*, "France is doomed to face its enemies with the worst tank of any major military power in the world."[21] Other *lacunae* in the French arsenal include anti-tank weapons like the Milan, which has an unfortunate tendency to bounce off new types of armor, the radar-guided Roland anti-aircraft missile which, though excellent, is too heavy for use by FAR, and a shortage of modern 155 mm self-propelled artillery, which the new AUF-1 seeks to rectify. The French need more attack helicopters like the Super-Puma to replace the aging Franco-German Gazelle-Hot.[22] Equipment for the reserve divisions is also looking distinctly long in the tooth.

The current trend in French force structure, and one which has been accelerated by the Socialists, is to replace a bloated army with a leaner, more potent force — "equipment rather than men." As a consequence, the army has been slashed from over 400,000 men barely a decade ago to one of about 290,000 today. The most radical innovation instituted by Hernu has been the creation of the Force d'action rapide (FAR) — 47,000 Foreign Legionnaires, paratroops, marines, air-mobile and light armored troops whose job would be to destroy Soviet tanks in Europe. It also has the mission of intervening in Africa if, that is, the French can get them there. The French are desperately short of transport aircraft, so that their recent intervention in Chad had to be accomplished courtesy of the USAF. So, without help, Germany is about as far as FAR can be. French units have proven their worth in Chad, stopping cold Ghadaffi's attempts to invade the south of the country, and in the brief, ill-fated intervention in Lebanon. The French prefer to send either the marines or the Foreign Legion to these spots — both have a tradition of intervention outside Europe, a thirst for action, and an intense rivalry which dates from the heroic period of French imperial expansion before World War I. But FAR has other problems — it is not a force in being, but a collection of separate, often contrasting, units which must be cobbled together in wartime. Also, it is fairly riven with intraservice rivalries over its proper function. One school argues that FAR should be a French contribution to a conventional European defense effort, fighting by the side of France's NATO allies in a "deep strike" against Warsaw Pact forces. Others see FAR as a "trip wire" which will release a French nuclear strike in line with France's concept of protecting its "vital interests."

Much of the French army's fighting power resides with the First Army, which is divided into three corps — the first in eastern France contains two armored, one air-mobile, and one school division. The second corps, in West Germany, counts three armored divisions, and the third, in northern France, has one armored, one infanry, and a school division. French divisions are smaller than their American and most of their European counterparts — an armored division, for instance, consists of two tank, two mechanized infantry, one artillery, one engineer and one logistics regiment, and an anti-tank company, making a total of 7,000 men. (A French regiment numbers about 800 men, the size of an American battalion.) One hundred and forty-eight battle tanks, 245 armored personnel carriers, 24 155 mm self-propelled artillery pieces and 50 anti-tank missile launchers make up its equipment. A mechanized division has three infantry and one tank regiment as well as artillery, logistics, and engineer units, and counts almost the same number of men as an armored division. It includes 36 tanks, 370 APCs, 24 howitzers and 84 anti-tank missile launchers. Up to 19,000 French troops are stationed overseas in the Caribbean, Tahiti, Djibouti, and Senegal, and lately in Chad and the Lebanon. The 83,000 strong *gendarmerie nationale,* which falls under the war ministry, has been assigned the task of territorial defense (DOT).[23]

French professional forces, though under-equipped, are as good as any and better than most — French paratroopers, marines, and, especially, the 8,000-man French Foreign Legion are highly professional and have few, if any, equals. The Achilles heel of French defense is its reserve organisation. Upon mobilization, many line units would be doubled in size with the addition of reservists. While most reservists are assigned to logistical and rear-area roles, large and unwieldy reserve units exist on paper which the government, in the event of war, would be hard-pressed to equip.[24]

The French would give a good account of themselves in any

encounter with the Soviets in Central Europe. Their divisions are small, highly mobile and heavily armed. However, as Stephen Ross has pointed out, the destructive intensity of modern warfare would mean that, within a matter of weeks at most, these units would be forced "to retreat or face annihilation . . . In fact, the army is structured in such a manner as to require the employment of nuclear weapons after a brief period of conventional warfare."[25]

While the French Socialist government has been surprisingly innovative in its restructuring of the French army, it has not altogether kept its promise to substitute equipment for manpower. Much of the money saved by reductions in personnel have been put into nuclear, not conventional, forces. That more has not been done for the army has been due to economic mismanagement rather than to ideology or strategic theory. Within one year of taking office, the Mitterand government had wiped out the trade surplus bequeathed by its predecessor, frittered away France's cash reserves, pushed up inflation, and turned France into the world's third debtor nation behind Mexico and Brazil. As a consequence, it was forced to introduce a policy of austerity far more draconian than anything the conservatives had dared attempt.[26] The defense budget was the first to feel the bite. Initially, the government intended to increase money for defense so that by 1983 it would account for 3.94 percent of GNP. However, austerity measures hit the army especially hard, so that increases in the defense budget have hardly kept up with inflation. The government has lopped off 1,300 million francs from the 1985 defense budget and announced that it plans to reduce the forces by another 6,707 conscripts, 1,759 regulars, and 650 civilian employees.[27] This has delayed plans to convert two armored divisions into more specialized infantry divisions trained to fight against armor in urbanized environments, a light armored division, and several air-mobile anti-tank regiments — the army is attempting to commit the government to purchase the Super-Puma combat helicopter for the 4th airmobile division which is to be ready for service in July 1985, as well as other combat helicopters to replace the aging Franco-German Gazelle-Hot.[28]

The cold winds of poverty have left the service chiefs disgruntled. In 1982, chief of the army General Delauney resigned amidst great publicity over the savage manpower cuts in his service. On 9 October 1982, the newspaper *Le Matin* published a confidential report which complained of an army whose "manpower is reduced, whose organization is weakened, whose equipment is old, and whose morale is low." The chief of the air force said that, if Socialist military policies were allowed to continue, the number of combat aircraft would be reduced from 450 to 300 before the twenty-first century. The chief of the navy also complained that, by the next decade, his service would not be able to carry out its assigned missions. Nor was their anger focussed only on the Socialists — in chorus they complained that, since 1969, France's military budget "has not been that of a great power."[29] Therefore, successive French governments have failed to provide the cash to allow France to play the world role to which it aspires. The major charge that one can lay at the feet of the present government is that, despite a mature interest in remodeling French forces, it has so debilitated the economy that fundamental re-equipping and restructuring may now be impossible.

A second factor which militates against a coherent French defense structure is that no one is quite certain of France's role in the defense of Europe. It has been argued that the Gaullist heritage has been good for the Socialists, for it forced them to follow in the wake of past policies rather than sail off into the uncharted and storm-tossed waters of Socialist ideology, those same seas that left the economy swamped and the crew fighting to save the ship. Popular consensus has forced the Parti socialiste to respect the basic tenets of Gaullist policy — independence in national defense, France's special status as an Atlantic ally, reliance on a national nuclear force, and opposition to a rigid bipolar international system.[30] However, tinkering with the force structure, especially that of the army, has raised questions about how far the Socialists are prepared to stretch a very brittle Gaullist foreign policy and defense doctrine to accommodate changes in international relations and in weapons systems.

When, from 1958, de Gaulle began to take his distance from NATO and announced that henceforth France would initiate an all-round defense, "à tous azimuts," many thought that his romantic vision of France "like the Madonna in the frescos" had got the better of his reason. But while it is true that the furtherance of French greatness was never far from the General's mind, his actions did rest on a national assessment of big power realities — namely that American interest in Europe might one day weaken, leaving Europe virtually defenseless against a powerful Soviet Union. He espoused a vision of Europe united in common defense as a third force between the two superpowers. On the face of it, it would appear that his arguments might have had a better chance of being accepted in Europe than in his own country, where attachment to the Atlantic Alliance was strong. In fact, quite the opposite occurred. While Europe is frequently exasperated by

American "hegemony," they are not so discontented that they are prepared to abandon the Alliance in favor of a laudatory but unproven system vulnerable to squabbling and national division. Whatever its faults, the Alliance is seen as an expression of the cultural and political ties between Europe and North America. It has stabilized Western Europe and integrated the Federal Republic of Germany into the state system. A strong American presence is seen as a guarantee against German resurgence, and an American commanding general as a way to prevent the bickering that would certainly occur if Europe were to choose a commander from its own ranks — the size of armed forces would indicate a German, which would be unacceptable to the rest of Europe for historical reasons, while a commander from a smaller country would not have the power base necessary to impose his authority.[31]

The initial reaction to de Gaulle's policies in France was incredulity. For almost a hundred years, France had sought security in alliance systems, and an independent nuclear force seemed to offer a dangerously isolationist course of action. Socialist leader Gaston Deferre blasted "an arrogant diplomacy in the service of a haughty policy which leads to insecurity."[32] However, de Gaulle was aided by several factors in gaining popular acceptance for his new direction in defense policy. De Gaulle's independent course helped to allay the feeling among Frenchmen that they were merely pawns between the two superpowers. The age of détente was dawning which made the Soviet Union appear to be less of a menace.[33] Anti-American attitudes among French intellectuals (a broad and active class) which dated from the Cold War helped to ease acceptance on the left. The French Communist Party supported by de Gaulle wholeheartedly, for they saw France slipping into a neutralist stance which could only help the Soviet Union. The SFIO, on the other hand, was in its final stages of decay, so that violent complaints that de Gaulle's policies would lead to a "confrontation of nations" packed little political punch. Indeed, it rather tended to demonstrate how little the left had actually thought about defense questions.[34]

Even before de Gaulle's resignation in 1969, the credibility of his independent policies had begun to slip. How far de Gaulle really wanted to distance France from the Atlantic Alliance is a matter of conjecture — certainly his all-round defense rang a trifle hollow. The 1968 Soviet invasion of Czechoslovakia helped to end the illusion that Moscow might allow the Warsaw Pact to wither away and be replaced by a pan-European entity. Georges Pompidou hedged closer to the US, but objected to SALT and test ban and nuclear proliferation treaties as part of a superpower "collusion" to retain their hegemony by disarming smaller powers.[35] French defense continued to rely principally on a policy called "sanctuarization," or a threat to unleash its nuclear arsenal if the "sanctuary" of France were threatened.

By 1974, when Valéry Giscard d'Estaing became President, it had become apparent that France was not an island, that a European "Third Force" was not an immediate possibility, and that some accommodation must be made with France's allies. The one which gave the most cause for concern, apart from the US, was West Germany. Germany, for a century the major threat to France, now provides that margin of security which means that, for the first time in its recent past, France is no longer in the front line. A stable Germany, then, has become almost as important for French peace of mind as a credible American presence in Europe. Here, again, the paradox of Gaullist logic confuses, rather than enlightens, the situation. When West German leaders questioned France's willingness to defend West Germany, Giscard replied with a concept which he called the "sanctuaire élargi" — in other words, he extended the French nuclear umbrella to cover the Federal Republic. Quite predictably this set off a heated debate in France in which each side claimed in oracular fashion to be the true interpreters of the General's thoughts. The orthodox Gaullists and their allies on the Communist left saw the "sanctuaire élargi" as a betrayal of de Gaulle's independent defense and a dangerous slip toward *de facto* integration into the Alliance. Supporters argued that de Gaulle had never severed relations with the Alliance and that the defense "à tous azimuts" was simply a public relations gambit with no basis in reality. However, it soon became clear that French opinion was troubled by anything other than a strictly national posture, that any generalized political debate which stripped away the ambiguity of French defense policy was divisive and counter-productive, and the "sanctuaire élargi" quietly shed its adjective.

One of the advantages of the debate over the "sanctuaire élargi" was that it concentrated the minds of the Socialists on defense questions. Opinions divided broadly into three groups. Charles Hernu defended a quasi-Gaullist position, arguing that the bomb and the *force de frappe* were necessary to prevent France from being manipulated by the larger powers. France need not have a large number of missiles, but just enough to "make her rights respected." The left wing of the party grouped in the CERES and led by Jean-Pierre Chévènement also came round to the bomb, both as an umbrella beneath which a Jaurèsian "popular mobilization" could be organized, and as a way to guarantee a neutralist stance between the two superpowers. Robert Pontillon argued in defense of the Atlantic stance of the old SFIO, accepting that the bomb should remain national, but that, on the conventional level, France should commit to Europe, in particular West Germany. Although the anti-nuclear group in the party remained strong, the once derided "bombinette" had now become, in Socialist eyes, the best guarantee of French independence. Soon after taking power in May 1981, Mitterand established a defense committee which concluded in a statement worthy of de Gaulle himself that "Frenchmen would not feel they existed as Frenchmen unless they maintained important armed forces."[36]

As has been noted, the French consensus on defense has been based on ambiguity. How long the government may be able to maintain that ambiguity is an open question, for technical changes in armaments are narrowing France's range of strategic and political choices. Not only have tactical nuclear weapons introduced another level of combat choice between France's strategic strike and conventional capabilities which push it inexorably toward a Central European role, but also the deployment of these weapons has shaken the two pillars upon which French security rests — a stable Germany and a credible American guarantee. The arrival of the Pershing II missiles in Europe accentuated the fears of many Europeans that their land might become a nuclear battleground, and set bucolic American legislators grumbling about European ingrates who were not even prepared to allow someone else to do their fighting for them. The peace movement, which has had a substantial political impact in Britain, Belgium, Holland, and especially in West Germany, has left France virtually untouched. This is due in part to the fact that these American missiles were not deployed in France and that, as France is the proprietor of its own nuclear arsenal, it has not mortgaged its defense completely to a foreign power. While there is no doubt a strong element of truth in this, it is equally worthy of note that France has never had a potent pacifist tradition, the population, even on the left, accepting the need for a strong defense. The support of the PS and the Catholic church for a nuclear deterrent, and the active participation of the French Communist Party in the peace movement which has helped to discredit it in French eyes, put out any sparks of discontent caused by the Pershing II question.

Faltering German resolve and the threat of American "decoupling" have, ironically perhaps, made Mitterand into one of Reagan's staunchest European advocates, to the point that the French President even travelled to Bonn to lecture the West German Parliament on their responsibilities to European defense. Although the jury is still out, the creation of the FAR and the transformation of French forces into a leaner, more muscular organization indicates that France has edged closer to acceptance of a "forward battle" concept. The French Prime Minister attended the NATO summit in 1982, and offered to host it in Paris in 1983. Mitterand has stated categorically that France intends to respect Article 5 of the Treaty of Paris, which obliges each member of the Alliance to come to the aid of a member who is attacked.[37] However, as the domestic consensus on defense depends upon its ambiguity, the French have so far declined to occupy a designated sector of the NATO front. France has also rejected the Rodgers doctrine of "flexible response," insisting on treating tactical nuclear weapons as if they were strategic ones. They are reserved for use only on the President's order and, consistent with French doctrine, are to be fi.ed as a "final warning" to the Warsaw Pact if they threaten the "sanctuary" of the hexagon.[38]

The Future

Despite the logic of military change that has pushed France *à petits pas* toward a Central European defense role, its commitment to NATO remains in dispute. Some argue that a revitalized Parti socialiste is far more radical in this regard than the old SFIO. Mitterand's primary concern has been to re-establish the military balance of power in Europe which was upset by the deployment of Soviet SS-20s. Once this is achieved, the French left might lapse back into its old anti-Americanism.[39] There seems little firm evidence to support this view. While the rhetoric of the party is sometimes strong, much of its grass roots support is conservative and provincial, and sees a vote for the Socialists as a protest against a strongly centralist French state ruled from Paris. Also, the leadership — Mitterand and Hernu — seem firmly committed to realism rather than radicalism in defense questions. If an anti-American, anti-NATO attitude does revive on the Socialist left, it may result from a defeat in the 1986 elections. It appears that the Independent Republicans (RPR) and especially the Gaullist UDF are committed to greater cooperation with West Germany and perhaps even a re-nuclearization of French conventional forces by returning "pre-strategic" weapons to the field.[40] If this happens, then the Socialists may adopt a more neutralist stance to define their policy clearly from that of the right. However, it must be remembered that on defense questions no party offers a united front. There is no classic left–right split on defense, and all parties contain those who see the independent deterrent as *de facto* armed neutrality and those who remain committed to Europe and the Alliance.[41] But whichever party is in power, it is certain that nuclear armaments, especially strategic ones, are those which divide French opinion the least.[42]

Because its defense policy rests on an ambiguous consensus, France has every interest in preserving the status quo in Europe. However, the evolution of nuclear armaments makes the Gaullist legacy that all parties are struggling to maintain appear increasingly fragile. The French have resisted the logical implications of tactical nuclear weapons, retaining their threat to retaliate against the population of the Soviet Union rather than against its forces. However, tactical weapons are essentially "counter-force" in character, and French claims that they merely form part of the "final warning shot" appear increasingly threadbare. Also, advances in Soviet technology have made the French deterrent appear increasingly vulnerable, while the vastness of the USSR makes the French threat to retaliate against its population appear less credible. The Soviets might also act on the periphery of Europe against strategic interests rather than carry out a frontal assault against the West, condemning the French arsenal to remain in its silos and bases.

Nor do challenges to French independence come only from the East — the Strategic Defense Initiative announced by President Reagan, provided it actually works, threatens to render the French deterrent obsolete at a stoke and create a super-nucleur league in which France would not be able to compete. In this case, the illusion of independence would be shattered and the French might fall prey to the same doubts and fears as many other Europeans. It is also possible that NATO may in future shift its conventional strategy from one of "forward defense" in West Germany to interdictory attacks into Eastern Europe. This could complicate things for France in at least two ways: firstly, French opinion will almost certainly be unwilling to support an offensive strategy against the Warsaw Pact. Secondly, it may mean that France's "final warning shot" could be loosed upon its friends rather than its enemies.[43]

Political, geographical, and technical realities, therefore, are threatening to solve the French defense dilemma for it. When forced to choose between neutralism and independence, and a defense commitment to West Germany and the Alliance, France is being drawn toward the latter. However, it is important within the context of French domestic politics that this shift be accomplished as far as possible by stealth. While the pacifist movement is not strong in France, there remains the very real danger of a protest "at the top" which might drive France into a sort of neutralist posture.[44] Any abrupt or well publicized move toward the Alliance would provoke a debate over doctrine which would confuse, rather than enlighten, the issues. As things now stand, political and technical changes may soon mean that ambiguity is not enough to maintain the French consensus on defense. Were this to happen, French policy may shade off into confusion and improvisation.[45] While the French recognize that they are no longer the world's most powerful nation, they still believe themselves the most intelligent. If keeping everyone, allies and enemies alike, guessing is a sign of intelligence, then perhaps they are right. Until then, France must remain the master of the paradox.

Notes

1. J.P. Thomas and R. Girardet, "Problèmes de recrutement" in R. Giradet (ed.), *La crise militaire française, 1945–1962* (Paris, 1964), p. 22.
2. Christopher Andrew and A.S. Kanya-Forstner, *France Overseas* (London, 1981), p. 29.
3. *L'Express*, 13–19 July 1984, pp. 44–50.
4. See, for instance, A.W. DePorte, "France's New Realism," *Foreign Affairs*, no. 63 (Fall 1984), pp. 144–165.
5. Pascal Krop, *Les socialistes et l'armée* (Paris, 1983), pp. 42–44.
6. Jean Jaurès, *L'armée nouvelle* (Paris, 1977).
7. Michel Martin, *Warriors into Managers: The French Military Establishment since 1945* (Chapel Hill, NC, 1981), 311–315.
8. Ibid, pp. 244–245.
9. François Cailleteau, Contrôleur des armées, "Les principaux problèmes de la politique du personnel militaire en France dans les années 80," unpublished paper, Centre d'études et le recherche de l'armée, Colloque de Toulouse, 1–4 October 1980, p. 5.
10. Krop, *Les socialistes et l'armée*, p. 73.
11. A poor example, as the Portuguese soldiers revolted for professional, not political reasons. See Douglas Porch, *The Portuguese Armed Forces and the Revolution* (Stanford and London, 1977).
12. Krop, *Les socialistes et l'armée*, p. 73.
13. Dominique Moisi, "Les limites du consensus" in Pierre Lellouche (ed.), *La contestation pacifiste et l'avenir de la sécurité de l'Europe* (IFRI, Paris, 1983), p. 258.
14. Martin, *Warriors into Managers*, p. 140.
15. Ibid., p. 129.
16. Ibid., pp. 148–152.
17. *Le Monde*, 20 July 1984.
18. Ibid., 19 September 1984.
19. Steven Ross, "French Defense Policy," *Naval War College Review* (May-June 1983), p. 31.

20. Cailleteau, "Les principaux problèmes," p. 2.
21. "The French Army. Shield and Sword for Europe?" *The Economist*, 23 June 1984, p. 39.
22. *Le Monde*, 16–17 September 1984.
23. Ross, "French Defense Policy," pp. 32–33.
24. "The French Army. Shield and Sword for Europe?" p. 39.
25. Stephen Ross, "France" in Richard Gabriel (ed.), *Fighting Armies, NATO and the Warsaw Pact* (Westport, Conn., 1983), p. 100.
26. Michael H. Harrison, "Mitterand's France in the Atlantic System: A Foreign Policy of Accommodation," *Political Science Quarterly*, no. 99 (Summer 1984), pp. 239–240.
27. *Le Monde*, 19 September 1984.
28. Ibid., 16–17 September 1984.
29. Krop, *Les socialistes et l'armée*, pp. 143–144.
30. Harrison, "Mitterand's France," p. 244.
31. A.W. DePorte, *The Atlantic Alliance at 35* (Foreign Policy Association, March/April 1984), pp. 33, 58, 12–13.
32. Krop, *Les socialistes et l'armée*, p. 42.
33. DePorte, "France's New Realism," pp. 151, 146.
34. Krop, *Les socialistes et l'armée*, p. 44.
35. Martin, *Warriors into Managers*, pp. 25–26.
36. Krop, *Les socialistes et l'armée*, pp. 85–93, 123–124.
37. Ibid, pp. 148–149.
38. *Le Monde*, 8 November 1984; see also Jonathan Macus and Bruce George, "The Ambiguous Consensus: French Defense Policy under Mitterand," *World Today* (October 1983), p. 376.
39. Harrison, "Mitterand's France," p. 225.
40. *L'Express*, 13–19 July 1984, p. 49.
41. Pierre Lellouche, "France and the Euromissiles: The Limits of Immunity," *Foreign Affairs* (Winter 1983–84), p. 324.
42. Moisi, "Les limites du consensus," p. 254.
43. Robin F. Laird, "The French Strategic Dilemma," *Orbis* (Summer 1984), pp. 314–318.
44. Moisi, "Les limites du consensus," p. 254.
45. Ibid., p. 264.

8 THE BUNDESWEHR OF THE FEDERAL REPUBLIC OF GERMANY

Dennis E. Showalter

The Bundeswehr of the Federal Republic of Germany is an institutionalized network of paradoxes. The linchpin of Western Europe's conventional defense, it exists in a society significantly uncomfortable with the concept and the reality of armed force. This in part reflects a belief, far more prevalent in the Federal Republic than in the United States, that conventional forces will never again be meaningful in a great-power conflict.[1] Relative indifference to the Bundeswehr as a military instrument incorporates a deeper and older faith as well, a faith accepting the German as a natural soldier whose societies, no matter what their structure, naturally produce armed forces far too efficient for their own good and their neighbors' peace of mind.[2]

In this context what becomes important is not nurturing but restriction, not fostering but control. West Germany's military establishment spends most of its public energy demonstrating innocuousness. Vacuity is a principle of conduct; visibility is a cardinal sin. The Bundeswehr's operational efficiency is discussed far less than its commitment to democracy, its role in institutionalizing civic virtues, its contribution to the mastering of Germany's past.

Outside Germany defense analysts approach the subject from quite a different perspective. The German question, the Nazi legacy, World War II itself, seem increasingly abstract, increasingly remote. What is important is the Federal Republic's current ability to participate in defending Western Europe. Budgets and force structures, doctrines and equipment are the stuff of presentations on the Bundeswehr for British and American readers, civil or military.[3]

This essay seeks to strike a balance between the concepts. Limited in its search for tradition, West Germany's military establishment nevertheless does not exist in a vacuum. It is the product of history as well as politics. Its current roles are best understood when presented in an historical/philosophical framework. And that framework rests on the fact that the notion of any institution remotely resembling the Bundeswehr would have been dismissed as absurd in 1945 by victors and vanquished alike. The destruction of Hitler's Reich was seen as a definitive break with Germany's military past. No proposals for

The Bundeswehr of the Federal Republic of Germany

reconstruction included rearmament — certainly not in the Western zones. Even as the wartime coalition weakened and collapsed, Germany did not appear a likely participant in an anti-Soviet alliance. This perspective was practical as well as moral. The Soviet Union's conventional forces were considered strong enough to make conventional resistance at the start of any future war futile. Direct defense of Western Europe gave way to the necessary optimism of the US air force and its hollow deterrent, the atom bomb.[4]

Postwar Legacy

European concern for the implications of this approach developed almost immediately. US planners made no secret of — indeed could not conceal — the fact that major American reinforcements for the continent would be available only on national mobilization, a process that might take years.[5] Anxiety about the possible costs of occupation and liberation in turn encouraged questioning the high US evaluation of the Soviet Union's military capacity.

Was it in fact possible to stop the Soviet army on the ground, as opposed to destroying the Soviet Union from the air or strangling it from the sea? Affirmative evidence was ready at hand in the experience of the Wehrmacht on the Eastern Front. But the first tentative consultation of German experience was not particularly comforting from a German perspective. To the Mansteins and the Guderians, success against a Russian attack involved trading space for time, allowing the enemy to push forward to the exact limits of his strength before counter-attacking, slashing into his flanks to threaten supply lines and communications networks. Standing in place against the kinds of hammer blows the Red Army could mount was an invitation to destruction.[6]

This in turn only reinforced arguments that the best immediate response to a Soviet grand attack was a fighting withdrawal to the Rhine. Space was indeed to be traded for time — but it would be German space.[7] The single consolation in the situation from a German perspective involved the capacity of Europe to increase its military strength to a point where such an option was even remotely feasible. Pre-NATO plans for conventional defense of Western Europe had a common Alice-in-Wonderland quality reflecting the wide gulf between their announced goals and the means available to realize them.[8]

Even these tentative discussions generated increasing demands from the emerging Federal Republic of Germany that its erstwhile conquerors give systematic thought to its future security. As long as German territory remained a mere glacis, then West Germany was a political no-man's land. Under international law it was not recognized as able to wage war; any troops it might raise would be considered guerrillas.[9] As early as 1949, Konrad Adenauer was unsubtly suggesting that if West Germany were to be successfully integrated into a reconstituted Europe, it must be given a positive stake in the process. Repentance for a Nazi past was not sufficient to motivate permanent commitment. The Federal Republic's integrity must be guaranteed; the forces stationed on its territory must be increased as proof of good faith.[10]

The issue of direct West German participation in a European security network had been raised even earlier by the conquering powers. By 1947 United States and British planners were evaluating technical aspects of West Germany's military potential. In the spring of 1948, the Brussels Pact addressed the political ramifications of West German rearmament. Charles de Gaulle indicated the utility of German participation in Europe's defense, albeit in a suitably distant future. By 1950, Winston Churchill was rising from the benches of Parliament to advocate the arming of the Federal Republic.

For its supporters, this policy increased the spectrum of possible connections between West Germany and the states of a still-developing Atlantic confederation. It correspondingly reduced the risks of neutralism or, less likely but always possible, an eastward orientation pursued for the sake of national reunification. It responded to US demands that Europe accept responsibility for its own security and its own development. Rearmament under controlled circumstances might also prove a homeopathic treatment for militarism. International order based on the rule of law appeared further away than ever. West Germany was virtually certain to acquire a military capacity sooner or later; better that it happen under Western auspices and Western influences. Perhaps repetition of the post-Versailles fiasco of disarmament could be avoided.[11]

A familiar German proverb advises never to calculate the bill without consulting the waiter. In the immediate aftermath of World War II, nothing seemed less likely than German acceptance of a call to arms from any quarter. The dominant spirit in the Western zones of occupation involved a search for new lives and new identities. This attitude was encouraged by the failure of radical-democratic initiatives combined with an occupation policy, particularly in the British and US zones, varying from the unpredictable to the erratic. But individualism and privatism were not mere manifestations of defeat and occupation. The Third Reich owed its popularity to promises, not demands. For all the rhetoric of *Gemeinnutz vor Eigennutz,* the Nazi regime at its grass roots sustained itself largely by appealing to special interests and balancing discontents. Wartime morale had depended less on commitment to a cause than on vague hopes of miracles and concrete fears of alternatives. If the stunned acquiescence of 1945 was by 1947 giving way to renewed public activity on local and regional levels, western Germany still seemed a long way from possessing a suitable social foundation for a recreated military capacity.[12]

Nor were Germany's ex-soldiers sounding a certain trumpet on the question of rearmament. They had failed, utterly and unmistakably, to fulfill the professional responsibility ultimately justifying their existence. Germany's defeat in 1945 was total, without even the skimpy fig leaves offered by the armistice terms of 1918. For all the senior officers' anxious denials, their submission to the Third Reich had been too clear and too complete to make them post-war rallying points for their disillusioned juniors. Hitler's generals saw their comrades vilified, dismissed, and hanged from meat-hooks, took their grants of cash or property, and held their tongues through it all. Small wonder that the best of the Wehrmacht's majors and colonels, like their counterparts in the American South after 1865, turned their backs on a way of life that seemed a dead end professionally and morally, seeking new careers with no serious thoughts of ever again donning uniform in Germany's service.[13]

Yet, paradoxically, this unlikely matrix facilitated the work of those military and political specialists willing to raise military issues in the context of the future rather than the past. The emerging Federal Republic might have been a second-best solution to many of its citizens. But it was a new government. It had correspondingly favorable prospects of integration into a Euro-Atlantic network providing security, reconstruction, and democratization within a framework of mutually supporting sovereign states. Until 1945 Germany's socioeconomic structure had been stronger than its political institutions, and any successful administration needed to respond to that fact. Now none of the interest and pressure groups possessed anything like the *gaudiam certaminis* of their imperial, republican, or National Socialist forebears.[14] In particular, the Social Democrats' traditional tension between an ideology stressing peace and cooperation and a *Realpolitik* affirming the legitimacy of national defense was exacerbated by the post-war leadership's focus on the issues of German unity and German independence from both principled and pragmatic motives. Never again, asserted Kurt Schumacher, must socialism abandon national questions to its right-wing opponents. But if that premise is accepted, asked his critics inside and outside the party, what remains of Social Democracy?[15] Answering that question required the best part of a decade — a decade in which Chancellor Konrad Adenauer had a correspondingly free hand in structuring West Germany's rearmament.

More than any of his predecessors since Bismarck, Adenauer was contemptuous of soldiers and their value systems. Armed forces to him were a means to an end, their roles as much symbolic as practical. Their existence would prove commitment to Europe on one hand, and on the other affirm the Federal Republic's status as an independent, sovereign state.[16] Yet the final catalyst for the Federal Republic's creation of its own armed forces lay not only outside Germany, but outside Europe as well. The outbreak of the Korean War in June 1950 at once distracted US strength from Europe and focussed its attention there. Neither American nor European advocates of continental self-defense could any longer avoid serious consideration of German participation in the process. By the fall of 1950 the Federal Republic of Germany was no longer a subject of security discussions, but a partner in those discussions.[17]

This removed the taint of illegality still clinging to questions of rearming the new state. It by no means made rearmament certain, or determined its nature. French Foreign Minister Robert Schumann argued eloquently and cogently for the risks of Germany's erstwhile conquerors appearing before her as suppliants, and for the dangers of an emerging NATO being swamped by German troops. The French counter-proposal had the appeal of audacity and imagination: a unified European army with a common Defense Minister, permitting national contingents no larger than regimental combat teams. These battle groups would in turn be integrated into higher formations with multinational command and staff structures.[18]

Such an approach had little appeal in a German military environment which for over a century had stressed the necessity of incorporating the community rather than standing apart from it. Nor was Adenauer enthusiastic about a proposal so easily lending itself to interpretation of West Germany as a milk cow for its ostensible allies, good enough to provide cannon fodder for tomorrow's wars, but not really acceptable as a full partner. Unlike some of his conservative critics, however, Adenauer was willing to bide his time and hold his tongue. Practical considerations of doctrine, training, and equipment suggested that a European army was likely to remain a chimera. The Soviet Union, moreover, was being conveniently cooperative. Its strident calls for German neutralization, unaccompanied by any significant gestures of reconciliation, lent added weight to the developing US position that Germany must become a full partner in the Atlantic Alliance. Eventually the Amis would get what they wanted. Better by far to let them carry the brunt of the debate. Events justified Adenauer's approach. On 9 May 1955 the Federal Republic of Germany was admitted to NATO as its fifteenth member, with the responsibility for contributing armed forces to the alliance on a national basis.[19]

Origins and Doctrine

The Bundeswehr was a means to the ends of Atlantic security and West German sovereignty. But the implication of the network of agreements legitimating its existence was that West Germany deliver an efficient armed force as quickly and with as little upheaval as possible. In one sense, "rearmament" is a misleading term; the Federal Republic's military establishment was a new creation. Yet time constraints required that it be based at least to some extent on existing and experienced talent.[20] At the same time the Federal Republic dared not alarm its allies and neighbors by producing soldiers *too* quickly and painlessly. That was the sort of conjuring trick already closely associated with the German military tradition. West Germany's situation in the early 1950s resembled a child's riddle: how to get a wolf, a cabbage, and a goat safely across a river in a boat too small to carry all three simultaneously.

Adenauer initally considered the concept of a militia, which at least would be politically secure.[21] But two world wars seemed to indicate the need for skills that could not be inculcated by spending a few weeks at a time in uniform. At the other end of the spectrum of possibilities was a volunteer force. The concept blended well with the Federal Republic's principled encouragement of free choice, and would sidestep a mushrooming domestic controversy surrounding compulsory military service. Volunteers could also be recruited quickly — an increasingly important point to a US government seeking quick results from a Europe seemingly still bogged down in details of numbers and formation size.[22]

This approach, however, challenged both tradition and experience.

From 1871 to 1914 the German army had been a successful positive instrument of socialization. Only during World War I did the relationship between the army and its soldiers break down, and then the phenomenon was seen as temporary. Throughout the Weimar era the Reichswehr's leaders insisted on national service as a necessary element of national integration as well as national security.[23] Paradoxically, it was in just this area where National Socialist military policies met their most significant failure. The Wehrmacht of 1945 was a far cry from a people's army in the German sense of that concept. Its morale and fighting power depended increasingly on institutional rather than national factors: group cohesion, professional skill, the courage of desperation.[24] Given that matrix, relying on volunteers might attract a disproportionate number of *Landsknechts* who enjoyed their work all too well, and who would be hardly likely to fulfill the increasing list of civic and professional requirements being set for the new security force.[25]

In May 1950 Adenauer began the process of systematizing the debate by organizing the *Zentrale für Heimatdienst* as a think tank and clearing house for viewpoints on the nature of the Federal Republic's proposed armed forces. In October 1950 it sponsored a conference of civil and military specialists whose report, the *Himmeroder Denkschrift,* described peace as depending on the strongest possible defense of Western Europe. This in turn involved full participation of the Federal Republic as a sovereign state with its own military establishment. The memorandum recommended a conscript-based armed force, firmly under political control, incorporating the link between soldier and citizen traditional in Germany but perverted by National Socialism. Its personnel policy should be based on democratic principles, with ultimate authority vested in Parliament and the executive. Its senior positions were to be filled by decision of a special committee.[26]

The *Himmeroder Denkschrift* laid the Bundeswehr's foundation. But it was to be translated into institutional realities by new men. The *ZfH* was dissolved in October, replaced rather than succeeded by *Dienststelle Blank.* This was a clear sign of the new government's determination to maintain control over its emerging armed forces. While Generals Hans Speidel and Adolf Heusinger played key roles in the new agency, it took its tone as well as its name from the civilian chief. On the surface Theodor Blank's major qualification for the appointment was his absence of qualifications. A Christian Democrat and trade unionist who had risen to the executive council of the Miner's Federation, he had served as a junior officer in World War II, but was otherwise unconnected to either the military or its critics. His major initial contribution was his conviction that the defense of a sovereign, democratic Federal Republic could not be the monopoly of a single estate, a single profession, or a single point of view. And this was enough to place him squarely in the mainstream of West German political practice.

From its inception the Federal Republic was a state of realities rather than dreams. Lacking powerful general elements of integration, it sought consensus on immediate concerns. This process manifested itself above all in a concern for institutionalizing cooperation among interest groups — a pattern familiar in form, if not necessarily content, in Germany since the Bismarckian era.[27] For Blank this involved acting in two directions. If the new Bundeswehr was to fulfill Adenauer's foreign policy goals, it needed competent senior officers. They must not, however, be treated as hired guns, technocrats serving yet alienated from the political structure. At the same time the Bundeswehr could not become the household troops of the Christian Democrats, with the Socialists maintaining an ideologically pure, hands-off stance. It was correspondingly important to establish common ground between the ex-soldiers of the Wehrmacht and the leaders of the Social Democratic Party, men like Kurt Schumacher and Carlo Schmidt — to integrate their respective positions, if at all possible, into the structure of the new military.[28]

The process of integration was facilitated by *Dienststelle Blank's* approach to personnel selection. The committee appointed to screen applications for senior posts considered 601 candidates. One hundred and one were rejected or withdrew their application. This relatively low rate reflected the committee's open affirmation of its intention to keep out of leadership positions anyone whose attitudes or behavior might give the new armed forces a tone encouraging the denial of previous bitter experience. It also reflected frequent and pointed charges of opportunism and careerism levelled against the men who sought to don the Federal Republic's uniform. As a result, they had to develop a systematic set of justifications, emphasizing not merely service to the state as an idea in the tradition of Hans von Seeckt, but service to a particular form of state: political democracy. They also had to present these justifications coherently and convincingly.

Whether individual candidates acted from principle or pragmatism must remain a subject for debate. More important for the history of the Bundeswehr is the selection committee's manifesting direct acceptance of responsibility for the military leaders by the political system. Bonn was far more willing than Weimar to confront the "dirty hands problem." Adenauer was not the man to recoil from unpleasant choices, or to let the best become the enemy of the good. Mistakes in judgment could be corrected. Failure of will in such a crucial area could never be recovered.[29]

As the Bundeswehr's cadres began to emerge, its framers confronted the more general challenge of considering and establishing the relationships between democracy and armed force. German intellectuals tend towards intolerance of ambiguities and are correspondingly prone to equate friction with failure. While recognizing in principle that complete integration of military and society is impossible in a dynamic system, the Federal Republic's soldiers and politicians, bureaucrats and academicians, were and are significantly uncomfortable with the concept of permanent tension between the normative requirements of armed forces and the value systems and behavior patterns of a democratic, industrial society. This discomfort has been reinforced by continued insistence, inside and outside the Federal Republic, on the relative newness and weakness of democratic traditions in Germany — particularly when compared to the historically high level of the military's integration into public life, and the relative competitiveness of the military's values in anything resembling an open market of ideas.

The Federal Republic's solution owes far more to Hegel than to Jefferson or Locke. It presents civil and military worlds as integrated, and mutually reinforcing. Military service must not become an end in itself, but neither must it be a mere break in the course of ordinary life, a task to be performed and then remembered with fondness or anger. Instead the months in uniform must develop and reinforce democratic consciousness.

This is an essentially conservative perspective. The Bundeswehr has never been viewed as an instrument of social change. Its political role is to preserve or restore conditions legitimated by the public will as expressed through Parliament. This cautious approach initially reflected an attitude, common and influential among West German elites in the 1950s, that it was the masses, the little men, who had been most susceptible to Nazi blandishments in the 1930s, and who had underwritten the Third Reich until its collapse.[30] The makers of the Federal Republic were in no sense populists. If the Bundeswehr as an institution was not to be the exclusive property of any interest group, neither were its rank and file to be left to their own devices. They might be "citizens in uniform" — but both nouns in the phrase would be carefully defined.

In assigning the military a significant role in citizen forming, soldiers and civilians alike were responding to a belief with deep German roots: that military service shaped civic character. The issue was complicated by the almost deliberate effort of West Germany's founding fathers to create an unexciting government and an unexciting society. Passions of any kind were at a discount in the climate of postwar Germany, and the Federal Republic had no desire to assume the risks involved in rekindling them. To sustain this approach, the military must be correspondingly unexciting. Yet this in turn seemed to run counter to the tendency of modern industrial society to stress productivity, growth, and achievement — a tendency especially marked in Germany during the *Wiederaufbau,* and continuing ever since.[31] A quasi-utilitarian ethic, stressing personal initiative based on rational calculation in terms of production and consumption, is as close to an ideology as the Federal Republic allows itself.[32] In such a context, is it possible to justify a military establishment that simply exists? And is it possible to make that military *salonfähig* for a spectrum of critics ranging from those hostile in principle to the concept of armed force, through those seeing the Bundeswehr as symbol of a social order that has been a sequence of missed opportunities, to those obsessed by the differences between an army barracks and an alternative commune?

One road of integration was closed to the Bundeswehr from the beginning: tradition. The Federal Republic remains significantly uncomfortable with its history in general. The "unmastered past" is a concept continually discussed in conferences and publications from all points of the political system. West Germany lacks the insouciant cynicism of the DDR, with its massive, integrated, and flexible program for putting the past at the service of a new order by rewriting history wherever necessary.[33] Nor is that history always easy to discover. Much of imperial Germany's military tradition was artificial, introduced or revived at the turn of the twentieth century from a mixture of William II's romanticism and the practical desire to create an instant identity for the new formations of a rapidly expanding army.[34] Turning to the Reichswehr or the Wehrmacht for models presents risks best described by Manfred Messerschmidt when he warns against concentrating on achievements at the expense of intentions.[35] Even focussing on 20 July 1944 can be challenged by critics who present the would-be assassins as right-wing advocates of an already moribund order, as well as by those who stress the risks of glorifying military mutiny as a moral principle.[36] Some of the Bundeswehr's air wings and many of its barracks bear names from the military past. Attempts to highlight anti-Nazi features of the Wehrmacht have remained muted, however, since the mid-1960s controversy surrounding the naming of three destroyers after purported *nur-Soldaten*. Erwin Rommel, Günther Lütgens, and Werner Mölders promptly became targets for the kind of scrutiny few careers made in the Third Reich can survive. Since then the Bundeswehr has been at pains to name its ships innocuously. Its unit designations are starkly functional, with no significant efforts made to foster elite or in-group attitudes. Even its airborne and mountain troops are consciously unselfconscious compared to their counterparts in other NATO armies. As for dress, the Bundeswehr extended the Wehrmacht's World War II evolution towards stark functionalism and corresponding de-emphasis of smart turnout into a virtual art form. One possible reason for the army's often-noted reluctance to wear uniforms off-duty might be that uniform's suggestion of a doorman at a moderately priced hotel. One officer recalls being asked in his first days of service if the German Automobile Club's highway service had taken to wearing rank insignia — a far cry from the *Glanz und Gloria* of earlier eras.[37]

If tradition posed risks as a means of integrating the military into society, then mission offered an alternative possibility. The Bundeswehr as conceived and organized has existed from the beginning to fight one set of enemies: the Soviet Union and her allies, satellites, and/or clients. Images of West German soldiers as crusading warriors protecting European civilization against an alien enemy were frequent in the early 1950s but remained unofficial.[38] The possiblities of using anti-Communism as a basis for legitimating military service and reinforcing civic identity in the new Germany were from the beginning restricted by the government's refusal to allow its defense forces a *Feindbild*. The political risks of such a measure were seen as outweighing its advantages. Direct reference to Russia or the Warsaw Pact as enemies threatened the principle of German unity and offered too many propaganda opportunities to an Eastern bloc already beating the drums of German revanchism at every opportunity. The Bundeswehr may be an objective symbol of the Cold War to its critics, but its anti-Communism has been more an attitude than a principle, carefully kept below the level of an integrating ideology.[39]

With mission and tradition limited as instruments of integration, the Bundeswehr's creators put correspondingly high hopes in the concept of *Innere Führung*. Defying translation into English, explained in as many ways as it has interpreters, *Innere Führung* remains a subject fitter for description than definition. Yet from its inception *Innere Führung* was regarded by neither advocates nor critics as an abstraction. The Bundeswehr was seen as demanding a new set of norms and virtues for professional as well as civic reasons. Historically, armed forces prepared for war, even if only in the most remote sense. They justified their existence on the grounds of their operational efficiency, even if that justification involved the crudest forms of self-deception. Under the circumstances of the Bundeswehr's creation, however, deterrence of a Warsaw Pact attack was the military's most important function — arguably, indeed, its only function. Given West Germany's geographic position, even a conventional war might well mean destruction of the state and the annihilation of society. At the same time, constitutional law and common sense continue to reject the concept of any more general roles for German forces. UN peacekeeping or intervention to protect the Federal Republic's interests in, for example, the Middle East remain equally remote possibilities. In such contexts the description of Bundeswehr recruits as "soldiers for peace" is anything but a simple exercise in public relations.

West Germany was also deeply concerned with the risks of politicizing the army in a partisan sense. The Social Democrats' principled hostility to militarism as a concept was reinforced by a political role which, even after the adoption of the Bad Godesberg Program of 1959, seemed to be one of permanent opposition. This position was not wholly uncongenial to that section of the party which saw itself freed alike from the risks of decision-making and the obloquy of compromise. To men like Willy Brandt or Helmut Schmidt, however, Social Democracy's chances of influencing West Germany's future development depended heavily on accepting responsibility for its security. What held the factions together was their reluctance to see the Bundeswehr shaped, whether deliberately or by default, along the anti-Socialist lines so familiar in Germany's past.[40]

The CDU and its coalition partners were equally concerned. Efforts to maintain the SPD as a "state-sustaining opposition" were not likely to be enhanced if the party and its followers saw the military as closed to them. An even more effective partisan of non-partisanship was, however, the Bundeswehr itself. Apart from any newly developed commitments to pluralist democracy, the limits of the anti-Socialism of the imperial and Weimar eras were all too clear. Even under the empire the policy could be sustained only because Germany's population of draft-eligible males far exceeded the numbers that could actually be inducted each year.[41] A smaller population and a more comprehensive conscription legislation meant that the Bundeswehr could not afford the luxury of prejudging or alienating any of its prospective soldiers. This meant acceptance of the broadest possible spectrum of political convictions and personal lifestyles. And such acceptance in turn posed the problem of finding a set of common denominators, civic values so generally accepted that their emphasis by the military would not generate a storm of protest.

Innere Führung has evolved in terms of generalizations rather than specifics. It involves establishing, in the context of military life, principles of conduct enabling the soldier to act as an autonomous moral being, able to balance the claims of subordination against the demands of conscience. A democratic society is based on a dialectic of rights and responsibilities. Its citizens have a duty to defend their country. If this requires temporary suspension or modification of such civic rights as free speech and unrestricted assembly, soldiers retain other basic rights: the right of complaint, the right to continuing education, the right to human dignity. At the same time, *Innere Führung* stresses the common soldier's responsibility for sustaining his rights by exercising his initiative. Citizenship depends on participation. As a citizen in uniform, the Bundeswehr soldier must be an involved member of both the wider community and the smaller, specifically military community to which he belongs, whatever the risks and discomforts such involvement might entail.[42]

This stress on moral autonomy and moral initiative is considered to have military as well as civic virtues. In two world wars a major element of German successes was the willingness of junior officers and enlisted men to accept responsibility, to act on their own initiative in constantly changing operational circumstances. British and American soldiers expecting to confront robots helpless without higher orders faced a particularly rude series of shocks. One of the less analyzed paradoxes of modern military history, indeed, has been the capacity of the allegedly "semi-authoritarian" German society to nurture a level of grassroots initiative foreign to the armies of the Western democracies.[43]

Innere Führung incorporates that experience. It was not intended to create a non-martial military, a *Marzipan-Bundeswehr* of exquisitely sensitive chocolate-cream soldiers contemplating their rights and grievances. In the words of its most familiar spokesman, General Wolf von Baudissin, it is an ethic of free men accepting common responsibility for a common purpose. An effective modern solider can be produced neither by indoctrination nor by discipline. Efficiency is a product of conscious commitment at all levels. In this context *Innere*

The Bundeswehr of the Federal Republic of Germany 225

Führung nurtures a relationship between freedom and obedience, between individual and collective, that replicates and reinforces the dynamics of a plural, open, late-industrial society where the isolated entrepreneur and the uncritical human cog in a factory or political party are alike anachronisms.[44]

Political Context

The internal dynamics of the Bundeswehr have also been shaped by the process of instutionalizing its operational responsibilities. The strength projected in the 1950s, half a million men in twelve divisions, represented to both domestic and foreign observers a defensible balance between a meaningful and a non-threatening German commitment to Atlantic security, particularly in the context of projections describing a ninety-division NATO. Even as the latter dream faded, the Bundeswehr emerged in essentially the same category as the armed forces of Britain and France — stronger than those of Benelux, Denmark, or Norway, better equipped than those of Greece or Turkey, but essentially unable to function independently without the tacit consent of its allies. In general strategic terms, West Germany's position in NATO is analgous to that of Prussia in the German Confederation during the age of Metternich. That too was a league of small and middle-sized states cooperating in a defensive alliance dominated by one power whose interests were essentially limited to Germany proper, and another whose policies were not only broader, but determined by a volatile mixture of interest and ideology, making them correspondingly unpredictable.

The comparison of the US with Metternich's Austria can be extended in the context of West Germany's continued determination to link its security with US commitments to Europe. The 1950s were the years of the New Look in Western defense policy: the substitution of atomic weapons, specifically American weapons, for conventional forces as far as possible. The Federal Republic's support for this concept in part made a virtue of necessity. The image of a Federal Republic with its own warheads generated anxiety on all points of the West German political spectrum. It created almost as much alarm in NATO capitals as among the states of the Warsaw Pact. Three decades later West German renunciation of the building and acquisition of nuclear weapons remains a cornerstone of domestic as well as foreign policy. Advocacy of an independent nuclear deterrent for West Germany remains confined to the pages of academic journals.

Accepting massive retaliation, however, raised another question. If West Germany depended on the US nuclear umbrella, what exactly was a conventionally equipped Bundeswehr good for? The answer was suggested in 1955, when NATO conducted a war game under the name of "Carte Blanche." Over 350 nuclear warheads were employed against a simulated Russian offensive in Central Europe. The attack was halted, but only at the cost of over 5 million civilian casualties, a third of them deaths. As information about the exercise became public, West Germany experienced a groundswell of protest. Pacifist and antinuclear groups proliferated. Socialist leaders argued that their party's support for Atlantic defense did not underwrite a suicide pact. Yet for all the fury of protest, the Federal Republic's continued participation in NATO was never seriously questioned.[45]

This seeming contradiction in part reflected the Bundeswehr's developing ability to respond to the nuclear challenge. The comparison of conventional Western forces to a tripwire in general carried less weight with European soldiers and defense analysts than among their US counterparts. The most extreme adherents of nuclear deterrence conceded that NATO's conventional military strength must suffice to deter adventurism: the seizure of Berlin or the occupation of northern Norway. The same lines of reasoning suggested that the West should be able to repel Warsaw Pact attacks that did not immediately threaten a break-through without having to escalate to a nuclear option.[46]

From the Bundeswehr's specific perspective, it was ironic that the tripwire concept, especially in its modified form, encouraged concentration on the tactics demanded by Hitler in World War II: hold on to forward positions, check the enemy's offensives immediately, drive him back to his own start lines in the contingency of a breakthrough with the resources immediately available. NATO's increasing emphasis on tactical nuclear weapons similarly suggested German experience on the Eastern Front. NATO's conventional forces were expected to play their powerful enemy as a matador plays a bull, encouraging the concentration of Warsaw Pact formations in masses large enough to be profitable targets for a battlefield atomic bomb. In this sense tactical nuclear weapons might be said to provide the shock power the Wehrmacht had increasingly lacked after the Battle of Kursk. Their existence was the other half of a combat equation Nazi Germany's overextension and limited resource base had rendered insoluble a decade earlier.[47]

The developing combination of massive retaliation with tactical nuclear capacity also encouraged reconsideration of force structures. As the Bundeswehr's first few divisions moved from training grounds to garrisons, questions arose regarding the balance between its political and its military responsibilities. Conscription as part of the process of citizen formation might be a sound principle. But were draftees a suitable basis for a modern military? As weapons and equipment grew more complex, as preparation for the human demands of combat grew more intense, conscripts often no sooner learned their skills and integrated themselves into their units then they were replaced by a fresh intake of recruits. Rapid turnover of personnel also handicapped the institutionalization of *Innere Führung* by diminishing the stability required for its practical implementation.[48]

One way of compensating was to increase the numbers of *Zeitsoldaten*, men willing to serve for periods of from 2 to 15 years. Critics suggested, however, that the Bundeswehr should move even further in the direction of a quality force emphasizing technology at the expense of numbers. This proposed shift from a personnel-intensive to a capital-intensive military offered three advantages. Militarily it could enhance NATO deterrence by creating a force better able to check an attack before it became a penetration. Socially it would reflect the Federal Republic's nature: a developed industrial state whose human resources were becoming increasingly correspondingly scarce. The traditional concept that manpower was cheap no longer fitted a modern market environment — particularly one so short of labor that it was importing hundreds of thousands of aliens each year. Economically, a shift of emphasis to technology would offer major opportunities for establishing an independent German defense industry.

For Franz Josef Strauss, Adenauer's Minister of Defense from 1956 to 1962, the last point was the most significant. A healthy German defense industry would give renewed impetus to an economy already showing signs of slackening its post-war pace. It would also ensure the Federal Republic's participation in the spinoff process — the proliferation of techniques and ideas generated by military technology. It would enable the Federal Republic to play an equal role in projected multinational design projects. And it would free the Bundeswehr from depending on equipment, much of it American-designed, that seemed at best marginally suited for Central European conditions.

Strauss' emphasis on technical development included laying at least a theoretical groundwork for a German nuclear capacity. He defended the principle that German troops should have the best weapons available, whatever their secondary capacities might be. He advocated and encouraged the acquisition of weapons systems, especially aircraft, able to deliver atomic weapons. This in turn brought the Federal Republic much too close to the nuclear issue for comfort — its own, its allies', or its adversaries'.[49]

The Kennedy/Johnson administration's increasing advocacy of flexible response, on one level a welcome alternative to the scenario of Operation Carte Blanche, had generated significant anxiety among the Federal Republic's policy makers because of its possible impact on the credibility of the US nuclear deterrent. Deepening US involvement in Vietnam further heightened Bonn's concern for its alliance position — arguably to the point of encouraging, if not inspiring, the Brandt–Schmidt governments' vigorous pursuit of *Ostpolitik* in the 1970s.[50] The logic of a high-tech military in the era of massive retaliation involved incorporation of a broad spectrum of atomic weapons from the medium-range rockets of an army corps to the portable launchers assigned to an infantry battalion. If the matrix existed, might not the substance follow? And apart from its impact on both halves of Europe, might not even a potentially enhanced West German nuclear delivery capacity encourage further US disengagement from Europe?

At the same time, none of the Federal Republic's chancellors from 1966 to 1974 — Ehrhard, Kiesinger, Brandt — had a base of support solid enough to encourage massive reorientation of the Bundeswehr. This was even more true of the SPD, on its accession to power in 1969, than of the Christian Democrats. As a participant in the Grand Coalition of 1966, the party had consistently asserted its commitment to the Western alliance and a strong national defense — not least as a means of demonstrating its flexibility and its respectability to a society still suspicious. The appointment of Helmut Schmidt in 1969 as first Social Democratic Minister of Defense set the seal on the party's approach. Schmidt, one of the party's leading experts on military questions, was more concerned with improving the Bundeswehr's performance than criticizing its parameters, an attitude shared by his 1972 successor, Georg Leber. This pragmatic stance was reinforced by the increasingly hostile position of the West German left, inside and outside the SPD. Defense questions were only part of a comprehensive challenge encouraging many of the party's moderate leaders to insist on maintaining Socialism's new position in the political mainstream.

The success of this policy was indicated by the increasing recognition of the Socialist and non-parliamentary left during the 1970s that the Federal Republic's armed forces were likely neither to be abolished nor *umfunktioniert*. While continuing half-hearted efforts at socializing the military from within, often with a level of approval from the government that removed much of the pleasure from the process, the Federal Republic's radicals increasingly turned to more general questions of national security. The neutron bomb and the Pershing missile were safer targets than the Bundeswehr, despite their contributions to a level and intensity of anti-Americanism hitherto foreign to post-war German politics.[51]

Restructuring the German military was also handicapped by the Bundeswehr's steady evolution into a pressure group along essentially bureaucratic lines. This is not a unique pattern. Since 1945 scholars have emphasized the converging needs of military and civil institutions in modern societies, and the corresponding tendency for military leaders to develop the skills and attitudes common to their counterparts in the world of business or politics.[52] More specifically, bureaucratization also served as an administrative counterpart of *Innere Führung*: a means of integrating the Bundeswehr as an institution into the Federal Republic on an everyday basis. The Bundeswehr was never intended as an institution excluded from the give and take of a plural democratic society, with its purpose and its budgets alike above mundane political and administrative infighting. The competitive symbiosis existing among the interest groups of West Germany's society and the branches of West Germany's government make it virtually impossible to stay aloof from an ongoing struggle for resources and influence increasingly exacerbated by arguments that military spending adversely affects domestic prosperity, specifically social welfare rights.[53]

The Bundeswehr's bureaucratization has also been fostered by the degree of its integration into NATO. Here too the Federal Republic's situation is a paradox. The concept initially developed by Adenauer, of close identification and involvement with the West, continues to be a focal point of West German foreign policy. The Atlantic Alliance, in the words of Defense Minister Manfred Wörner, remains the ultimate "guarantor of peace and security."[54] With its active forces exclusively under NATO control, with no General Staff and no field commands higher than a corps, the Bundeswehr is arguably more a NATO force than an army of the Federal Republic.

At the same time Germany's sustained economic strength has made it Europe's "banker and economic spokesman . . . the once and present king" of the continent. This position was enhanced by France's withdrawal from NATO and by Britain's seemingly endemic state of economic crisis. West Germany has found itself increasingly pushed by its US ally to become the European pillar of Atlantic security and to make corresponding increases in its defense budget and the size of its armed forces.⁵⁵

Apart from the likely domestic repercussions of such a change, its probable impact on West Germany's position within the Alliance has been perceived as devastating by the Federal Republic's policy makers. A significant aspect of their commitment to reassuring their lesser partners has been enhusiastic participation in making ever more complicated a NATO network best defined as command by committee. The plethora of carefully defined spheres of authority, the delicate balances involved in making appointments, might well be cited as ultimate proof of the Alliance's peaceful intentions. No would-be aggressor would dare take the field with such a command structure. And the absence of a national structure of senior command and staff appointments has meant that the career ambitions of the Federal Republic's best and brightest lead into the jungles of NATO's flow charts. Here indeed West Germany has won mighty victories. The well filled briefcases of Bundeswehr generals have often proved far more potent than the Tiger tanks of their Wehrmacht forebears. As in any *nomenklatura*, these victories tend to be negative. They involve preventing things from happening. They consist of the checkmating of rivals and the preservation of turf, as opposed to moving the NATO dinosaur in any specific, positive direction.⁵⁶ In the area of NATO politics, however, the Bundeswehr's bureaucratization is an important diplomatic asset, sustaining the original grounds for West German rearmament.

Domestically too bureaucratization has proved a virtue. The Federal Republic has experienced no significant assertion of a military position independent of the political system. Even the notorious Spiegel Affair of 1962 reflected more the antagonism between Franz Josef Strauss and Rudolf Augstein than any will of the soldiers, who sought to distance themselves from the conflict with a haste that might well be described as indecent.⁵⁷ Bundeswehr support for the controversial Emergency Legislation of 1968 reflected less crypto-Fascist desire to create machinery facilitating a military takeover than bureaucratic concern for legitimating action should the normal government channels be unable to function.⁵⁸ Like good civil servants everywhere, West Germany's military men accept abuse in relative silence, comforted by the notion that politicians and journalists pass, governments fall, opinions change, but public institutions go on forever — as do the people who staff them.

Force Structure and NATO Relations

Forcing a modern bureaucracy to accept major change requires focussed attention, constancy of purpose, pettifogging attention to detail, and a developed sense of alternatives. For all the sound and fury surrounding it, the Bundeswehr's force structure has remained remarkably consistent. This in part reflects the fact that the restricted missions of the air force and the navy offer correspondingly restricted opportunities for manipulating inter-service rivalries. The navy is currently in the process of modernizing its 1960s destroyers while adding a new generation of the Dutch-designed Frigate 122, strengthening its force of fast attack craft and strike aircraft and increasing its mine warfare capacities. It remains committed to limited coastal operations in the North and Baltic Seas. The air force likewise may be structurally independent, but continues to play essentially a tactical role as Thunderjets, G-91s, and Starfighters gave way first to Phantoms, then to Tornadoes and Alpha Jets in the air superiority, strike, and reconnaissance roles. But the heart of the Bundeswehr is still the army: 345,000 men organized into the same twelve divisions projected at NATO's inception.[59]

They are the same, but not the same. The US concept of flexible response generated support as well as opposition in West Germany. Helmut Schmidt was only the most familiar voice arguing that the capacity to halt invasion on the ground at subnuclear levels was itself becoming an important element of a meaningful deterrent. And if that deterrent failed, conventional defense would buy time, giving political leaders on both sides opportunity for reflection before escalating to the ultimate unpredictabilities of nuclear warfare.[60]

This line of argument was in itself a challenge to concepts of high-tech defense that seemed so closely linked to atomic weapons. At the same time, the costs of such a policy, presented as given even by its supporters, seemed increasingly unattractive, not to say unattainable, in the context of a slowed-down economy. With military expenses absorbing almost a third of the state's budget and over 5 percent of GNP by 1967, with both the costs and the lead time of advanced weaponry escalating geometrically, the times were scarcely auspicious for the military to demand an even bigger share of the national pie, even apart from social questions.[61]

Nor was it proving quite as easy in practice as in theory to provide personnel for such a system. Since the mid-1960s the pool of potential *Zeitsoldaten* had been steadily shrinking. The psychic appeals of military life, never widely invoked in the Federal Republic, were at an all-time discount. Nor could the military offer educational and training opportunities to compete with those available in the larger society. Technically skilled, well motivated young men were not affected negatively enough by the stabilizing economy to encourage a military career. The late 1960s also marked the onset of the *Pillenknicks* — a decline in the West German birthrate steep enough by 1974 to give the Federal Republic the lowest natural increase of any state in Europe. From the Bundeswehr's point of view it seemed corresponding folly to risk exclusive dependence on long-term enlistments.

Direct pressure on the ethic of national service declined in the 1970s as a once-interlocking spectrum of protest movements turned to privatism on one hand and Parliament on the other. Sober calculation of career prospects combined with allowances, benefits, and conditions of service to increase significantly the number of extended-service volunteers. By March 1985 the Bundeswehr boasted of having 194,400 *Zeitsoldaten*, with 172,500 of them enlisted for over three years. Yet the Bundeswehr is by no means convinced that it can obtain enough true volunteers to fill even its technical requirements in the absence of the pressures imposed by conscription. Covering projected shortfalls by requiring national service from women and resident aliens remains a subject too controversial for serious advocacy. The Federal Republic is correspondingly unwilling to face the ultimate risk that neither volunteers nor draftees will be forthcoming in numbers sufficient to maintain the armed forces' strength at levels set by state policy.[62]

The issue of numbers was by no means an abstract problem for the Bundeswehr. Advocates of high-tech defense argued that increasingly complicated weapons systems combined with shrinking lead times to make reservists at best marginally useful in any future conflict. Their most likely roles were seen as fillers and replacements. This negative perception was reinforced by the status of West Germany's Territorial Army. Unlike the Bundeswehr's active forces, it was under national command — a fact making it both a political football and a poor relation. It was a direct symbol of West German sovereignty that the right was unwilling to relinquish and the left was correspondingly unwilling to nurture. A government still heavily concerned with placating its allies devoted neither money nor energy to any military force even faintly hinting at an independent defense policy. And the active forces' demands for more of everything set what seemed a final seal on the reserves' relegation to local security and home guard missions.[63]

Signs of change, however, emerged even during the 1960s. Perhaps the greatest paradox in an armed force of paradoxes is that the parliamentary democracy of West Germany makes the same kinds of operational demands on its military as those made by Adolf Hitler in the last years of World War II. The Bundeswehr functions in a firm, continuing context of commitment to a forward defense of West Germany. This commitment is both strategic and political. While its roots are by no means entirely German, it has been fostered by the Federal Republic's long-term policy of encouraging settlement and development along the frontier. Thirty percent of West Germany's population and a quarter of its industrial capacity are within 100 kilometers of the DDR frontier. Defending this strip has been rendered even more difficult by the refusal of successive governments to consider the systematic construction of prepared defenses, whether from fear of their impact on relations with the Warsaw Pact or from concern with their implications for the issue of German unity.[64]

Beginning in the 1960s, an increasingly crucial question involved the relationship between forward defense and conventional defense. An increasing number of the Federal Republic's soldiers and defense analysts wondered whether the Bundeswehr was not preparing to fight the last war in the wrong theater. The concept of a *Qualitätsarmee*, critics argued, assumed significant human and technical superiority. But such superiority depends heavily on the weaknesses of an enemy, and those weaknesses lay outside the control of the Western alliance. Nothing could prevent Soviet study and Soviet institutionalization of the lessons of World War II. The argument that the military shortcomings of the Russian character and the Soviet system were inherent did not fit the facts. From the heavy, blunt instrument that had hammered down the Wehrmacht, the Soviet army was developing into a sophisticated, modern fighting force. Nor could NATO's and West Germany's armies rely on the intangibles of leadership and initiative. They would enter combat after decades of routine service in barracks and on maneuver grounds, unlikely to match the combat skills of the Wehrmacht's veterans, unlikely to repeat performances that had been the fruit of years of experience.

The logical, not to say the inevitable, result would be an almost immediate crossing of the nuclear threshold by NATO. The risks of this could, however, be obviated by taking advantage of developments in geography and technology. Bavaria and Lower Saxony were not Manstein's Ukraine. Urban sprawl was combining with an increasingly complex geography in the rural areas to make West Germany more suited to defense in place — not a tripwire, not a static Maginot Line, but an elastic structure able to stop an attack without massively damaging the battleground. Forward defense of the Federal Republic was best entrusted not to tanks and missiles, but to infantry formations with strong local elements, depending heavily on newly designed light vehicles for transportation and newly designed anti-tank missiles for fire-power.

In an era of détente and *Ostpolitik,* this adjusted defense structure seemed to offer solutions for a broad spectrum of military and diplomatic problems. It utilized developments in weapons technology that bade fair to render the by now traditional concept of blitzkrieg obsolete. It also presented the advantage of removing even West Germany's theoretical capacity for doing anything but defending itself, thereby eliminating much of the underpinning for criticism of the Federal Republic's institutions and policies.[65]

Whatever its military and diplomatic prospects, this lower technical profile would require both high levels of manpower and increased integration of reserves with the active army. In 1969 the previously independent Territorial Defense Command was placed under the Inspector-General of the Army. Its Home Guard Commands began organizing large tactical units: *Jäger* brigades whose light infantry battalions were supported by tank destroyers and heavy mortars. These formations, while existing largely on paper, were a major step in the process of integrating field and reserve forces. They were also a major element in freeing the active army from responsibility for rear security, and from operating in terrain unsuited to mechanized warfare. At the same time Army Structure 3, adopted in 1972, converted two mechanized divisions into *Jäger*, equipped and organized for elastic defense in broken or built-up country.[66]

Continued evolution along these lines was, however, challenged by an increasing number of German studies of the "hammer and anvil" defensive battles on the Eastern Front from 1943 to 1945. Academic reconstruction of the chaotic events of the Wehrmacht's long retreat blended with and underwrote the personal experience of Bundeswehr officers who had led platoons, companies, or battalions in Russia during that period. From a West German perspective, extrapolations from the tactical and operational evidence of the war's final years strongly suggested that conventional mechanized forces, properly trained, equipped, and commanded, retained the capacity to check any conventional offensive in central Europe before the attacker could achieve more than limited, temporary successes.[67]

This approach owed as much to NATO deployments as it did to the alleged lessons of history. The Alliance is integrated at army corps

The Bundeswehr of the Federal Republic of Germany 235

level. Instead of being deployed as an entity, the West German army is organized in three separate corps sectors, with one independent division. From north to south, the Bundeswehr's 6th Panzer Grenadier Division garrisons Schleswig-Holstein and cooperates with the Danish army to screen the Danish peninsula. On its right flank is I Netherlands Corps. Then comes I West German Corps, with headquarters at Münster, and one mechanized and three armored divisions covering the north German plain. Great Britain's Army of the Rhine and I Belgian Corps continue the line southward until III Corps assumes the missions of covering the direct route to the Ruhr and protecting the right flank of the US 7th Army with two armored and a mechanized division. V and VII US Corps screen the Fulda Gap; and the Central Front's line is closed by II West German Corps, deploying an armored, a mechanized, and a mountain division against any attacks from Czechoslovakia.

These dispositions owe little either to coherent strategic thought or to a deliberate policy of keeping West German forces divided. They reflect rather the positions held by the allied armies in 1945, with Bundeswehr units introduced as they were formed into the most obvious gaps and weak spots. Their principal significance from a West German perspective is that they render impossible any serious independent strategic thinking. This is not necessarily unwelcome to the Bundeswehr. An historic weakness of the German military has been an inability or an unwillingness to ask what happens next. From the days of Frederick the Great, German generals have planned to win campaigns rather than wars and battles rather than campaigns. Now the Federal Republic's geopolitical circumstances combine with NATO's deployment to tranform a flaw into both a virtue and a necessity.

To be defended successfully, West Germany must be defended on its frontiers. This does not mean a cordon deployment of the kind that Napoleon suggested was most suitable for stopping smugglers; but it also obviates opportunities for those virtuoso performances at army level characteristic of the Wehrmacht in Russia. The numerical strength and the high overall quality of Warsaw Pact forces make it excessively risky to give them any operating room at all. What is needed instead are quick ripostes, trip-hammer blows executed at the lowest possible levels. This decentralization is fostered by the nature of the terrain: West Germany offers less and less open space for the maneuvering of large formations under one command. And it is rendered imperative by an increasingly sophisticated electronic warfare that bids increasingly to make communication on the future battlefield a matter of voice and vision. Army corps, even divisions, take too long to react under modern conditions. It is at brigade, battalion, and company level that the next war will be won or lost.[68]

Accompanying this conviction is a renewed emphasis on "mission tactics" (*Auftragstaktik*) — the necessity for subordinate commanders to act independently within a general framework, responding to specific conditions and exploiting specific opportunities without reference to higher headquarters. Bundeswehr planners increasingly refer to the Eastern Front after 1943, where a few tanks and a handful of men on the right spot at the right time frequently proved worth more than ten times their number even a few hours later. US defense analysts were given a demonstration of the process at work, at least in theory, in May 1980, when Hermann Balck and his one-time chief of staff, F.W. von Mellenthin, defended a division sector of a US Corps against a Warsaw Pact attack in a simulation. The old Wehrmacht hands made it look easy as they crippled two enemy tank divisions and counter-attacked towards the West German border.[69]

Implemented along NATO's Central Front, these local counter-attacks would stablize the battle line quickly enough to make the use of nuclear weapons by either side a calculable option, as opposed to a logical extension of ongoing circumstances. Critics sometimes describe the lesser NATO contingents as breakthroughs waiting to happen. This position, while by no means unknown in the Bundeswehr, has not affected its operational doctrine — at least not to the extent that it sees its formations playing the role of "corset stays" for unreliable allies. Each corps is expected to fight its own battles successfully. Ideally there will be no single decisive point (*Schwerpunkt*) for the theater; but rather a series of them, developing in response to Warsaw Pact initiatives checked by NATO's backhand game — a game designed to seize the initiative at operational levels for the purpose of restoring as far as possible the *status quo ante bellum*.[70]

As for going further than the old frontier, such proposals as Samuel P. Huntington's, that the occupation of Warsaw Pact territory would substantially enhance the credibility of conventional deterrence, have found no open doctrinal echo in the Bundeswehr. Defense Minister Wörner's recent statement that "In the 1990s, both [West German] ground and air forces will have the capability to take the battle deep into the enemy's rear" may be a straw in the wind. Certainly current NATO air doctrine calls for strikes deep into the Warsaw Pact rear areas to disrupt the flow of reinforcements to the battle zone. Apart from doctrine, it violates every canon of common sense to assume that in wartime the West German armed forces would simply stand their ground like overchivalrous duelists, waiting patiently for the next wave of enemies. Nevertheless the concept of West German ground troops crossing existing borders, into Czechoslovakia or the German Democratic Republic, remain informal and off the record, the stuff of late-night conversations and cocktail-party speculations.[71]

This caution is in good part a manifestation of the Bundeswehr's conviction that an effective forward defense poses quite enough operational challenges without adding political ones. The high-tech concepts of the Bundeswehr's early years had been too close to Wehrmacht realities in that their projections paid too little attention to numbers, creating a corresponding dependence on nuclear weapons. The alternate approach of anti-tank guerrilla warfare also ignored military and political realities. For all the hopes accompanying the introduction of the *Jäger* divisions, maneuver results in Germany combined with experience in the Middle East to indicate that light infantry was a poor man's weapon in a high-intensity combat environment. Whether deployed as mobile tank-killers or in hedgehogs on close terrain, it remained ultimately static and ultimately passive, lacking above all the capacity to mount counter-attacks without significant reinforcements — reinforcements unlikely to reach the scene in time to be effective.[72] And a Bundeswehr unable to mount counter-attacks meant a Federal Republic sure to be defeated even if future conflict remained at subnuclear levels. The question of US willingness to trade New York for Hamburg is only part of the equation. West Germany is not Switzerland. Its society is neither organized nor prepared to conduct a multi-level attritional war against a would-be occupier.[73] Images of *retiarius* and *secutor* fade before the reality that any territorial changes under such circumstances are likely to be permanent.

What was required, then, was a Bundeswehr strong enough to displace nuclear weapons as a direct factor in German defense, a Bundeswehr strong enough to support both specific West German interests and the general policies of NATO, without having to choose between them. This in turn demanded three changes. One was technical: a higher level of mechanization. One was organizational: an improved articulation of West German tactical units. One was psychological: an increased emphasis on those non-quantifiable combat multipliers, fighting spirit and command style, initiative and self-confidence, that had historically proved so important in fighting the Russians.

The Bundeswehr's Army Structure 4, developed in the late 1970s and adopted in 1982, reorganized the ground forces into six armored, four mechanized, one airborne, and one mountain division. Armored divisions consist of two tank brigades and a mechanized brigade; mechanized divisions reverse the ratio; the mountain division is for all practical purposes a mechanized formation with some high-altitude capabilities. Of the Bundeswehr's 36 active brigades, 17 are armored and 16 mechanized; the airborne division's three brigades function essentially as air-mobile anti-tank formations.

Reserves have also been overhauled and updated. The Territorial Army's principal missions remain the securing of operational freedom for the forward units and the preservation of rear security. But increasing recognition of the possibilities of systematic sabotage, combined with the likelihood of extensive airborne and *Spetsnaz* operations in NATO's rear, has led to significant upgrading of the capacities of this force. It remains organized on a regional basis, and under West German as opposed to NATO command. But its principal operational force is now twelve Home Guard Brigades, each of two full-strength tank battalions and two *Jäger* battalions. Six of these have some peacetime cadres. Two are attached to active divisions, not as round-outs in the US pattern, but as supplementary formations. These units automatically come under NATO command, as would, presumably, most of the other Home Guard Brigades on mobilization. The process of integrating field and territorial armies can be expected to continue. It reflects corresponding West German conviction that in practical terms the Federal Republic's security depends on its commitment to NATO, as opposed to any unilateral initiatives.[74]

The Territorial Army's increasing tank strength also manifests Bundeswehr conviction that reserve formations are exactly the troops most likely to need armored support even on secondary missions. Their tanks are likely to be welcomed by any American light infantry who encounter the heavily mechanized airborne and deep-penetration troops of the Warsaw Pact. From a West German perspective, current US enthusiasm for deploying light divisions on the NATO Central Front resembles a hermit's discovery of sex: enthusiasm unaccompanied by finesse. To his advocates, the modern light infantryman is an updated version of the Homeric hero, combining the warrior's traditional skills with a spectrum of one-man weapons prefiguring the Mobile Infantry of Robert Heinlein's *Starship Troopers*. West Germans refer informally and sarcastically to *Rambo-Soldaten,* and suggest that Sylvester Stallone's film character at least has the virtue of being an imaginary creation.

Light infantry has its uses in secondary roles. It is a way of increasing the US commitment to Europe. The Bundeswehr, however, does not consider the survivability of an individual soldier to be particularly high on the modern battlefield, no matter how developed his combat skills. Nor does it consider even the "all-weather infantryman" to incorporate enough striking power to be an effective military instrument. In part this attitude reflects the likelihood that West German soldiers, conscript or volunteer, are collectively less suitable material for modern light infantry than are US, British, or Canadian professionals.[75] Sour grapes is, however, only part of the story. The West German army has all too complete a heritage of the results of pitting men against machines. Particularly on the Russian front, the heroic deeds of the Wehrmacht's *Landser*, the deeds that so inspire Western romantics, were usually performed *faute de mieux*. They reflected a lack of suitable equipment, especially tanks. They represent the misuse of fighting power, an error to be avoided rather than an ideal to be emulated from misplaced military vitalism or excessively clever armchair analysis.[76]

The Bundeswehr's continued mechanization is based on a coherent structure of weapons systems. If initial hopes for high-level defense technology have not quite been fulfilled, the Federal Republic nevertheless emerged during the 1970s as a significant middle-level arms producer. Its submarines and small arms, its patrol boats and electronic equipment have been widely purchased outside Europe. They would be even more familiar in Third World inventories were it not for continued governmental concern for the political ramifications of extensive West German involvement in the arms trade. The pride of West Germany's military designers, however, is their stable of armored fighting vehicles, in particular the Leopard main battle tank and the Marder infantry combat vehicle.

Work on both began in the 1960s, and their introduction as replacements for US-designed M-48s and M-113s was greeted with sighs of relief in the Bundeswehr. Each in its own way realizes the dreams of Wehrmacht commanders after Stalingrad. The Leopard is close to an optimal combination of gunpower, mobility, and mechanical reliability. It is also sufficiently cost-effective to be in service throughout NATO's smaller contingents. Canada, Belgium, and the Netherlands, Greece and Turkey all feature Leopards in their order of battle. In its updated Mark 2 version it remains at least competitive with the US Abrams MBT — and few Bundeswehr tank commanders would agree to an exchange. The Marder is more specifically German. A combat vehicle as opposed to a battle taxi, it carries a rifle squad that is expected to fight from the vehicle under most circumstances. While the Marder has been subject to more criticism than the Leopard, its survivability, amphibious capactiy and cross-country abilities have won general approval at operational levels. Leopard and Marder chassis also serve as the basis for a comprehensive family of supporting weapons, notably the Gepard anti-aircraft tank and the Jaguar rocket tank destroyer.[77]

As for fire support, the Bundeswehr was until recently the only NATO force equipped with multiple rocket launchers, the successors to the World War II *Katyushas*. Its tube artillery is oriented towards delivering saturation fire against area targets, with prompt response considered more important than delayed volume. And while the Bundeswehr does not quite share the US faith in combat helicopters as offensive weapons, the West German army includes three regiments, each with 56 PAH-1 light helicopters, in the anti-tank role.[78]

Maximising the potential of mechanization demands enhanced flexibility. This process began for the Bundeswehr in the 1970s, when its airborne division was divided for operational purposes into its three component brigades, one assigned to each corps as an air-mobile reaction and anti-tank force. Army Structure 4 carried the policy further. Instead of the division, the brigade has become the principal operational unit. Instead of the familiar three combat battalions, each brigade on mobilization will have four. The battalions are smaller. Companies have no significant administrative functions. Their strengths have been correspondingly reduced — a policy considered both to enhance unit cohesion and to encourage initiative and responsibility at junior command levels. The new structure also provides for greater use of reservists in front-line units. The fourth battalion of each brigade forms its staff and supporting units on mobilization. It draws its three combat companies from the brigade's active battalions, which in peacetime command four companies instead of three.[79]

This represents a significant reversal of traditional approaches, which usually maintain headquarters of reserve units in peacetime and complete the fighting units with men recalled to duty. It also gives each Bundeswehr brigade a combined arms battalion of two tank companies and one mechanized company in a mechanized brigade, the reverse in an armored brigade. This reflects the increasing West German commitment to combined arms operations, particularly the cross-posting and the integration of companies into the successors of those hard-hitting Wehrmacht *Kampfgruppen* that did so much to discomfit allied

The Bundeswehr of the Federal Republic of Germany 241

advances everywhere in Europe.

The reorganization of the West German army and the upgrading of its heavy equipment have generated an increasing concentration on the cutting edge. Officially, at least, 90 percent of the active soldiers are assigned to troop units, and 75 percent of those are in combat and combat support formations, as opposed to headquarters, logistic, or medical units.[80] This teeth-to-tail ratio is somewhat diminished in practice by a policy of carrying detached men on unit rolls, much in the pattern of the Union and Confederate armies. Nevertheless it follows Soviet as opposed to US models, to the point where critics periodically accuse the Bundeswehr of ignoring sustainability for the sake of an immediate battle.[81] It also involves depending on reservists to man a high proportion of service and support units, particularly at corps level and above. Reserve stocks of fighting vehicles, ammunition, and spare parts are lower than the Bundeswehr would prefer in an ideal world. But even if a future war should be "not over by Christmas," as a recent book argues, the Bundeswehr is convinced that it could all too easily be lost in the first few days.[82] Particularly with the ever-present threat of nuclear escalation, the sharpness of the sword's edge counts for more than the weight of the blade.

Function and Ethos

British operational analyst Richard Simpkin misses the point when he describes the Bundeswehr as one of NATO's "rotten planks," committing itself in practice to "ever deeper dugouts and ever more ponderous equipment" in pursuit of the militarily futile policy of forward defense.[83] A better metaphor is that of a bar-room fighter facing a stronger, heavier opponent in a confined space. An experienced brawler in such a situation seeks to close with his more powerful enemy, eschewing a knockout punch in favor of lesser, but still painful, combinations of hooks and jabs, while at the same time keeping his foe from employing his full strength. Surviving such a fight, however, depends heavily on intelligence, skill, and reflexes — in other words, on those intangibles that are the third element of the Bundeswehr's approach to the defense of the Federal Republic.

How successful have the West Germans been in encouraging and inculcating flexibility and initiative in their military establishment? This kind of military vitalism is significantly attractive in a state increasingly uncomfortable with demanding service of any kind from its citizens, and significantly unwilling to pay the costs of parity. It offers the hope of a free military lunch. Instead of building tanks, build morale. Instead of improving force ratios, improve quality. And this can be done without cutting civilian entitlements. It only requires emphasis on the virtues of the soldier — virtues which, in the context of a bureaucratized Bundeswehr that appears to know its place, are seen as unlikely to threaten the Federal Republic's ordered comfort under normal circumstances.[84]

Martin van Creveld comes closer to the mark by questioning whether a self-conscious, bureaucratized military establishment, integrated into a society stressing comfort and risk-avoidance as norms, can be expected to sustain in combat an operational doctrine calling for initiative, sacrifice, and risk-taking at all levels.[85] The West German officer corps is closely assimilated at all levels to the model of the civil servant. This dominant *Beamtenmentalität*, cultivated among the Wehrmacht generation, has become increasingly natural. From the beginning the Bundeswehr rejected the concept of a socially homogeneous officer corps — a concept that had been more a myth than a reality even under the empire, to say nothing of the Nazi years. Instead, the Bundeswehr's officers were to reflect the structure of West German society as a whole. From being a way of life, an officer's career was to become a profession, one open to classes and groups historically underrepresented. Ambition and execution would become the determinants of success — determinants subsumed, of course, by the moral integrating factor of loyalty to the state.

This process involved a significant alteration in principles of selection. Prior to 1945, subjective factors tended to outweigh objective ones in a candidate's evaluation. "Character" was considered far more important than formal qualifications. The concept could mean as little as having the right surname or the right connections. It could mean as much as an examiner's sense that with this young man one threw the paperwork away. But the approach was impossible to implant in the Bundeswehr for two reasons. The line between judgment and prejudice was always fine enough to raise charges of discrimination. A military with a strong power base and a generally positive image might be able to ignore or refute such charges. The Bundeswehr's position in the Federal Republic in no way supported anything but deferential behavior on controversial issues. At the same time, subjective selection involved a level of professional confidence difficult for an army with the Bundeswehr's heritage of total defeat — a heritage no less significant for being informal and unofficial.

The result has been an increasing emphasis on credentials: specifically formal education as a criterion for both commissioning and advancement. The number of *Abiturienten* among the officers has risen steadily, not least because the Bundeswehr's officer corps is perceived by its members as comparing very favorably to other areas of West German society in offering careers open to talents and chances to develop these talents while in uniform. The Bundeswehr draws a high and increasing proportion of its officers from those social groups with the greatest opportunities to move their sons through the school system: upper-level white-collar employees, bureaucrats, administrators, executives. But the often-raised question of whether Bundeswehr officers are best described as a class or a caste involves a false dichotomy. The crucial factor in selecting a military career is less likely to be heritage than prospects.[86]

This emphasis on formal education as the basic criterion for career progress diminishes the role of the field soldier, the ranker, the mustang, as a role model. Potential Anthony Herberts or Charles Beckwiths find little encouragement in a Bundeswehr dominated by colorless men carrying briefcases. The exclusion as a matter of state policy of West German forces from any operational experience of its own has correspondingly circumscribed its ability to produce leaders from an operational environment. In this sense at least West Germany's military is closer to Dutch or Scandinavian models than to its French, British, or US counterparts. With a few spectacular exceptions, notably Luftwaffe Inspector-General Johannes Steinhoff and his army counterpart Heinz Trettner, senior German officers have been most likely to become visible negatively, by personal behavior or political opinions seen as deviating from accepted norms of innocuousness.

The question is how well officers formed in such a mold will be able to lead troops in battle, much less implement current Bundeswehr doctrines. The Western world in general, the US in particular, is going through a phase generally critical of credentialism as a means of defining competence. Nor is tradition particularly helpful in this area. The German stereotype of leadership emerging from World War I was that of the warrior isolated by his experience from the civilian world. The *Fronterlebnis* of 1914–18 blended naturally, if not automatically, with the propaganda of a Third Reich which presented its *Ritterkreuzträger* as men whose feats set them apart in essence from their fellows. This was a sharp contrast to Soviet and Western cultural images of a war fought by everyman in uniform.[87] It has been nurtured by a growing tendency everywhere in the West to make World War II a mythic experience. The catalogues of Stuttgart's *Motorbuch-Verlag* may profitably be compared to the respectable American hobbyists' magazine that made it briefly possible to send away for a poster of SS tank commander Michael Wittmann, executed in living color.[88] A further cry from the concept of *Staatsbürger in Uniform* can hardly be imagined — or one less likely to encourage replication in the Federal Republic.

Yet at the same time West Germany's military faces nothing like the current dispute over management versus leadership raging in the US. In part this reflects confidence in the potential of doctrine to shape behavior. Military establishments have historically been more flexible, more responsive to altered internal dynamics, than is generally understood by contemporary scholars focussing on the links between armies and societies. In operational, as opposed to political, matters, the Bundeswehr seems increasingly willing to allow junior officers the freedom to make mistakes and learn from them. The risks of overcontrolling remain. Nevertheless West German units regularly perform well in maneuvers and competitions; West German soldiers regularly earn the praise of their NATO counterparts. Peacetime achievements offer no guarantee of success in war, but cannot be summarily dismissed.

Nor does confidence depend entirely on rehearsal performances. Since its creation the Bundeswehr has focussed on one operational mission: large-scale conventional defensive war on its home ground. Attitudes borrowed from other military environments, France in Algeria, the US in Vietnam, or Russia in Afghanistan, are seen as at best marginally appropriate to the conditions obtaining should the Warsaw Pact roll westwards. Sustaining that kind of fighting even for a few weeks will require more than technical skill, more than primary group cohesion, and far more than the *Landsknecht* mentality generated by the Wehrmacht experience.

It is exactly here where operational factors depend in essence on philosophical considerations. In practice *Innere Führung* has demonstrated limits, but these have essentially resembled the limits of similar concepts in previous regimes. Soldiers tend towards an exaggerated faith in the capacity of their milieu to alter consciousness, as opposed to modifying behavior — a faith generally shared by the military's critics. This assumed degree of influence over young adults is not, however, justified by significant supporting data. An overwhelming weight of evidence indicates that most essential processes of value and attitude formation occur well before the individual is draft-eligible. A period in uniform that in West Germany has never exceeded 18 months is hardly likely to alter that consciousness, particularly when that period is the product of compulsion rather than the reflection of choice.[89]

Since the late 1960s, moreover, principled criticism of the Bundeswehr among German youth has tended to be expressed by rejection of the military as an institution. The challenge is not to improve the system by participation, but to avoid contamination as far as possible. The Federal Republic's generous conscientious objector legislation and provisions for alternative service play much the same objective role as anti-Socialist discrimination in Bismarck's Reich, by significantly reducing the number of potential boat-rockers in uniform. Their counterparts who do don uniform are correspondingly likely to feel a bit ashamed of themselves for having accepted a compromise, and to do their service with as little involvement as possible. *Durchsitzen* and *durchbüffeln* are common expressions of attitude. Neither suggests principled participation.[90]

The absence, physically or psychologically, from the Bundeswehr's ranks of a disproportionate number of those to whom *Innere Führung* might be more than an avant-garde concept is not necessarily a major weakness. Ideally, *Innere Führung* implies a positive state of mind, institutionalized in a military committed to internalizing democratic values in its members. It involves a constant process of challenge, criticism, and affirmation. Yet while this process may be desirable as a principle, it counters most of the everyday, commonsense experience of young people in the Federal Republic — particularly those outside the influence of the intellectual community. The normal demands of life in West Germany, the requirements of schools, jobs, and even social activities, are increasingly likely to condition positive acceptance of institutional structures reasonably administered and of authority reasonably exercised.[91]

In the 1960s Herbert Marcuse wrote of "repressive tolerance." Ralf Dahrendorf described the Germans' search for consensus, their dislike of conflict, as necessarily inimical to democracy. Twenty years later Ernst Renan's epigrammatic definition of nationalism as a daily plebiscite seems more appropriate for the Federal Republic of Germany. The state has endured almost as long as the Second Empire, without anything like the same domestic challenges to its legitimacy. The principles of *Innere Führung* fit objectively into a society with a self-image as a network of interdependent specialists functioning best when not divided by abstractions. Voltaire's dislike of heroes for making too much noise in the world seems well on the way to balancing, if not outweighing, those Nietzschean calls for living largely that exercised such an influence over German culture for the past century.

"Democracies," in the words of Graf Baudissin, "may be in peace markedly unheroic and plural, but on the field of battle they are remarkably efficient. In any case, in two world wars they beat hell out of us." When his interviewer suggested that in the decisive moment West Germany's conscripts would emerge as warriors, that Babylonians would become Spartans, Baudissin eagerly answered, "Right! Right!"[92] On one level the Bundeswehr's mission is simple: to buy time before the missiles start flying. West Germany and NATO ask no more of their conventional forces. Yet Baudissin's outburst also reflects the fact that the Bundeswehr is not the psychological counterpart of U.S. conventional forces. It is rather the Federal Republic's equivalent of American strategic nuclear capabilities. To use it at all represents defeat and the only question remaining will be the extent of the disaster.[93]

Being cast as an ultimate weapon is likely to generate a correspondingly general sense of responsibilities. For the Bundeswehr, the task of buying time is seen as necessarily engaging West Germany's fighting men at a level calling for what F. Scott Fitzgerald described as "a whole-souled sentimental equipment going back further than you could remember." *Innere Führung* may not be the equivalent of Fitzgerald's "tremendous sureties." Forty years of freedom and prosperity may not replace ". . . beer gardens in Unter den Linden and weddings at the *mairie*, and going to the Derby, and your grandfather's whiskers."[94] They are the best the Federal Republic of Germany has been able to do to prepare its citizen-soldiers for the kind of war its experts believe they will have to fight if deterrence fails. In this sense not Babylon or Sparta, but Athens, stands as a fitting model for the men of the Bundeswehr. In the words of Pericles, "where our rivals from their very cradles seek after manliness, at Athens we live exactly as we please, and yet are just as ready to encounter every legitimate danger."[95] The Federal Republic's aspirations are no less high. May its achievements ever remain untested.

Notes

1. Karl Kaiser, Georg Leber, Alois Mertes, and Franz-Josef Schulze, "Nuclear Weapons and the Preservation of Peace: A Response to an American Proposal for

Renouncing the First Use of Nuclear Weapons," *Foreign Affairs*, 60, 1982, pp. 1157–1170; and Helga Haftendorn, "Das doppelte Missverständnis. Zur Vorgeschichte des Nato-Doppelbeschlusses von 1979," *Vierteljahrsheft e für Zeitgeschichte*, 33 (1985), pp. 244–287.

2. Peter Loewenberg, "Psychological Perspectives on Modern German History," *Journal of Modern History*, 47 (1975), pp. 229–279.

3. Cf. *inter alia* Alex A. Vardamis, "German–American Military Fissures," *Foreign Policy*, 34 (1979), pp. 87–106.

4. Cf. E. J. F. Thomas, "The European Advisory Commission and Allied Planning for a Defeated Germany," PhD dissertation, American University, Washington DC 1981; Robert McGeehan, *The German Rearmament Question: American Diplomacy and European Defense after World War II* (Urbana, Ill., 1971); Harry F. Borowski, *A Hollow Threat: Strategic Air Power and Containment before Korea* (Westport, Conn., 1982); and Samuel F. Wells, Jr., "The Origins of Massive Retaliation," *Political Science Quarterly*, 96 (1981), pp. 31–52. Christian Greiner, "Die alliierten militärstrategischen Planungen zur Verteidigung Westeuropas 1947–1950" in R. G. Foester, Christian Greiner, Georg Meyer, Hans-Jügen Rautenberg, and Norbert Wiggershaus, *Anfänge westdeutscher Sicherheitspolitik 1945–1956*, vol. 1 of *Von der Kapitulation zum Plevin-Plan* (Munich, 1982), pp. 131ff, presents US policy from a West German perspective.

5. US Congress, Joint Hearings before the Committee on Foreign Relations and the Committee on Armed Services, US Senate, 81st Congress, 1st Session on S. 2388 (Washington, DC, 1949), *passim*

6. B. H. Liddell Hart, *The German Generals Talk* (New York, 1948); Erich von Manstein, *Verlorene Siege* (Bonn, 1955); Heinz Guderian, *Kann Westeuropa verteidigt werden?* (Heidelberg, 1950); and Felix Steiner, *Die Wehridee des Abendlandes* (Wiesbaden, 1951) are representative examples of this approach.

7. Greiner, "Die Alliierten militärstrategischen Planungen," pp. 206ff.

8. Gruenther to Hickerson, 16 July 1948, and accompanying "Instructions for the U.S. Representatives Attending the London Western Union Talks," *Foreign Relations of the United States*, 1948, vol. 3 (Washington, DC, 1974), pp. 188ff (hereafter cited as *FRUS*); *The Memoirs of Field-Marshal the Viscount Montgomery of Alamein* (New York, 1958), pp. 447ff *passim*; Geoffrey Warner, "The Reconstruction and Defence of Western Europe after 1945" in N. Waites (ed.), *Troubled Neighbours: Franco-British Relations in the Twentieth Century* (London, 1971), pp. 259–292.

9. Hays to Acheson, 17 January 1951, *FRUS*, 1951, vol. 3, pp. 996ff.

10. Comments of John J. McCloy, "Summary Record of a Meeting of United States Ambassadors at Paris, October 21–22," *FRUS*, 1949, vol. 4, pp. 487f; McCloy to Acheson, 14 July and 25 September 1950, *FRUS* 1950, vol.4, pp. 696ff, 724ff.

11. Gerhard Wettig, *Entmilitarisierung und Wiederbewaffnung in Deutschland, 1943–1955. Internationale Auseinandersetzungen um die Rolle der Deutschen in Europa* (Munich, 1967) remains the most detailed analysis of the debate. Cf. Wilhelm Cornides and Hermann Volle, "Die Vorgeschichte des Brüsseler Fünfmächte-Paktes (1948)," *Europa-Archiv*, 4 (1949), pp. 1755–1767; A. C. Azzola, *Die Diskussion um die Aufrüstung der Bundesrepublik Deutschland im Unterhaus und in der presse Grossbritanniens, November 1949–Juli 1952* (Meisenheim, 1971); and Lawrence W. Martin, "The American Decision to Rearm Germany" in H. Stein (ed.), *American Civil–Military Decisions* (Tuscaloosa, Ala., 1963), pp. 643–666.

12. Marlis Steinert, *Hitlers Krieg und die Deutschen* (Düsseldorf, 1970); and Gerald Kerwin, "Waiting for Retaliation" A Study in Nazi Propaganda Behaviour and German Civilian Morale," *Journal of Contemporary History*, 16 (1981), pp. 565–583, document the collapse of public interest under Hitler. On the alleged failure to reorder German society after the war cf. recently Carolyn Eisenberg, "Working-Class Politics and the Cold War: American Intervention in the German Labor Movement, 1945–49," *Diplomatic History*, 7 (1983), pp. 283–306; and Wolfgang Benz, "Versuche zur Reform

des öffentlichen Dienstes in Deutschland 1945–1952: Deutsche Opposition gegen alliierte Initiativen," *Vierteljahrshefte für Zeitgeschichte*, 29 (1981), pp. 216–245. Lothar Gall, "Die Bundesrepublik in der Kontinuität der deutschen Geschichte," *Historische Zeitschrift*, 239 (1984), pp. 605–613, perceptively challenges the concept of "zero hour." Diethelm Prowe, "The New Nachkriegsgeschichte (1945–49): West Germans in Search of their Historical Origins," *Central European History*, 10 (1977), pp. 312–328, surveys a proliferating literature on the general theme of reconstruction.

13. Georg Meyer, "Zur Situation der deutschen militärischen Führungsschicht im Vorfeld des westdeutschen Verteidigungsbeitrages 1945–1950/51" in Foerster *et al.*, *Anfänge westdeutscher Sicherheitspolitik*, pp. 579ff; and Manfred Messerschmidt, *Die Wehrmacht im NS-Staat. Zeit der Indoktrination* (Hamburg, 1969).

14. Hans-Jürgen Rautenberg, "Zur Standortbestimmung für künftige deutsche Streitkräfte" in Foerster *et al Anfänge westdeutscher Sicherheit*, pp. 739ff, particularly stresses this break with the past. Cf. Hans Speidel, *Aus unserer Zeit. Erinnerungen* (Berlin, 1977), pp. 254ff *passim*.

15. For Social Democratic defense conceptions at this period cf. particularly Udo Loewke, *Für den Fall dass: SPD und Wehrfrage, 1949–1955* (Hanover, 1969); G. D. Drummond, *The German Social Democrats in Opposition, 1949–1960: The Case Against Rearmament* (Norman, Okla., 1982); and Hartmut Soell, *Fritz Erler: Eine politische Biographie* (Berlin, 1976).

16. On Adenauer's relationship to the military see particularly Klaus Schwabe, "Konrad Adenauer und die Aufrüstung der Bundesrepublik (1949–1955)" in D. Blumenwitz *et al.* (eds.), *Konrad Adenauer und seine Zeit*, 2 vols. (Stuttgart, 1976), vol. 2, pp. 15–36.

17. Norbert Wiggershaus, "Bedrohungsvorstellungen Bundeskanzler Adenauers nach Ausbruch der Korea-Krieges," *Militärgeschichtliche Mitteilungen*, 25 (1979), pp. 79–122; and Günther Mai, *Westliche Sicherheit im Kalten Krieg. Der Korea-Krieg und die deutsche Wiederbewaffnung, 1950* (Boppard, 1977).

18. For the Plevin Plan cf. Acheson to Bruce, 27 October 1950, *FRUS*, 1950, vol. 3, pp. 410ff; and "Minutes of the US–UK Political–Military Conversations," 26 October 1950 ibid., pp. 1689ff. Jules Moch, *Histoire du réarmement allemand depuis 1950* (Paris, 1965), offers a French perspective. Cf. Edward Furdson, *The European Defence Community. A History* (New York, 1980), pp. 50ff.

19. McCloy to Acheson, 25 September and 22 December 1950, *FRUS*, 1950, vol. 4, pp. 724ff, 813ff. The Germans' views on operational problems confronting multinational divisions are presented in McCloy to Acheson, 2 March 1951, *FRUS*, 1951, vol. 3, pp. 1022ff. Cf. in general Klaus von Schubert, *Wiederbewaffnung und westliche Orientierung der Bundesrepublik 1950–1959* (Stuttgart, 1970).

20. Memorandum of 7 August 1950 in Speidel, *Aus unserer Zeit*, pp. 477ff.

21. Rautenberg, "Standortbestimmung," pp. 778ff *passim*.

22. This impatience is particularly expressed in Acheson's telegram to the US Embasssy in France, 21 June 1951; and McCloy's memorandum of 1 September 1951, *FRUS*, 1951, vol. 3, pp. 501ff and 874ff.

23. Dennis E. Showalter, "Army and Society in Imperial Germany: The Pains of Modernization," *Journal of Contemporary History*, 18 (1983), pp. 583–618; and Michael Geyer, "The Dynamics of Military Revisionism in the Interwar Years. Military Politics between Rearmament and Diplomacy" in W. Deist (ed.), *The German Military in the Age of Total War* (Dover, NH, 1985), pp. 100–151.

24. Cf. W. V. Madej, "Effectiveness and Cohesion of the German Ground Forces in World War II," *Journal of Political and Military Sociology*, 6 (1978), pp. 233–248; and Martin van Creveld, *Fighting Power* (Westport, Conn., 1982), *passim*.

25. Similar anxieties about volunteers were expressed by US High Commissioner John H. McCloy and SPD leader Kurt Schumacher. Cf. Speidel, *Aus unserer Zeit*, p. 278; and Drummond, *Social Democrats in Opposition*, p. 60. The subsequent SPD

reversal on the question is analyzed in ibid., pp. 163ff *passim*.

26. Hans-Jürgen Rautenberg and Norbert Wiggershaus, "Die 'Himmeroder Denkschrift' vom Oktober 1950. Politische und militärische Überlegung für einen Beitrage der Bundesrepublik Deutschland zur westeuropäischen Verteidigung," *Militärgeschichtliche Mitteilungen*, 20 (1977), pp. 135–206.

27. For recent treatments of this issue cf. Diethlem Prowe, "Economic Democracy in Post-World War II Germany: Corporalist Crisis Response, 1945–1948," *Journal of Modern History*, 57 (1985), pp. 451–482; and Klaus von Beyme, "The Power Structure in the Federal Republic of Germany" in C. Burdick, H-A. Jacobsen and W. Kudszus (eds.), *Contemporary Germany: Politics and Culture* (Boulder, Colo., 1984), pp. 77–106.

28. The most focussed treatment remains Christian Greiner, "Die Dienststelle Blank. Regierungspraxis bei der Vorbereitung des deutschen Verteidigungsbeitrages von 1950–1955," *Militärgeschichtliche Mitteilungen*, 17 (1975), pp. 99–124. Cf. also Dietrich Genschel, *Wehrreform und Reaktion: Die Vorbereitung der Inneren Führung 1951–1956* (Hamburg, 1972).

29. Rautenberg, "Standortbestimmung," pp. 788ff, is the most recent summary of the selection process. Cf. also Alfred Grosser, *Germany in our Time*, trans. P. Stephenson (New York, 1971), p. 224.

30. Cf. *inter alia* Gerhard Ritter, *Europa und die deutsche Frage* (Munich, 1947); Hans Rothfels, *The German Opposition to Hitler* (Hillside, Ill., 1948); Hannah Arendt, *The Origins of Totalitarianism* (New York, 1957).

31. See particularly Gerald Ambrosius, *Die Durchsetzung der sozialen Marktwirtschaft in Westdeutschland 1945–1949* (Stuttgart, 1977).

32. Familiar statements of this thesis include Ralf Dahrendorf, *Society and Democracy in Germany* (New York, 1967); Jürgen Leinemann, *Die Angst der Deutschen: Beobachtungen zur Bewusstseinlage der Nation* (Hamburg, 1982); Peter Brückner, *Versuch uns und Anderen die Bundesrepublik zu erklären* (Berlin, 1978); and, far more optimistically, Walter Laqueur, *Germany Today: a Personal Report* (Boston, 1985).

33. Recent typical statements include Heinz Hoffmann, "Militärgeschichte im Klassenkampf unserer Zeit," *Militärgeschichte*, 22 (1983), pp. 389–396; and Paul Heider, "Erbe und Tradition der DDR aus militärhistorischer Zeit," ibid., 24 (1985), pp. 73–76.

34. Gunter Will, "Zur Praxis der 'Traditionshandhabung.' Erlebnisse, Beobachtungen, Betrachtungen" in Klaus-M. Kodalle (ed.), *Tradition als Last? Legitimationsprobleme der Bundeswehr* (Cologne, 1981), pp. 183–188.

35. Manfred Messerschmidt, "Das Verhältnis von Wehrmacht und NS-Staat und die Frage der Traditionsbildung" ibid., pp. 57–78.

36. Cf. *inter alia* Wolfgang von Groote, "Bundeswehr und 20 Juli," *Vierteljahrshefte für Zeitgeschichte*, 12 (1964), pp. 285–289; and Klaus Donate, "Deutscher Widerstand gegen den Nationalsozialismus aus der Sicht der Bundeswehr," PhD dissertation, University of Freiburg, 1975.

37. Colonel Hans-Joachim Krug, "Der erste Artillerist" in H.-J. Krug (ed.), *25 Jahre Artillerie der Bundeswehr* (Bad Nauheim, 1982), pp. 14–15.

38. Cf. Günther Blumentritt, *Deutsches Soldatentum im europäischen Rahmen* (Giessen, 1952); and Günther Krauss, "Christ und Wiederbewaffnung," *Wehrwissenschaftliche Rundschau*, 2 (1952), pp. 100–110.

39. Cf. Axel Hartmann, "Das Feindbild im Spiegel der Bundeswehrpublikationen," Dissertation Jurisprudence, University of Würzburg, 1975; Wilfried von Bredow, "Asymmetric Images of the Enemy: The Problem of Political Education in the Armed Forces of the Two German States," *Journal of Political and Military Sociology*, 9 (1981), pp. 31–41; and Ralf Zoll, "The German Armed Forces" in M. Janowitz and S.D. Wesbrook (eds.), *The Political Education of Soldiers* (Beverly Hills, Calif., 1983), pp. 209–248.

40. Cf. *inter alia* David Childs, *From Schumacher to Brandt: The Story of German Socialism, 1945–1965* (Oxford, 1966); Susanne Miller, *Die SPD vor und nach Godesberg* (Bonn-Bad Godesberg, 1974) and Klaas Günther, *Sozialdemokratie und Demokratie, 1949–1966: Die SPD und das Problem des Verschränkung Innenparteilicher und bundesrepublikanischer Demokratie* (Bonn-Bad Godesberg, 1979); Stephen J. Artner, "The SPD and NATO: The Transformation of Social Democratic Alliance Policy 1957–1961," PhD dissertation, John Hopkins University, 1983), is also useful on military issues in general.

41. Wiegand Schmidt-Richberg, "Die Regierungszeit Wilhelms II" in W. Schmidt-Richberg and E. Graf von Matuschka (eds.), *Von der Entlassung Bismarcks bis zum Ende des Ersten Weltkrieges (1890–1914)*, vol. 5 of *Handbuch zur deutschen Militärgeschichte* (Frankfurt, 1968), pp. 51–52, 113ff.

42. *Innere Führung* has generated an immense body of critical literature. Major recent treatments include Ulrich Simon, *Die Integration der Bundeswehr in die Gesellschaft: Das Ringen um die Innere Führung* (Heidelberg and Hamburg, 1980); Karl Gero Ilsemann, *Die Innere Führung in den Streitkräften* (Regensburg, 1981); Peter Wullich, *Die Konzeption der "Inneren Führung" der Bundeswehr als Grundlage einer allgemeinen Wehrpädagogik* (Regensburg, 1981).

43. Van Creveld, *Fighting Power*, especially pp. 28ff *passim*.

44. Wolf Graf von Bundissen, *Soldat für den Frieden. Entwürfe für eine zeitgemässe Bundeswehr*, ed. P. v. Schubert (Munich, 1969), remains the most complete collection of his views.

45. On the evolution of West German defense policies in the era of massive retaliation cf. R. F. Driscoll, "West German Nuclear Politics: A Study of Interpersonal Cooperative Behavior," PhD dissertation, American University, Washington, DC, 1981; Catherine M. Kelleher, *Germany and the Politics of Nuclear Weapons* (New York, 1975); and H. K. Rupp, *Opposition in der Ära Adenauer. Der Kampf gegen die Atombewaffnung in den fünfziger Jahren* (Cologne, 1970);. Hans Speier, *German Rearmament and Atomic War: The Views of German Military and Political Leaders* (Evanston, Ill., 1957) is a contemporary treatment of the question.

46. A point made as early as 1950 in B. H. Liddell Hart, *Defense of the West* (New York, 1950), p. 115.

47. Glenn H. Snyder, *Deterrence and Defense. Toward a Theory of National Security* (Princeton, NJ, 1961), pp. 137ff; and Lawrence Friedman, *The Evolution of Nuclear Strategy* (London, 1981), pp. 107ff are representative critiques of the doctrine.

48. Catherine M. Kelleher, "Mass Armies in the 1970's: The Debate in Western Europe," *Armed Forces and Society*, 4 (1978), pp. 3–30; Alan Ned Sabrosky, "Societal Values, Military Institutions, and the Western Dilemma," *Orbis*, 22 (1978), pp. 37–45.

49. Michael Geyer, *Deutsche Rüstungspolitik 1860–1980* (Frankfurt, 1984), pp. 210ff, surveys the relationship of high-tech defense to an emerging West German military–industrial complex. Fritz Vilmar, *Rüstung und Abrüstung im Spätkapitalismus. Ein sozioökonomische Analyse des Militarismus*, 2nd edn (Reinbeck, 1973) fits the Federal Republic into a universal model of late capitalism. Carola Bielfeldt, *Rüstungsausgaben und Staatsinterventionismus. Am Beispiel der Bundesrepublik Deutschland 1950–1971* (Frankfurt, 1977); and Manfred Schmidt, *Staatsapparat und Rüstungspolitik in der Bundesrepublik Deutschland (1966–1973)* (Giessen/Lollar, 1975) are among the best concrete treatments of the relationship between defense budgets and economic development in West Germany.

50. Cf. Walter F. Hahn, *Between Westpolitik and Ostpolitik* (Beverly Hills, Calif., 1975); and William E. Griffith, *The Ostpolitik of the Federal Republic of Germany* (Cambridge, Mass., 1978), especially pp. 108ff.

51. Gerard Braunthal, *The West German Social Democrats, 1969–1982: Profile of a Party in Power* (Boulder, Colo., 1983), pp. 277ff., is a good brief summary of the party's position on defense issues. Cf. also Jeffrey Boutwell, "Politics and the Peace Movement in West Germany," *International Security*, 5 (1983), pp. 72–92; and Günther

Schmid, *Sicherheitspolitik und Friedensbewegung. Der Konflikt um die "Nachrüstung"* (Munich, 1982).

52. Morris Janowitz, *The Professional Soldier: A Social and Political Portrait* (New York, 1960).

53. James A. Linger, "The Emergence of the Bundeswehr as a Pressure Group," *Armed Forces and Society*, 5 (1979), pp. 560–589, provides a series of case studies as well as a useful structural model. Cf. also Kenneth H. F. Dyson, "Party, State, and Bureaucracy in Western Germany," Sage Professional Paper in Comparative Politics, 6, 01–063 (Beverly Hills and London, 1977). The myths and realities of the guns-and-butter issue are admirably presented in R. C. Eichenberg, "Defense–Welfare Tradeoffs in German Budgeting," PhD dissertation, University of Michigan, 1981.

54. Manfred Wörner, "The Atlantic Alliance — Guarantor of Freedom and Security" in H.-J. Veen (ed.), *Arguments for Peace and Freedom*, trans. E. Martin (Melle, 1983), pp. 109–116.

55. For Germany's position in NATO and in Western Europe generally, cf. inter alia Wolfram Hanreider and Graeme P. Auton, *The Foreign Policies of West Germany, France and Britain* (Englewood Cliffs, NJ, 1980); Catherine M. Kelleher, "The Federal Republic and NATO: Change and Continuity" in R. G. Livingstone (ed.), *The Federal Republic of Germany in the 1980s: Foreign Policies and Domestic Changes* (New York, 1983), pp. 7–10; and Helmut Haftendorn, *Abrüstungs- und Entspanungspolitik zwischen Sicherheitsbefriedigung und Friedenssicherung. Zur Aussenpolitik der BRD 1955–1973* (Düsseldorf, 1974). The quotations are from Catherine M. Kelleher, "The Defense Policy of the Federal Republic of Germany" in D. J. Murray and P. R. Viotti (eds.), *The Defense Policies of Nations. A Comparative Study* (Baltimore, 1982), p. 271.

56. While NATO's Circumlocution Offices and Ministries of Truth yet await their Charles Dickens or George Orwell, Johannes Steinhoff, *Wohin treibt die NATO?* (Hamburg, 1976) and Gerd Schmückle, *Ohne Pauken und Trompeten. Erinnerungen an Krieg und Frieden* (Stuttgart, 1984), esp. pp. 271ff, offer scathing and perceptive insiders' accounts.

57. Cf. David Schoenbaum, *The Spiegel Affair* (Garden City, NY, 1968); and Ronald Bunn, *German Politics and the Spiegel Affair: A Case Study of the Bonn System* (Baton Rouge, LA, 1968).

58. Linger, "Bundeswehr as a Pressure Group," pp. 584–585.

59. *Weissbuch 1985: Zur Lage und Entwicklung der Bundeswehr*, ed. Federal Ministry of Defense (Bonn, 1985), pp. 202ff. For specific treatments of the lesser services see "Vice Admiral Bethge, Former Inspector of the German Navy, Talks to IDR," *International Defense Review*, 18, no. 8 (1985), pp. 1227–1228; Wolfgang Flume, "Die Zerstörerflotille," *Wehrtechnik*, 17 (May 1985), pp. 14–23; and Jörg Kulbart, "Die Luftflotte," ibid. (August 1985), pp. 34–40.

60. Helmut Schmidt, *The Balance of Power: Germany's Peace Policy and the Super Powers*, trans. E. Thomas (London, 1971).

61. Cf. Eichenberg, "Defense–Welfare Tradeoffs"; and the far more critical treatments by Peter Schlotter, *Rüstungspolitik in der Bundesrepublik Deutschland, Die Beispiele Starfighter und Phantom* (Frankfurt, 1975); and A. Mechtersheimer, *Rüstung und Politik in der Bundesrepublik. MRCA Tornado* (Bad Hannef, 1977).

62. For statistics and projections cf. *White Paper 1970: On the security of the Federal Republic of Germany and on the State of the Federal German Armed Forces*, ed. Federal Ministry of Defense (Bonn, 1970), p. 88; *White Paper 1979: The Security of the Federal Republic of Germany and the Development of the Federal Armed Forces*, ed. Federal Ministry of Defense (Bonn, 1979), pp. 223ff; and *Weissbuch 1985*, pp. 138ff, 249ff.

63. Cf. *White Paper 1971/1972: The Security of the Federal Republic of Germany and the Development of The Federal Armed Forces*, ed. Federal Ministry of Defense (Bonn, 1971), pp. 27, 50ff; Clemens Range, *Das Heer der Bundeswehr: Geschichte, Organisation, Laufbahn* (Stuttgart, 1978), pp. 93ff; and Wolfgang Roschlau's DDR summary, "Grundzüge der strukturellen Entwicklung der BRD-Landstreitkräfte in den

letzten 30 Jahren," *Militärgeschichte*, 22 (1983), p. 408.

64. For the genesis of forward defense, see James A. Blackwell, Jr., "In the Laps of the Gods: The Origins of NATO Forward Defense," *Parameters: Journal of the U.S. Army War College*, 15 (Winter 1985), pp. 64–75. Its current problems and implications are presented in J. C. F. Tillson, "The Forward Defense of Europe," *Military Affairs*, 61 (May, 1981), pp. 66–76; and John Keegan, "Soviet Blitzkrieg: Who Wins?" *Harper's* (May 1982), pp. 46–53.

65. The evolution of this line of argument is best followed through F. O. Mischke, *Die Zukunft der Bundeswehr. Gedanken über den Umbau der Westdeutschen Verteidigung* (Stuttgart, 1967); Horst Ahlfeldt, *Verteidigung und Frieden: Politik mit Militärischen Mitteln* (Munich, 1967); Franz Uhle-Wettler, *Gefechtsfeld Mitteleuropa-Gefahr der Übertechnisierung von Streitkräften* (Munich, 1980); and the contributions in J. Löser (ed.), *Weder Rot noch Tot-Überleben ohne Atomkrieg. Eine sicherheitspolitische Alternative* (Munich, 1981).

66. *White Paper 1973/1974, The Security of the Federal Republic of Germany and the Development of the Federal Armed Forces*, ed. Federal Ministry of Defense (Bonn, 1974), pp. 53ff, 78–79, 177; Siegfried Schulz, *Das neue Heer* (Koblenz, 1974), pp. 58–59, 133ff; and Franz Uhle-Wettler, "Die Jägertruppe. Das Wiedergeburt der Infanterie," *Jahrbuch des Heeres*, 3 (1971), pp. 29–34.

67. Representative accounts include F. W. von Mellenthin, *Panzer Battles* (Norman, Okla., 1956); F. M. von Senger und Etterlin, *Der Gegenschlag: Kampfbeispiele und Führungsgrundsätze der beweglichen Abwehr* (Neckargemünd, 1959); Hans Kessel, *Die Panzerschlachten in der Puszta* (Neckargemünd, 1960); and H. Magenheimer, *Abwehrschlacht an der Weichsel 1945* (Freiburg, 1970).

68. Paul A. Dipter, "In the Wake of the Tank: The 20th-Century Evolution of the Theory of Armored Warfare," PhD dissertation, John Hopkins, University 1984, pp.. 421ff; John J. Measrsheimer, *Conventional Deterrence* (Ithaca, NY, 1983), pp. 165ff passim; and James M. Garrett, "Conventional Force Deterrence in the Presence of Theater Nuclear Weapons," *Armed Forces and Society*, 11 (1984), pp. 59–83, provide a more general doctrinal and technical context for an ongoing debate. Recent updates include Lt.-Gen. Hans Henning von Sandrart, "Forward Defense. Mobility and the Use of Barriers," *NATO's Sixteen Nations*, 30 (Special Issue No. 1, 1985), pp. 37–43; and Major T. Cross, "Forward Defence. A Time for Change?" *RUSI*, 130 (June 1985), pp. 19–24.

69. BDM Corporation, *Generals Balck and Von Mellenthin on Tactics: Implications for NATO Military Doctrine* (McLean, Va., 1980), passim. Cf. also Richard A. Timmons, "Lessons from the Past for NATO," *Parameters* (Autumn 1984), pp. 3–11; and Michael A. Phipps, "A Forgotten War," *Infantry* (November/December 1984), pp. 38–40.

70. *Weissbuch 1985*, pp. 190ff.

71. "Dr Manfred Wörner Talks to IDR," *International Defense Review*, 18, no. 9 (1985), p. 1393. Cf. Samuel P. Huntington, "Conventional Deterrence and Conventional Retaliation in Europe," *International Security*, 8 (Winter 1983–84), pp. 32–56. For a representative contemporary set of critiques of the deep-penetration concept see C.F. von Weizsäcker (ed.), *Die Praxis der defensiven Verteidigung* (Hameln, 1984).

72. Typical, though unofficial, is the critique in F. W. von Mellenthin and R. H. S. Stolfi with E. Sobik, *NATO under Attack* (Durham, NC, 1984), pp. 127–128.

73. For the Swiss approach cf. Alfred Ernst, *Die Konzeption der schweizerischen Landesverteidigung 1815 bis 1966* (Frauenfeld, 1971), and the more recent and popular John McPhee, *La Place de la Concorde Suisse* (New York, 1984).

74. Data on Army Structure 4 and its implementation are from *White Paper 1979*, pp. 52ff; *Weissbuch 1985*, pp. 188ff; and William C. Remagel, "West Germany" in R. A. Gabriel (ed.), *Fighting Armies: NATO and the Warsaw Pact* (Westport, Conn., 1983), pp. 104–128.

75. John A. English, *On Infantry* (New York, 1981), pp. 185ff *passim*, surveys the debate and is the source of the aphorism. In a rapidly proliferating literature, Major Petei N. Kafkalas, "The Light Divisions and Low-Intensity Conflict: Are They Losing Sight of Each Other?" *Military Review*, 66 (January 1986), pp. 18–27, is a useful corrective to some of the more extreme flights of fancy. Cf. also Gen. William E. De Puy, "The Light Infantry: — Indispensable Element of a Balanced Force," *Army*, 35 (June 1985), pp. 26–41. The difficulty of training the West German light infantryman is mentioned in Schulz, *Das neue Heer*, pp. 71–72.

76. See in particular Maximilian von der Fretter-Pico, *Missbrauchte Infanterie* (Frankfurt, 1957) (rev. edn issued Wiesbaden, 1969, under the title . . . *verlassen von des Sieges Göttern*); and F. von Senger und Etterlin, *Die Panzergrenadiere* (Munich, 1961), pp. 77ff *passim*.

77. On the evolution of armored fighting vehicles in West Germany see in particular Walter J. Spielberger, *From Half-Track to Leopard 2*, trans. T. W. Fuchs and W. J. Spielberger (Munich, 1979); and Wolfgang Flume, "Die zukünftige Kampfwagenfamilie," *Wehrtechnik*, 18 (March 1985), pp. 28–35. The Federal Republic's arms export industry is surveyed in Frederick S. Pearson, "Of Leopards and Cheetahs: West Germany's Role as a Mid-Sized Arms Supplier," *Orbis*, 29 (1985), pp. 165–181.

78. Germain Chambost and K. G. Benz "The Franco-German Combat Helicopter," *International Defense Review*, 17, no. 5 (1984), pp. 575–578; Wolfgang Bäder, "Neugliederung der PAH-Regimenter?" *Wehrtechnik*, 17 (July 1985), pp. 38–39. A reduced squadron of 21 helicopters is also directly assigned to the 6th Panzer Grenadier Division.

79. *Weissbuch 1985*, pp. 193ff. The current mission of the airborne division is presented in Inge Dose-Krolin, "Einsatz für Spezialaufgaben. Die Luftlandedivision," *Wehrtechnik*, 17 (August 1985), pp. 26–31.

80. *Weissbuch 1985*, p. 198.

81. As in Rennagel, "West Germany," pp. 120–121. The completion of major payments for several weapons systems permitted, however, increased allocation in the 1985 budget for munitions, signal, and logistics equipment. *Weissbuch 1985*, p. 129.

82. Elmar Dinter and Paddy Griffith, *Not Over by Christmas: NATO's Central Front in World War III* (New York, 1983).

83. Richard Simpkin, *Race to the Swift. Thoughts on Twenty-First Century Warfare* (London, 1985), pp. 298–299.

84. The essays in Gwyn Harries-Jenkins (ed.), *Armed Forces and the Welfare Societies: Challenges in the 1980s* (New York, 1983) provide a comparative perspective on the problem of legitimating armed forces in modern consumer societies.

85. Martin van Creveld, "Bundeswehr Manpower Management," *RUSI and Brassey's Defense Yearbook* (Oxford, 1983), pp. 47–72.

86. On the Bundeswehr's officer corps cf. in particular Detlev Bald, "Sozialgeschichte der Rekrutierung des deutschen Offizierkorps von der Reichsgründung bis zur Gegenwart"; Ekkehard Lippert and Rosemarie Zabel, "Bildungsreform und Offizierkorps," in *Zur sozialen Herkunft des Offiziers, Schriftenreihe Innere Führung*, no. 29, ed. Federal Ministry of Defense (Bonn, 1977), pp. 15–47 and 49–155; and Detlev Bald, "The German Officer Corps: Caste or Class?" *Armed Forces and Society*, 5 (1975), pp. 642–668.

87. Cf. Eric Leed, *No Man's Land* (New York, 1979); and Jay Baird, *The Mythical World of Nazi Propaganda* (Minneapolis, 1974); with Bernard F. Dick, *The Star-Spangled Screen: The American World War II Film* (Lexington, Ky., 1985).

88. *AFV-62: A Magazine for Military Vehicle Enthusiasts*, 6 (April 1978).

89. The most comprehensive study of the limits of socialization through military service is Ekhehard Lippert, Paul Schneider, and Ralf Zoll, "Sozialisation in der Bundeswehr. Der Einfluss des Wehrdienstes auf soziale und politische Einstellung der Wehrpflichtigen," *Schriftenreihe Innere Führung*, no. 26 (Bonn, 1976). An abridged version appeared as "The Influence of Military Service on Political and Social Attitudes:

A Study of Socialization in the German Bundeswehr," *Armed Forces and Society*, 4 (1978), pp. 265–282. Cf. also Klaus Roghmann and Wolfgang Sodeur, "The Impact of Military Service on Authoritarian Attitudes: Evidence from West Germany," *American Journal of Sociology*, 78 (1972), pp. 418–433; Roland Wakenhut, "Effect of Military Service on the Political Socialization of Draftees," *Armed Forces and Society*, 5 (1979), pp. 626–641; and Ralf Zoll, "The German Armed Forces" in *The Political Education of Soldiers*, pp. 209–248.

90. Albert Krölls, *Kriegsdienstverweigerung. Das unbequeme Grundrecht* (Frankfurt, 1980); and Volker Möhle and Christian Rabe, *Kriegsdienstverweigerer in der BRD* (Opladen, 1972) survey the issue of conscientious objection. More generally on West German youth in the post-industrial era, see Thomas Ziehe, *Pubertät and Nazismus. Sind Jugendliche entpolisiert?* (Frankfurt, 1977).

91. Jugendwerk der Deutschen Shell, *Jugend zwischen Anpassumg und Ausstieg* (Hamburg, 1980) and *Die Einstellung der jungen Generation zur Arbeitswelt und Wirtschaftsordnung* (Hamburg, 1980) and the Federal Ministry for Youth, Family, and Health, *Jugend in der Bundesrepublik heute* (Bonn, 1981) provide relevant statistics. Klaus von Beyme surveys "Political Culture and Electoral Behavior in West Germany," *German Studies Review*, 3 (1980), pp. 415–434. Wolf Dieter Narr, "Toward a Society of Conditioned Reflexes" in J. Habermas (ed.), *Observations on The Spiritual Situation of the Age: Contemporary German Perspectives*, trans. A. Buchwalter (Cambridge, Mass., 1984), pp. 31–66, offers a critical perspective. Direct applications to the Bundeswehr are suggested in Ralf Zoll, "German Civil–Military Relations: The Problems of Legimacy," *Armed Forces and Society*, 2 (1979), pp. 523–559.

92. Quoted in Simon, *Integration der Bundeswehr*, p. 182.

93. Peter Schmidt, "Public Opinion and Security Policy in the Federal Republic of Germany," *Orbis*, 28 (1985), pp. 719–742, is a reasonably up-to-date overview.

94. F. Scott Fitzgerald, *Tender is the Night*, preface M. Cowley (New York, 1951), pp. 117–118.

95. Thucydides, *The Peloponnesian War*, trans., R. Crawley rev. and intro. T. E. Wiek (New York, 1982), p. 109.

9 THE DEFENSE FORCES OF THE LOW COUNTRIES

John H. Skinner

Known for long as the "cockpit" of Europe, modern Belgium and the Netherlands share more than a common history. In 1815 the former Spanish and Dutch Netherlands were combined in order to establish a "buffer" state between France and Germany — only to be divided again, 16 years later, when the European Powers guaranteed them both perpetual neutrality. This guarantee failed dramatically twice in quick succession, in 1914 and 1940; but this was due partly to their own military unpreparedness.

The Background

These two small, highly populated countries share even more than a chequered career, geographical contiguity, and flat land. Both are strategically wedged by powerful neighbors against a busy sea; a sea where shipping and sources of oil and natural gas proliferate; countries where many routes and nodal points, as well as key ports and airports, provide commerce and defense forces with access and communications to the hinterland of Europe.

Only the canal network and major river esturaries, together with some notably high and difficult ground in the Ardennes in southeast Belgium, present potential obstacles to the movement of military forces; always provided that decisions were to be made in time to blow bridges and breach dykes. Such timely decisions would be hard to take during an international crisis when tension could be protracted and the climate could blow hot and cold. The results of such decisions might escalate other measures, but at least they would surely create conditions to impede would-be defenders just as much as would-be attackers.

An enemy could blockade NATO's key maritime entry points along the coast, seaborne landings might further disrupt and endanger strategic reinforcement and resupply as well as homeland security, aerial attacks would also hamper or even prevent airlift and other operations. Even if a conventional land/air battle was being fought some distance away, say, near the *neue Grenze* between East and West Germany, the Low Countries would provide NATO with an essential platform on which to land and from which to launch reinforcements. Belgium and the Netherlands form part of this vital communications zone; one or both could eventually become an enforced refuge prior to a second Dunkirk. In peacetime, they already accomodate important allied command, control, communications, and logistic installations, in addition to their own national bases and facilities.

Against this background, it is crucial to the West that not only Belgium and the Netherlands remain staunch allies of each other and NATO, but that their governments also remain stable and steadfast in politico-military terms. This means maintaining their defense forces at the ready in peace, affording facilities to others particularly during transition-to-war, and giving unflinching support to land, sea, and air operations in war, should deterrence fail and war occur in Europe. By assigning or earmarking their forces to NATO, they also pledge to become engaged in the fighting to defend their allies' sovereign territory, quite apart from their own, should Warsaw Pact or any other forces invade.

Though consistently steadfast in their verbal support for NATO as a defensive alliance to which they wish to belong, Belgium and the Netherlands alike have suffered from some domestic instability. Extensive unemployment and sluggish industrial growth have not helped to allocate sufficient Belgian francs or Dutch guilders for the upkeep of effective conventional forces in the broadest sense and by all the measures that are applied to such judgements. Defense spending has decreased considerably, and has not increased at the annual rate of 3 percent required by NATO. The miscellany of political parties, all with strong and sometimes discordant voices on defense and defense-related subjects, have bred tenuous and uneasy coalitions for many years in both Belgium and the Netherlands. The nations themselves project quite pronounced anti-military, anti-establishment, not only anti-nuclear, images and feelings. It is not surprising that such tough decisions as whether or not to accept the deployment of cruise missiles on their soil have threatened national stability and steadfastness. The same has happened among other Alliance partners faced with the same decisions.

The Belgian and Dutch governments have made some valuable efforts to share the NATO burden; however tentatively, they have grasped the nettles of nuclear doctrine and weapons deployment; they have played their part in that policy of deterrence which has kept Europe at peace for over forty years — albeit an uneasy peace. Neither the Dutch nor the Belgians, however, are martial peoples by tradition, nature, or inclination. Only the Dutch navy has a long history and long standing status in the major league. Thus the temptation to return to some sort of neutrality between East and West, or even to project and encourage pacifism, shows strongly from time to time.

There are real, outward, and visible signs of real, inward, and spiritual protest against military service in general, and against such dogmas as a last-ditch or even an early first use of nuclear weapons in particular — just as there are in some other countries. The vestiges of neutralism are stronger in the Low Countries than in many others, and have been so over quite a prolonged period of years. It is the accumulation and the strength of projection of these various attitudes of protest that cause deep concern from time to time among allies, politicians, and military commanders. They can and they do undermine in a way the strong stance and stand that NATO must democratically take against its potential enemy; against the growing offensive capability and military superiority of the Warsaw Pact; and against the sometimes devious, often blatant, Soviet-led propaganda and maneuverings aimed at weakening the will of individual government of free nations.

Belgium and the Netherlands share yet more common ground. They were co-signatories of the Brussels Treaty, founder members of NATO and the Western European Union; they joined the Common Market together, they both play a prominent part within the European Economic Community, and they participate in a number of agencies including Eurogroup. With Luxembourg, they have long been a force for free trade, further meaningful union within Western Europe, and human rights. The Benelux voice is always strong in support of the Third World and for the gradual lessening of tension between East and West.

Belgium and the Netherlands also find themselves closely aligned: they face similar pressure over cruise and other weapon issues; similar difficulties with keeping a satisfactory equilibrium between keen regulars and not-nearly-so-keen conscripts in their small armed services; the same socio-economic and military reconciliation between the need to retain an adequate peacetime military presence in the Federal Republic of Germany and the desire to station their formations at home; the same intractable problems of finding enough money to maintain their present force levels and structures intact, and at anything like operational readiness; the same hard decisions about whether to buy Patriot missiles to replace the ageing NIKE/Hercules, thereby continuing to contribute to Western Europe's vital air defenses. Their air crews have shared the vagaries of flying the F-104 Starfighter; their armed services lack training areas and the opportunities to take part in really testing field exercises. Recently their governments and their nations have had to face the rising threat and to deal with the hidden dangers of bombing campaigns, as well as militant minority fringe groups at home.

There can be absolutely no doubt that NATO needs their political, diplomatic, military, economic, and moral support; they themselves also need NATO. Nevertheless significant and various sections of the Belgian and Dutch people tend to question whether they do really need NATO, and this places something of a question-mark behind their resolve; that is to say, the resolve of their governments which, as finely and delicately balanced coalitions, are vulnerable to sharp expressions of public opinion on defense as with other issues. Whatever the people and the governments say or do, there is no lack of resolve among the small regular cadres of the armed forces. They clearly recognize the need to play their part in the defense of Western Europe, as well as maintaining the security of their homelands and bases.

Even so, there is a lack of resources with which to play this part and this must discourage national commanders just as much as it concerns NATO staffs. Even the staunchest and most professional Belgian and Dutch servicemen must have also been severely discouraged, just as NATO has been concerned, with the deliberate disobedience and unsoldierly appearance of conscripts in intake after intake, particularly young Dutchmen. Several incidents have caused unease over the years. For instance, in March 1980 senior officers from the Breda Military College — the Dutch equivalent of Sandhurst and West Point — publicly preached unilateral disarmament, against only muted official reaction. To mention a different example which illustrates the same general point: on 21 July 1981 a Belgian general had to lead 3,400 soldiers on foot to a training area in order to save fuel. Moreover, for a number of years now, the activities of trade unions within their forces have openly disrupted standards of military discipline, behavior and performance normally accepted in the forces of most other nations. All this has quite considerably harmed morale, quite apart from overall competence.

These, and many other instances like them, can only sap the collective professional strength of their otherwise proud and keen armed services. Still more, the Belgian and Dutch people show a somewhat traditional lack of sympathy, understanding, and support for standing regular forces and the role they have to play. Many in both nations have insistently questioned the need to station any military units in West Germany in peacetime. These critics have undoubtedly exerted pressure on successive governments, thereby occasioning significant, damaging reductions of "in place" operational land forces — despite the requirements to locate them in peacetime reasonably near to their battle positions in sufficient numbers. The Belgian and Dutch land forces are now too weak on the ground in the Federal Republic. Furthermore their training state, operational readiness, and reinforcement capabilities would diminish their ability to make a timely response in a crisis, and NATO's potential overall effectiveness. The physical siting of their air forces is not crucial in these terms though, again, fitness for role assessments show up operational deficiencies. The Royal Netherlands Navy is larger and traditionally and professionally stronger than its Belgian counterpart, but both make a valuable contribution in their own way to Alliance maritime capabilities. Both nations would be able to send mobile forces to the flanks of NATO and still have the wherewithal to provide a reasonable, but not strong, home defense.

Belgium

Belgium has a population of nearly 10 million. In 1984 its armed forces totalled more than 93,000, with about 25,000 serving in the Federal Republic; they also comprised over 3,000 women and nearly 32,000 conscripts. Conscripts represent one-third of all those in uniform; they serve for eight months if posted to Germany or ten months if stationed at home. With an overall defense budget in 1984 of $2.572 billion, the government spent $257 per head of population on its military forces, military aid to other nations, military pensions, tenant force expenses, NATO infrastructure contributions, civilian staff costs, and paramilitary forces. That same year the combined strength of the army and the separate Medical Service was over 65,000 (26,000 conscripts), the navy more than 4,000 (1,000 conscripts), the air force nearly 20,000 (nearly 5,000 conscripts) and the Gendarmerie in excess of 16,000. The Gendarmerie is a paramilitary police force jointly responsible to the Ministers of Defense, Interior, and Justice.

The King of the Belgians is the titular Commander-in-Chief of the armed services, though national control is vested in the Ministerial Defense Committee (CMD), chaired by the Prime Minister with the Ministers of Defense, Foreign Affairs, Interior, Justice, and Communications as principal members. The Permanent Committee of Defense Affairs (CPMD) sits more frequently to deal with policy

Figure 9.1: Outline Organization of Belgian Ministry of Defense and Principal Army Commands

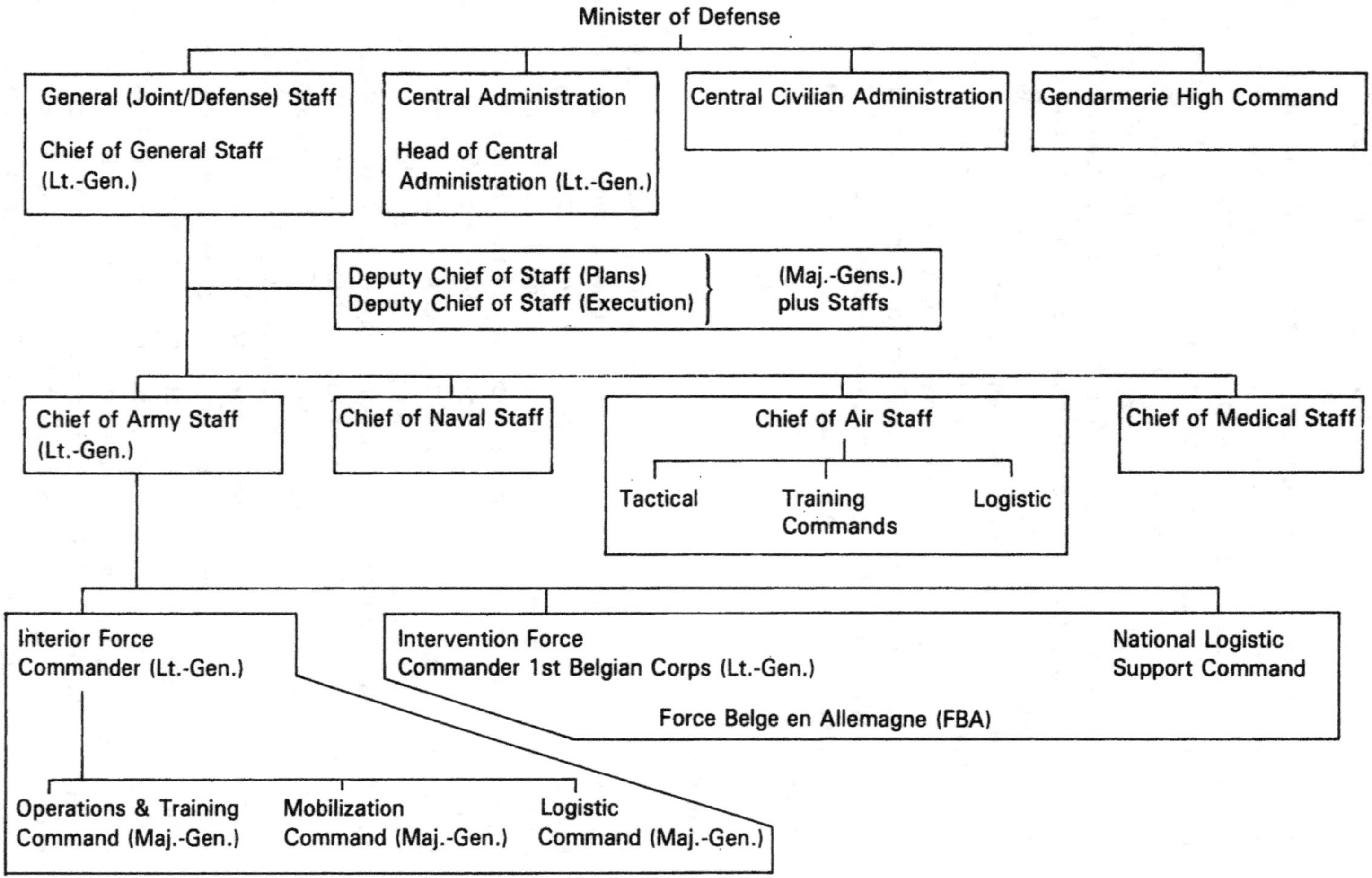

Minister of Defense
- General (Joint/Defense) Staff — Chief of General Staff (Lt.-Gen.)
  - Deputy Chief of Staff (Plans) (Maj.-Gens.) plus Staffs
  - Deputy Chief of Staff (Execution) (Maj.-Gens.) plus Staffs
  - Chief of Naval Staff
  - Chief of Army Staff (Lt.-Gen.)
    - Interior Force Commander (Lt.-Gen.)
      - Operations & Training Command (Maj.-Gen.)
      - Mobilization Command (Maj.-Gen.)
      - Logistic Command (Maj.-Gen.)
    - Intervention Force Commander 1st Belgian Corps (Lt.-Gen.) — Force Belge en Allemagne (FBA)
  - Chief of Air Staff
    - Tactical
    - Training
    - Logistic Commands
  - Chief of Medical Staff
    - National Logistic Support Command
- Central Administration — Head of Central Administration (Lt.-Gen.)
- Central Civilian Administration
- Gendarmerie High Command

affairs and executive business.

The Ministry of Defense is in Brussels and its outline organization is illustrated in Figure 9.1. The four service and medical Chiefs of Staff act as Commanders as well, responsible to the Chief of General Staff (other nations may use the titles of Chief of Defense or Joint Staff) for the command, control, management, and efficiency of their own services. First and second line medical support are matters for each service, with the higher echelons and overall control being the concern of the Chief of Medical Staff.

Following several reorganizations during the past 25 years, the Belgian General Staff is responsible for the formulation and coordination of defense policy, joint plans, programs, personnel, and logistics. The so-called NATO staff organization and system, derived from previous Prussian and French models, is hardly accepted or adopted as "standard" within the Alliance and this degrades interoperability. However, the Belgians come close to its original structure and concept for staff work in higher as well as field headquarters. To provide a basis of explanation, the General Staff deals only with "operational" planning and its duties largely correspond with those shown in Table 9.1.

Table 9.1: Organization and Tasks of General Staff Branches

G-1	Operational Staff Coordination
	Operational Organization, Equipment, and Personnel Matters
	Mobilization and Reinforcement Planning
	Operational Information Systems and Computer Development
G-2	Operational Intelligence and Security
G-3	Combat Planning
	Collective Operational Training
G-4	Logistic Planning
	Operational Movement and Infrastructure
G-5	Operational Civil and Military Cooperation (CIMIC)

In most armed services the general or "G" staff relates to army, "J" to joint or defense, "N" to naval and "A" to air staffs. The prefix letter "S" relates to the same duties at unit, rather than at formation, level.

Administrative or peacetime staff duties are not included in the General Staff organization or system. They are dealt with by an administrative staff in the majority of armed services. The separation is well illustrated in Belgium's case, as a quick glance at Figure 9.1 will show. It is a feature of the Belgian defense structure that military staffs predominantly manage military administrative and financial affairs. In 1834 the Ecole Royale Militaire was formed to train young officers and close by the Ecole d'Application was established separately to complete the training of those officers destined for technical or administrative employment; here was the start of a most useful specialized arm. The Ecole de Guerre began General Staff training in 1868 and these three colleges remain in Brussels today. All regular officers attend the Military Academy before receiving special-to-service and special-to-arm training at single service schools. Similarly the Staff College is a joint concern.

Belgium's defense forces are structured according to their missions. The army and the air force have formations assigned or earmarked to the Supreme Allied Commander Europe (SACEUR) and include land/air units for the Central Front and flanks of NATO. Ships of the Belgian navy sail in peacetime under the flags of allied operational commanders, and train closely with components of other nations like their army and air force counterparts. The plans and arrangements to mobilize, deploy, reinforce, and support national forces are national matters monitored by NATO's international staffs. Joint preparations have to be made in peacetime to receive, sustain, and move the large numbers of British, Canadian, and United States forces that may pass through NATO's vital communications zone in a time of crisis.

Belgium may no longer be the natural battlefield of Europe in any future continental conflict, but most of the country will certainly become a congested, vulnerable support base in the event of action further east. Therefore home defense is of crucial significance and interest to its allies as well as itself; it is equally as crucial as allocating forces to NATO commands.

Originally Belgian forces were conscripted on a selective basis with only a small regular cadre of officers and NCOs. Not until the post-war requirement arose for them to make a permanent contribution to the Alliance was any major change necessary or made. No Belgian government since the late 1940s has wished to have armed forces comprised solely of regulars, hence the Belgian forces comprise volunteers on short (temporary) or long (career) engagements, and conscripted personnel. For this "mixed service" system to work well some 3,500 volunteers are required each year. Officers represent about 10 percent of career personnel.

The *Auditeur-Generaal's* report in June 1980 showed that the previous five years had seen a quintupling of desertions. In 1979 the figure reached 1,333, including 1 officer, 24 regular NCOs, 860 volunteers, and 448 conscripts; of the volunteers who deserted the majority were serving 2 to 10 year engagements. Desertion was most prevalent in the army, where 3.3 percent of active soldiers were absent without leave for periods during 1979, most of them aged 18–21. The report analyzed the problem, and improvements were subsequently made which helped to correct deficiencies caused largely by lack of resources, falling standards of training, and the unprofessional attitudes and practices that stem from them. Just after the announcement of these statistics, much attention and publicity were given to halting and reversing Belgium's "military decline" as it was called at the time.

In 1981 a commission investigated defense problems and, particularly, how economic stringencies could be reconciled with military operational readiness. Between 1970 and 1980 the numerical strength of the Belgian army had been reduced from 70,000 to 54,000 men. The number of volunteers in the new complement should have been 21,000, but recruiting never achieved this. It had been the intention, until then, to reduce the conscription term to six months by increasing the proportion of regulars; it was decided to retain the eight or ten months. Quite apart from the serious doubt that surrounds the question of what can actually, constructively and militarily be achieved during such short periods of conscripted service, the army in 1981 was still short of more than 1,000 regular NCOs alone. Economic crises hardly helped solve these almost endemic problems, though high and rising unemployment in civilian life helped with military recruitment in Belgium as it did in other countries. Suggestions were made that the Federal Republic of Germany should pay for Belgian troops stationed on its territory.

In 1982 and 1983 many morale-sapping economies were imposed. By 1984, however, things had gradually improved and some larger-scale collective military training was resumed: for instance, in September of that year Exercise "Roaring Lion" took place in West Germany involving 22,000 troops with 1,500 tracked and 5,700 wheeled vehicles. Yet the air force was still beset with such severe heating oil problems during the 1984/85 winter that a "prolonged holiday" had to be authorized for airmen. A national newspaper at that time recalled that the entire Belgian air force had been destroyed by the Germans in 1940 and asked whether it would be any different if the Russians attacked. With budget cuts of more than 6 percent, the Belgian forces were said to be capable of meeting their NATO commitments and mounting a reasonable home defense, but it would be "a close run thing."

Conscription will almost certainly continue. The number of 18-year-olds will decline by 25 percent by 1994, in common with the projected rate in other countries, and unemployment throughout the EEC has hit the young particularly hard. In principle, universal service is a compulsory feature of Belgian life: *tout citoyen belge doit accomplir le service militaire.* The basic law fixes an obligation of 15 years of reserve service unless indefinitely extended by mobilization. In practice, however, there have been many exemptions made for men considered indispensable to their civilian occupations, quite apart from those excused or barred for other reasons. Also, in practice, it is probable that an individual reservist will only complete about one period of 21 days' training during his whole reserve service. Compare this lenient, short-term conscription with, for instance, the Federal Republic's much more robust system of selective national service when the young, with the very skills or aptitudes needed by the forces, are called up for a longer period. There is also far more stringent continuation training for West German reservists.

Many Belgians have felt for long that armed services composed predominantly of conscripts integrate more easily with the populace, becase the conscript is a citizen doing his national service. Draftees are cheaper than regulars, and of course the system does produce reservists of a sort. Some people mistrust armed forces with a high proportion of long-serving regulars. They feel that the military could grow apart from the nation. This probably gives rise to the social arguments for bringing even more troops back from Germany and some concern that a government might use volunteers against industrial strikes. On the other hand, there are Belgians who would welcome a more dominantly regular army for reasons of effectiveness. As things stand at present, operational formations and units may have to be further reduced in size, capability, and strength, if regular recruiting does not improve and resources are not increased.

Nevertheless, Belgians are firm supporters of NATO. They could hardly be unaware of its existence with the large Alliance Headquarters in Brussels and the sprawling Supreme Headquarters Allied Powers Europe (SHAPE) only some 30 kms away near Mons. Not only do these bureaucratic institutions provide useful local employment, government policy is also verbally supportive of NATO. The Belgians tend to regard "rationalization" and "specialization" within allied forces as practical ways to contain costs while providing overall

Alliance capabilities. There is much to be said for this approach *per se*. It is a valid and practical way of helping smaller nations, like their own, to continue making worthwhile military contributions. They recognize that military credibility is not achieved by spreading limited manpower and financial resources across too wide a range of military roles, particularly when costs are spiralling. The unification of their Medical Services was a national rationalization measure and this has been achieved without degrading specialization. Clearly, Belgium will continue to press for multinational innovation of this kind.

Another factor which has caused internal problems in the forces is the schism over language. The division of the country into distinctly Flemish- and French-speaking provinces, with the majority of *Bruxellois* using French, has led to political and social difficulties significant for the nation as a whole. Language has military repercussions too: for instance, a 50-50 promotion system is said to retain linguistic balance, fluency in both languages is a prerequisite to officers' promotion, and the order of battle contains Flemish- and French- speaking formations and units. These problems are not easy to solve, as other countries with similar challenges have found, but the divisions are indelibly drawn in Belgium.

As shown in Figure 9.1, the Belgian army comprises an Intervention Force; this is 1st Belgian Corps and a small supporting logistic increment. The operational deployment of multinational formations in NATO's Central Region is "layer cake" in concept and construction; forward elements at the eastern end of each "layer" would become engaged early and possibly simultaneously were Warsaw Pacts forces to assault. This is instrumental to the way the North Atlantic Charter provisions are meant to work, since all allies are bound to come to the aid of a member or members threatened or invaded. Therefore, 1st Belgian Corps would deploy in depth to defend its own sector of the central-northern part of the front, with flanking allied land formations on both sides, all beneath the NATO air "umbrella." This defense is planned to be conventional in form, mobile and aggressive in character; nuclear release being ordered, later perhaps rather than earlier, by SACEUR after agreement by national governments. The same applies to the Netherlands and its national corps further north along the front.

Headquarters 1st Belgian Corps is based near Cologne in West Germany and the formation as a whole, together with the small co-located logistic staff, is controlled nationally in peacetime. They would be transferred to NATO's Northern Army Group, which would then exercise operational command from an early stage during transition-to-war; this procedure is practiced on peacetime collective exercises. The Army Group's Headquarters, close to Cologne near Düsseldorf, coordinates operational planning and runs exercises for all multinational formations assigned or earmarked to it: American, Belgian, British, Dutch, and West German.

The Belgian Corps has a peacetime strength of 34,000 troops; this is scheduled to double when it is placed on full war footing. Basically it consists of two divisions, one based in Germany and the other at home, as well as corps troops units: these include reconnaissance, artillery, air defense, engineer, signal, aviation, and logistic elements. Each division consists of two brigades at maximum readiness, though this must be assessed to a certain extent by where they are located permanently in peacetime. Another two brigades are in reserve in Belgium for commitment as required, but they are skeletal formations requiring embodiment, reinforcement, and training before becoming fully operational. Indeed some specialized corps troops units would also require considerable time to mobilize, move, and sort themselves out before becoming role-ready. The key questions are: how long would all this really take and how long would NATO actually have?

In the 1950s there was much experimentation with formation structures within NATO and individual nations. Although the zest for this type of innovation has slackened, the requirement which it is meant to satisfy still very much exists: why, over time, does the structure of field armies even within the same integrated allied command become more dissimilar instead of more similar within NATO? This is another question worth asking. Some thirty years ago, NATO suggested a "standard" division of three brigades in the Central Region. Today, there still is no uniformity of operational structures or operational procedures with which to fulfill the same mission; just as there is preciously little equipment standardization, compatibility or interoperability. However, it should be recorded that Belgium strongly supported NATO when its international staff tried to introduce a standard division in 1958.

The Belgians, like the Dutch, adopted the American "pentomic" structure. For this particular experiment, a division had no conventional brigades at all; it had instead five strong battle groups, each with an enlarged infantry battalion, and organic tank and artillery support. This division was to be capable of mobile and independent operations. The Americans found this structure unsuitable for use in the Central Region so, in the late 1950s, they reverted to a more orthodox division normally comprising three brigades; the Germans had already done this by that time, and the British were trying to do so as well. Therefore the Belgians, with the Dutch, gave up their pentomic divisions. This did not deter the British from trying some twenty years later a similar arrangement, for economic rather than any sound military reasons; this was also doomed to failure even before the experiment was started.

Thus a golden opportunity to standardize — that most hypocritically overused and tragically undervalued NATO word — was missed long ago. The Belgian army went its own way: a way which has suited the size of its purse rather than military operational requirements. But in that respect it is not alone among allies.

Belgian, as well as Dutch, divisions were reorganized during the 1960s to save money, manpower, and *matériel*. A small tactical command post replaced divisional headquarters; no specialized combat support, communications, or logistics were provided at divisional level. The divisional commander would, and still does, conduct the tactical battle drawing forward whatever specialized corps troops resources are made available to him. His brigades have a limited amount of integral artillery, engineer, communications, and logistic support; they are thus moderately self-contained and reasonably self-sufficient for combat. 1st Belgian Corps will receive an integrated land-based command, control, and communications (C^3) system this year which will operate compatibly with NATO's field equivalent.

The single division based permanently in the Federal Republic has one armored and one mechanized infantry brigade. Its counterpart stationed at home has two mechanized infantry brigades. The range of field equipment is listed by the International Institute for Strategic Studies in its regularly published pamphlet, *The Military Balance*. The 1984/85 editions shows that Belgian combat land force units have the German Leopard I main battle tank, British tracked combat vehicles such as Scorpion light tanks and Scimitar armored fighting vehicles as well as other carriers, the German *Jagd-panzer* tank destroyer and Gepard tracked air defense weapon system, and the normal variety of self-propelled artillery and the Lance tactical missile system all of American derivation. The Belgian army uses Milan and Tow anti-tank guided weapons and hopes to introduce an anti-armor helicopter.

The fact that only about half of 1st Belgian Corps is "in place" in Germany, still some appreciable distance from forward battle positions, causes less concern to NATO's operational commanders and planners than the other half, which would have to travel all the way from the home base along congested routes. In times of tension, chaos is unavoidable; indeed present movement programs are thought, rather cynically by some, to organize chaos. The reinforcement formations would have to move by road or be moved by rail across or along the lines of communication of other allied forces. Belgian supply depots are positioned on both sides of the Rhine. The main bridges over that major waterway could well be blown before any Warsaw Pact onslaught starts further east. A superior enemy usually attacks weakest points, while containing and then outflanking strong points along a front. The lack of strength and capability on the ground early enough is an undeniable problem for NATO in the Belgian Corps' area: it is even more of a problem in the Dutch Corps' area, where only the rudiments of one brigade are "in place" in Germany in peacetime and the remainder of three divisions would have to move from home base, again, after mobilization.

To return to Belgium. In peacetime the Interior or Home Defense Force (see Figure 9.1) of 27,000 troops helps to run army training schools and prepares mobilization procedures for reserve units and reservists. There are 160,000 army and 40,000 medical service reservists on the books and some of these are now at immediate recall status. In wartime these troops are required to reinforce the Intervention Force and to defend Belgium itself. Home Defense units include nine provincial infantry regiments, two motorized infantry regiments, and four guard battalions. These are allocated and grouped together to cover this highly developed, heavily populated, inevitably congested, and vitally important country measuring 250 kms north to south and the same distance east to west. None of these units are maintained on an operational footing in peacetime. There is also some doubt as to whether reservists are "double-earmarked" to fill these units and to reinforce 1st Belgian Corps. Improvements are under way; and there is always the gendarmerie.

The very small Belgian navy mans and operates four frigates armed with Exocet and Sea Sparrow. It has ocean-going minehunters and minesweepers, coastal and river patrol boats, command and logistic ships, and helicopters. It doubles its strength when 4,500 reservists at immediate recall status are embodied. The frigates were commissioned in 1979 as a contribution towards NATO's defense of the Channel, North Sea, and Eastern Atlantic; until then the navy had specialized in mine counter-measures and mine-laying, and these capabilities still exist. Virtually all resources are assigned or earmarked to NATO as part of Standing Naval Force Channel (STANAVFORCHAN) and Standing Naval Force Atlantic (STANAVFORLANT), with Belgian officers serving in the respective headquarters at Northwood in England and Norfolk in Virginia. Naval bases are at Zeebrugge, Ostend, and Antwerp and the School of Mine Warfare is also at Ostend.

The Belgian air force has three components. The Tactical Air Command flies combat and transport aircraft and operationally forms part of the 2nd Allied Tactical Air Force (2 ATAF) whose headquarters is alongside Northern Army Group's near Düsseldorf in West Germany. The Command has three tactical wings equipped with F-16 and Mirage, and a transport wing flying C-130 Hercules, Boeing 727 and smaller aircraft. The Hercules are tasked to move and support the army's parachute–commando battalion assigned to the Allied Central Europe Mobile Force (AMF) and they have also been used for African disaster relief operations. The Training Command instructs pilots and advanced courses, and the Logistic Command is the third component. When fully mobilized, the Belgian air force receives 14,000 reservists. It participates in the NATO Air Defence Ground Environment (NADGE) system and the AWACS airborne early warning system. The air base at Florennes is planned to be the base for 48 ground-launched cruise missiles if they are deployed in Belgium by 1987 as scheduled.

The medical service and gendarmerie are separately controlled by the Ministry of Defense. The medical role needs no further explanation. The gendarmerie is a disciplined paramilitary force equipped with armored cars, helicopters, and small arms. It provides military police, security guards, escorts, and assistance to the civilian police with traffic and crowd control.

The Netherlands

The Netherlands is the most densely populated country in Europe with over 14 million people packed into a comparatively small area. In 1984 the armed forces totalled more than 103,000 with some 5,500 serving in the Federal Republic; it comprised nearly 1,500 women and over 46,000 conscripts. Conscripts represent almost half of all those in uniform; they serve for 14 months, or slightly longer if they are undergoing officer training and in certain cases NCO training. With an overall defense budget in 1984 of $4.216 billion, the government spent $300 per head of population on its military forces, military aid to other nations, military pensions, tenant force expenses, NATO infrastructure contributions, civilian staff costs (over 27,000 civilians are employed in defense establishments), and paramilitary forces. In 1984 the strength of the navy was nearly 17,000 (just less than 1,500 conscripts), the army was well over 64,000 (nearly 41,000 conscripts), the air force almost 17,000 (just over 3,500 conscripts), and the Military Constabulary over 4,000 (with some 300 conscripts).

Political responsibility for the organization and control of the armed forces lies with the Minister of Defense. The highest consultative body is the Defense Council which, under the chairmanship of the Minister, makes policy decisions. The Ministry of Defense is in The Hague and its outline organization is illustrated in Figure 9.2.

The individual responsibilities of the Chiefs of Defense, Navy, Army, and Air Staffs are similar to those in the Belgian structure. Single service chiefs are also Commanders-in-Chief, but the major exception is that they report directly to the Minister and not through the Chief of Defense Staff. Comparing the Belgian and Dutch organizations, there is more evidence of direct political influence on the control of the services in the Netherlands. Each single service chief/commander has a headquarters provided with directors of personnel, *matériel*, and economic management which mirror the central staff organization. The NATO staff organization and system are quite closely followed in higher echelons and followed even more closely in field headquarters.

The Netherlands Defense Planning Process (NDPP) has been gradually introduced since 1976 with the objective of determining, preparing, implementing, and evaluating policy in a balanced way. Experience so far emphasizes what many nations have found: that alternative policies, planning standards, operating, and maintenance costs, as well as military operational functions, need to be given special attention. The quality and affordability of the Dutch defense effort, and how the armed forces are accepted in Dutch society, both feature prominently and are also being specifically examined as part of the NDPP process.

The Netherlands forces are small, modern, and excellently equipped. Maritime, land, and air elements are assigned or earmarked to NATO's central front, flanks, and sea lanes. Ships of the Royal Netherlands Navy sail in peacetime under the flags of allied operational commanders and they train closely with other national components in common with their sister service counterparts. As in the case of Belgium, mobilization, deployment, and reinforcement planning are vital constituents of national defense efforts and arrangements; they are even more vital in the Netherlands' case since dependence on reservists and quite a complicated mobilization system is much greater. Like Belgium, the Netherlands forms part of the Alliance's vital

Figure 9.2: Outline Organization of Dutch Ministry of Defence

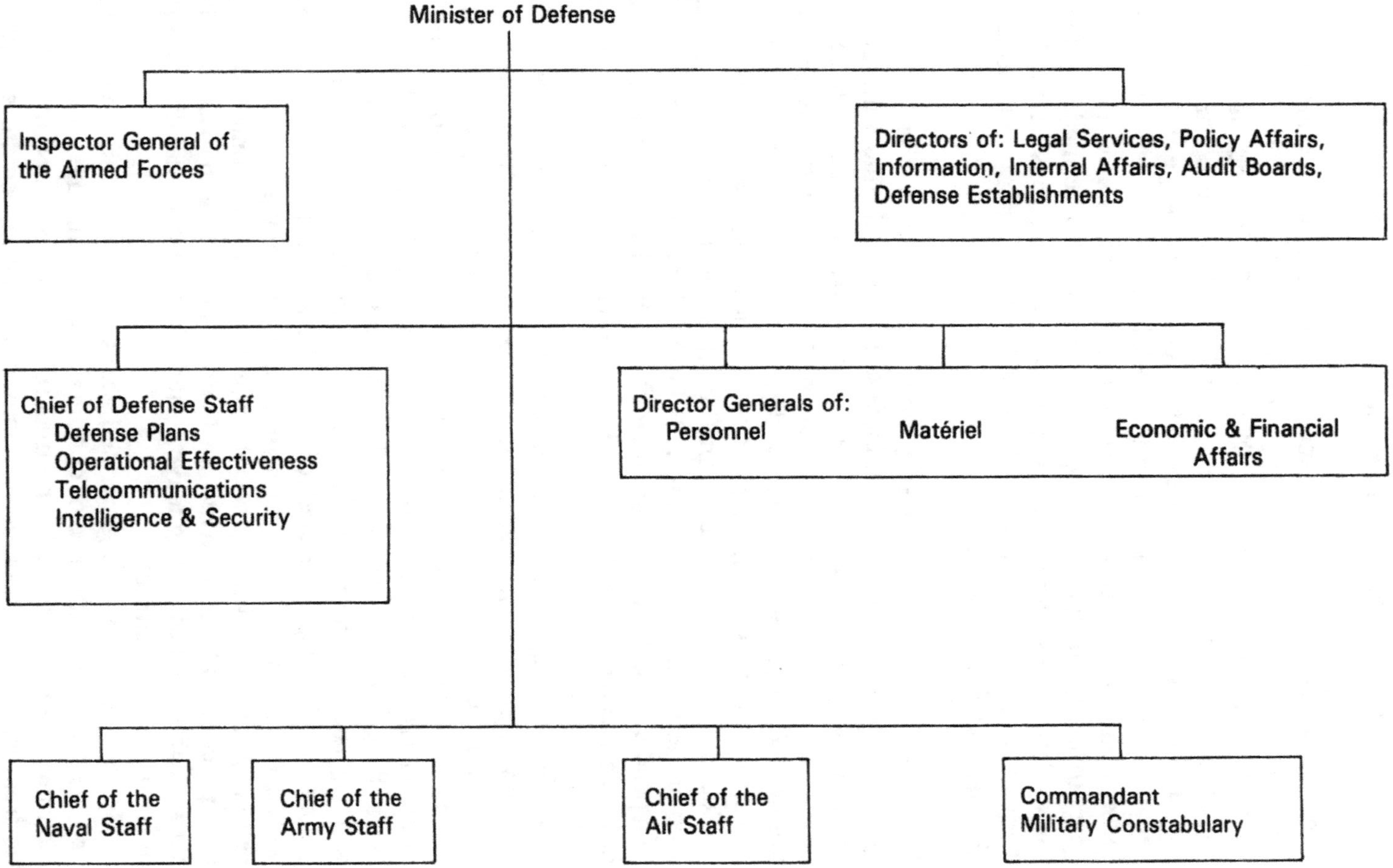

Minister of Defense

- Inspector General of the Armed Forces
- Directors of: Legal Services, Policy Affairs, Information, Internal Affairs, Audit Boards, Defense Establishments
- Director Generals of: Personnel, Matériel, Economic & Financial Affairs
- Chief of Defense Staff
  - Defense Plans
  - Operational Effectiveness
  - Telecommunications
  - Intelligence & Security
- Chief of the Naval Staff
- Chief of the Army Staff
- Chief of the Air Staff
- Commandant Military Constabulary

communication zone; its role and capabilities in this connection, are coordinated and monitored by international staffs. Memoranda of Understanding were signed in 1982 with the British and United States governments regulating the use of Dutch facilities during transition-to-war and major peacetime exercises. Again, like Belgium, it too will become a heavily congested and key link in the complex arrangements for moving NATO reinforcements and supplies forward. This is quite apart from the substantial deployments required to be made by Dutch forces themselves which are, with very few exceptions, home-based. They would also be moving forward to their operational areas in Germany at the same time.

Universal service is compulsory and it works on a highly selective system. Many young conscripts have found and still find various ways to protest against military service. Over the past decade or more there has been a great deal of unease among the elders of the nation about military service, about the way military service has been carried out, and about the ways conscripts have demonstrated their protests.

Section 134 of the Dutch Constitution states that all Netherlanders who are able shall be bound to collaborate for the maintenance of the independence of the Kingdom and for the defense of its territory. Dutch law also recognises political motives as serious grounds for rejecting military service.

In 1976 it was reported that, of all young Dutchmen who registered for conscription each year up to that point, about 40 percent were exempted; yet 75 percent of those who were not exempted were then rejected on medical grounds. Many have also objected to the use of arms on grounds of conscience over the years. In late 1980 a survey showed that the number of conscientious objectors continued to grow, with so-called nuclear pacifists especially active. About 28 percent of young men between the ages of 18 and 24 at that time claimed they would refuse to take part in armed military combat. Those actually called up for their 14 months' conscripted service (16 months for some) then proceed on "short leave" for 8 months at the end of their full-time service, followed by "long leave," until their reserve liability expires, as a rule at 35 years old.

So much concern was generated about the state of the armed forces and the disruptive influence of certain conscripts that the Mommersteeg Commission was set up, in the mid-1970s, to examine the feasibility, desirability, and acceptability of introducing an all-regular army. The Commission addressed such questions as: how 40,000 men of the right quality could be recruited as volunteers; the financial implications; the organizational structure required; and how to make the transition if it were decided to proceed. The findings recommended no change, mainly because of recruiting problems. Therefore, the 14-month conscription period, the reservist mobilization system, and trade unionism would remain intact.

Clearly, the Dutch army in particular found itself in a precarious situation, especially around that time. Instances of unmilitary behavior and flagrant ill discipline by conscripts were supported by trade unions as being part of a "democratization" process, quite irrespective of any unit's or any individual's military fitness for role. Proponents of an all-regular army within the nation seemed to be divided between those who urged change and those who, though sympathetic to change, considered that "democratization" had probably gone too far, or done too much damage already for the scheme to be practicable. Opponents of the proposal argued that the army should remain predominantly conscript-based so that it reflected the character of the population. Any foreigner who knew that proud nation at all well could see that these shaggy, sloppy, undisciplined, unmilitary conscripts in no way identified with the majority of the population at that time or any other. There were also Dutch people who opposed the idea of an all-regular army because they feared that a professional force would grow away from the nation and become an élite. In 1974 even the Minister of Defense himself asked: "In any case do we really want to create a purely professional army composed of old warriors forming a potential military class?" He had obviously not been briefed about how certain other armies achieved professionalism; there were very few "old warriors" on the British side in the Falklands campaign.

Anyway, saluting became no longer obligatory, a 40-hour week was introduced with bonus pay incentives, and "sleepers" were known to be actively subverting their less militant conscript colleagues. The *NATO Review* of October 1975 published an article on "Defence Motivation in the Netherlands." At that time part of the well respected author's thesis was that basic principles of military service had been challenged by large numbers of young Dutchmen. He claimed that the concept of authority was changing, that conscripts were exerting more and more pressure to take part in decision-making processes, and that armed forces should be compared more closely in these respects with industrial undertakings. He described the organization and activities of conscripts' trade unions, and the prominent part they were playing in questioning former values and institutions. He reported on an increasing preparedness among representatives of younger generations to speak out more openly in favor of certain new values and institutions, and thus, in the military context, against the former ones. He then proceeded to discount the sort of symptoms that led to such critical expressions as the "Dutch Hair Force" as valueless as assessments of military competence. He claimed that the Dutch soldier often showed during NATO maneuvers that he met the requirements and not infrequently achieved more than was expected of him. It must be said that requirements sometimes are a matter of perception, and expectations can be set low as well as high.

Yet the author of that article was no maverick; he was seriously representing a prevalent mood and an existing situation. Though long hair, earrings, and trade unions are no longer as prominent as they used to be, there is no doubt that former subversive activities and unkempt appearances have cumulatively done a great deal of harm which will take a long time to cure totally.

In March 1981 some Dutch soldiers warned that they would not continue to serve if nuclear weapons were deployed on the soil of their homeland, whatever the political decision. In January 1982 it was reported that three soldiers had been notionally "executed" by a firing squad using "blanks" during an exercise; when one soldier refused to take part in the firing squad he apparently became one of the "corpses" which were than carried a few hundred meters away and ordered to lie prone for a while. In July 1982 it was alleged that two representatives of the conscripts' trade union, *Nederlandse Vereniging van Dienstplichtige Militairen*, were involved in serious security breaches, possibly designed to cause deliberate embarrassement to the military authorities rather than to pass any secrets to a potential enemy. In August 1983 it was reported that most armed forces' trade unions had moved gently to the right politically; it was suggested that this could have been caused by the recession, but it was helping to make a job in the armed services desirable again. Later that year there was an authoritative demand for conscripts to remain in uniform long enough to learn their jobs, especially if these were in any way technical. Yet, even more recently, there have been loud protests about the movement of ammunition through the Netherlands, which does not bode well for what might happen in a real emergency.

Unlike Belgium which has no Defense White Paper, the Netherlands publishes one periodically. The document produced in 1984 also has a useful "summary and excerpts" pamphlet. It is worth quoting from page 5 of that pamphlet:

Well equipped and trained forces can fulfil their tasks properly only if they have the support of the society of which they are part.

Especially since the sixties the issue of the relationship between the armed forces and society has received much attention.

Changes in society and the disputed nature of some military weapons have made acceptance of the armed forces as an indispensable instrument for the protection of our way of life less self-evident. Social acceptance is above all a matter for society itself. For it is society, reflected in parliament and government, that decides whether, and if so to what extent, it regards the armed forces as the appropriate and indispensable instrument to protect the territory itself from external attack. The forces and the individuals who form part of them should likewise contribute to their own acceptance by society. This can be done by, among other things, participating in all sectors of community life, but this is limited by the fact that the armed forces have the task of being prepared for acts of war. This places special demands on those forces.

Effective as the defense organisation may be, if the armed forces are not sufficiently accepted by society, their continued existence, and thus the very things we want to defend, will be in jeopardy. Hence, the pursuit of social acceptance will also have to be a guiding principle in the entire defense policy.

Perhaps this is an appropriate point at which to bring this particular commentary about conscription, unions, and all the unfortunate turmoil to a close. However, the more that quotation is read, the cleverer its drafting seems to be; for it appears to sum up not only both sides of the story, but also summarizes the pressures to protect the basic principles and freedoms of Dutch life while still giving armed forces a role and a chance to play that role.

Successive Dutch governments have repeated their avowed support for NATO. They have expressed the firm intention to continue making military contributions to its allied commands, as well as providing home defense. Together with Belgium and other small countries of the Alliance, the Netherlands has also stressed for more than ten years the merits of "rationalization" and "specialization." These measures would assist with meeting military commitments when costs are rising so steeply. Certain medical functions were amalgamated within the Dutch armed services in the interests of internal rationalization. The government at one time suggested that the Royal Netherlands Navy might offer to take over certain West German maritime commitments in return for the Bundeswehr reciprocally undertaking some land force roles within Northern Army Group, as a way of introducing external specialization.

Recent Defense White Papers have all emphasized that the future composition of the armed forces, as well as the extent and nature of the adjustments needed to maintain well equipped and well manned forces at an adequate level of training, should be viewed in the context and perspective of a relatively small member country of the Alliance. As an increasing price will have to be paid for defense, so the small member nations will have to confine themselves more and more to a limited number of military tasks. The 1984 document explains: "That is why the Netherlands will continue to strive for a higher degree of task specialization, standardisation and rationalisation in the Alliance. However, experience shows that it takes time to accomplish fundamental change." The first sentence of this extract must be welcomed as a restatement of a constructive proposal; the second sentence is profoundly and sadly true.

Another factor which has caused over recent years widespread internal as well as external problems for successive Dutch governments, and for NATO as a whole, has been the doubts cast about cruise missile deployment on Dutch soil. Politicians, churchmen, servicemen, and citizens have all had their say. These weapons will be accepted by 1987 provided arms control agreements bring about a freeze or reduction of the numbers deployed by both sides, East and West, and provided other confidence-building measures are effectively fostered. Despite the trouble and concern this debate has caused, it is significant to note that the Dutch government has pronounced officially that: "Nuclear weapons exist and cannot be removed; nuclear weapons are notably weapons of mass destruction, but have the effect of preventing war; and there are no alternatives for the present strategy, which is based on nuclear deterrence."

The Royal Netherlands Navy is a "conventional" instrument of deterrence. Its tasks in time of tension and war would be to safeguard the free and unhindered use of the sea and to guarantee safe access to the country's ports. It trains for these roles and would undertake these tasks both for national protection and in collaboration with allies. Other Alliance partners also have primary interest in the Eastern Atlantic, Channel, North Sea, and Norwegian Sea, but keeping such vital ports as Rotterdam and Europort open will be crucial for reinforcement and logistic reasons should an emergency arise. The Royal Netherlands

Navy keeps surface ships, submarines, and maritime patrol aircraft at constant readiness in peace, but not without manning difficulties.

The naval Commander-in-Chief has three subordinates. The Admiral, Netherlands Home Command, is based at Den Helder. He controls: five groups of escort ships, submarines, maritime patrol aircraft, helicopters, and the mines service; four main shore stations — Texel, Ijmond, Rijnmond, and Schelde; and a number of training schools, support services, and other shore establishments. The Flag Officer, Netherlands Antilles, discharges the responsibility for externally defending these Caribbean islands with a force of marines, a frigate, and two maritime patrol aircraft. The third subordinate is Commander, Royal Netherlands Marine Corps, who controls two amphibious combat groups and an arctic/mountain trained infantry company.

Ships, aircraft, and main weapon systems are listed by the International Institute for Strategic Studies in its 1984/85 edition of *The Military Balance*. This list includes: 2 destroyers with Harpoon, Standard, and Sea Sparrow; 16 frigates with quite similar weapon fits; 6 submarines; 4 corvettes; and a number of patrol craft, coastal minesweepers, minehunters, combat support, and survey ships. The Naval Air Arm flies the Orion maritime patrol aircraft and Lynx helicopters. Several new submarines, ships, and aircraft are on order.

The Royal Netherlands Navy has units deployed with STANAVFORLAND and STANAVFORCHAN. It is represented by officers serving at both NATO headquarters, as in the case of the Belgian navy. Dutch and British marines train and operate in close cooperation on amphibious tasks, including those in the far north of Europe; their predecessors developed an admirable relationship during World War II which has lasted ever since.

The Royal Netherlands Army (RNLA) has two main tasks: to contribute forces to the forward defense of Western Europe against ground attack within NATO's strategic concept and integrated allied command organization; and to secure and defend the homeland, also ensuring that the vital lines of communication that cross the narrow and congested country are kept open and protected. The army's organisation is outlined in Figure 9.3.

The RNLA would reach a total strength of well over 200,000 when mobilized and placed on a war footing; this is considerably more than three times its peacetime size. Yet, for every regular officer and NCO — and the majority of these are in some way part of a training "machine" — there are two conscripts on active service and another

Figure 9.3: Outline Organization of the Royal Netherlands Army

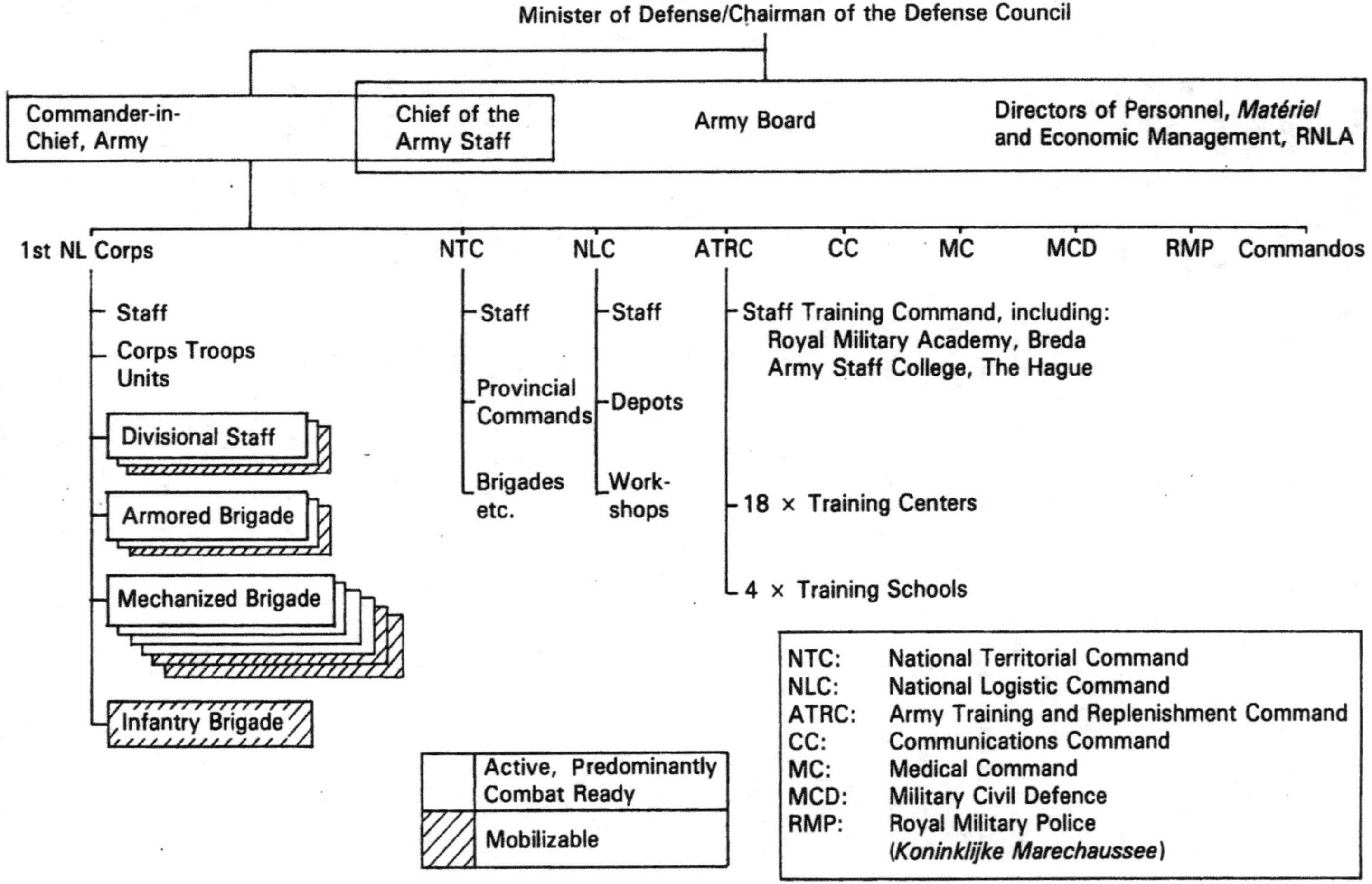

Minister of Defense/Chairman of the Defense Council

- Commander-in-Chief, Army
- Chief of the Army Staff
- Army Board
- Directors of Personnel, *Matériel* and Economic Management, RNLA

Army Board branches: NTC | NLC | ATRC | CC | MC | MCD | RMP | Commandos

- NTC — Staff; Provincial Commands; Brigades etc.
- NLC — Staff; Depots; Workshops
- ATRC — Staff Training Command, including: Royal Military Academy, Breda; Army Staff College, The Hague; 18 × Training Centers; 4 × Training Schools

NTC: National Territorial Command
NLC: National Logistic Command
ATRC: Army Training and Replenishment Command
CC: Communications Command
MC: Medical Command
MCD: Military Civil Defence
RMP: Royal Military Police (*Koninklijke Marechaussee*)

1st NL Corps
- Staff
- Corps Troops Units
- Divisional Staff
- Armored Brigade
- Mechanized Brigade
- Infantry Brigade

Legend:
- Active, Predominantly Combat Ready
- Mobilizable

seven former conscripts in the reserve. To achieve as high a combat readiness rating as possible in the circumstances, a complex and unique manning system is worked.

Each year about 36,000 conscripts join the army; every two months some 6,000 put on uniform for the first time. Potential officers, certain potential NCOs, and some personnel in highly technical fields are called up two months earlier than others to start a longer basic training period and thus serve for 16 months in all. Most soldiers serve for 14 months, consisting of 4 months' basic training followed by 10 months at combat-ready status. Infantry and artillery battalions do their own basic training, but for all other arms it is completed in central schools.

Taking an infantry battalion as an example, conscripts joining together start basic training as a complete company and move through their active and the first part of their reserve service as an entity. Each infantry battalion comprises three companies, three mortar platoons, three anti-tank platoons and so on. Therefore, after four months of basic training, the last joined company moves up in seniority by becoming combat-ready at the same time as the most senior company goes on "short leave" and then moves into a reserve, affiliated battalion, on "long leave" as it is termed. These affiliated reserve battalions (in the infantry and all other arms that use the system) receive intakes and are mobilizable; abbreviated in Dutch these "long leave" units are known as RIM. Later, when "long leave" finishes, former conscripts may be individually posted to mobilizable units which do not keep intakes together as sub-units and which may not have an immediate standby readiness status. Later still, they may be assigned to mobile civil defense columns prior to finishing their liability on the general reserve.

The differentiation between active, RIM, and mobilizable units forming part of 1st Netherlands Corps, as illustrated in Figure 9.3, is an important indication of combat readiness. The manning system used by the Dutch does create units, even active units, at varying degrees of training and operational efficiency. Thus, at any one time, a unit such as an infantry battalion or any other on this scheme is never actually complete, quite apart from the unsettling fact that its short-serving complement constantly changes. Figure 9.4 illustrates the problem.

At the 20-month point, for instance, only two companies are in the battalion and the third is on "short leave," albeit immediately recallable. Moreover, only a reinforced brigade is stationed permanently in Germany in peacetime, with the remainder of 1st Netherlands Corps having to deploy to battle positions from home

Figure 9.4: Dutch Manning System as Illustrated in a Battalion-Size Unit

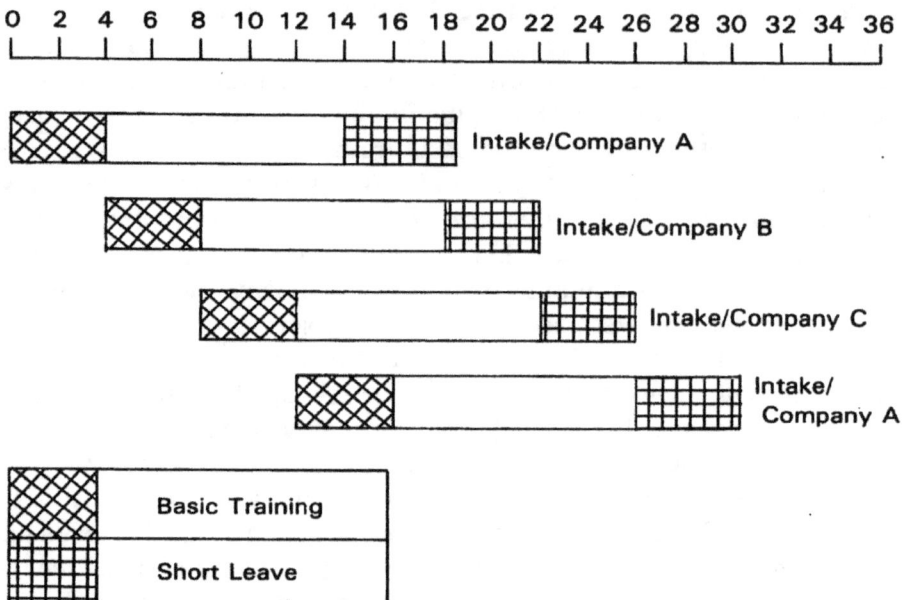

bases. SACEUR has asked for a second brigade to be located in the Federal Republic but this has not been agreed. This goes some way towards explaining concern about lack of operational readiness, quite apart from the lack of professionalism and military competence which stems from such short periods of conscripted service. All appropriate regular officers and NCOs have "shadow" mobilization roles in field units and headquarters, which improves readiness to a degree. However, the same question must be repeated that was asked about 1st Belgian Corps: would mobilization and deployment procedures be too late?

1st Netherlands Corps, like its Belgian counterpart, does not have divisions as formations. The three divisional headquarters are really sets of divisional staffs which, with the commander, man tactical command posts. There is no fixed composition of brigades, no automatic allocation of corps troops units, and no permanent divisional level support. Each armored brigade has two tank battalions and one mechanized infantry battalion, each mechanized brigade has the reverse mix, and both have a tracked artillery battalion, an engineer company, some reconnaissance and anti-tank capabilities, and a logistic battalion composed of medical, supply, and maintenance companies. In addition to the ten "front line" brigades an infantry brigade is in reserve, may become mechanized soon, and would require complete mobilization. Corps troops units, partly active or wholly mobilizable elements, include: reconnaissance battalions with tracked or light vehicles; an artillery brigade with the normal range of self-propelled artillery, Lance missiles, and some air defense consisting of 35 mm self-propelled Gepard with tracking radar (Caesar) and Stinger missiles replacing a considerable amount of L40/70 low level air defense guns; engineer, signal, and aviation groups; a corps logistic support group of medical, supply, maintenance, and transport units; and a battalion of military police. Main battle tanks are Leopard I and II and the armored infantry fighting vehicle YPR 765 is in service or is being introduced into service in many variants: command, infantry carrier, anti-tank with Tow mounted, mortar, radar, observation, ambulance, and load carrier. Other details of equipment are to be found in *The Military Balance*.

Operational readiness is being considerably enhanced as the Dutch take over and stock more forward storage sites located within their assigned combat area in Germany. More depots for storing mobilization equipment are being taken into use which are nearer deployment areas. A larger quantity of training equipment and railway rolling stock is becoming available, to assist with the quick embodiment and movement of very large forces. The mobilization, reinforcement, and support of these forces would fall on a number of functional RNLA commands, as shown in Figure 9.3. The National Territorial Command has 5,500 troops in peace and 40,000 when placed on a war footing. Apart from security and home defense tasks, it has an important mobilization role and is responsible for organizing the military aspects of Host Nation Support and lines of communication for other NATO forces in transit or stationed in the Netherlands. It includes two infantry brigades, a number of independent infantry units and sub-units, and an engineer group to help keep routes open within its order of battle. The country is divided into eight provincial military commands and the infantry would be allocated according to the circumstances that were found to exist during transition-to-war and war.

The information in Figure 9.3 requires supplementing in respect of the military civil defense, police, and commandos. The MCD comprises mobile columns of reservists which undertake civil tasks including disaster relief, working in the home base in close cooperation with provincial military commands. The *Koniklijke Marechaussee* performs military police duties for all three armed services. Apart from providing a battalion of nearly 700 men (with very few conscripts) within 1st Netherlands Corps, as an armed and mobile paramilitary force it also assists with security, traffic control, and border passport checks. The RNLA Commandos are formed into a 500-strong parachute trained unit for special operations.

The Royal Netherlands Air Force has close air support as its main mission and also contributes towards air defense, mainly by ground-launched missiles (Hawk and Patriot) deployed in Germany and at home. F-16 in fighter ground attack and tactical air reconnaissance roles is replacing the F-104 and the NF-5. Fokker Friendship F-27 and helicopters are in transport service. Except for transport aircraft, all resources are integrated within 2 ATAF and NATO's NADGE system. The Tactical Air Command comprises aircraft and missile systems and the Air Logistics and Training Command consists mainly of supply and maintenance depots and schools for pilot, basic, and specialist instruction.

Luxembourg

Luxembourg has a population of well under 400,000 and spent almost $117 per capita on defense in 1983 (expenditure details for 1984 are not yet available). It maintains a light infantry battalion of 720 officers and men, a gendarmerie of 470 armed and mobile paramilitary police, and voluntary military service.

Conclusion

Future historians will surely have cause to admire, and perhaps to praise, NATO's longevity, endurance, and deterrent value — despite the weaknesses displayed at present by unmilitary member states such as Belgium and the Netherlands. NATO remains a singularly potent force for peace in the world. After all, it has helped significantly to keep apart the strongest military adversaries ever known in and around the centre of Western Europe, where they confront each other most closely and dangerously. The historians will place in perspective difficult, and hopefully transitory, political problems and military weaknesses in two particular small countries, which are certainly not alone in these circumstances. Nor are they unique by any means in their struggle to find the resources needed to maintain their defense commitments during a prolonged period of economic depression.

NATO is not the Warsaw Pact. It features no equivalent to Soviet political hegemony and military domination; no policies of "limited soverignty." NATO is an Alliance of free, truly sovereign states of different size, character, wealth, and military capacity. Together, as allies, partner states have pledged to help defend each other's territorial integrity and, in the context of Belgium and the Netherlands, to defend Western Europe, which includes their homelands and contiguous sea and air space. The continuity of strong Belgian and Dutch support as Alliance members contributing land, sea, and air forces to allied commands, as well as providing home defense which will also secure NATO's vital lines of communication, is *politically* crucial.

Militarily, their forces may have comparatively low combat readiness ratings; they may comprise too large a proportion of short-serving conscripts and too small a cadre of regular volunteers; their formations, units, and individual reservists may lack training and fitness for role; most of their semi-active land forces may be mal-deployed in peacetime. Yet, it is fundamentally important they are in fact assigned, earmarked, and would be available to NATO in a crisis. Their availability is just as important politically as militarily.

The longer the extensive and democratic membership of the Alliance lasts, the more disparate and at times dishevelled it can appear; so the more attention and concern is focussed on any divergencies, dissensions, and deficiencies. Nevertheless, it remains the most remarkable invention of the twentieth century. The fact that NATO exists is more remarkable than computers and space travel. And it will continue to exist all the time Soviet overt and covert threats trouble this traditionally troublesome part of our world, namely the centre of peninsular Europe. California, Kansas, and Conneticut have been securely linked to Cornwall and Kassel by this Alliance for nearly forty years. It is against this background that temporary concern about Belgium and the Netherlands has to be viewed.

Perhaps three main observations are in order about the defense forces of Belgium and the Netherlands. First, it will be obvious that it would take time — too long, in fact — to embody, equip, and reinforce the semi-active peacetime contingents, form them up into cohesive units and formations, move them substantial distances, and finally deploy them as key operational components in Northern Army Group's coordinated defense system — even if the political decision to mobilize was made without procrastination. Intact routes and bridges over major waterways could still mean serious disruption because of the mass and concurrent movement of more land forces than their own, quite apart from refugees travelling west.

The second observation also concentrates upon their armies, though it has some applicability to their navies and air forces as well. It can be encapsulated in these two questions. Just what expectation should NATO planners and commanders have of Belgian and Dutch operational performance? Would the lack of professionals, training, experience, expertise, and morale enable their forces, if they arrived in time, to withstand for long enough the ferocity and fluidity of enemy echelons assaulting with vastly superior numbers and weapon systems? Long enough, that is, to help engineer some form of territorially defendable "stalemate" across a long and difficult front in Europe in order to give politicians of both sides an opportunity to consider other alternatives before releasing nuclear weapons. If that sounds dramatic, then it serves adequately to emphasize the vital part Belgians, Dutch, and their allies will individually and collectively have to play in trying to solve that conundrum.

The third is a happier observation. There are sure signs that conscientious measures are being taken to halt the so-called "military decline" in Belgium, the Netherlands, and their armed services, which presage better days ahead. Better days can arrive sooner if NATO grasps yet another "nettle." This is the one which would help the smaller member nations with limited resources by introducing "rationalization" and "specialization" of roles within the military structure. It may be necessary to consider integrating Belgian and Dutch brigades or divisions within multinational divisions or corps in Northern Army Group. To achieve this not impracticable feat would emulate the interoperability currently attained by allied naval and air forces. Such a move would give the impetus NATO has needed for years to introduce the organizational and procedural conformity, the compatibility or standardization of weapon systems, and the operational cohesion required to enable its formations "to fit together to fight together."

Select Bibliography

Dodd, Norman L. "The Belgian Armed Forces," *Defence* (March 1982)
——— "The Netherlands Armed Forces," *Defence* (December 1980)

Donnet, Baron M. "Cross Hands of Europe," *NATO's Fifteen Nations* (February-March 1979)
International Institute for Strategic Studies *The Military Balance, 1984–1985* (IISS, London, 1984), pp. 31–32 and 44–45
Ministry of Defence of the Netherlands *Defence in the Netherlands* (Ministry of Defence, The Hague, September 1983)
──── *The Netherlands Defence White Paper 1984: Summary and Excerpts* (Ministry of Defence, The Hague, 1984)
Roos, J.G. "Rapid Mobilisation for War," *NATO's Sixteen Nations*, Special Edition No. 1 (1983)
Skinner, John H. "Belgium" and "The Netherlands" in John Keegan (ed.), *World Armies* (Macmillan, London, 1979; reprinted 1983)
──── "NATO Organisational Structure," M. Litt. Dissertation, Oxford University, 1978
van Vuren, A.J. "The Royal Netherlands Army Today," *Military Review* (April 1982)

10 UNITED STATES ARMED FORCES IN EUROPE
Harry G. Summers, Jr.

Will the United States "be expected to send substantial numbers of troops [to Europe] as a more or less permanent contribution to the development of [Western Europe's] capacity to resist?" asked Senator Bourne Hickenlooper of Iowa during the 1949 Senate hearing on the North Atlantic Treaty. "The answer to that question," replied Secretary of State Dean Acheson, "is a clear and absolute 'No.'"[1]

"More or less permanent" is difficult to define, but the fact is that 36 years later, 216,700 of the army's 780,800 soldiers, 26,600 of the navy's 564,800 sailors, 89,800 of the air force's 594,500 airmen, and 1,900 of the nation's 196,600 marines are forward-deployed in Europe and a substantial number of the remainder are earmarked for reinforcement there in the event of war.[2] According to a *New York Times* analysis of a 1984 Pentagon study:

> The total cost of European-deployed United States forces and all of the United States-based forces that we have pledged to contribute as NATO reinforcements over the course of a conflict amounts to about $177 billion. That would be 58 percent of the fiscal year 1985 military budget of the United States.[3]

How and why did this remarkable change in American foreign and military policy take place? To provide an answer to that important question, this chapter will examine the United States commitment to European Defense since the end of World War II in terms of five distinct periods: 1945–50, 1950–53, 1953–64, 1964–73, and 1973 to the present. Each will be analyzed in terms of the peculiar political–military environment that made the period unique, the military policies that grew out of that environment, and the composition and capabilities of the force that was deployed to execute these policies. Because the army provided (and provides) the bulk of America's commitment to NATO and because — unlike the other services — the army's internal composition varied widely from period to period, the analysis will concentrate on that service.

1945-50: the Cold War Begins

The Political–Military Environment

"In May of 1945," Theodore White wrote in his 1953 analysis of American policy toward Europe, "the Army of the United States had stood in Central Europe with a force of 3,500,000 men, organized into 68 veteran divisions, supported by 149 air groups of planes, supplied by one of the most elaborate logistical systems ever flung over the globe." But he went on to say, "By March of 1946, ten months later, the American forces had dwindled to 400,000 men, with homeland reserves insufficient to keep them at strength. The Air Force had disappeared."[4] It was destined to get worse. By the end of the period in 1950, army strength in Europe would fall to just over 81,000 soldiers.

This was no accident, but a deliberate reaction to the prevailing attitudes of the American people. Tired of war, their cry was "Bring the Boys Home," and the government had no choice but to comply. As the army's official history relates:

> Pressure for faster mobilization from an articulate public, the Congress, and the troops themselves upset the plans for an orderly demobilization. The Army, which felt greatest pressure, responded by . . . releasing half its eight million troops at the end of 1945. Early in 1946, when the Army cut down the return of troops from abroad in order to meet its overseas responsibilities, a crescendo of protest greeted the move, including troop demonstrations in the Philippines, China, England, France, Germany, Hawaii and even California. The public cry diminished only after the Army more than halved its remaining strength during the first six months of 1946 . . . [To reach the dollar ceilings imposed by President Truman for fiscal year 1947] the Army issued no more draft calls and released all postwar draftees along with the remaining troops and 306,000 airmen [the Air Force did not become a separate service until the following September]. The Navy was meanwhile reduced to a strength of 484,000 and Marine Corps to 92,000 . . . [In the Army in the field] shortages of capable maintenance troops resulted in a widespread deterioration of equipment, and remaining Army units, understrength and infused with briefly trained replacements, were only shadows of the efficient organizations they had been at the end of the war.[5]

At first these developments were not particularly disturbing, for the primary concern in Europe was to provide sufficient forces to police the American zone of occupation as agreed at the Yalta and Potsdam Conferences, and the division-equivalent Constabulary and the First Infantry Division were considered sufficient for that purpose. But by 1947, concerns changed from the occupation of Germany to the more ominous problem of deterrring Soviet expansion into Western Europe. When President Harry S. Truman announced the "Truman Doctrine" in March 1947, which committed the United States "to help free peoples to maintain . . . their national integrity against aggressive movements that seek to impose upon them totalitarian regimes,"[6] the deterioration of America's armed forces took on new meaning. As Theodore White noted, "the Russians massed 40 divisions of combat troops in combat position in Central Europe with over 100 divisions behind them in reserve, while America's forces stood at two divisions and its homeland reserve counted no more than six ready battalions." As if that were not bad enough,

> the Russians had moved their divisions north to the critically sensitive German flatlands and so overmatched Allied strength that our intelligence reports gravely doubted whether, if a clash came, our troops could be capable of making an effective retreat to the North German ports where they might be evacuated without catastrophe . . . Russian fighting strength in Europe outweighed Western fighting strength by more than three to one. "All the Russians need to get to the Channel," observed one American military statesman at that time, "is shoes."[7]

Military Policy

"To counter this enemy strength," White wrote, "the West had but one weapon — the Strategic Air Force of the United States, *laden* with atomic bombs."[8] White could not know when he wrote those words in 1953 that "laden" was hardly the right word. As more recent accounts make clear, "As late as 1949, the United States could have assembled fewer than 200 atomic bombs." Not only that, but of the "around fifty trained crews and properly equipped aircraft," it was found that at the time "not one crew could place a weapon on target in conditions approaching wartime."[9]

But:

> the nation's nuclear weakness did not prevent policy makers from

putting the atomic bomb at the center of the nation's strategy . . . the threat of nuclear retaliation was the cornerstone of defense policy . . . The military planners believed that Western Europe could not be defended in a general war. Instead, the United States would have to depend upon air strikes mounted from Great Britain, the Middle East, and Japan to defeat the Russians. The only commitment of non-nuclear air and ground forces would be related to holding air bases and the oil resources of the Middle East . . . Truman paled at the prospect, but he approved the military's concept of fighting a nuclear war if deterrence failed.[10]

Although he did not say so, it was these realities that were behind Secretary of State Acheson's reply to Senator Hickenlooper in 1949 that the United States did not intend to station American troops in Western Europe permanently. What Acheson did say ten years later in his autobiography was that:

> even as a short-range prediction [the] answer was deplorably wrong. It was almost equally stupid. But it was not intended to deceive. [It came] a year before the united command was thought of, at a time when our troops were regarded as occupation forces for Germany and not part of a defense force for Europe.[11]

Composition of the Force

While there was a significant air force build up to counter the Berlin Blockade from June 1948 to May 1949, the army comprised the bulk of direct American military involvement in Europe — the First Infantry Division and the Constabulary together with their supporting units in the American zone of occupation in West Germany, a regiment in Berlin, a regiment in Trieste (then in dispute between Italy and Yugoslavia) and an occupation force in the American zone in Austria.

As noted above, by 1947 this was almost exclusively a "regular" force. For the officer corps, "regular" was something of a misnomer, since large numbers of reserve officers had been voluntarily retained on active duty after World War II. The non-commissioned officer corps, however, was comprised exclusively of regulars, the majority combat veterans who had re-enlisted after World War II. Although the draft was reinstituted in June 1948 (primarily to spur enlistments), few of the 300,000 men drafted between 1948 and the beginning of the Korean War saw service in Europe, for an attempt was made to send only experienced soldiers there. The author, for example, enlisted in June 1947 specifically for assignment to what was still called the "European Theatre of Operations (ETO)" over the advice of the recruiting sergeant who warned that, no matter what the advertising said, only second-term enlistees were being sent to Europe. His counsel proved only too sound, for the only "ETO" that materialized was Korea — the "Eastern Tip of the Orient."

Capabilities of the Force

The problem with the army in Europe prior to the Korean War was the lack of a sense of mission, not the quality of the force. As the noted military historian Russell F. Weigley observed:

> Despite the opening of the Cold War, the American Army faded to near impotence after World War II, at least in relation to the country's responsibilities . . . So pervasive was this attitude that the Army itself appears to have suffered increasingly under a sense of its own irrelevance, with consequent damage to energy and efficiency. To the extent that Americans saw the communist threat as a military threat, their answer to it was simply the American atomic monopoly.[12]

The effect of this loss of sense of purpose was devastating. In an address to the Army War College in 1973, then Army Chief of Staff General Creighton Abrams described conditions in the field:

> I remember in 1949 I went over to Germany and it was a tremendous disappointment . . . Well, they assigned me to command a tank battalion in Germany. A job, you known, I had had about 3½ years doing when it counted. [General Abrams was one of the most famous armor commanders of World War II; it was his tanks that broke through to the besieged forces in Bastogne during the Battle of the Bulge in 1944.] That is the way I looked at it.
>
> I went to this tank battalion. That was in 1949. I got there on the 29th of August. I will never forget it. Right after my first day, I got a letter from the division commander. It said something like this, "The 63rd Tank Battalion which had previously held the highest record for venereal disease of any battalion-sized unit in Europe, broke that record in the month of August. This has raised serious doubts about your qualifications for command."
>
> Well, I am like everybody else . . . the injustice! I had only been

there two days in August. I spent a couple of days contemplating a severe rebuke, one that would sizzle right back through the same message centers that the letter had come down through. I wanted to give it to him. Then I got to thinking. It is already September, then was going to come October, November, December. Whatever I said about August . . . what was I going to say? I had no place to go. So I got the letter out and looked at it again. This time I looked at the statistics. Well, I had one company with 90 men in it and 110 new cases in the month of August. So I could see that the problem was real.

My family was staying down at Bad Tolz. I was staying at the bachelor officers' hotel. One week-end I went to see them. Coming back, driving the Autobahn in a terrible rain, the windshield wipers were not working very well. They had gotten old and cracked. So they were not clearing off the water the way they should. I pulled into this big German gasoline station. I was in the repair part trying to find somebody to see if I could get some windshield wipers.

This soldier came running up to me, saluted, and said, "It's not my fault, sir." My eyes had now grown accustomed to the dim light in there and I could see that there was a 2½ ton truck out of the 63rd Tank Battalion. This fellow was the driver. On further examination, it is loaded full up to the top sides with 5-gallon cans of gas. He is down there selling it to the filling station. We went back together. It was really an accident of fate. I was ahead of the CID by a mile. They were selling about 100,000 gallons a month. They were a tank battalion and drew a lot of gas, then pocketed the money. A few officers, a few noncoms and so on.

One thing led to another. I found out that they were also selling rations, the rations they drew for the men . . .

Walking one day with the adjutant, we came to a sports car. It had these tiny swastikas on it. I said to the adjutant, "What's that?" "Oh," he said, "that's Lieutentant so-and-so's car." I said, "What are the swastikas?" He said, "Each one represents a German female conquest." . . .

I don't mean that the battalion I had joined in August of '49 was typical of every battalion in the American Army, but it wasn't far from it . . .[13]

In his masterful account of the Korean War, *This Kind of War* (Macmillan, New York, 1963), T. R. Fehrenbach related what happened to such an army when it was committed to combat. It was the troops in Korea who paid the price in blood for the army's decline, but, as will be seen, it was Europe which ultimately profited from their terrible ordeal.

1950–53: The Korean War

The Political–Military Environment

By 1950 momentous changes had radically altered America's military relationships with Western Europe. What had begun as a commitment to the post-World War II occupation of Germany akin to the temporary stationing of American forces in Germany from 1918 to 1919 after World War I hardened into more permanent guarantees for the defense of Western Europe. While America still had not committed itself to the permanent stationing of American forces in Europe, (see Secretary of State Acheson's comments above) and while US army forward-deployed forces in Europe had declined from 316,500 in 1946 to 90,600 in 1948 to 81,200 in 1950, these levels in fact represented not so much a lessening US commitment in Europe but instead a decline in overall army strength, for in each instance these levels represented over one-third of army forces stationed abroad.[14]

Although troop levels had declined, military assistance increased dramatically when the North Atlantic Treaty (and the concomitant military assistance program) won Congressional approval in 1949.[15] The approval of this treaty marked a revolutionary shift in American foreign policy. From the beginning of the Republic, George Washington's advice that it was America's "true policy to steer clear of permanent alliances with any portion of the foreign world" had remained a tenet of US foreign policy. This especially applied to Europe, for, as Washington had warned:

> Europe has a set of primary interests which, to us, have none or a very remote relation. Hence she must be engaged in frequent controversies, the causes of which are essentially foreign to our concerns. Hence, therefore, it must be unwise for us to implicate ourselves by artificial ties in the ordinary vicissitudes of her politics or the ordinary combinations and collisions of her friendships or enmities.[16]

This was more than just ancient history, for the late Senator Robert A. Taft of Ohio and others used these very arguments unsuccessfully against ratification of the North Atlantic Treaty. As Senator Taft warned, "By executing a treaty of this kind, we put ourselves at the mercy of the foreign policies of 11 other nations."[17]

What overrode traditional American fears of entangling alliances was the growing perception of the threat posed by the Soviet Union. Describing the world situation to a joint session of the Congress on 17 March 1948, President Harry Truman noted that:

> Since the close of hostilities, the Soviet Union and its agents have destroyed the independence and democratic character of a whole series of nations in eastern and central Europe. It is this ruthless course of action, and the clear design to extend it to the remaining free nations of Europe, that have brought about the critical situation in Europe today.[18]

The comforting illusion that America's nuclear monopoly would be sufficient to deal with this situation was called into question when the Soviet Union broke that monopoly with the development and testing of its own nuclear weapon in 1949, and was shattered completely in June 1950 with the North Korean invasion of South Korea.

It appeared at the time that — American nuclear superiority notwithstanding — "monolithic world communism" controlled by the Soviet Union was prepared to use force of arms to extend its domination over the world. As President Truman said, "The attack upon Korea makes it plain beyond all doubt that Communism has passed beyond the use of subversion to conquer independent nations and will now use armed invasion and war." Not only did Truman dispatch troops to Korea to check this invasion (and send the Seventh Fleet into the Straits of Formosa, increase aid to the Philippines, and — in what would prove to be a momentous move — increase aid and send a military mission to "the forces of France and the Associated States in Indo-China"), he also began a major force buildup in Europe.[19]

Military Policy

The North Korean attack on South Korea caused a major shift in America's military policies. As was noted earlier, it was assumed that America's nuclear monopoly and, after 1949, America's nuclear superiority were sufficient not only to protect the American homeland but also to guarantee America's overseas interests. While the initial attack on South Korea was ambiguous (since earlier erroneous signals had made it clear that Korea had been excluded from America's security sphere), the continuation of the attack after US military forces had been committed to combat there demonstrated that US nuclear superiority in and of itself had not proved to be a credible deterrent.[20]

While the immediate concern was to hold the line in Korea, there was also concern about US force levels in Europe, since it was assumed at the time that the attack in Korea was merely a diversion, and that the real Communist objective was Western Europe. To shore up defenses there, the US secured allied agreement to the appointment of General Dwight D. Eisenhower as NATO Supreme Commander and activated and brought up to strength a field army — Seventh Army — to mount a conventional defense in Europe. The mission of US forces was no longer occupation but the forward defense of the United States. The American–British–French zones of occupation were tranformed into a defensive alliance and American lines of communication and supply were rerouted from the vulnerable north German ports through what had been the French zone of occupation west of the Rhine and across France to the sea.

As America mobilized for the Korean War, numerous army reserve units were sent to Europe (the 320th General Hospital from New York, for example, established what was to become the Landstuhl Army Medical Center), and of the eight National Guard divisions mobilized for the Korean War, two (the 28th and 43rd Infantry Divisions) were forward-deployed to Europe, the same number as were sent to Korea. After the battle lines stabilized in Korea, there was an almost equal allocation of military assets to the war zone in Korea and to the reinforcement of NATO. By 1951, army strength in Europe had increased to 124,300, as compared to 229,300 soldiers in Korea, but by 1952 troop strength in Europe had increased to 260,800, slightly more than the 238,600 soldiers in combat in Korea.[21]

Composition of the Force

With the Korean War buildup, the composition of the force in Europe underwent a radical change. While (although reinforced by reservists called to active duty) the officers and non-commissioned officers remained predominantly volunteers, the enlisted ranks were filled not only by reservists and the National Guard but also by conscripts raised by the reinstituted Selective Service Act of 1948 as later amended by the Universal Military Training and Service Act of 1951. Unlike the earlier enlistees, these draftees represented a major cross-section of American society. Senator Ted Kennedy, for example, served as a military policeman at NATO headquarters, former *Foreign Affairs* editor James Chace as a translator in France, and *US News & World Report* deputy foreign editor Gerson Yalowitz began his journalistic career on a post newspaper in Germany.

Capabilities of the Force

What had been, as General Creighton Abrams' comments above testified, a garrison army of doubtful combat ability was transformed into a credible fighting force. Writing at that time, Theodore White described the remarkable change that had taken place:

> Our line of battle in the critical central area counts six American divisions . . . No longer are the troops scattered in hopeless garrisons, helter-skelter through Germany. They are poised on a known line, with presited positions and deployment areas, with avenues of attack and withdrawal surveyed, engineered and zeroed in. No longer must American suplies move down the dangerously vulnerable north-south routes form the North Sea to Bavaria. They are beginning now to enter by the safe ports of the Bay of Biscay, deep in the French rear, and then move horizontally across France to Germany over an enormous American communications system . . . Four million tons of American military supplies, plus 503 planes and 82 warships, had arrived in Europe between the beginning of NATO, in the spring of 1949, and January of 1953 . . . American divisions in Europe are the best equipped of American history.[22]

1953–64: Inter-War Years

The Political–Military Environment

The more than a decade between the end of the war in Korea and the beginning of the war in Vietnam that spanned the Eisenhower, Kennedy, and Johnson administrations was marked (as will be seen below) by two major changes in military policy, and witnessed several significant world events. Viewed from the perspective of American military force presence in Europe, however, it was a period of remarkable stability.

One of the reasons for this stability is that world events tended to reinforce the foundations of the NATO Alliance. Even the Korean War fitted this pattern. The willingness of the United States to commit its forces for the defense of an ally was affirmed, both by the commitment of American forces to combat in Korea and (perhaps more importantly) by Congressional recognition that America's days of isolation from world events were at an end, as evidenced by their appropriating funds for America's forward defense in both Europe and Asia.[23] Further, the defensive nature of the NATO Alliance was reinforced by US actions after the Chinese intervention in Korea. On the urgings of its European allies, the United States deliberately rejected strategic offensive measures against China but instead (as with the NATO Alliance) adopted the strategic defensive. The objective was to hold the line and to bring the war to a close — not by taking the war to the enemy's homeland, destroying his army, and breaking his will to resist — but by diplomatic negotiations (albeit diplomatic negotiations reinforced by the hint of nuclear escalation). In 1956, this national policy of containment of Communist expansion (in military terms, the strategic defensive) rather than roll-back or liberation (the strategic offensive) was made explicit when President Eisenhower opted against intervention in the Hungarian uprising.

The Soviet launching of Sputnik in 1957, while initially unsettling, ultimately had the effect of drawing the Alliance together, since only the United States had the capability to counter what would become the Soviet intercontinental ballistic missile (ICBM) threat. That proved to be the case five years later when, during the Cuban missile crisis in October 1962, "the United States had about 200 to 250 ICBMs, Russia probably only 50 to 75 . . . The total nuclear balance remained overwhelmingly in America's favor." The result, as Russell Weigley has noted, was that, for a while at least, "Soviet policy had to tread cautiously in the face of assertive American nuclear power, in Berlin as well as in Cuba."[24]

Military Policy

During the inter-war years, US declaratory military policy underwent two significant changes. In 1954, then Secretary of State John Foster Dulles announced what was to become known as the strategy of "massive retaliation." He stated:

> The Soviet Communists are planning for what they call "an entire historical era" . . . they seek, through many types of maneuvers, gradually to divide and weaken the free nations by overextending them in efforts which, as Lenin put it, are "beyond their strength, so that they come to practical bankruptcy" . . . In the face of this strategy . . . it is not sound to become permanently committed to military expenditures so vast that they lead to "practical bankruptcy" . . .

We want a maximum deterrent at a bearable cost.[25]

the answer appeared to lie in almost total reliance on strategic nuclear weapons as the basis of not only primary deterrence of attacks on the American homeland but also extended deterrence of attacks on America's interests in the world, especially including interests in Western Europe.

But this change was more apparent than real. "The new look of 'massive retaliation' was, in fact, the old look of the Truman adminstration's pre-Korean policy of reliance on the atomic deterrent alone," observed historian Russell Weigley:

> If air-atomic power had failed to deter a Communist adventure on the military frontier in 1950, because the threat of atomic war was not credible in a peripheral crisis, the nuclear deterrent alone was hardly likely to be more successful in the mid-1950's, now that the Soviet Union had acquired a substantial nuclear arsenal of its own ... Behind the screen of rhetoric, therefore, the Eisenhower administration had to retain much of the increase in ground strength created during the Korean war.[26]

Although army strength in Europe declined from a high of 262,700 in 1955 to a low of 226,600 in 1960, even at its lowest level it was still 100,000 higher than it had been before the Korean War. Further, while army strength in Europe through 1954 represented some one-third of the army's overseas strength, from 1955 onward it represented over one-half of such strength and by 1960 had increased to almost two-thirds.[27]

This gap between America's declaratory military policy and its actual policy became part of the debate in the 1960 presidential election, and soon after he won office, President John F. Kennedy changed US military policy from "massive retaliation" to one of "flexible response." Unlike its predecessor, "flexible response" would not rely on nuclear weapons alone, but would "meet Communist threats with an appropriate level of matching force . . . At the center of 'flexible response' theory was the assumption that deterring and fighting with nonnuclear forces would reduce the likelihood of nuclear escalation."[28]

Reflecting this emphasis on conventional forces, army troop strength in Europe (although remaining at about two-thirds of army overseas strength) increased from 226,600 in 1960 to 278,000 by 1962, then fell off to 240,100 by 1964. More significantly, as far as NATO was concerned, "weapons modernization continued apace to give the alliance more fighting power [and] in 1963 NATO's annual exercises included troops flown to Germany from the United States; the Army then accelerated a plan to preposition weapons, vehicles, and supplies in Europe for the reinforcing troops."[29]

Composition of Force

As was noted above, changes in military policy during the inter-war years had only marginal impact on the overall composition of the force. Internally, however, there were some significant changes. With the end of the war in Korea, the army National Guard and army reserve units that had bolstered America's commitment to NATO reverted to inactive status, and were replaced by regular units deployed from the United States. In addition, active duty-reservists within the officer corps who had remained on active duty after World War II or who had been recalled for the Korean War were vetted by a severe reduction-in-force. In the author's experience (from 1953 to 1957, acting Sergeant Major of Western Area Command which was responsible for all US forces west of the Rhine in what had been the French zone of occupation), these cuts (which included some regular officers as well) at first eliminated many sub-standard and marginal performers from the officer corps, although what began as a laudable attempt to get rid of the "worst of the worst" ended up, as the reductions continued, by forcing out "the worst of the best." Although some good officers were lost, overall there was a significant improvement in quality and professionalism.

Within the enlisted ranks, the non-commissioned officers continued to be primarily an all-volunteer force, and the majority of the senior NCOs were combat veterans of World War II and the Korean War. Racial integration, which had begun in 1948, was fully realized by 1954.[30] The draft, which remained in force after the end of the war in Korea, continued to leaven the ranks with a representative cross-section of American society. The eminent military sociologist, Northwestern University Professor Charles Moskos, for example, as well as *Commentary* editor Norman Podhoretz served with the United States army in Europe during this period.[31]

Attempts were made to replace the individual replacement system (where units remained in place but their personnel were rotated in and out after fixed overseas tours of duty) with a unit replacement system where units deployed from the United States would replace like units in Europe. In the 1950s, a system called "Gyroscope" involved the exchange of entire divisions where, for example, the 2nd Armored Division stationed in West Germany was replaced by the 8th Infantry

Division from its base in the United States. Designed to decrease personnel turbulence, the effect was an increase in such turbulence, for to make the system work efficiently the entire army personnel system had to be revamped, a move the army bureaucracy was not willing to undertake.

Force moderniziation, which began during the Korean War when World War II vintage arms and equipment were replaced by a new generation of weapons, continued throughout the period. M-46, and M-48, and, later, M-60 tanks were deployed in Europe, as was the M-79 and later the M-113 Armored Personnel Carrier. As part of NATO standardization, the World War II and Korean War 30-caliber M-1 rifle was replaced with the M-14 rifle, which fired 7.65 mm NATO standard ammunition. Particularly significant was the introduction of nuclear-capable field artillery, first with the 280 mm "atomic cannon," and later with nuclear-capable 155 mm and 8-inch howitzers and Pershing and Sergeant missiles. This army modernization was matched by similar modernization of combat aircraft and, by the end of the period, USAF Europe was equipped with the latest F-111 and F-4 fighter-bombers and fighters.[32]

Capabilities of the Force

Judged from the perspective of the composition of the force, US armed forces in Europe were at their zenith during the inter-war period. Logistically supported by a "Communications Zone" in France with protected lines of supply, reinforced by tactical air force units based in England and on the Continent, the primary ground combat unit — the US Seventh Army — was acknowledged as one of the most combat-ready units in the American army. Fully equipped, highly disciplined and highly motivated, the United States armed forces in Europe were maintained at a high level of readiness, their battlefield skills honed by rigorous training and frequent field exercises.

1964–73: the Vietnam War

The Political–Military Environment

From the Tonkin Gulf incident in August 1964 to the Paris peace accords of 1973, the political–military environment was dominated by the war in Vietnam. It colored America's relations with its NATO allies, particularly with France; affected (as will be seen below) not only American military policy but also troop levels in Europe and the composition and capabilities of the force. In the meantime, the Soviet Union consolidated its hold over Eastern Europe, enforcing the "Brezhnev doctrine" that Communist control was irreversible with its invasion of Czechoslovakia in 1968, and continuing its drive to reach nuclear parity with the United States.

From 1946 to 1954, America's involvement in Vietnam coincided with its involvement in Europe. Military aid and assistance were provided initially in an attempt to assist France in Indochina so as to obtain French cooperation in the defense of Western Europe. In 1950, as part of America's worldwide response to what was then perceived as attempts by "monolithic world Communism" to expand its control by force-of-arms (a response which, as was discussed earlier, included a major US commitment to the defense of Europe), aid to French forces in Indochina was increased and a military assistance team was dispatched there. After the French withdrawal from Indochina in 1954, however, America's interests and those of its NATO allies began to diverge. With the loss of their colonies, European nations were primarily concerned with regional issues. As a world power, America's interests and those of its NATO allies began to diverge. With the loss of their colonies, European nations were primarily concerned with regional issues. As a world power, America's interests were global and included interests in the Pacific as well as in Europe. A major rationale for US involvement in Vietnam, for example, was the containment of Chinese Communist expansion.[33] While the United States, as a Pacific power, saw China as a threat, Western Europe saw China (especially after the Sino-Soviet split in the early 1960s) as a natural ally which siphoned off Soviet power to the defense of the Sino-Soviet border and the Soviet Far East, thus relieving the pressure on Western Europe. This divergence of interests was matched by a divergence on strategy, especially with France. Arguments over the applicability of "flexible response" to the defense of NATO led France in 1966 to announce its withdrawal from NATO's integrated military organization, a move which "deprived the alliance of geographic depth for its logistical system and closed French air bases to NATO aircraft."[34]

Military Policy

Although not formally adopted by the North Atlantic Council until December 1967, "flexible response" (defined as "a strategy predicated on meeting aggression at an appropriate level or place with the capability of escalating the level of conflict if required or desired"[35]) remained US military policy throughout this period. But from the first the emphasis of flexible response was not on Europe. It was

> the [Kennedy] adminstration's belief that nuclear deterrence and the complementary balance of power between NATO and the Warsaw Pact had driven the military competition to different techniques and different places. The most likely challenges would be "people's war" . . . Kennedy did not undervalue NATO, but he thought the great conflicts of the future . . . would come outside Europe.[36]

Thus, beginning in 1960, and especially after the commitment of US ground forces to combat in Vietnam in 1965, the emphasis was on "counterinsurgency" at the lower end of the flexible-response scale, an emphasis that had little relevance for NATO. This emphasis would begin to fade in 1969 with the beginning of the US phase-down of the war and the gradual withdrawal of US forces from Vietnam, but it would not completely disappear until after the withdrawal of US forces from Vietnam in 1973.

Composition of the Force

In numerical terms, the effect of the war in Vietnam on US force levels in Europe was reflected in their decline from 374,000 personnel in 1964 to a low of 291,000 in 1970.[37] Because of college deferment and the activities of the anti-war movement, the draft, which earlier had provided a cross-section of the American public, was no longer representational. Leadership declined as captains, majors, and lieutenant-colonels were diverted to Vietnam, leaving some units to be commanded by junior lieutenants. Equipment was not replaced and maintenance was deferred. Quality of life also declined. As a 1973 study reported, "Troop housing and family quarters had been allowed to deteriorate for years, largely because of diversion of Army resources to Vietnam. Soldier morale was terribly low as a result of living in 'slums' in the midst of German affluence."[38]

Capabilities of the Force

US forces in Europe, which had been at their peak during the 1954–64 period, had reached the depths by the end of the war in Vietnam. With outdated equipment, inadequate maintenance, poor leadership, and low morale, it was in danger of becoming a drug-ridden and undisciplined rabble rather than an effective fighting force. A 1977 report to

Congress confirmed that "in the early 1970s . . . disciplinary difficulties devitalized US armed forces: drug abuse, 'underground activity,' crime, racial friction, irresponsibility, and rebellion against authority were common manifestations."[39]

1973–85: the Post-Vietnam Era

The Political–Military Environment

After the US military withdrawal from Vietnam in January 1973 in accordance with the Paris peace accords, American security concerns once again focussed on Western Europe. Then Army Chief of Staff General Creighton Abrams, for example, formed a study group within the Pentagon in the fall of 1973 to examine the post-Vietnam need for military force. The findings of this study group (the so-called "Astarita Report," named for the head of the study group, Colonel Edward Astarita, USA) were briefed extensively throughout the Washington national security establishment. Essentially, the report held that the United States was in a position of relative advantage in the world, allied with the two major economic power centers (West Europe and Japan), while its potential adversaries, the Soviet Union and China, were also adversaries with each other. The role of military power, therefore, was to assist in maintaining the US in that relatively advantageous position. In a very real sense, the report validated American forward deployments in both Northeast Asia and Western Europe as essential for the foreign policy of the United States.[40] As will be seen below, this revalidation of NATO was soon reflected in official military doctrine.

The most important political–military development, however, was not the end of the war in Vietnam; it was Soviet attainment of nuclear parity with the United States. With American nuclear forces checkmated at every level — strategic (i.e., intercontinental), theater (mid-range), and tactical (short-range) — conventional forces regained an importance they had not had since the beginning of the nuclear age.

Military Policy

While offical NATO military policy remained (and remains) "flexible response," under that heading significant changes took place in American military doctrine. As the war in Vietnam ended, counterinsurgency doctrine, which had dominated army thinking for over a decade, virtually disappeared. Under the leadership of General William

E. Depuy, commander of the army's newly formed Training and Doctrine Command, a whole new series of "How to Fight" manuals were produced. Given the deplorable condition of US forces, emphasis was on holding the line through what was called the mobile defense — actually wearing any enemy attack down through attrition.[41] This doctrine was severly criticised but it was not until the quality of the force improved, and better arms and equipment became available, that maneuver doctrine — attacking the enemy's weak points by highly mobile forces — was formally adopted.[42] To take maximum advantage of this doctrine, some have called for abandoning NATO's defensive orientation and carrying the war to the enemy through deep strikes into Eastern Europe.[43]

Although Soviet nuclear parity did not result in changes to NATO's military policy of flexible response, it did cause the United States to abandon what had been called the "short war" theory with its notion that any war would rapidly become nuclear and be quickly terminated. This theory made some sense when the United States had escalation dominance — the ability to escalate a crisis to a level at which the adversary could not respond — but with Soviet nuclear parity escalation dominance was lost. Conventional, not nuclear, forces now held center stage. As then Army Chief of Staff General Edward C. Meyer put it:

> We have . . . witnessed a concerted and successful effort by the Soviets to checkmate all previously existing Western military advantages . . . Our great nuclear advantage, for example, once offered a presumably economical option to land forces . . . [But] the Soviets' achievement of rough nuclear parity has . . . open[ed] the door for the Soviet Union to employ more actively long-held advantages of its own in conventional forces. In this regard, the USSR's investments in strategic forces have tended to serve its traditional focus on the primacy of land warfare.[44]

In the early 1980s, the guidance given to America's armed forces was to prepare for a "long war." This guidance made official the trend that had been developing since the end of the war in Vietnam — the revitalization of America's reserve forces and their orientation toward the wartime reinforcement of forward-deployed active forces, especially in Western Europe.[45]

Composition of the Force
Draftees peaked to 42 percent of the army's total force in 1967 and then

began to decline. By 1971, more men were volunteering than were being inducted, and in 1973 the draft was officially ended.[46] The end of the draft did not immediately end personnel problems in Europe, however. It would take until 1977 before the indiscipline, drug, and racial problems were brought under control.[47]

As was the case with the period 1945–50, forces in Europe are once again an all-volunteer force. But that would be a false comparison. For one thing, the size of the force is much larger. From a low of 291,000 in 1970, US military forces in Europe have been maintained at over 325,000 since 1978.[48] For another, it is a much more capable force.

Capabilities of the Force

Just as the lack of a sense of mission was the underlying reason for the lack of motivation in the 1945–50 force, so a strong sense of mission has been a major factor in the vitalization of today's force. Increased funding and agreements with the West German government have resulted in significant improvements in housing and base facilities. Modern arms and equipment, such as the new M-1 tank, have improved conventional combat capabilities, and the 1980–84 deployment of new Pershing II intermediate range missiles as well as ground-launched cruise missiles has upgraded theater nuclear capabilities.

Visiting Western Europe in 1977, the "overriding impression" of Professor Charles Moskos, one of the best of the military sociologists, "was the noticeable improvement since 1973." "By whatever indicator one chooses," he reported, "whether unit effectiveness, soldierly morale, disciplinary rates, or race relations, there has been a decided change for the better." But he went on to warn that because the years just before and after the end of the war in Vietnam were a low point in the US army generally as well as in USAREUR, "it would be misguided to use the 1971–74 period as a sole reference point." He went on to say that "If one used the 1961–64 period as an alternative benchmark, comparison might be less favorable."[49]

Using just that benchmark, *Worldview* columnist Jeremiah Novak, who commanded a tank company in Europe from 1964 to 1965, returned to his old unit in June 1984. What he saw was an army with "a laid-back attitude" that took six hours to make a routine river crossing. "The Army you served in died at Tet in Vietnam," the division commander, Major-General (now Lieutenant-General) Crosby E. Saint, explained.

After that, we went through a period of drug-takers and hoodlums. Today's new Army is comprised of volunteers, who are more dedicated than the post-Tet Army, but they are nothing like the soldiers you served with . . . We lost a lot more in Vietnam than a war. We're rebuilding the American Army, and that takes time.[50]

Conclusion

From a political point of view, America's commitment to NATO has been remarkably constant. Against every tenet of its isolationist past, America has maintained forces in Europe for literally over a generation. The author's own son was born in Landstuhl, Germany, in 1955 while he was serving as a member of the United States Army Europe (USAREUR). Twenty-two years later, in Wiesbaden, Germany, a daughter was born to that son, then serving as a lieutenant with USAREUR's 8th Infantry Division.

And not only are those forces still there, they are there in strength. When NATO was founded in 1949, the United States had one infantry division in Europe. In 1985, it had 216,700 soldiers stationed in Europe, including those assigned to the two armored divisions, two mechanized infantry divisions, two armored cavalry regiments and three infantry brigades of the Seventh US Army. Supporting these ground forces are the 89,800 airmen of the USAF Europe with their 729 combat aircraft and 32 ground-launched cruise missiles, as well as the navy and marine combat elements of the Second US Fleet in the Atlantic and the Sixth US Fleet in the Mediterranean.[51]

Strength figures aside, from a military point of view America's contribution to NATO has undergone profound changes. When NATO was formed, American military power was not only the backbone of the NATO alliance, for all practical purposes, it *was* NATO. Even though relatively small in number, American forces were the "tripwire" in America's nuclear arsenal, and it was these nuclear forces that were NATO's primary counter to the massive Soviet/Warsaw Pact advantage in conventional forces. Although, as was seen earlier, American conventional force levels in Europe were increased during the Korean War, and maintained at a relatively high level ever since, NATO defenses continued to be built on the foundation of American strategic, theater, and tactical nuclear weapons. In fact, the relationship between US conventional force levels and the declaratory strategy of the United States was ambiguous. As Jeffrey Record has noted, "Paradoxically, the United States maintained larger general purpose force levels in Europe during the era of massive retaliation — a strategy calling for 'trip wire' conventional forces — than it has since the inception of flexible response."[52]

One reason for this seeming disparity was the increase in the conventional forces of other NATO nations. In the early days, European NATO nations were continuing the post-World War II rebuilding of their nations and their armed forces. Now they provide the majority of the ground forces deployed in NATO. In 1985, for example, on the Central Front of NATO alone, the US deploys the equivalent of 6 divisions. Other NATO allies field some 22. These conventional force levels are especially significant, for today NATO faces a twofold challenge — to maintain the nuclear balance so as to continue to deter a nuclear attack in Europe and to build a conventional capability so as to be able to turn back a Soviet/Warsaw Pact conventional attack without resorting to nuclear weapons.

The first challenge is complicated by the enormous change in the strategic balance caused by Soviet attainment of nuclear parity with the United States in the late 1970s. American nuclear forces — strategic, theater, and tactical — are as necessary as they ever were, but they are not nearly so useful. Once they served both to deter a Soviet nuclear attack on Western Europe and at the same time to compensate for the Soviet/Warsaw Pact advantage in conventional forces and thus to deter a Soviet/Warsaw Pact conventional attack. Today, checkmated by Soviet nuclear weapons, their value lies solely in their ability to, in turn, checkmate Soviet nuclear weapons. While British and French nuclear weapons play a part in this nuclear deterrence, the United States still has the key role. America provides the primary strategic deterrence and US theater and tactical nuclear forces in Europe remain critical. American deployments of ground-launched cruise missiles and Pershing IIs, for example, restored the balance disrupted by the deployment of the Soviet SS-20 missiles.

But while America continues to have the primary role in meeting the first challenge, when it comes to the second challenge the roles are reversed. While American conventional forces are an important part of the response, it is the conventional forces of the European NATO nations that carry the main burden of turning back a Soviet/Warsaw Pact conventional attack without resorting to nuclear weapons. Unfortunately, too-long reliance on the American nuclear shield has inhibited their ability to meet that challenge. As Jeffrey Record concludes, "Key allies continue to exhibit a nostalgic and unwarranted confidence in the

US nuclear deterrent as a means both of preventing war and of excusing all but token efforts on their part to remedy NATO's conventional force weaknesses."[53]

Testifying before Congress in March 1984, General Bernard W. Rogers, Supreme Allied Commander Europe, noted the need for NATO nations to do more for defense. But he went on to say that

> In seeking greater European contributions to NATO security, the United States should challenge, not threaten, its allies . . . Cuts in United States spending and troop commitments to NATO play into the hands of those Europeans who promise a formula for peace that somehow does not require military strength. The heavy commitment of United States troops in Europe provides critical reassurance to its allies. Decreases in American commitments would, I believe, prompt some European leaders to consider seeking compensation through greater accommodation with the Soviet Union. Such a development clearly would not be in America's interest.[54]

America's armed forces deployed in Western Europe have a dual role. As General Rogers pointed out, they not only *deter* an attack by the Soviet Union and its Warsaw Pact allies on Western Europe, but they also *assure* America's European allies that the United States remains firmly committed to their defense. Since the very beginning of NATO, stationing America's sons and daughters potentially "in harm's way" on European soil has been proof-positive of that committment. "Many things have changed since 1949," said Vice-President George Bush on 20 May 1984, in ceremonies honoring the 35th anniversary of the signing of the North Atlantic Treaty, "but many things remain unchanged. The solidarity of the North Atlantic Alliance is still the pole around which peace and security revolve."[55]

Notes

1. Dean Acheson, *Present at the Creation: My Years in the State Department* (W. W. Norton, New York, 1969), p. 285.
2. *The Military Balance 1984–1985* (International Institute for Strategic Studies, London, 1984), pp. 6–11.
3. Richard Halloran, "Europe Called Main U.S. Arms Cost," *New York Times*, 20 July, 1984.
4. Theodore White, *Fire in the Ashes: Europe in Mid-Century* (William Sloan

Associates, New York, 1953), p. 32.
   5. Maurice Matloff *Army Historical Series: American Military History* (Office of the Chief of Military History, United States Army, Washington, DC, 1969), pp. 530–531.
   6. Allan R. Millett and Peter Maslowski, *For the Common Defense: A Military History of the United States* (The Free Press, New York, 1984), p. 474.
   7. White, *Fire in the Ashes*, pp. 33, 295.
   8. Ibid., p. 296 (emphasis added).
   9. Millett and Maslowski, *For the Common Defense*, p. 477.
   10. Ibid., pp. 477–478.
   11. Acheson, *Present at the Creation*, p. 285.
   12. Russell F. Weigley, *History of the United States Army* (Macmillan, New York, 1967), p. 501.
   13. General Creighton W. Abrams, Address to the US Army War College, 7 August 1973.
   14. John P. Lovell, "Table 5, Priorities in Army Overseas Commitments as Indicated by Number of Personnel Assigned or Attached to Overseas Commands, 1946–1965" in *The American Army and Revolutionary Conflict, 1946–1965: The Tortuous Process of Foreign Policy Learning* (Strategic Studies Institute, US Army War College, Carlisle Barracks, March 1985), p. 40.
   15. Acheson, *Present at the Creation*, pp. 307–313.
   16. George Washington, "Farewell Address, September 17, 1796," quoted in Henry Steel Commager (ed.), *Documents of American History* (Appleton-Century Crofts, New York, 1963), p. 174.
   17. Senator Robert A. Taft (R–Ohio), quoted in Ambassador Jeane J. Kirkpatrick, "The Atlantic Alliance and the American National Interest," *Current Policy No. 581* (Department of State, Washington DC, 30 April, 1984), p. 2.
   18. Harry S. Truman, quoted in ibid.
   19. Harry S. Truman, "Statement on the Korean War, June 27, 1950" in Commager, *Documents of American History*, pp. 560–561.
   20. Russell F. Weigley, *The American Way of War: A History of United States Military Strategy and Policy* (Macmillan, New York, 1973), p. 396.
   21. Lovell, *American Army and Revolutionary Conflict*, p. 40.
   22. White, *Fire in the Ashes*, pp. 296–298.
   23. See "The Impact of the Korean War" in Lawrence S. Kaplan's *The United States and NATO: The Formative Years* (The University of Kentucky Press, Lexington, 1984), pp. 145–175.
   24. Weigley, *The American Way of War*, p. 453.
   25. Secretary of State John Foster Dulles, *Department of State Bulletin*, vol. 30, 12 January 1954, pp. 107–110.
   26. Weigley, *History of the United States Army*, p. 526.
   27. Lovell, *The American Army and Revolutionary Conflict*, p. 40.
   28. Millett and Maslowski, *For the Common Defense*, pp. 530, 535.
   29. Ibid., pp. 535–536.
   30. William L. Houser, *America's Army in Crisis: A Study in Civil–Military Relations* (The John Hopkins Press, Baltimore, 1973), p. 60.
   31. See Norman Podhoretz's *Making It* (Random House, New York, 1967), pp. 184–193, for an account of his experiences as a draftee in Europe.
   32. For precise data on arms and equipment, see *The Military Balance*, published each year by the London-based International Institute for Strategic Studies.
   33. See my *On Strategy: A Critical Analysis of the Vietnam War* (Dell, New York, 1984), p. 238.
   34. Millett and Maslowski, *For the Common Defense*, p. 536.
   35. John M. Collins, *United States/Soviet Military Balance: A Frame of Reference for Congress* (US Government Printing Office, Washington, DC, 1976), p. 61.

36. Millett and Maslowski, *For the Common Defense*, p. 530.
37. Jeffrey Record, *Revising U.S. Military Strategy: Tailoring Means to Ends* (Pergamon-Brassey, Washington, DC, 1984), p. 104.
38. Hauser, *America's Army in Crisis*, p. 145.
39. Collins, *United States/Soviet Military Balance*, p. 10.
40. Harry G. Summers, Jr., *The Astarita Report: A Military Strategy for the Multipolar World*, (Occasional Paper, US Army War College, Carlisle Barracks, Pa., 30 April, 1981).
41. Field Manual 100-5, *Operations* (US Government Printing Office, Washington, DC, 1976).
42. Field Manual 100-5, *Operations* (US Goverment Printing Office, Washington, DC, 1982).
43. Samuel Huntington, "Conventional Deterrence and Conventional Retaliation in Europe," *International Security*, vol. 8, no. 3 (1984), pp. 32–56.
44. General Edward C. Meyer, "A Ready Land Force," *Defense 83* (April 1983), p. 3.
45. "American Military is in 'A Race to Prevent War,'" interview with Chairman of the Joint Chiefs of Staff General John W. Vessey, Jr., *US News & World Report*, 14 October, 1985, pp. 37–38.
46. Eliot A. Cohen, *Citizens and Soldiers: The Dilemmas of Military Service* (Cornell University Press, Ithaca, NY, 1985), p. 170.
47. Charles C. Moskos, Jr., "US Soldiers in Germany–1977," unpublished research report, Department of Sociology, Northwestern University, October 1977.
48. Jeffrey Record, *Revising U.S. Military Strategy: Tailoring Means to Ends* (Pergamon-Brassey, Washington, DC, 1984), p. 104.
49. Moskos, "US Soldiers in Germany–1977."
50. Jeremiah Novak, "Is NATO Necessary?" *Worldview* (February 1985), p. 7.
51. *The Military Balance 1984–1985*, pp. 10–11.
52. Record, *Revising U.S. Military Strategy*, p. 24.
53. Ibid., p. 99.
54. General Bernard W. Rogers, Congressional testimony, 6 March 1984, quoted in "Raising the Nuclear Threshold," *Defense 84* (June 1984), pp. 6–7.
55. Vice President George Bush, "Opening Session, North Atlantic Council, May 29, 1984," *Department of State Bulletin* (July 1984).

NOTES ON CONTRIBUTORS

Roger Beaumont is a Professor of History at Texas A & M University, as well as the North American Editor of *Defence Analysis*. His many works include *Military Elites* (1975), *Sword of the Raj* (1977), and *The Next Decade* (1975), of which latter work he is co-editor.

Nigel de Lee is a Senior Lecturer in War Studies and International Affairs at the Royal Military Academy Sandhurst. He has worked on major research projects for the Imperial War Museum, and has published extensively on military history and strategic affairs, especially with regard to the Nordic countries.

H. R. Fuhrer, a serving officer in the Swiss army, is editor of the *Allgemeine Schweizerische Militärzeitschrift,* and has published widely on the military affairs of Switzerland and Austria, including *Spionage gegen die Schweiz, . . .* (1982).

John Keegan taught at the Royal Military Academy Sandhurst, and is author of numerous major works, including *The Face of Battle* (1976), *The Nature of War* (1981), and *Six Armies in Normandy* (1982). He is also editor of the *Rand McNally Encyclopedia of World War II* (1977), of *World Armies* (1983), and other works.

Matthew Midlane is a lecturer in Politics at the Royal Military Academy Sandhurst. He has written on military affairs, South African politics, and other political and strategic topics.

Vittorfranco S. Pisano is an attorney-at-law and a consultant in international security affairs. His most recent monographs include *Terrorism and Security: The Italian Experience* (1984), and *France as a Setting for Domestic and International Terrorism* (1985).

Douglas Porch is Mark W. Clark Professor of History at the Citadel, Military College of South Carolina. His publications include, among others, *Army and Revolution, France 1815–1848* (1975), *The Portuguese Armed Forces and the Revolution* (1977), *The March to the Marne: The French Army, 1871–1914* (1981), *The Conquest of*

Morocco (1983), and *The Conquest of the Sahara* (1984).

Dennis E. Showalter is Professor of History at Colorado College. He has published extensively on German history, for instance *German Military History, 1648–1982: A Critical Bibliography* (1984); and *Little Man, What Now? Der Stürmer in the Weimar Republic* (1982).

Bridadier John H. Skinner retired from the British army in 1985 to take up public service in the United Kingdom, having served in numerous military capacities as far afield as the Far East, Germany and Great Britain. A former Defence Fellow at Oxford University, he has written widely on defense matters.

Colonel Harry G. Summers taught at the Department of the Army, US Army War College, Strategic Studies Institute, Carlisle Barracks, Pa. He is also Senior Military Correspondent for *U.S. News & World Report*. His publications comprise, among others, *On Strategy: A Critical Analysis of the Vietnam War* (1982).

INDEX

Acheson, Dean 286, 289
Adenauer, Konrad 214, 216–17
air force
    Austria 112
    Belgium 269
    Britain 39–40
    Denmark 70–3
    France 200, 203–4
    Italy 170
    Netherlands 282
    Norway 85–7
    Portugal 150, 153
    Spain 137
    Switzerland 118
    West Germany 231
anti-nuclear sentiment
    and neutron bomb 29
    Belgium 256–7
    Britain 33
    Committee for Nuclear
        Disarmament 28–9
    France 207
    Italy 160–1
    Netherlands 256–7, 274, 276
    Norway 75
    West Germany 226
army
    Austria 19, 111–12
    Belgium 19, 265–8
    Britain 7–9, 34–9
    Denmark 18–19, 61–7
    Finland 18
    France 6–7, 200–3
    Ireland 19–20
    Italy 15–16, 164–8
    Netherlands 19, 277–82
    Norway 18, 77–81
    operational experience 5–6
    Portugal 15, 149–50, 153
    recruiting 2–5
        officers 4–5
    Spain 13–15, 136–7
    Sweden 17–18
    Switzerland 16–17, 115, 118–21
    United States 20–2, 287–305
    West Germany 10–13, 237–41

Astarita Report 302
Attlee, Clement 25
Austria 95–112, 121–3
    anti-military sentiment 122
    armed forces 111–12
    civil-military relations 19
    conscription 111
    defense budget 123
    defense policy 102–12; and politics 104–5; comprehensive territorial defense plan 106–7; concept 108–11; rearmament 105–6; weaknesses 121–3
    neutrality 97–102
    strategic position 96, 108

Belgium 255–69, 282–4
    armed forces 259–69; air force 269; army 265–8; conscription 262–4; in West Germany 265–6, 267–88; language difficulties 265; matériel 267; navy 268–9; operational readiness 263–4; organization 259–62; role 265; strength 259; training 262
    background 255–9
    civil-military relations 19
    defense budget 259
    strategic position 255–6
Blum, Léon 194
Britain 24–53
    armed forces 24–53; air force 39–40; army 34–9; British Army of the Rhine (BAOR) 34–6; civil aid 51–2; command-and-control 46–7; conscription 28–9; in Egypt 27; in India 25; in Ireland 29–31; in Korean conflict 26–7; matériel 34–5; mystique 49–51; navy 41–3; operational experience 5; operational readiness 35, 40, 43; retrenchment 29–31, 34, 41; roles 34, 39, 42; statistics 47–9; strength 35; training

313

44-6
civil-military relations 7-9
Committee for Nuclear
   Disarmament 28-9
conventional forces 27, 33
Defence Operational Analysis
   Establishment 27
defense budget 28
Falklands War 35, 40, 41, 42-3, 47
imperial retrenchment 24-8
military innovation 52-3
National Service 28-9, 45
nuclear deterrence 27, 31-4
Secret Service 43-4
Bush, George 307

Caetano, Marcello 142-5
Churchill, Winston 214
civil-military relations 1-23
   Austria 19
   Belgium 19
   Britain 7-9
   Denmark 18-19
   Finland 18
   France 6-7
   Ireland 19-20
   Italy 15-16, 158-61
   Netherlands 19
   Norway 18
   Portugal 15, 146-9
   Spain 13-15, 131-4
   Sweden 17-18
   Switzerland 16-17
   West Germany 10-13
Committee for Nuclear Disarmament 28-9
comprehensive territorial defense plan 106-7
conscription
   aspects of 3
   Austria 111
   Belgium 262-4
   Britain 28-9
   Denmark 63-4
   France 195-9
   Italy 170-1, 183
   Netherlands 272-5
   Norway 78-9, 83
   Portugal 150
   Spain 129
   United States 303-4
   viewed as obsolete 27, 195

West Germany 218, 227, 232
containment, doctrine of 31
conventional forces
   as tripwire 226, 305-6
   British reduction 27
   French lack of modernization 200-1
   renewed importance 302, 303
   Warsaw Pact superiority 306
   see also nuclear deterrence
Cuban missile crisis 296

de Gaulle, Charles 191-4, 204-5, 214
de Rivera, Miguel Primo 127
Defence Operational Analysis
   Establishment 27
Denmark 58-73
   air force 70-3
      forces 70-1; matériel 71-2;
      roles 72-3; strength 71;
      training 71
   and NATO 59-61
   army 61-7
      conscription 63-4; matériel
      64-5; officers 64; roles
      65-7; strength 62-4;
      training 62
   civil-military relations 18-19
   defense policy 58-61
   navy 67-70
      forces 67-8; roles 68-70;
      strength 68
détente
   Denmark 60
   Norway 74
Dulles, John Foster 296

Eanes, Ramallio 148-9
Eisenhower, Dwight 294, 296
European Defense Community 33
European theater nuclear force 160

Falklands War
   British infantry 35
   Royal Air Force 40
   Royal Navy 41, 42-3
Federal Republic of Germany
   see West Germany
Finland civil-military relations 18
flexible response 208, 228, 297, 300-1, 302
   see also massive retaliation,

Index

nuclear deterrence
Force d'action rapide (FAR) 201–2
forward defense 233–4, 237
France 188–210
  armed forces 200–3
    army 200–3; conscription
      195–9; conventional 200–3;
      matériel 201; modernization
      200–1; nuclear 200; officers
      195–6; operational
      experience 5; strength 201;
      training 196
  arms industry 200
  civil-military relations 6–7
  colonial wars 189–90
  defense budget 203–4
  defense policy 188–210
    and politics 191–5, 208–10;
      background 188–95; nuclear
      versus conventional
      199–208; social context
      195–9
  withdrawn from NATO 28
Franco, Francisco 127–9

Giscard d'Estang, Valéry 206
Gonzales, Vasco 146
Gonzalez, Felipe 138

Hernu, Charles 194–5, 197–9, 206

India 25, 27
Ireland
  British armed forces in 29–31
  civil-military relations 19–20
Italy 158–85
  and NATO 180–2
  armed forces 158–85
    air force 170; and politics 158,
      183; and society 158–61;
      army 164–8; assessment
      182–5; background 161–3;
      conscription 170–1, 183;
      defense establishment
      163–4; government control
      163; matériel 168, 183–4;
      navy 169: roles 175–80;
      strength 171–2
  arms industry 185
  civil-military relations 15–16,
    158–61
  intelligence 172–5
  strategic position 181

Juan Carlos 131, 133

Kennedy, John 27, 297
Kissinger, Henry 27
Korean War
  British forces 26–7
  United States forces 292–5

Lascaze, Jeannou 193
Liddell Hart, B.H. 28
Luxembourg 257, 282

MacArthur, Douglas 26
McMahon Act 31, 32
Macmillan, Harold 27
Malta 160
Marshall Plan 31, 34
massive retaliation 296–7
  see also flexible response, nuclear
    deterrence
medical facilities 36
mission tactics 236
Mitterand, Francois 193–4, 207–8
mobile defense 303
Mountbatten, Louis 46

navy
  Belgium 268–9
  Britain 41–3
  Denmark 67–70
  France 200, 204
  Italy 169
  Netherlands 276–7
  Norway 81–5
  Portugal 150, 153
  Spain 137
  West Germany 231
Netherlands 25–9, 269–84
  anti-military sentiment 272–5
  armed forces 269–82
    air force 282; army 277–82;
      conscription 272–5; in West
      Germany 279–80; matériel
      281; navy 276–7;
      operational readiness
      279–80, 281; organization
      270; roles 276, 277;
      strength 269–70
  background 255–9
  civil-military relations 19
  defense budget 269
  Netherlands Defense Planning
    Process (NDPP) 270

strategic position 255–6, 271–2
neutrality armed 100–2
  Austria 97–102
  definition 97–8
  Switzerland 97–102
neutron bomb 29
North Atlantic Treaty Organization (NATO)
  Belgian attitude 256–9, 264
  Danish policy 59–61
  Dutch attitude 256–9, 275–6
  French withdrawal 28, 192, 229
  impetus for growth of 32
  increase of European forces 306
  Italian participation 162–3, 180–2
  Norwegian policy 74
  Portuguese commitment 150–2, 155
  Spanish participation 138–40, 154–5
  standardization 266–7
  United States commitment 286, 305–7
  West German role 225–6
Norway 73–87
  air force 85–7
    forces 85–6; matériel 86; roles 87; training 86
  army 77–81
    conscription 78–9; matériel 78; officers 79; roles 79–81; strength 77–8; training 78–9
  civil-military relations 18
  defense policy 73–6
  navy 81–5
    conscription 83; forces 82–3; roles 84–5; strength 82; training 83–4
nuclear deterrence
  Britain 27, 31–4
  France 199–208
  United States 288–9, 296–7, 302–3, 305–7
  see also conventional forces, flexible response, massive retaliation
Nuclear Non-Proliferation Agreement 175

Ostpolitik
  Austria 96
  West Germany 228

Pompidou, Georges 205–6
Portugal 142–55
  and NATO 150–2
  armed forces 142–54
    air force 150, 153; army 149–50, 153; conscription 150; historical background 142–4; matériel 152–4; modernization 152–4; navy 150, 153; officers 144–5, 149–50; operational experience 6; organization 149–50; social structure 144–5; strength 149–50
  arms industry 154
  civil-military relations 15, 146–9
  defense budget 152–3
  strategic position 151–2

Reagan, Ronald 30, 209
regimentality 8–9, 27, 36–7

Salazar, António de Oliveira 142–4
Schmidt, Helmut 228, 231
Soares, Mario 149
Spain 126–42, 154–5
  and NATO 137–40
  armed forces 126–42
    air force 137; army 136–7; conscription 129; historical legacy 126–9; matériel 141–2; modernization 137–8, 140; navy 137; officers 129–30, 135; organization 134–7; social structure 130–1; strength 129–30
  arms industry 140–2
  civil-military relations 13–15, 131–4
  defense budget 140–1
  strategic position 139
  United States forces in 137–8
Spannochi doctrine 108–11
Spinola, António de 145–6
Strategic Air Command 32
strategic bases
  British reduction 24–8
  Italy 181
  Lajes (Portugal) 151
  Norway 76
  Spain 137–8
Strategic Defense Initiative 209

Strauss, Franz Josef 227–8
Sweden civil-military relations 17–18
Switzerland 95–103, 112–23
   armed forces 115, 118–21
   civil-military relations 16–17
   defense budget 122–3
   defense policy 102–3, 112–21
      concept 113–18; weaknesses 121–3
   neutrality 97–102
   strategic position 115

tactical nuclear weapons 200, 208, 226–7
Truman Doctrine 288
Truman, Harry 31, 288, 293

United States 286–307
   armed forces in Europe 231, 305
      strength 286
   army 287–305; 1945–50 287–92; 1955–64 295–9; capabilities 304–5; composition 303–4; conscription 303–4; Korean War 292–5; post-Vietnam era 302–5; Vietnam War 299–302
   contribution to NATO 286, 305–7
   defense policy
      1945–50 288–9; 1953–64 296–8; Korean War 293–4; post-Vietnam era 302–3, 305–7; Vietnam War 300–1
   political-military environment 302
   relations with Portugal 150–1
   relations with Spain 137–8

V-bomber force 32
Vietnam War 21–2, 299–302

Warsaw Pact
   forces for attacking Italy 176
   forces in Baltic 67
   superiority in conventional forces 306
West Germany 212–46
   armed forces 212–46
      air force 231; and politics 223–4; army 5–6, 237–41; background 213–17; bureaucratization 229–30; conscription 218, 227, 232; development 217–25; *Innere Führung* 224–5, 245–6; navy 231; officers 242–3; roles 223, 235; strength 231
   arms industry 239
   Belgian army in 265–6, 257–88
   British army in 34–6
   civil-military relations 10–13
   defense policy 231–7
   Dutch army in 279–80
   United States army in 305

For Product Safety Concerns and Information please contact our EU representative GPSR@taylorandfrancis.com
Taylor & Francis Verlag GmbH, Kaufingerstraße 24, 80331 München, Germany

www.ingramcontent.com/pod-product-compliance
Lightning Source LLC
Chambersburg PA
CBHW071801300426
44116CB00009B/1168